MY LIFE WITH OSHO

Seven Doors to Self-Realisation

Azima V. Rosciano, MD

⊙ DIAMOND BOOKS

Published by Diamond Pocket Books Pvt. Ltd.
X-30, Okhla Industrial Area, Phase-2, New Delhi-20
Tel : 011-40712100 Fax : 011-41611866
e-mail : sales@dpb.in website : www.diamondbook.in

Copyright ©2013 by Azima V. Rosciano

Copyright © 2013 by Azima V. Rosciano. All rights reserved.

Azima V. Rosciano asserts the moral right to be identified as the author of this work.

No portion of this book, except for brief review, may be reproduced, stored in a retrieval system, or transmitted in any form or by any means – electronic, mechanical, photocopying, recording, or otherwise – without the written permission of the publisher.

Nor may this work be circulated in any form of binding or cover other than that in which it is published and without a similar condition being imposed on a subsequent purchaser.
For information contact Diamond Books.

Printed in India by G.S. Enterprises
ISBN 978-93-5083-633-0

Dedicated to the spiritual Master Osho

Foreword

This is a very personal story about my love affair with an enlightened mystic, Osho. It's an account of all the incredible dramas, adventures, twists and turns that happened to me when I became Osho's disciple.

I don't pretend to be a historian, so maybe not all of my facts are right. Wherever I have put Osho's words in quotation marks, I am quoting him from memory. I am not saying these are his exact words. I don't pretend to represent anyone except myself, so maybe some people will disagree or take offense at what I say.

But I'm happy with my story. I do my best to convey to you, as honestly and accurately as I can, everything that happened in the company of the most amazing being I ever met. I wish you joy in reading it.

A.R., April 2013

Acknowledgments

I want to thank my friends who helped me with this English edition of my book.

Anurag David, who translated the original Italian version.

Anand Subhuti, who did a wonderful job making the English version smooth, easy to read and in tune with my heart.

Prem Sheelu, who out of her dedication to the Master, did a final edit.

Atit Maria, my partner, who supports me always with cheerfulness and high spirit.

And Diamond Books, my publisher, who trusted this work.

Preface

If you have never met a spiritual master like Osho, it is difficult to understand the power and intensity of living near a source of pure consciousness.

But anyway, I will make the effort to talk about my life with him, because after my body has returned to the cosmic wind that pervades the universe, all of these amazing experiences will be lost forever.

Humanity is facing the greatest challenge of its history on this planet. Our greedy and unconscious way of life is threatening all our essential resources: the water, the air, the soil and the incredible variety of wildlife that makes this planet so precious and so beautiful.

At the same time, the great organisations that are supposed to take care of us – religious, political, financial, social – are being nakedly exposed as nothing more than opportunists and exploiters with no vision to guide us through the coming storm.

It is my understanding that Osho has given us a new message, a new blueprint, of immense value not just for our generation but for generations to come.

I hope my book will bring more clarity to the image of this controversial mystic, who I am sure one day will be recognised as the most original and significant visionary of the 20th century – and perhaps one of the greatest human beings of all time.

Contents

1. The Observer 1
2. The Year of '68 7
3. Leaving For the Orient 27
4. The Mystery Begins 39
5. India Comes Closer 52
6. Meeting the Master 63
7. The Alchemy of Transformation 78
8. Deconditioning 93
9. The Past Revived 108
10. The Only Alternative 120
11. Home Again 131
12. The Conscious Beehive 140
13. Switzerland 154
14. America 160
15. The Return of the Doctor 179
16. J. Krishnamurti 186
17. The Visit 191
18. The Second Try 196
19. Trust 214

xi

20. Lake Tahoe	224
21. The Dream Ends	233
22. Osho Arrested	247
23. Leaving America	259
24. Turning Point	266
25. Return to India	277
26. The Close Encounter	294
27. Out of Lao Tzu House	310
28. The Blows Keep Coming	318
29. The Osho Robes	329
30. My New Identity	333
31. Meeting with Poonjaji	344
32. The White Robe Brotherhood	350
33. The Last Teaching	363
34. The Last Celebration	371
ABOUT THE AUTHOR	382

book start here

1 The Observer

July 2010:
After more than 30 years I finally got to the island – nature, birds, the sea, the forests, wind, fresh air...and sun...so much sun. I had lived the preceding years so intensely that my energy was at the brink of complete exhaustion. The candle of my life felt like it was burning out.

I began to take stock of the enormous quantity of energy used only four years earlier, when I was dying, once more from a chronic disease, from which current medical practice did not hold out much hope for recovery, so much so that medical colleagues who treated me gave me only a few years to live.

I am still here and with a remarkable resurgence of energy. Nevertheless, something in me had changed, and the change was so drastic, so unexpected and intense, that my state of awareness is now very far from the point at which I found myself before this dying experience

But in a way, this was not new to me. It seems as if I had already entered into an altered state of consciousness in my early childhood, at the age of six months, as a result of contracting acute pneumonia. But this event tends to get lost in unreliable memories of my family life.

What I know for sure is that, at the age of five, I entered into coma. From that event there remains an indelible mark on my body that will be there as long as I live: an enormous scar that disfigures my chest from one side to the other, created by a pan of boiling water that I spilled all over me. It took three years of transactional analysis and many millions of Italian lira to establish that the person really responsible for this horrible event, though unintentional, was actually my mother.

But the analysis and the lira were not only for that purpose. They were also useful in shedding light on my relationship with my ex-wife and the cracks in the marriage that started showing after a few years as the relationship deteriorated and went to ruin.

From psychoanalysis emerged a picture of a weak mother, insecure and full of fear, the fears typical of a girl born at the beginning of the twentieth century, when women could not leave the house alone or even look into a man's eyes.

Now this could seem medieval, but nevertheless my mother lived like that, even in a big city like Palermo, sequestered in the house with her sister, her mother, and the memory of a father who committed suicide because of his gambling debts when she was only four years old.

I think the sense of abandonment the little four-year old girl received from her father's death never left her. A large portion of the fears she experienced as an adult woman were surely attributable to the sensations of being 'alone' and 'small' and completely insecure, above all during the hard years that followed the Second World War.

It was a family composed of three women and one man, my uncle, who at the tender age of 13 was forced to take responsibility for the whole family. I imagine it caused him a great deal of anguish, because the former head of the family threw on the green poker table not only his life, but all his property too.

What happened was that a well-off family suddenly lost its centre, with all its security, its economic and emotional stability. So at 13, my uncle Mimmo was taken on at the bank of a relative in order to maintain the orphaned family.

However, this didn't last long because, after a few years, Uncle Mimmo decided to risk everything, learn a commercial trade and go into business for himself. The gamble paid off. His business did well, initiating a period of well being that enabled him to live comfortably and take care of the family.

With his sisters he behaved like a father, giving them both practical and financial help until they were married. But as for my mother, at least until the day of her wedding, she was not permitted to leave the house or to meet friends, or to walk in the streets, as was the case with all Sicilian women of that age.

She saw her future husband through the window of her house and it was 'love at first sight,' an instantaneous love, the type of love that lasts a lifetime, in fact, forever – 'until death do us part'. Her death that came just ten days ago, as I am beginning to write this book, after sixty years of living with her husband.

When she was young, my mother was a robust Sicilian woman, apparently secure in herself and greatly respected by her husband who loved her. She was dedicated to the family, especially – to tell the truth – in the kitchen, because in all my memories of her I see her in the kitchen, cleaning, tidying up, and preparing the next meal for all four members of our family.

I think the room in which she cooked gave her security and wrapped her in a kind of second skin. In fact, she loved to cook: that was her gift of love to us. Like all those who appreciate good food, she was jovial and expansive with everyone. When I was a teenager and started having relationships with girls, she never had any problem with me bringing them home, because they were immediately accepted by her and showered with gifts. This made us great friends and for many of my teenage years she was my sole confidante and my only guide.

I saw my father exclusively at lunch and dinner. There was no exchange of words or ideas between us—he was only interested in maintaining the family financially. From the emotional standpoint, he didn't seem to care very much, neither when he was young, nor as he grew older. My emotional life was centered on my mother.

However, her tender and thoughtful preparations in the kitchen did once again take me into a state of suspended animation, in the form of another coma, at the age of 13, caused by appendicitis and a resultant festering peritonitis. The recurring infection that attacked my intestines may well have been induced by my diet. I was continuously stuffed with fried Sicilian food and sweet tomato sauce, the base of every dish in my native land. At lunch, at dinner – two, three, four times a day – there was always fried food and tomato sauce.

I went regularly to the church in our neighbourhood, where I sang as an altar boy until one day I felt my usual stomachaches and was forced to stay in bed and eat light food. I spent a lot of time in this condition when I was little, suffering from severe intestinal problems and moving from one antibiotic to the next. Just for a change, I also had a tonsil infection.

Convinced by the therapeutic value of maternal care, my mother used these periods of my forced immobility to shower me with cuddles and attention, and later fill me with more tomato sauce. So to her, on the day I came home from the choir, suffering from my usual ailment, it wasn't a cause for much concern, except this time the pains didn't go away, even after the usual bombardment of antibiotics.

Let me repeat, throughout my whole childhood I was consuming almost as many antibiotics as I did portions of my mother's tomato sauce. In fact, to be honest, I really don't know if I swallowed more tomatoes or more antibiotics. What I do know is that all these medicines had a long-lasting effect more dramatic and damaging than Mama's well-intended supply of tomato sauce.

This time the family doctor had to surrender: the antibiotics he was giving me were not working. It was dark when they rushed me into the emergency room, for the second, or more exactly, the third time, if we want to give credence to the fantasies of my mother. Once again in coma....

That event, which happened at the age of thirteen, still stays imprinted clearly on my memory in an indelible way. Why? Because that was the first time I consciously experienced the sensation of 'going out' of my body. I was seeing myself from above, without experiencing any attachment to my body or my emotions. Everything appeared as a series of images that did not belong to me. In that dimension there weren't any emotions or thoughts: only a witnessing consciousness that observes.

From above, I was seeing my father who was speaking to the doctor on duty while the nurses, their faces covered with surgical masks, wheeled me into the elevator. From above, I followed the steps of my dad, who was heading toward a meeting with the surgeon.

"No, Mr Rosciano, it is not possible to operate as long as the coma persists. It is good that the boy remains under observation. We will continue with the medication and hope he survives. In any case, we can only operate after a few months."

It was the first out-of-body experience of my life and the memory of it is always vivid, still today, as happens for all deep experiences that leave a mark on the lives of human beings. Thousands of days dissolve in the camera of memory, like snow in the sun, but spiritual experiences remain imprinted with fire on men's souls. These are the events that will condition our present life and the ones that follow.

The memory of this dimension, in which I was seeing my lifeless body and my dad hopefully seeking comforting information, is crystal clear, as clear as was – and still is – the sensation that he who was 'observing' found himself in a dimension where *there doesn't exist the slightest emotion*.

I didn't understand why all these people were so agitated and so desperately worried about that body on the gurney, which I was observing from about 20 feet above. I could see that the body was that of a young person, which gave me the understanding that the observer was also far beyond time, beyond the temporal dimension, where men and events were perceived like a sequence of photographs.

I was feeling the *intense emotions* of my parents and I perceived the drama painted on the faces of the people around me, who were getting so worked up, but I wasn't really getting the point. It was like two separate realities appearing as one in the eyes of the observer.

Why were they so worried about this body? From that dimension, it seemed the acts and lives of men were wasted in doing things that made no sense, that the beings 'down there beneath me' were being forcefully directed toward a reality that constitutes only a small aspect of existence.

On reflection, with all the experiences of my life up to now, I would say that this perception is true. Man has indeed managed and oriented his life in only one direction, motivated by the fear of death, the fear of suffering and disease. He uses all his energy to feel secure, surrounding himself protectively with home and family, with work that gives him the means of survival, sheltering him from potential risks and dangers such as poverty, hunger and want.

In the dimension that I was passing through, time and space do not exist. There are no dangers; there is no death or suffering. There are no emotions that drag you into the darkness of despair, no sense of separation or of belonging, no sense of mine and yours, no chaos and no harmony. The only thing I can remember is a great sense of *detachment* and a great infinite *space* without time and without emotion.

Spiritual experiences can be more easily described by negation than by affirmation– or, to say it another way, from the point of view of emptiness, rather than fullness. In his lifelong teachings, Gautama Buddha gave more emphasis to negation than to affirmation, and one of his most famous *sutras* corresponds exactly to the concept of *'neti-neti,'* which means 'neither this nor that,' seeing that in emptiness there is neither object nor subject, neither objectivity nor subjectivity.

From that moment it became a quality present in my life, like an undercurrent, this sense of detachment with respect to events that happened to me. And if I look deeper inside myself, in any serious moment, or when daily life subjects me to so-called tests, serving up every type of 'problem,' there is always a part inside of me that observes with detachment what is happening.

In any case, I came out of the coma the next day, was given an appendectomy operation a few months later and after that my body didn't get sick for many years. At sixteen years of age, I passed the exam to be admitted to the last three years of high school for classical studies, but more importantly, I passed into what is recorded in history as 'The Year of '68.'

2   The Year of '68

In Italy, the year of '68 happened in 1969, especially in Palermo. But still we call it 'the year of '68' because this revolutionary period was initiated by the famous month of May 1968 in Paris. That was the time when thousands of students at the Sorbonne University and millions of French workers triggered a series of mass protests against authoritarian government and caused an entire nation to examine its basic social values.

At the time, I was young, thin, intelligent, timid and determined to change the values of the world, along with all the other young people on the planet who were doing the same thing. From Vietnam to Prague, from Paris to Berlin, there was a single wish, a single desire – that of changing the values of our social and political life.

None of us wanted any more of this capitalism that swallowed up every human value for a fistful of dollars. We were tired of war, of duties and limitations, of useless studies and repressive education, of taboos around sex and drugs. We wanted to change everything; we wanted a more human world.

Women wanted to be as free as men and to show the world they were smart, even smarter than the repressed and stupid males. In this way, the image of the vagina was raised during demonstrations all over the world, along with the clenched fist, as a symbol of freedom for both the body and the mind.

For a long time we thought change was really possible. We were living in a dream where everything was permitted, from Woodstock to smoking joints in school meetings, from playing guitar at school to spending hours in student meetings to discuss the issues of the day.

Women were liberating themselves, showing their breasts openly, and for us men it seemed too good to be true – this abundance of femininity all around us. I discovered sex in these years, and it was a liberation to be able to use this powerful energy that exploded inside, that you couldn't control.

If I want to describe these years, I don't have any reservations about comparing them to the buds of a tree that open, then flower and allow their seeds to be carried everywhere by the wind.

The spirit of '68 was created by the young, by millions of us discovering together the sexual freedom and the joy of finding satisfaction here and now, in the present moment. We were tired of hearing how you need to suffer in life, like our parents had done. We wanted to be joyful; we wanted to enjoy life – all of it at once.

This basic urge, so fundamental, was surely stronger than the parallel political effort that was gathering momentum. To me, it was a much deeper and wider demand for freedom, sexual freedom and liberation from deep-seated ancient attitudes and beliefs. Politics was the vehicle with which we hoped to get our new ideals accepted.

Nevertheless, many of these ideals were absorbed and manipulated by the establishment that I am part of today, so much so that the present generation takes them for granted. The real meaning of the ideal of liberty has been skilfully camouflaged by the system that today would have you believe that being free means having a beautiful car, an iPod and the possibility to communicate with the rest of the world in real time.

Looking back at '68, our biggest mistake was to address our demands to the wrong people. The demands for social and personal freedom should not have been addressed to the political class and the powerful. They should have been addressed to ourselves. If we ask the politicians and the corporate executives, they can only give us material freedom – in other words, more stuff – nothing more profound than that.

Deeper freedoms are subjective. They have to be experienced.

They cannot be packaged and sold as objects. Nor can they be organized and sanctified as social rights. The year of '68 opened a door, or better yet an enormous storm gate, where the potential 'to be free' appeared on the horizon. What we didn't understand then was that this gate to freedom can only be entered by an individual, walking alone.

It would take me nine hot revolutionary years to be able to arrive at the end of the adventure begun in '68. Some of my companions have carried on, still committed to politics and work that is consistent with their ideals. Others abandoned the crusade out of exhaustion, opportunism or lack of conviction. Some continued with violent actions against others and against the state, while others turned to violence against themselves through drugs like heroin that killed many bodies and many souls.

In those years, many personal and social dreams were born and also wrecked. We wanted to discover the world and change it at the same time. But when it came to constructing something new, as an alternative social model, we could find no practical, common ground. Romantic ideas and hopeless ideals ran amok in this juvenile and chaotic period.

We had no alternative, so we turned to the model posited by Karl Marx and the thinkers that followed him: 'the communist model,' which was being applied in the real world in Russia, in China, in a newly born Cuba and other revolutionary campaigns in South America.

"Long live Mao, long live Lenin and Che!" These were the slogans that filled the main squares of our cities. We were convinced that communism was the alternative to capitalism. But we were wrong. In every case, time has demonstrated the errors of the communist systems, which in fact were run by dictators, or by pseudo-social organizations manipulated by the same international financial system as capitalism itself.

Communism, both in China and Russia, has caused millions of unnecessary deaths, people swept away by arrogant revolutionaries who pretended to have the truth in their hands. All the truth that was needed was condensed in Mao's 'little red book' where it was explained how the less affluent classes, like the workers, would crush the established power structure, installing a communist regime first and a socialist regime thereafter.

It never happened. Neither in China, nor in Russia. What we see today in these two enormous 'socialist' countries is a mean and rampant capitalism that manages international finance by buying economic and commercial power at every level, in every country, in every region of the globe.

Paradoxically, if the old capitalism of the post-war period once had at least a minimum of respect for human beings and for the planet, the two ex-communist colossi don't seem to have any interest in respecting even a minimal social and ecological state of wellbeing. On the contrary, they are among those now participating most heavily in the destruction of the planet.

* * * *

We wanted a cleaner world, more beautiful, more joyous, and we found ourselves on a planet of total social and economic greed, without a way back, without alternative possibilities. So everything was being gambled in a disastrous way, whether by the powerful or by the masses.

We wanted to change the world and the world is changed, but for the worse, so much worse that we have very few years of life left to us as a human society.

We have arrived at the end of egoism and of nature, which is supreme because it is our cosmic mother, and she will be forced to drastically reduce the number of inhabitants on the planet, either by cataclysms or by wars that never make any sense except to those few who enrich themselves by producing and selling their products to the masses.

Seven billion unaware human beings are clearly too much for this amazing planet. We already have widespread starvation and billions of human beings who are dying, now, in this instant, or that will die soon of hunger. Food will cost more and more, just as water and food supplies will increasingly be obtainable only for the few.

The atmosphere has been polluted - earth, sky and water are polluted as never before in the history of the planet. A small continent of floating plastic is constantly growing in the ocean and there is no way to clean it up.

Hundreds of thousands of cubic metres of radioactive waste don't have a secure place to be stored, nor is it known in heaven or on earth how to get rid of the various national mafias that get rich from exploiting every human weakness.

Nothing is manageable anymore and all governments can do is take turns giving ridiculous hopes to a dying body.

* * * *

In these hot years when I was a university student and often talked to the student assembly, it was already being said that capitalism could not be fought with communism, or with other political systems. It had to 'self-destruct.' But I didn't think I would have the pleasure and terror of seeing it fall in my lifetime.

The capitalist system is based on the individual, the lone man who can do it 'by himself.' In fact, the concept of the loner who goes boldly into the future by himself is also at the heart of this political system that is called 'democracy.' It's not a mistaken concept, but the point is always the same, and it's the same error we made in those student years. It's not important which system you use for organizing society; what counts is the individual.

The international left, which is now adrift because it no longer has a philosophical or economic credo, desperately seeks to give itself a 'leftist' appearance, but cannot manage because the leftist model has failed. It is necessary to accept this defeat and the consequences of this defeat. Communism, as an idealistic structure, doesn't exist anymore. All that exists is the climbing to power of the strongest, the richest and the most powerful, who are buying up national governments as a way of constructing a shield to hide their economic swindles.

Politics today is a business and the real power is money. The only real goal, the only real intent, is profit, the personal profit of one against all and against any obstacles. Whether the obstacle is a man, thousands of men, or nature itself, is of absolutely no importance in the eyes of those who want to grab more power and more money.

Society has changed drastically in the last thirty years and class divisions have dissolved in the solvent of individual opportunism: men who start from nothing and become very rich in a few years are immediately accepted into the highest levels of the power structure. People who didn't even come out from behind their national borders, who were living at survival level just a few years ago, like the Russians, can now be found in all the big hotels, in all the best vacation spots, in all the centres of economic power, and continue to spend millions of dollars ostentatiously in front of the eyes of those who once were the world's rich.

In our time it was clear who were the enemies, who were the people to fight against, or with whom to initiate a dialogue and organize a platform for discussion. It was clear who was an industry boss, who was the owner to confront, but today you no longer know who is running a company – there are so many powerful subgroups that it is no longer possible to begin a dialogue. The bigger the urban areas, the larger the cities, the more alienated and self-destructive they become, and the more complicated it gets to manage a decent standard of living.

In the '70s life was a lot simpler. This brave new world of globalization – promising a state of well-being more apparent than real – has brought suffering, alienation, more acute emotional disturbances and increasing social discontent. Maybe it would be more sensible for us to go back to living in small urban areas, as in the old countries where everyone knew each other and helped one another. Such areas could be independent of outside control and could manage their problems at the local level.

But the trend is exactly opposite. There is a tendency to put more and more people in spaces that are bigger and more impersonal, as in China with its skyscrapers and megamalls, where now they are constructing a city for 300 million inhabitants.

If at first there were social classes with clear distinctions, today there seems to emerge a kind of amorphous urban conglomeration with the main characteristic that everyone works all day in order to survive. Whether they are employees, workers or self-employed professionals, people today use almost all of their energy for survival – that's to say, to maintain a house with a mortgage, a family with children – and all for the reward of a good credit rating that will allow them to possess the objects they believe will make them happy.

The social levelling enables everyone to have the same machines, the same clothes, the same designer shoes. They can go to the same vacation spots and appear to be rich and beautiful in the eyes of others, when inside they are anxious, insecure and full of worry for the future. But the ostrich puts his head in the sand and thinks the enemy doesn't see him – and he continues like that, making it appear on the outside that all goes well.

Then there is a social strata that becomes ever more subtle, a class of human beings, of single individuals and families, that get wealthier and wealthier and that manage the money of the world. Economists have calculated that no more than 300 families manage 90 per cent of all the money in the world.

What to say? Political discourse in these conditions is useless, hypocritical and hard to digest. Politics is not the solution, politics has failed, both from the left and the right, and it doesn't have any answer for our enormous social and ecological problems.

That's why, over 40 years ago, I recommended waiting for capitalism to eliminate itself. I repeat my vision today, with one important difference: I can now say, from my own personal experience, that each individual human being has in his hands the responsibility to manage his life for the best, and that he alone has the possibility to find fulfilment, happiness and peace.

How?

If he changes his point of view from the outside to the inside, if he looks inside his consciousness and his human heart, where the solution to every problem is found.

Once again, as in the '70s when the doors of social change opened, now, even more than then, the doors are open for **an enormous individual spiritual change**. Not mass changes, since the masses don't exist except as collections of individuals. And not political changes either, but rather spiritual changes, changes of awareness. Human beings have inside them an enormous potential, a potential for light and infinite love, when they turn their attention toward the inner dimensions, toward the shores of awareness and divinity that they have inside themselves.

Man is an animal and a divine being at the same time: it depends on whether the individual turns his attention toward his animal nature or toward his spiritual being. A human being that looks only toward the flesh and toward material success can never be happy. He could be one of those 300 families that rule the world but he will never have peace inside.

Peace is reached by moving the goal posts from the outside to the inside, by moving the responsibility for your own life from others to yourself. There is no one outside ourselves who can give us something, because it all depends on us – to see or not to see, to feel or not to feel. Jesus said, "He who has eyes to see will see, he who has ears to hear will hear." What does it mean? That men are deaf and blind? That they don't have sense organs? No. It means that there are five sense organs that keep us in contact with the outside, and in a similar way we also have five senses that keep us in contact with our inner world.

But no one has said that to us, no one teaches us how to listen from the inside and see the inner world and shift our focus from outside. No one has established a framework for developing human potential as the unity of body and mind. Society is interested only in developing the mental faculties of man in order to make him a more efficient unit, a better cog in the wheel.

At the same time, the religious components of society condition human beings to follow established paths that are very limiting spiritually. We need to go back to the time of Ancient Greece to find social structures that provide access to inner research and the development of human potential. Since then the world, the Western world at least, has been organized around economic and material growth, losing sight of the inner component of being.

****

In these 2000 to 2500 years only the great masters have taught how to go inside and discover the divine that is in us. Only the great masters have illuminated the inner path. Only a real master can reach us. Only an authentic master can indicate the path and bring light to the darkness of the mind, but it is we alone who have to get up and walk the path along which these masters point.

****

Stand up and walk means to take the first step toward freedom and the first step toward taking responsibility for everything that happens in our life. This means, among other things, not running around in circles in an effort to get somewhere else, but standing still for a moment and becoming aware of where we find ourselves... And the plain fact is that millions of people find themselves in total suffering.

We need to remember the four Noble Truths of Buddha:
- The first noble truth is that all humans experience suffering.
- The second noble truth is that this suffering has a cause – our craving.
- The third noble truth is that the cessation of suffering is possible.
- The fourth noble truth is the path that leads to the cessation of suffering.

The first truth consists in recognizing the suffering inside us and starting a process to resolve this enormous emptiness that we carry within us, bridging this black hole where ultimately everything disappears; where every love story disappears, where success disappears, where all our strength disappears, where family disappears, where every attempt to be happy disappears, where nothing endures, always leaving us with the feeling that something is missing and with a sensation of dissatisfaction that endures as an underlying theme for our whole life.

Spiritual dissatisfaction was, in my opinion, the underlying motivation and impulse in the Humanistic Movement born in the 1970s; a desire to discover who we are and to bring our potential out into the light, an attempt to go beyond the barriers of social conditioning, to discover our inner self.

At the beginning of the movement everything was confused. We wanted only to break every pattern, break the chains of family and of society that anchored us to obsolete, worn out roles that were centuries old. While this process of destruction was going on, many of us realized that the enemy we were fighting against was a chameleon and that it was impossible to defeat it. It was for this reason that many of us went into the personal experiences of drugs, which by the end of the '70s would take over the movement.

In that period, the first drug that entered my circle of friends in Italy was cannabis, which arrived from Morocco, or from India, or Afghanistan. The drug represented the discovery of new mental spaces that were often experienced when relaxing and sharing with friends. Little by little the outer world disappeared, leaving a more credible personal world in which change appeared more possible.

I have to say that the substantial presence of women naturally brought a shift of attention away from the outer and toward the inner, creating a significant impact on this process of transformation. The feminist movement surely constituted an essential component in those years. It was women, together with so-called 'therapy' groups supporting self-analysis and self-care, that brought to the forefront our interest in a more personal and private sphere.

Soon, however, there arrived on the market a drug that created a big split in the humanistic movement: LSD. Lysergic acid, a psychedelic drug, had an even greater impact than ordinary dope, opening doors of perception and exalting the individualistic dimension. An LSD trip could be taken in the company of others, could have an external dimension, but in the vast majority of cases it was an internal and private experience. You were only with yourself.

Not only did the social world and its problems disappear, but so did the sense of communion when sharing with others. Music also had a powerful influence. Bands like the Pink Floyd, whose members had done a lot of acid, became the idols of cerebral isolation and total rebellion, rebellion in all directions, without any program and without wanting to resolve anything on the outside. The outer dimension was simply rejected. It was no longer of any interest...

In this way, at the beginning of the '70s, there was a big split in the movement between those who were continuing to work hard in politics and social action, and those who were going further and further inside into their inner world.

Personally, in all this, I was lurching from one side to the other, unable to choose. Physically, I continued to be thin, but after turning sixteen I grew unexpectedly to the astonishing height of 180 cm (nearly six feet), from where I truly did see the world in a different way. And if I already felt disconnected from my adolescence, in view of my experiences of being in a coma, I now felt as if standing high on the mountain peaks, observing with a few friends what was happening to us.

I liked the drugs but with 'acid' I went slowly. I felt LSD could burn out my brain. This tendency toward self-control was probably the result of the military education I'd received from my father.

I have to say that with time I have learned to recognize many, many good qualities in my father that were once the target of my personal struggle against the family. I could not stand his mute presence, his deliberate and obstinate silence. I could not stand his authoritarian ways, imposing his decisions on me without giving me the slightest explanation. I could not stand his lack of joy and the climate of austerity in which he lived.

So, this habit of self-control, ingrained in me by my father, functioned as a deterrent in respect to the new psychedelic awakenings that were being enthusiastically explored by my contemporaries.

When drugs entered Italy and Europe it would signal the ultimate destruction of the movement, or at least many of its components. Almost without us noticing it, heroin suddenly arrived and became part of our world. The first time I saw my friends reduced to derelicts and junkies, with no vital energy, I was very upset and it was clear to me I would never take such a path, or any similar one.

More and more, I preferred to stay alone and throw myself headlong into my medical studies. Ironically, magically, the polarisation of the movement into extremes – both of which were unacceptable to me – brought maximum benefit to me in terms of driving me into my education.

I succeeded in getting accepted into medical school, even though it was one of the most difficult courses. The scientific world of the human body grabbed me totally, in a way that made me study day and night. I received the highest exam scores and graduated with honors a year earlier than expected, with special recognition for my thesis and other accolades. My mind was open, and through the study of cells and organs I encountered the mystery of the divine that is innate in human beings.

In the meantime, the movement splintered even more and for the first time skirmishes including real violence began to manifest, with the creation of revolutionary organizations intent on destruction, violence and murder. As for me, I could never accept the idea of violence toward others and so, when these armed groups were born, I completely separated myself from them. Change the world? Yes, but not by killing other human beings.

On one side, many of my friends were starting to die of overdoses; on the other side, many were joining armed groups to defeat the powerful with their own weapon: violence. I hated being caught between the two and the sense of separation between me and my former colleagues plunged me into a deep existential crisis.

I didn't know any longer who I was or what I was supposed to do, but luckily, once again, my father met with me. He met me in his own way, for sure, but it was nevertheless effective. And, on that occasion, I received the most beautiful gift that he could offer to me: *he gave me the space to be free and to choose my own life.*

It was the last year of university and my medical education was missing only a few easy clinical exams. But I was in such a crisis that I decided not to take my degree, because nothing made sense to me anymore. I couldn't see myself as a doctor, employed in a hospital, running behind the head physician for years before being able to open my mouth.

The world I had been struggling against didn't interest me. Now that I had to decide whether to enter it or not, I decided absolutely for the 'no.' I announced this decision to my parents, who with so much joy had made many sacrifices to support me while I was at university and who were rewarded by my brilliant results. I told them I was stopping my studies and that I didn't know what to do.

After a few days of heavy silence in the house, my father talked to me. It was one of the rare times in his life that his wall of silence crumbled. He didn't judge me, he didn't criticize me, or try to analyse my choice. He simply said he thought it would be more useful if I finished university and then made my choice.

He said that if I didn't want to be a doctor that was fine by him, but it was important for me to complete the project I'd started, because otherwise my life would always be lacking something – something I could never again reclaim. He made me understand the respect he had for me, which he'd never shared with me before. For the first time, he let me know that he really appreciated me and that he left me free to choose – and for that I have remained grateful my whole life.

I started feeling the goodness and the love of this man who'd been in the war and who'd lived at a time in which his village, when he was young, didn't even have electricity. This silent man had lived without electricity, without newspapers, without a telephone... without all the other infernal devices society has since constructed.

He was and always had been a real man, gruff but honest and sincere. His silences filled the house, and when he returned from the office we all had to be calm because 'papa had to rest.' In his apparent immobility, which I hated, he supported a family with his work for the state government, bought houses for his children and maintained all of us in the best way he knew how.

Notwithstanding the emotional void, this man succeeded in giving us values, at least to me, so much so that I observe them now, at a distance of many decades, understanding that he raised me in a way that saved me from many dangers in which I could have been easily caught.

Even now at 94 years of age, he continues to be upright and firm, like an old oak tree that is now slowly abandoning the ground where it grew up.

I remember when I was about 40 years old I had a car accident, with my then-wife. Following the crash, the car turned over on us. It was one of many accidents I had in my life. Once again I saw my body from above, just before the crash and immediately after. Also then, there was no fear in the observer. I returned to my body after a few minutes because of the severe pains that were racking me. I had various broken bones, in the head, in the shoulder, in the arm and elsewhere.

I was taken to a small hospital close to where we'd been vacationing for several weeks. In all the period of recovery, especially when I was in intensive care, the only person I wanted near me was my father. He was the only calm person, managing to be near me without projecting fears and other emotions I couldn't handle in that state. I was partly in my body and partly out of my body, seeing everything from above. Only my father stayed with me without saying anything, while holding my hand... I felt him there with me as a pure presence, once again without judging me or making me feel guilty for what had happened.

My father was like that, silent and present for his whole life, a life that was lived - as he himself said a few years ago when I asked him if he was satisfied with his life - without regrets, a life in which he had realized his dream of creating a family and bringing up his children so they could have decent work and be independent. He had very simple values that nevertheless made him content and satisfied, without the slightest doubt about his choices.

After that long-ago conversation with my father, my dubious decision to interrupt my university studies vanished and thanks to him I completed my studies, received my degree with the highest marks and was soon being interviewed by three different hospitals which all offered me work.

Immediately, I started working as a doctor in the emergency unit of the largest hospital in the province. I went to work with a red bicycle, the mythical Bianchi, my t-shirt tied in a knot to the handlebars as a way of being different — intentionally ostentatious in front of my colleagues and others working there.

I felt different and wanted to show the world that even though

I was working in one of those terrible institutions against which I'd been fighting until a few months ago, 'inside' I wasn't buying it. I forged ahead with my hospital work and met with the few friends I still valued. I was living with one friend who'd graduated with me and like me had chosen to begin working. We lived in a working class neighbourhood of the city with the door always open to other friends, day and night.

In reality, the movement didn't exist any longer. There were groups that still met, but they were disconnected from each other. It was 1977. Eight years had passed, eight years of intense search accompanied by thousands of other young people. The illusion that we could change the outside world had faded, and inside we felt worse than when it had all started.

If at the beginning we had enthusiasm to push toward our ideals, now we had neither enthusiasm nor ideals. What remained were young people drifting in a social world that had been torn apart, thrown into crisis, crushed in its basic beliefs, that hadn't given any practical new openings – neither to the collective, nor to individuals.

In '76, if I remember correctly, there was one last attempt to keep the movement alive. A demonstration against the government was organized throughout the whole of Italy. The idea of many friends was to arrive in Rome at Palazzo Montecitorio – roughly the equivalent of the Capitol building in Washington – and take this palace of power by storm and then see.... Maybe, memories of the storming of the Bastille still resonated within us.

Many were leaving for Rome and the message from other revolutionaries all over Italy was,'Go for it!' As usual, however, the groups were disconnected and badly organized. There were the really violent ones, the less violent, the intellectuals, the ideologues, the feminists and so on. And each one had a different strategy, created in the moment, to deal with the situation.

They were arriving in big numbers. I think there was something like 200,000, or may be only 199,999, because I was missing. I didn't want to go because I didn't feel 'in' – a key term that was part of the vocabulary with which we expressed ourselves in those days. Not feeling 'in' meant, "I don't want to do this thing and I don't know why, I don't have a logical reason, but I don't want to do it." The taking of the Bastille seemed to me an absurdity and I knew the chronically bad organization of my political companions. How could they think of repeating history in this way?

So I followed the demonstrations on television and became for the first time a spectator, watching the movement that I had once supported so fervently. The clashes were tough and went on all through the night. The violent factions vented their feelings using guns and Molotov cocktails, the less violent shouted slogans against the government, while others ran like crazy through the streets of Rome and managed to arrive at the Bastille (Palazzo Montecitorio).

Many were arrested, many escaped, many were wounded and I truly cannot remember if there were any deaths. I don't think so, but in any case the events seemed far away from me. I remember this as the last big action of a movement that was born from love of liberty and the desire to break the old structures that conditioned us in society. Now it had dissolved into fights without ideals, splintered into factions without shared objectives – problems that even now still persist in the so-called Italian left.

My inner observer developed slowly in the course of those years and continued to take more space inside of me, space created by my refusal to join the armed struggle and my resistance to the drift toward heavy drugs that were spreading like an oil stain.

Two previous episodes deepened the damage done to my revolutionary convictions. They happened between '75 and '76, before my graduation from medical school. The first happened during a big demonstration in Palermo, one of many by the movement in support of some social cause. It was a beautiful demonstration, there was a big crowd of us in the piazza and we were definitely feeling superior to the ordinary citizens passing by on their way to work.

We were at the cutting edge of a movement that was hoping to change the way of life for everybody, improving social conditions, demanding change, even for those ordinary people who were watching on the edges of the city squares.

The demonstration was beautiful, but it was also long and tiring. We had met early in the morning to discuss what to do, to choose the route of the demonstration and other details that constituted the so-called 'orders of the day.' It was also necessary to organize speeches and build platforms. So halfway through the demonstration we were already pretty tired and many of us stopped in a few bars along the way to have a drink or eat a sandwich.

I stopped in a bar downtown, in the old city, where the baroque palaces interweave like cane in the wind, with a variety of architectural styles – Arab, Spanish, and Norman. I was watching, relaxed, eating my sandwich, and at that moment I saw a river of young people slowly coming down the street shouting pseudo-revolutionary slogans:

"Long Live Lenin! Long Live Mao! Long Live Che!"

Among these standard slogans, none stood out more than others. Rather, it was more like a series of nursery rhymes that I myself had been singing for years. But on this morning the observer in me simply watched and listened, without judgment or involvement.

Now they were shouting, "Power to the workers! Power to the workers! Power to the workers!" The words entered into my mind like dripping water, digging deeper inside of me.

"Power to the workers! Power to the workers!"

I was watching all these children of the upper middle class, a few of them very rich, who were shouting their hymn. Their goal was to give the power to a class that was not even represented here. If there were any representatives of the working class, they surely constituted a very small percentage of the demonstrators.

All of us, from the height of our social position of privileged offspring of the middle class, were shouting that we wanted to give power to a class that wasn't asking for anything. The workers weren't there. They were working in the factories. They had children and families to maintain, they had more important things to do – like earning money to survive. By the time I finished my sandwich I'd also finished believing in something that, in all these revolutionary years, seemed to have been overlooked: we middle class intellectuals wanted the working class to take care of managing power for all of us. That was the most absurd thing that I could imagine.

I was, quite suddenly, outside the context of my previous attitudes as a revolutionary. I saw the sandwich being eaten by the young university student, I saw the beautiful old city, rich in history, I saw thousands of young people herded together under a single hypnosis - that of communism.

Some months later - I don't remember the exact date - another episode took place that destroyed the foundations of my intellectual convictions. The singer Bennato, who was considered a friend of the movement, came to Palermo. We thought he would give the concert for free, or at least at a low price.

He surprised us by choosing to perform in a 'chic' theatre of Palermo, with a paid entrance fee that favoured the so-called bourgeoisie who could afford it. So I joined about a hundred companions outside the theatre to protest against this event we considered 'bourgeois.'

After a while, some of our group started to express their rage against the power structure by smashing everything in sight: shops, street signs, parked cars. I couldn't see the sense in this, and observed that the more violent members of our group were the ones who seemed to have the most authoritarian fathers.

After a short time, the police arrived. As usual, as soon as they started to attack, everyone ran away. So, escaping through the old alleys of the city, where we knew we would have protection from the working class inhabitants of the area, we thinned out and at a certain point we found ourselves in a small street that I didn't recognize. Only one of us knew how to get to Piazza Marina, an old city square that had enormous magnolia trees. So we went in that direction, but as soon as our street opened up into the spacious square we saw the police cars already parked there.

We all jumped back. The mind has no time to function in such moments. Seeing the police squad and hearing a bullet pass nearby and hit the wall in front of us, I had a moment of panic. The whining of that bullet penetrated into my mind and made me review and reorganize all the juvenile ideas I'd cultivated until that moment.

By 1977 the adventure that had begun as the so-called 'year of 68' was practically over. The movement had come in suddenly like a wave, surprising us all. It took us by the shoulders and raised us up, higher and higher. If you let it take you, as I did, you could relish the joy up there, with the swirling foam, together with many others, sparkling little bubbles that play in the wind.

But that big wave, after about nine years, finally crashed on the rocks of the collective unconscious, which has a dimension all of its own, heavy and difficult to handle – a collective unconscious that seems to need to pass through great suffering before it can open into the dimension of the heart, where we can welcome other beings as our sisters and brothers.However, the year of '68 has not been lost in the black hole of history, but has in fact entered the larger society as a conscious awakening to many issues that were formerlyoverlooked or even taboo.

In those years at the end of the wave and the ebbing of the movement many of us were hurting, really hurting. Those who had decided to continue by using force were certainly hurting, because it was absurd to fight against the whole world with the same arms they said they abhorred.

Those who were devoted to drugs were hurting because, when heroin arrived, they didn't have a way out. Even thougha few succeeded, over the years, in overcoming their addiction, with the help of community therapy or with strong family support, they were left with their minds dulled and with a constant tendency to search for other kinds of addictions.

The rest of us, like me, who weren't attracted to either violence or drugs, slowly moved into the working world, making careers, having children, forgetting that we were once dissatisfied youths.

A few continued to write in the newspapers or to be part of political movements, but that was a very small minority. Most of us were lost in a stagnant social life and in our personal problems. As for me, I simply thought about ending it all. I was depressed, gloomy, without hope.

My partner and I tried to help each other to stay alive, but it was really difficult. For the first time, I was thinking of committing suicide.

It didn't make sense to me to continue to work at the hospital, with all its insoluble problems, and with a career that had to advance by competition and comparison, by pushing ahead of others and getting good recommendations.

I didn't feel like having children; I couldn't see the point in bringing new human beings into this messed-up world. It didn't make sense to live in the enormous old house I occupied. It didn't make sense to remain in that city which now seemed dead to me and without interest. It didn't make sense to live without a dream, without a future.

I had lived a dream of sharing with so many other companions, sharing a world of new values, hoping for change and freedom. Now alone, without any goal or any hope, it was no longer really worthwhile to continue to live. The only thought that stayed with me was to put an end to my life.

❏❏❏

3   Leaving For the Orient

My physical death didn't happen, but the death of the ego I had constructed up to now definitely did. It happened slowly, hour after hour, during the days and weeks while travelling over land to India. I left in the month of March 1978 with hands empty of the past and a small blue backpack on my shoulders.

Beside me was my companion at the time, Donatella, who had also recently graduated from medical school and who'd entered the revolutionary movement in recent years, mainly because I was a part of it – as I later discovered.

After less than a year she realized that her trip to India was a result of her choice to follow me. It didn't come from any deep feelings on her part. She was in love and like many women in love she wanted to merge with her man, filling herself with dreams and desires that weren't really her own: first, the idea of revolution, then later the life of a disciple.

After the end of my involvement in the movement, I worked in the emergency ward for a few months. But I found it very difficult to be in this structure that I'd rejected and fought against during all my university years. Professional success didn't interest me, nor did making money just to survive, and I didn't want to work in a hospital.

Around this time, in similar situations, my companions were saying "I don't feel it inside," but this was a very approximate way of expressing our inner feelings. It was the best we could do, but it was childish. We were taking a position without knowing the origin from where the decision was coming. With the subsequent years lived in the Master's commune and its therapy work, the 'inside' became more obvious and clear. Feelings were transformed into living experience - with emotions, with eyes, with odours, with kinaesthetic sensations.

Normally, people live with fixed goals and proceed in a certain direction without feeling anything of their emotions and sensations. For example, on the way, we may meet a person and feel an immediate sense of repulsion, irrational rejection, but we don't pay attention to that feeling. On the contrary, we may even establish a friendly relationship or some other kind of social connection – usually for utilitarian reasons.

Then it happens, after years or months, that we get wounded or damaged in some way by that person. In the moment that it happens, we feel a vibration, in the belly or in the chest, an unpleasant pang, or maybe an odour that provokes disgust, or a look that frightens us for a moment, a shiver that goes through our spine.

Because of our education or because of social convenience, we continue the relationship –as friends, lovers, employer-employee, co-worker, whatever – until one day, this person exposes who they are in such a way that we can no longer avoid seeing the violence, the hypocrisy, the dishonesty.

Millions of people live without listening to their own intuition and their feelings. The only thing that functions is their logical mind. Moreover, all our revolutionary years, as we called them, were lived at a purely intellectual level. We talked a lot, shared a lot of ideas – philosophical, political or existential thoughts – but these ideas were disconnected from our inner reality.

In the commune, on the other hand, Osho put at our disposition all the techniques imaginable for us to know and live our deeper truth – our emotions, feelings and sensations. This was no longer a world of ideas but a real world, our inner world, which allowed us to feel how our body-mind system actually works.

I didn't like working in the hospital. There was too much chaos, I didn't like the smells, and I was too sensitive to the pain of sick people whom other doctors treated like machines to repair and with whom they shared no empathic connection.

I could not stand the neon lights, or the heaviness that existed between employees. I could not stand the sick coming in and being left on a stretcher for hours before a specialist could care for them. I couldn't stand the prevailing attitude that the work of a doctor was confined to knowing which antibiotic or which anti-inflammatory to prescribe, or how big a dose of cortisone to give, followed by the final dismissive: "Go now! Next patient!"

The aim of therapy, for me, has always been to treat the person, not the sickness or the symptoms. The symptoms didn't interest me. What interested me was the sick person, the human being in whom, in this moment, sickness was manifesting. Otherwise everything becomes reductive, and this is exactly what has happened in the mainstream medical practice of today. It has become a series of protocols that almost everyone follows, a mechanical, automated system where a computer can perform better than a man.

So, not recognizing any respect for the values I believed in, I found myself isolated in the hospital, with a longing to escape from that infernal mechanism, and I did just that. One day, during my morning rounds, I came out of the ward and headed toward the office building. Shortly afterwards, among the hundreds of doors and corridors, I found the right one.

There was a kind woman in a bright room with tons of paperwork piled on tables. I told her that, in the interests of correctness, I had come to inform her that from this day on there would be a doctor missing in the emergency care ward because I had decided to leave work completely. She looked at me, took some papers, which were forms to fill out, and handed them to me. She told me I had to answer these questions and wait for the next board of directors meeting and that, if they agreed, I could present my request to resign.

I carefully explained to her that I was not filling out any forms, that I was there only to inform the hospital organization that from tomorrow there would be one doctor less in the emergency ward. It was up to them to manage the situation. I politely said good day to her, opened the door and started down the long corridor...

After a few moments I heard someone running behind me. It was the same woman, who ran after me saying, "Doctor! At least wait two weeks, till the end of the month, so that you get paid and then leave." I thanked her. "I'm going," I said, "and from tomorrow this hospital will not see me again." I left as if I was flying, with a strong sensation of lightness, of dropping a big weight from my life. I was free of work. Often choices, once they are made, turn out to be so simple.

That night, my companion Donatella and I decided to leave, go away from the city, away from all memories, away from family, away from friends, leaving everything behind to go to a new world, to places never seen or imagined. The idea was to stay away for at least a year, to live where we felt like living, in natural surroundings, and see what would happen. Our chosen destinations were in South America, especially Peru, where soon there would be a conference on ancient techniques of shamanic healing; or we would go east, in the direction of India and then the Maldives.

In these last few months, a book had come out that was to become a sort of bible for much of the worldwide alternative movement. The book was *The Teachings of Don Juan* by Carlos Castaneda. It described the shamanic view of life as including different levels of reality, which are all interconnected. I was fascinated by it. It was the first book I read that was not about politics or about *Psichiatria Democratica* – an Italian movement to free psychiatric patients from the segregation of mental hospitals.

Because of my interest in shamanism and healing, South America attracted me more than India. I wanted to go to Machu Picchu and other temple areas in order to meet the native peoples who had a background in shamanism.

The Orient, on the other hand, was a place I knew nothing about. I had never read anything about India, Buddha, Shiva, Krishna or reincarnation – absolutely nothing. For me, the East had simply never existed. But I didn't want to choose rationally. The logical mind had tired me out and I was stuffed with ideas that had brought me nothing but constant thoughts of suicide.

So we decided to leave it to 'fate.' We chose to let go completely, into the river of life, for the first time without the mind, without explanations, without organizations. We would decide simply because a coin fell on one side or the other. Heads for India, tails for South America. I really can't remember whether it was Donatella or me who tossed the coin but for sure, while the coin was flying in the air to decide our lives, a guardian angel was delicately and invisibly supporting the process; a guardian angel was guiding the coin that was deciding my life for the rest of its course. That coin made a path for the next 30 years of my life. The coin fell, showing the image of a head, an insignificant symbol up to now. This 'head' decided for us, and for the first time we didn't use our own heads.

Life is fascinating only when it is lived adventurously; otherwise it is reduced to a series of organized events that slowly take us toward death. I hated the example of my father who had always done the same thing in his whole life. Always the same work, always the same habits: getting up in the morning at 6:30...15 minutes for exercise...breakfast always with bread and milk...leaving the house at 7:30...coming home at 1:45...lunch and rest until 3:30...return to the office...coming home at 7:00 in the evening. And it was all carried out in a ghostly silence.

Obviously, I didn't succeed in loving or respecting the methodical nature of the life that emanated from this paternal image. Moreover, there was, and had always been in me, a desire to change everything, to let it all go and start again, which has helped me a lot when I had to make drastic decisions in my life.

So, together with this flip of the coin, we threw everything to the wind: medical career, family, friends, the city, the neighbourhood, revolutions, the emancipation of women, worker power, the proletariat rising to power, drugs opening up the mind, years of exhausting meetings, endless kilometres of citizen marches, and the possibility to make a lot of money and become good bourgeois citizens.

With regard to money....we didn't have any for leaving, neither she nor I. Donatella, however, who came from a more open family than mine, was able to ask her parents for money, with the excuse that she had finished her degree, was tired and needed some rest. I had a father who'd never given me a single gift, so there was no point in talking about it. The only time he promised me a trip was for qualifying for secondary school. When I went to collect the promised prize, he answered, "I don't have any money." Everything said in one line: no money, no enjoyment, no prizes.

So I didn't feel like going to my family and telling them that I wanted to let go of the hospital work in order to go on a trip around the world, without objectives or sure prospects, and top it all off by asking them for money. In any case, I knew my dad would find it impossible to talk about money.

So I decided to ask a friend. He was not really from the movement, but he enjoyed our company and our alternative ideas about the boring nature of middle class life. He was married, with children, but separated from his wife and lived in small villa outside Palermo, near the sea. He loved the sea. He loved it so much that a couple of years after I left he built a catamaran to go on trips by himself. He followed this by sailing the Atlantic alone. Eventually, he met a woman, fell in love and lived with her on the boat for years, traveling around.

I thought he would be the ideal person to turn to for a loan. Silvio had a beautiful heart and was very generous. When I asked him by phone if he could lend me some money for leaving and dropping everything, he didn't hesitate. After a pleasant evening at his house, where I shared my feelings and opened my broken heart to him, he gave me one million lira (about €1000)!

Donatella scraped together even more money from her family. Everything was going well and this was a good omen for the success of our adventure.

I had gained my first experience of independence a few years before, after finishing high school, when I left for London. I stayed there for a few months, supporting myself by selling ice cream from a van on the outskirts of the city.

For the young it is necessary, almost physiological, to rebel against the parents, who seem obsolete and boring. It is only later, with a wider perspective that comes from years of experience – and growing maturity – that we realize how much we should thank our parents for what they did for us.

During my London adventure, I didn't just sell gelato and make money. I also began to smoke joints, so much so that I was getting regularly stoned. I ended up living in a house in London where a feminist friend from Palermo lived with a group of Hare Krishna followers from all over the world. On the second floor of the house lived a modest Italian family with a young child of seven, and with kilos and kilos of hashish. The guy was very nice and willingly shared pieces of his excellent merchandise, which came from India.

London was really an exceptional place in those years and a great location in which to tentatively begin to explore my inner world, aided by dope. There was Pink Floyd, Jesus Christ Superstar, the Beatles and a series of explosive events that would continue to shake the rest of Europe for years to come. I felt I was in paradise. I was free to do what I pleased, to dress how I wanted to – no one judged you in London. Everybody seemed to be smoking dope or taking LSD. What a high those months were!

So when I came back to the narrow-minded provincial mentality of Palermo, I felt like I was in a cage and summarily announced that I was leaving the house. I stayed only because my parents agreed to accept my freedom, giving me an extra key and part of the apartment where I could be more independent. So I continued to smoke dope in the house with my friends, to study and come and go as I pleased until I graduated.

Before leaving for India, I'd completed a course of studies in Palermo that opened up the prospect of self-realization. Even so, I still felt such emptiness in my heart that I felt I had to leave Italy. I only wanted to escape and be free, free of this city and of everything and everyone who reminded me of the past.

But, to spare my poor parents, I didn't say that my intention was to stay a long time far from home, which would have made things a whole lot worse. So I prepared my small blue backpack, which was like a 'Linus blanket' for me, and busied myself with saying goodbye to my relatives: my parents, my sister and her husband and their two children, my nephews, with whom I had an especially joyful relationship. I left them when they were six and nine years old; by the time I returned they had grown up a lot.

My blue backpack was really small and I put very few objects into it: two or three pants and a few shirts; I figured I could buy other things on the road. In a few days we were ready for the big jump into the unknown, traveling to countries never seen or imagined, to people with a completely different type of unconscious mind. We left by train from Palermo to Trieste.

Once we left Italy, we entered the countries that were called friends of communism and moved toward the Soviet bloc, where we began to see things the books of Lenin never mentioned. The sights were beautiful and eloquent, but there was so much poverty in those countries, in those cities. How poor those people were. The misery was everywhere, even in the centre of cities that generally tried to hide the less agreeable aspects, showing off an image of wealth and prosperity that did not correspond to reality. That reality, on the other hand, was strikingly evident the moment you turned a corner into a square or a main street on the outskirts of the city, or in villages that foreigners visited less frequently, or only passed through. The villages, the countryside, the immediate suburbs of the cities all shamelessly revealed their misery without any reticence.

Everything I saw clashed with the social standards I was leaving behind. It made me think that Italy was a rich country that was flourishing and, above all else, ancient. I started understanding what it meant that Rome had been the capital of the Roman Empire. For us, there had already been a golden age of prosperity, some 2000 years ago.

Globalization had not yet created the levelling effects of homogenization that no longer makes us amazed to find Murano glass for sale in Hong Kong and African tribal masks for sale in Venice. At that time, each country was actually different from the rest, with its own characteristics, with definite cultural, mental, geographical, social and emotional features. What stayed with me from those places is not much, except for the impression of finding myself in an extremely poor, social and economic context that I think is still widespread in many ex-communist countries today.

We spent days and nights changing trains, one after the other in succession, finally arriving in a city that is still close to my heart: Istanbul.

Istanbul was the first impactful oriental experience I had and it was magnificent. The city resonated deeply in the strings of my heart, with a spherical vibration from the cupolas, and the soaring minarets that insolently sketched out a blue skyline that matched the shade of the Blue Mosque. The gold of the mosaics, mixed with the pastels of majolica, caught fire in the rays of intense sunlight.

This oriental world I'd hardly even met let me know I'd entered another dimension. The sea, the big port and the waters intertwining with the streets presented a dramatic site that reflected the light in a whole new way. There were millions of people everywhere, a huge variety of colours...and still more colours. The city appeared to me as something totally unique.

It was wonderful to land in this place that was so rich in history, colours and smells. That's it: the smells. Only the East regaled the sense of smell with such quantity and quality of aromas, the most diverse ones being spices, foods and flower essences. These odours stunned me and transported me to distant memories. I started to feel myself going back in time and this sensation continued to get steadily stronger as we gradually got closer to India.

Everything was different – the streets were different, the people had different physical features, the fruit was different - but what was really different was the mentality, a way of seeing and thinking that was totally different from what we knew and what we were used to in Italy and the West.

London had seemed like a dream to me because I could do anything I wanted there, a dream because in London, as well as in Paris, New York and San Francisco, we had already changed the history of the West. And yet fundamentally the mentality remained exactly the same. Even though the languages are different, there is uniformity to the Western mind, and it belongs to all of us: logical, systematic, and rational in all forms and structures of thought.

Here in Istanbul, however, in this first bastion of the Orient, the unconscious mind immediately revealed itself as something different. Deprived of the support of logic and rationality, things unfolded in a completely different way. People's actions appeared to be disconnected and chaos seemed to reign everywhere, especially in giving directions and explanations.

The buses could arrive, or not arrive at all, and any adherence to timetables seemed to be more the result of luck than the consequence of any organized reality. Life was tremendously chaotic and unpredictable: either you let go into this constant flow in which millions of diverse beings were floating, or you were struck by a real panic attack and ran away terrorized.

I was fascinated by this dimension that was so illogical, so different from what I was used to. I continued to smoke dope, which we found without difficulty, and it was really helpful for entering into this reality, for accepting it – so much so that I ended up completely absorbed by it. Nevertheless, we didn't stay many days in Istanbul. In reality, there was a tremendous force that was pushing us to keep going, to go forward, always further to the East.

The space that was opening up toward the Orient resonated in me like an acid trip. I liked acid, although I hadn't done much of it. I felt a strong attraction to those visionary journeys full of insights that could stay with you for a lifetime.

I remember one acid trip that I took on a property my father owned in the countryside. During the experience I entered into intense contact with a dog that my family kept there. The dog and I went on talking the whole night. We cried together and told each other our life stories. From that moment on, my connection to animals changed profoundly and I have no doubt an inner dialogue was created, a sort of silent communication.

Something similar would happen many years later, while walking in the Himalayas, when suddenly and unexpectedly there appeared before me the impressive form of a cobra. It was 1991, more than a year after Osho had left his body, and my future wife and I had gone to those mountains to find a disciple of Osho who'd withdrawn to a small village with a few of his followers.

This man was considered by many to be a realized being, or, as is said in the language of spiritual seekers, an enlightened one.

So now we settled near him for a few weeks in order to share the space of meditation and the life in the small community around the guru. In the morning we often took long walks.

But that morning we went higher into the hills, where the path became narrow and steep. I was walking far ahead when suddenly I felt a silence descend on me that was filled with reverence. I stopped, thinking that an eagle was flying over the area, but in the sky there was nothing, only the blue of the mountains. As if called by a living presence, I turned in the direction from where the impression came and found myself face-to-face with a very real cobra.

Seeing him, opening my arms and my heart, all happened at the same time. From my heart began to flow all the love of which I was capable, while inside my mind there were vibrations of words that didn't have a voice. It was almost as if I wanted to reassure him. I informed him that I was also a being of light, like him, and that I didn't want to do him any harm. On the contrary, I respected and loved him, because we were part of the same family. What came from my heart was a unique, intense vibration that took the form of a message, a message of love. I really felt it – it was not merely a thought. I felt love for that being.

After a few seconds, the cobra started to rise up, half his body erect and taut, while his tongue continued to go in and out very fast. I didn't take my eyes off of him, continuing to watch while sending him all the love that I could. We watched each other like that for a time that seemed interminable, after which he threw himself at me with lightning speed. I started running backwards in order to get away but not to lose sight of him. This strange pursuit lasted for the space of a few metres and then, just as he had appeared, the cobra slid over an embankment and disappeared. He didn't want to kill me, just get me away from his territory. Something was revealed between us.

Going back, for a moment, to my years with the movement, I knew that LSD could open up new horizons for me, but at the same time I was afraid to throw myself totally into the process. In those years of revolution and destroying old concepts, so much was changing that I felt I could easily have got lost in drug-related experiences. Some force in me, at the time unknown, restrained me from throwing myself headlong into the ravines in which I might, otherwise, have been trapped with extreme ease.

□□□

4   The Mystery Begins

    We continued our journey to the Orient. From Istanbul the trip continued by bus and various other means of transport. Bus trips included frequent stops that left the passengers not knowing when we would depart again. The guy who was driving the bus, or someone who suddenly appeared from nowhere to take his place, spent hours under the vehicle repairing breakdowns with imaginative tools, in very creative and ingenious ways, always emerging with a satisfied look on his face. Uncertainty was the cardinal rule.

    Inside these vehicles of transport there was a rich variety of beings of every kind. Men, women and children were consistent passengers, and then there were the changing passengers: pigs, chickens, goats, lambs, hunks of butchered meat, pieces of furniture, and many other objects unimaginable to a Westerner.

    We left Istanbul in daylight, and from that time on we wouldn't have the possibility to sleep regularly. The nights, in fact, almost always transformed themselves into incredible adventures. Our transport vehicles stopped, or broke down, or the driver went to sleep, or waited for hours in the middle of nowhere – for whom or for what no one knew – or someone got sick and had to be taken off.

    At daybreak there were prayers, at sunset there were prayers, during the day there were prayers. It was one continuous prayer, in places that became more and more bizarre. We crossed the Tigris or maybe the Euphrates – I was more inclined to think it was the

Tigris. The countryside was rocky, barren, dusty, inaccessible and steep, with unexpected holes that we entered and exited as if by a miracle. Rocks, rocks, rocks of various colours – predominantly a yellowish brown, with various shades of brownish grey tinged with ash.

Dust, so much dust. Even if those buses had had fireproof windows as now required by law in the West, I don't think I would have been able to avoid inhaling some of it. In any case, windows tended to be optional, often replaced by pieces of plastic jammed into ancient window frames of rusting metal. Our butts became two pieces of imitation leather shot through with the pain of continuous jolts. Donatella was stronger than I had thought and remained tough through these horrific experiences.

At a certain point, I started to draw with some coloured pencils I'd bought along the way. I was trying to insulate myself from the difficulties of the journey. I started drawing slowly, like a puzzle, very small areas of colour that, after some days of pulverizing jolts, gradually took the form of a face.

It was an Aztec face, exactly like the ones seen in National Geographic magazine articles on the pyramids of South America. The face seemed to come out of another unconscious reality. I had never had any contact with South America, but I thought I was being influenced by the only book I'd taken with me, *The Teachings of Don Juan* by Castaneda.

I started reading the book in Palermo and finished it during the trip. It was the first book in which I entered into contact with the world of energy, of astral body travel, of the spiritual master and the expansion of consciousness. I loved Don Juan. I felt filled up and nourished by him when he spoke to Castaneda and I would have immediately become his disciple had I known him. I didn't know exactly what that meant, to become a disciple of someone, but I would soon discover it for myself. I had no idea I was going to a Don Juan much more powerful than the one Castaneda had encountered. I still didn't know that this whole trip was guided by a mysterious force that was taking me home. Anyway, I finished my drawing and really liked it.

At a certain point, after days and days of travel in the middle of this rocky desert between Eastern Turkey and Western Iran, we arrived in a fairy-tale place that evoked the fantastic tales of *A Thousand and One Nights*.

It was almost sunset and shades of rose were starting to tinge all those dull brownish rocks. As the landscape took on an orange rose hue, the beauty of this rocky desert became indescribable. In the distance, we saw something similar to a building, and coming closer we saw columns in a style very similar to the Romanesque sculptured arches of bas-relief. Around the structure there was absolute emptiness – no people or village or houses or fields. There was nothing, only this beautiful arch of triumph in the middle of nowhere, an echo of some long forgotten emperor.

After a few kilometres, tents became visible and we stopped to spend the night. It was all very surreal: this marvellous arch with columns in the middle of the desert where, since time immemorial, sand had been the undisputed queen, and rocks of fantastic colours which were suddenly swallowed up by night into a black nothingness.

The desert night was impressive for the intensity of its darkness, the intensity of a sky filled with stars and all the wonders scattered across the galaxy. Pitch-black darkness all around us, a lavish sky, a body shocked by the withering blows of the bus.... We stretched out on the ground on an enormous mat that seemed to appear from Aladdin's lamp, along with a tent where a fat guy was selling beer.

Yes, my friends, in the middle of nowhere the fat man was selling beer, cold beer. So we enjoyed this fairy-tale scenery in silence, together with a few other people. The rest of the passengers slept inside the bus. Regularly someone would arrive from the darkness of the night and start chatting with the fat guy, as if we were in a bar in the centre of town.

Then, after a while, *he* arrived, a mysterious man dressed in blue. He was on a camel, with a boy who could have been eight or ten years old walking along beside him. He stopped before our mat, got down from the camel, or more accurately, the camel knelt down so he could dismount. The child helped him in everything, as if he was his personal caretaker. He was taller than me, dressed in beautiful clothes of wide material that surrounded his body and hung loosely on his shoulders, all in the colour of a celestial blue that shone brightly in the dark night.

He went toward a man who was already standing there and exchanged a greeting with him that I never forgot, because of the beauty of the male strength that emanated from both of them. Looking into each other's eyes, they embraced each other with their forearms intertwined while powerfully shaking their bodies. Then, putting their arms around each other's waist, by turns they hoisted each other off the ground. That hug was so full of joy and, at the same time so virile that any woman seeing them would fall in love with them.

I had never seen anything like it. The closest thing I had experienced was the Sicilian *vasata* for men – a kiss on the cheek – which was already a good step forward compared to the sterile handshake of Northern Italy and the rest of Western Europe.

He was really a beautiful man, with a strong and athletic body, a face tanned by the sun and an attractive smile etched on his lips, which were dark and full. After that ritual meeting, they sat down and started drinking beer, but *really* drinking, one beer after another. They placed the empty bottles carefully on the ground next to them and the boy gathered them up and took them to the fat man. The fat guy put away the empties and gave more full bottles to the boy who brought them to the two men...They went on like that for a long time, speaking a language I didn't understand. The whole scene was fantastic and I was fascinated by it.

After a period of time, he turned toward me and stared into my eyes, with me returning his gaze. We stayed that way for a long, long time. My mind did not have anything to hang onto and I didn't know what to do, or say. I couldn't imagine what was happening. I only knew that the energy I felt was good and I was not afraid, in fact, I felt charged with energy, male energy of the purest and most natural kind.

My mind stopped. That was the first time I experienced something that could be called No Mind. I was only an energetic presence, pure energy shared with this magnificent man. The boy was always near him, and this added something mystical to the whole experience, giving to me for the first time an understanding of devotion.

Both of these concepts – *No Mind* and *Devotion* – are absolutely unknown in the West and this constitutes an unbridgeable gap between two worldviews: the Orient being *mystical* and the Occident being *logical*. In our future on this planet there will not be any growth in our consciousness if these two concepts do not come together in our daily lives.

The Western mind is conditioned by the need to give a sense of purpose to our actions. For us Westerners, it is inconceivable to seek experiences that don't somehow give us the promise of a certain benefit in the future. Human relations are, fundamentally, oriented toward a particular purpose or a certain personal interest.

The concept of devotion is thousands of miles away. If a Westerner judges relationships that exist in the Orient, relationships that bind two people in a synthesis so different from our own, he may simply shrug and dismiss them as acts of subordination or slavery. A human being that freely chooses to serve and to totally respect another human being does not have a place in our belief system. The social values that predominate today are not real, they are not existential, and shift us further and further away from the light of being that is inside each of us, arriving finally at the opposite of what they should be.

Today, our society no longer respects older people. They have more experience of life, yet are considered obsolete. Lacking current information on the latest computer updates, they are pushed aside. Better to have a young person with you who knows all the information systems, even if he is a victim of an on-going process of robotization.

It doesn't make sense to live without an awareness of our interiority, without contact with the inner sense of the divine, without contact with the mystery, without contact with love, and love has nothing to do with information technology. You can know all the spiritual systems that have existed up to now but you will never find a direct experience on a web page. It doesn't matter if millions and millions of web pages speak of spirituality, of Christ consciousness, of chakras and angels, of light bodies and indigo children, of beings who help us find the right path, of those who have lost their way and found it again. In a web page, you will never find that which will make you grow spiritually.

We have so much information, but information is worth absolutely nothing in relation to direct experience. Direct experience nurtures and transforms every fibre of the body, every part of the brain and all our other organs, and above all our heart and our soul.

Until recently, in tribal cultures and in the Orient, old people were the sages of the village, of the tribe. This was the person who was most respected and who we trusted to make the big decisions, the person to whom we listened in silence because he had knowledge derived from long personal experience of life.

The person who has real knowledge combined with consciousness comes to be respected in the East and is rightly revered as a sage. From this reverence arises the attitude of *devotion* toward a person who knows, from whom you can learn the real things of life. But in the West today such a person is rare, and devotion is almost unknown.

Instead we have arrogance. And all our young people are affected by it because they no longer have an image of the sacred to respect, a sage to listen to, as a point of reference in their lives. It's useless to propose more social legislation if we don't give to human beings the opportunity to recover the healthy values of self-respect and respect for people who have life experience.

Devotion, as an act of recognition toward another human being who can help us travel on the difficult path of life, is in fact the first door to open in the temple of light that is found in human beings – a circular temple with spiral staircases that lead to deeper and deeper parts of our being. Along this path there are doors that open and lead to other spirals that also go deeper and deeper and from which we can gather fundamental knowledge.

The first door we must open in our inner temple is certainly the door of devotion.

The First Door
Devotion

The word devotion means divine action. It is a divine act to recognize real ignorance and respect a person who has direct experience. As long we don't change this and other paradigms that I will talk about little by little in the book, man is and will remain a machine that is devoted to self-destruction.

And so, on that magical night in the desert, with the mysterious man in blue, I remained with my gaze and my heart fixed on him for a long, long time. We were having a silent dialogue, through the eyes, the body and the energy we were sharing. He was curious about seeing a man so different and I was fascinated to have met a person who was not using the logical mind to communicate.

When man connects with nature he uses his heart, his senses and his intuition. The man in blue opened wider a portal in me than LSD had already set ajar. Now this opening was happening without the need of drugs. When this energetic connection ended he came toward me and I gave him my drawing.

He looked at it again and again while I was laughing, content to see him, the majestic blue man, curious as a child with a toy that he didn't understand. It was an act of love that had united us. I stood up, staggering a bit, because while we were looking at each other he continued to offer me beer and I certainly did not want to refuse this act of courtesy on his part.

I said good night to him and the boy and went to sleep filled with colours, with emotions and with so much pure energy that I had received and also rediscovered in myself – with thanks to the blue man who appeared in the tent of Aladdin.

In the morning, however, I felt more sober. I started to feel there was some purpose in this journey that had been completely hidden at the time we started out. It was a journey to know myself, not to know new places or to have new experiences. It was an inner journey that would unfold along the roads that were bringing me to India.

We continued to travel in vehicles that at home could be seen only in car dumps. Yet they continued to transport people from one place to another in the various deserts between Turkey and Iran. Our entry into Iran was really special, both for the circumstances in which it occurred and for the desolate terrain in which we were lost. I remember it being in the middle of the day, in a fierce yellow heat amid arid and rocky land. We hadn't seen green trees for a long time and the predominant colour was yellow in a whole gamut of shades – desert land with no apparent life forms.

We arrived after a rocky descent into a narrow valley that really only had one building. We all had to get out, being invited to enter this edifice in the middle of nowhere. It took a while for us to understand that this was the border between Turkey and Iran. We were in line. We had to pass between two tables where a few armed soldiers would check and stamp our passports. Behind the building, our bus, if you want to call it that, waited for us to depart again.

Donatella followed me, a few steps behind. All the procedures were slow and tiring. I thought they were intentionally playing with us, going slow in order to tire us out. Finally, my turn came. They checked my passport. Slowly, very slowly, they went through the pages, forward and back. Their movements were of a dull slowness that felt like stupidity, looking at each page as if it contained a religious tract. Finally, they returned the passport with a beautiful stamp on it.

As I passed the barrier of wooden chairs I turned to look at Donatella behind me, to give her some energy during these interminable minutes, but she was no longer there. She had disappeared. I looked everywhere. In that room we were only about fifty people, so she could not be hidden from my view. But I couldn't see her. It was as if she had suddenly dissolved into nothingness. I started to call out to her in a loud voice and tried to go back, but the soldiers blocked me because I was now in Iranian territory and could not re-enter Turkey.

I tried to make them understand that this was ridiculous and that she was in the same room, that I wanted to know where my companion had gone, but there was no way – they would not let me cross the line of tables that represented the impassable boundary.

So I started to insist, even to scream, but there was no way. Either they didn't understand, or they didn't want to understand, and they started to push me out of the room with force.

I waited outside, hoping that sooner or later she would come out, but I didn't see her. Everyone else was coming out and getting back on the bus, and when all passengers were aboard, the driver made a sign to me to get on the bus and leave. I tried to make him understand that my friend was missing and that I could not abandon her there. I put myself in front of the bus in order to block it.

The guy got more and more nervous and wanted to leave at all costs. I was desperate – what had happened? I couldn't leave without her, I couldn't leave her there in the hands of men who spoke another language and who had expressions on their faces that were less than reassuring. I didn't know what to do anymore. They didn't understand – they were like stubborn mules, impossible to speak to, and anyway I could not decipher their language.

When would we have the chance to board another bus going to Pakistan? And where was Donatella? These questions were hammering in my mind without any answer. After endless discussions with the driver, who insisted that he wanted to leave, she finally came running out of the building.

"Let's escape! Let's escape now! We must get out of here..."

We left immediately. She was very upset and in shock and she needed some time to calm down before she managed to tell me what had happened. Two guards had taken her forcefully from the line and brought her to a small room where they tried to rape her – that's what happened! She fought with all her strength to escape. In the end, she gave a hard kick in the balls to these two bullies, then managed to open the door and escape.

The further east we went, the more dominant became the male energy, and very little of the feminine could be detected anywhere. In these countries where sex is so violently repressed, the impact has been brutal, especially for women. It took Donatella many days to recover from this incident, and I do not know how much it affected her in later years. For millions of women these devastating episodes create a psychological trauma that affects their whole life.

Sex remains, and will always remain, the primary drive in human beings because the race has to reproduce and continue the species. But for centuries this basic drive has been distorted, repressed and massacred by religions that have the goal of keeping the masses subdued in order to manipulate them. Women have experienced the most devastating consequences of this. Both in the West and the East, female sexuality has been misinterpreted and exploited for the use of men.

In the energy system of the human body there are centres that accumulate energy, connected by the nerve plexus, which have the function of maintaining, accumulating and using certain types of energy. In the system of Indian Yoga these centres are called *chakras*, a Sanskrit word meaning 'wheels.' We have many chakras, but there are seven primary ones.

The first is found in the perineum, between the genitals and the rectum, at the muscular base of the pelvis. This is the centre that conserves sexual energy, the potent energy of reproduction for the species. In Kundalini Yoga, this chakra is represented by a sleeping cobra coiled up in itself. During yogic practices and meditation, this powerful energy wakes up and the serpent starts rising against gravity in order to activate the higher centres. So sexual energy constitutes the primary force for humans and when it's repressed it necessarily manifests in a variety of sexual perversions.

Sigmund Freud based his psychoanalytic work on the interpretation of sexual energy in dreams, in order to understand the human psyche. He observed that this energy is powerful and explosive, like a huge waterfall, and it is not possible to repress it. Or, to be more accurate, it is not possible to repress it without perverting it.

Any man who does not receive a healthy sexual education will repress this energy in diverse ways, working against this force of nature, turning the drive itself into something negative and destructive. The basis of war in the world is the repression of sexual energy. If a human being lives his sexual energy fully and has healthy orgasms, then homicidal instincts and violent urges would not manifest and our world would certainly be the better for it.

A healthy orgasm, the union of masculine and feminine reaching a peak together, brings inner peace. In 90% of cases, men and women don't have full orgasms. The majority of men suffer from premature ejaculation, meaning that they abandon the act of love after a few minutes. This has brought on the widespread use of Viagra, with which men try to compensate for their impotence. And by the way, ejaculation is not the same thing as orgasm.

Whoever speaks openly about sexual energy is denigrated and opposed. We urgently need to provide a healthy sexual education in schools. My feeling is that, by the end of primary school, kids should be informed about their most basic energy and understand how it operates.

For instance, they need to understand that the orgasmic energy for women rises very slowly, much more slowly than for men. For this reason, for a man to be able to follow and accompany the energy of a woman, he must enter into contact with his inner female. A healthy sexual act requires a lot of time and a protected, welcoming atmosphere where both partners can let go and share the intention to discover their energy without limitations. An orgasm might need hours to arrive and the more time together that precedes orgasm the better. Hours of intimacy in order to welcome this experience, even days together with all the time at your disposal, only in this way it is possible to experiment deeply with orgasm.

Who takes this much time? Who considers love-making important enough to stay together with another being in the depths of intimacy for so long? No one has time to spend days together; very few people give themselves this luxury. Sex is lived by us Westerners as a release valve, a quick energetic catharsis where the energy is dispersed and not accumulated. By not allowing themselves to fully live this explosive energy, men start to produce perversions.

For example, power is a form of perverted sexual energy. The desire to control others, the feeling of strength that comes with dominating the masses and deciding their fate is nothing other than sexual energy not lived in healthy way. A slogan from the hippies of the '60s in America was, "Make love not war." They were perfectly right.

Every day we read stories in the newspapers about incredible depravity, most of which is likely the result of repressed sexuality. It seems our society is built on hypocrisy, allowing the 'good' people to commit horrific but socially sanctioned acts.

For instance, in the time of war in Yugoslavia, when that country fragmented into Serbia, Croatia and Bosnia, a business was created with many offices in different parts of Europe that offered a week in the war zone for rich people seeking 'relaxation.' They were provided with all the necessary gear and they could shoot and kill people in order to release their tensions. After a week of killing, they returned relaxed to their workplace. And this is a healthy society?

Continually, we read in the newspapers about women or girls who are raped by packs of males who discharge their sexual aggression this way. As I see it, hiding behind this aggression is a deeper sense of impotence. Deep down, men feel impotent when comparing their single ejaculation to a woman's capacity for hours and hours of orgasm. In this situation, man knows he can dominate women only with brute physical force.

Men are afraid to let go into intimacy and contact their own female side. Many men who do acknowledge that feminine side choose to become homosexuals, but the truth is that a big percentage of every man's energy can manifest as a feminine expression if it is allowed a natural outlet. Likewise, every woman's energy has a strong masculine component that also needs to be lived.

It's the union of these two energies inside us that ultimately brings the joy and peace of connecting with the divine. If human beings don't contact and accept these two polarities inside, they remain forever 'mechanical men' and never develop the divine component.

Sex is the primary energy that we need to work with, in order to refine it and bring it to the heart where it starts to become divine. The Heart Chakra is in the centre of the chest. Its name in Sanskrit is *anahata*. Its colours are pink and green. The gland that sustains it is the thymus. The emotion that is released when the heart chakra is activated is love.

So, as we have seen, sex is the raw energy of human beings and can manifest in almost any form, either healthy or perverted. It can be used in an animalistic way, or it can be used to bring more awareness and consciousness.

The animalistic form serves only to release accumulated tensions and to start the procreation of another being. In the repressed form, it has created so much distortion that we would need volumes just to speak about it. Used with awareness, on the other hand, it creates a sublime energy and brings man more and more in contact with the experience of the divine.

Up to now, most of humanity has used this energy in an animalistic way and only a very small percentage of people have tried to use it in order to evolve: the Tantric schools in India, the Sufis in the East and the Taoists in China. The rest of the population continues to use it destructively.

***

So we arrive at the spiral in our inner temple of light where the second door, the door of sexuality, can be seen. At this door, the majority of people spend their lives trying to manipulate their sexual energy to feed their egos. This energy is so overpowering that to open it and enter it consciously, we need the help of a spiritual guide. Without this help, almost all human beings down the centuries have lost their way and self-destructed.

The Second Door
Transformation of Sexual Energy

The evolution of human beings happens through the creative use of their sexual energy and the transformation of this energy so that it is refined into its highest form, which is love.

5 India Comes Closer

In buses that were ever more damaged and precarious, we continued our journey toward the Orient. My most vivid memories are of stops in the middle of nowhere, when nothing was visible all the way to the horizon. Then suddenly there cropped up, seemingly out of the desert itself, kids selling tea to travel-weary passengers. Many stops were for prayers; they got off the bus, bowed down, prayed, got back on and departed.

Like that, after a really long trip, we arrived in Pakistan. We stopped a few days in Quetta, a city of low houses parched by the sun that was inhabited by millions of people. The heat was unimaginable, too much even for us Sicilians, going up to 120 degrees Fahrenheit in the shade.

It was April, the hottest month on the Indian subcontinent. In the city you couldn't walk until the evening, when the desert coolness arrived and lowered the temperature a little. The daytime was literally an inferno. The hotel in Quetta was our first after weeks of sleeping on the ground and shaking in the bus. The first night in the hotel, we finally ate something decent and went out on the terrace to take some fresh air under a fantastic sky, with a crescent moon riding low on the horizon.

It was the first time I saw an oriental crescent moon and understood we were in another collective unconscious where the symbolism was different from our own and the logical mind had very little space. In the East, the crescent moon is reclining gracefully in the evening sky, rather than standing upright as in the West.

The intense heat put my body in incredible stress. I wasn't hungry and drank only liquids, sweating continuously, and every movement was exhausting. After a few days of rest, we decided to keep going, with the idea of reaching Mumbai, where we would depart for the Maldives. Surely, on those beautiful islands, surrounded by the sea, we would feel better. We intended to stop there, in paradise, for a long, long time, at least two or three months, and then see.

More buses to the border, then trains, but this time *Indian* trains. Anyone who travelled through India in those days would put their head in their hands and start to laugh or cry at the mention of Indian trains.

Indian trains are locomotives with cars packed full of human beings, not only inside but also hanging on the outside and on the roof. When a train leaves the station, usually at least two or three hours late, you suddenly see hundreds of people – all men, to tell the truth – running with the train and then climbing up onto the roofs of the cars. They appear like a sudden swarm of locusts and jump on the train with a speed and agility that seems totally natural, almost as if handed down for generations.

So by the time the train left the station, it was carrying all the regular passengers inside, plus all those calmly attached to the outside. In time, some of them managed to enter the cars through the windows, others jumping off at the next station. It all happened in a climate of total chaos, acceptance and hellish heat.

I remember we took the train for India from Karachi, a chaotic city that, as I remember, only tired and depressed me. After Istanbul, it was the first big city we encountered. Nevertheless, we stopped there only to organize our travels to India. We arrived on Indian soil on rusty rails, one month after our initial departure. The train moved slowly, loaded down with human beings who, in spite of the oppressive conditions emanated a sense of peace and happiness. This was the first time on our journey to the East that I noticed this quality among the people.

I found the faces of Indians to be beautiful. Both men and women usually have graceful faces and, above all, shining eyes. Unfortunately, in those early days I felt exhausted and had very little energy to enjoy the new world in which we were arriving. We stopped in the first town to rest, because we felt really worn out. We took a small hotel in a city whose name I cannot remember. The heat persisted and increased, going up to 120 degrees, I think, and my body was really finished.

Thinner and more exhausted than ever, I asked myself for what purpose I'd come to these places so far away and so different. My body couldn't go on anymore. That night I thought I was dying, I was so completely exhausted, and in the late night I felt worse than when I had lost consciousness as a child. I passed out on the hotel bed.

In these latitudes a hotel meant a house swallowed up in the midst of millions of other two-storey houses without air conditioning, without a separate room for the bath, without a fridge, and with only the inexorable fan hanging from the ceiling of the room as it continued turning day and night.

Donatella dragged me to the corner where the shower was, turned it on and left me on the floor with the water running over me. I regained consciousness, but lacked any strength. I stayed on the ground – I didn't have the capacity to move. She was also at the end of her endurance and remained immobilized, stretched out on the bed under the fan. We spent the night in this condition until dawn came.

The whole night I was watching the water running over my body, lying flat on the floor in the corner of a dark room of an Indian hotel, where my death would go completely unnoticed in the midst of millions of beings who were surviving in precarious conditions where death could come at any moment.

Why, why, I asked myself, had I come to this strange country? To die here? Why had I pushed so far, to risk my own life? What was this hidden force that moved me as if I were a magnet attracted by the opposite pole?

Spirituality had never interested me, neither Hinduism, yoga nor any other discipline. Nothing could explain to me why I had left everything and headed toward a land unknown to me. That was how the night passed, with doubts running through my mind like the water running over my body. I think it was dawn when I fell asleep, or passed out again, I can't remember.

In the following days I felt I was in pieces, not only physically but also emotionally. I no longer knew what I was doing on this absurd trip. The world outside was too different from that of my origins. I didn't want to move, I didn't know what to do, and Donatella was just as confused. She was continually asking me what was the purpose of our trip. We had left because we wanted to live in nature, as far away from civilization as possible. But by now I realized the world is vast, diverse, multidimensional, and I was a tiny microorganism in an enormous universe, without the slightest understanding to whom this microorganism belonged.

For the first time, I felt insecure, weak and fragile. I no longer had any sense of certitude in my life. Here, I was really nobody, not a doctor, nor an Italian, nor did I have family or friends I could contact – I was literally at risk like a shipwrecked person lost in the middle of the sea.

After spending some time in the room to rest and eat, we set off again, for Mumbai – which at this point seemed like an oasis in the desert. We arrived in the daytime, so we could easily see the vastness of this immense city that seemed to have no limits.

Mumbai reminded me of the circles of Dante's hell. I had studied the *Divine Comedy* in classical school and was familiar with its different circles of hell. I think Dante must have succeeded in reaching this city by some mysterious means, in order to be able to describe his hell so well. In his allegory, there are circles of hell where the sinners are condemned to the worst hunger. Here in Mumbai, people often take opium to stave off hunger and be able to last a few days more. They live in streets full of mud. In fact, to be more accurate, they live in mud, in houses that are nothing more than sheets of plastic held together by string. They don't call them circles. They call them 'slums.'

Slum areas are located all over Mumbai, in the most surprising places. You can find yourself visiting these circles of hell with your own Caronte, who is the driver of your rickshaw, a kind of motorized cart with three wheels, covered by a tarp. And then suddenly you find yourself in the middle of a magnificent avenue filled with stupendous trees you have never seen before – even in your imagination – bursting with orange flowers that make you feel drunk just by passing near them.

That's Mumbai. Different levels of reality go on melting into each other, weaving continuously between hell, purgatory and paradise. We entered small lanes lined with colonial style English villas that offer all you could possibly want in the way of a rich and luxurious residence, with dozens of servants working in landscaped gardens, garages and outbuildings. There were equally magnificent cars, big, round and shining, so shiny, in fact, that they seem to have just been delivered from auto shows in Hollywood.

Some hotels were so big and luxurious you felt dizzy when you entered the reception halls with ornate doors and enormous spaces covered with satin, fragrant fresh flowers, statues of various Hindu gods and with sofas that were the most comfortable that had ever existed.

But when you exited from the back door of the hotel you found yourself immediately in the circle of hell reserved for beggars, who swarmed around you like flies, with outstretched palms, intoning the hymn, "*Baksheesh baba, baksheesh baba, baksheesh baba....*" They could go on singing their refrain for hours if necessary, trying all the tonalities, not abandoning this struggle to separate you from a rupee — until you give it just to end this persistent humiliation. It is for this reason that Indian beggars know how to sing so wonderfully well.

Mumbai is huge, chaotic and as steamy as a Turkish bath. The traffic in Palermo or Naples is a paradise compared to what it is in Mumbai, where you can find yourself stuck in an interminable line of cars, buses, rickshaws and cows, not to mention the encampments of the 'untouchable' families living in the midst of it all. Sometimes you are sure you will be stuck there forever, jammed between the vehicles and the pedestrians who move like herds around your taxi.

The various levels of existence in Mumbai continue to blend until you, the insignificant Western tourist, completely lose your sense of orientation and come to be manipulated with ease by the rickshaw and taxi drivers, who at the end of your journey, ask you for much more money than an Indian would pay. But the drivers are part of Dante's circle of greed, condemned to spend their whole lives in tin boxes, sweating and manipulating tourists in order to survive.

I understood that these driver-souls alleviated this terrible punishment of their occupation by making brief stops, during which they got out without saying anything to their passengers, started speaking to other beings from other circles of hell, went to have a *chai* and eventually returned lighter and ready to face, once again, the long journey through the labyrinth of the city.

Chai is the drink that is consumed by all Indians, regardless of what circle they belong to, regardless of what caste they belong to or what city they live in. It is a strong black tea, brimming with spices, primarily cardamom, ginger and cinnamon, and a lot of boiled milk, not only boiled by fire but also by the sun of the city. Oh yes...and sugar, lots and lots of sugar, not sprinkled on afterwards but cooked into the potent brew.

So an average Indian can drink a dozen cups of *chai* in a day – that is, when he is not busy with the time-honoured occupation of chewing *pan*, his other great love. A leaf from a pan tree is smeared with lime paste, then packed with boiled areca nut and spices, rolled into a quid then chewed until it colours the oral cavity with different tints ranging from red to an intense violet colour. Folded in a triangle, the leaf is offered ceremoniously from small, mobile vending stalls everywhere on the subcontinent.

Even the richest people have the same habits and the only difference is that their two fetishes, *chai* and *pan*, are served in porcelain plates by reverent servants in livery, in gilded kiosks. The substances are the same in this great democratic India, where everyone has their chance to stuff themselves with *chai* and *pan*.

We felt lost in this ocean of humanity, with red mouths and the blackest eyes and faces. All we could do was abandon ourselves into the hands of a bigger destiny.

We rested for quite a few days, enjoying the luxury of a city that was really rich and really poor at the same time. In India, I understood immediately that contradictions could easily coexist in the mind, unlike in the West, where we struggle to keep them separate, hiding from the ones we find unpleasant. In India, opposites are lived simultaneously and the most intense opposite to life is surely death, which is lived in a way unthinkable for a Westerner.

Death in this huge subcontinent stares everybody in the face every day—young and old, rich and poor, men and women, without any distinction. You can find a dead body in front of a house, lying patiently in the road, waiting for the family to collect enough money to buy wood to burn it. The more money, the more wood and the more effectively the corpse burns at the burning *ghat*. The relationship is very simple, meaning that, when the fire has burned out, the cadavers of the poor leave pieces of flesh and bone languishing in the smoke, or dragged around the countryside by animals and birds, food for dogs and vultures.

The Parsi religion has its own centre in Mumbai – historically, it was actually outside the city when members of this faith first arrived, centuries ago, fleeing from persecution in Iran – and its priests have avoided the practice of cremation. Rather, they place the corpse on a steel grate that covers a deep well, and the body is consumed by waiting vultures and crows.

In whatever part of India you care to visit, you will always find an enormous number of crows cawing from morning till night in a noisy and endless search of food. From sunrise to sunset their song, or strident screeching – depending on the mental state in which you find yourself – accompanies you everywhere in India. They are the all-purpose flying scavengers of this country.

Death is totally accepted by Indians; it is not taboo like in the West. It is received, respected and celebrated as the most important part of our lives. Death is regarded as a passage, like birth – two spokes of the wheel of life that is turning continuously in time and space. This vision of a wheel offers an enormous sense of relaxation to the Western mind because it no longer needs to consider life as a single trajectory lasting 70 or 80 years, but a vast circle, as vast as existence itself.

For Westerners, death is the end of everything; whatever we have done gets wiped out forever. So this short life gets transformed into two phases: the first, an indescribable stress and rush to somehow cram every experience into a short time; the second, an awesome emptiness waiting at the end of this mad race. Even though they tell us that paradise awaits us after death, in the collective unconscious mind there is doubt whether this place really exists. Over the centuries, no one has come to tell us they have been in paradise.

On the other hand, in India there are human beings who have ventured inside the personal and collective mind and have come out of it illuminated, realizing paradise in a totally different way. Indian history is full of human beings who have discovered paradise on earth, and the people who witnessed this have followed them, acknowledging them as spiritual Masters.

Over the centuries, millions of people have seen, touched and lived the experience that paradise, or Nirvana, exists. They have seen the Buddha walking and breathing as we all do, preaching and explaining that **paradise is inside of us**. They have seen Mahavira, Meera, Kabir, Farid, Chaitanya, Ramananda, Raidas, Ramakrishna...all living examples of this. These Buddhas that have existed have shown us that paradise is possible **here and now**, not in some other worldly paradise after death.

This, I think, is the fundamental difference between the Indians and us. They have accepted and respected these Buddhas, or Tirthankaras, while we, when we had one, crucified him. And although very few know about it, Jesus fled to India after the crucifixion and stayed there for the rest of his long life.

The acceptance of death, and allowing the possibility that each of us can become a Buddha/Christ, forms the line of demarcation between a stressed and materialistic Occident and an essentially spiritual and pacifist Orient. In the history of India there has never been an expansionist imperialistic war to inflict damage on other peoples, as so often happened in the West. India has never moved toward war with its neighbouring countries in order to expand its political or religious power. Over the centuries, invaders have entered India, from China, from Mongolia, from the Middle East, but India has never moved against other states.

India has an essentially pacifist culture because for centuries so many of its people have realized their inner divinity, sharing it compassionately with the general population. Krishna lived more than 5,000 years ago and in the sacred texts it is said that there were already Buddhas living before him, perhaps even as long as 10,000 years ago.

The Western mind is limited in comparison to the Indian mind, which has an ancient past illuminated by personalities that have profoundly influenced the path of human consciousness on this planet. Western history consists of wars, deaths, massacres, invasions, jealousies and continuous power games that have impoverished the lives of millions of human beings. Essentially, the West is so identified with the rational mind and with a pseudo-religion conceived as a set of childish beliefs, that it has had no choice but to live for centuries in a state of existential anguish and spiritual emptiness.

For millennia, India has always focused its attention on the realization of the divine, which is inside us, not outside us. Indians say the world, as we see it with our unaware eyes is *maya*, illusion, nothing more than a mental projection. Starting from these presuppositions, a single individual takes responsibility for his own life, which he can spend endlessly looking for material comforts, or he can focus on the interruption of *maya*, of the false projections we have of life.

In the West, the individual cannot take responsibility for his life because that life is like a helpless pawn in the hands of an omnipresent, all-powerful and totally aware God that decides everything for everyone. The individual can only submit and surrender, moaning and accepting it.

The Third Door
Free Choice

The divine is in us and not outside of us. And it is the responsibility and free choice of the individual to bring his attention to the light or to the darkness.

All the Buddhas, from time immemorial, have been living examples of this, showing the whole world this is the truth because they have experienced it.

Mumbai constituted the first approach to a new world, a reality that was different in almost every way from what I had known. I was open and began to feel and see new colours that were more alive, more intense than in the West. My rational mind had started to dry up like clay in the hot oriental sun. The old mask I had worn for so many years began to crack and break up.

After some days in Mumbai, we were ready to take the boat that would finally deliver us to our oasis. In the Maldives, we would give free rein to our Western dream of rest and relaxation. There, we would be able to live in a simple and natural way for a long time, so long that eventually we would come to understand what we wanted to do with our lives.

The port of Mumbai is enormously chaotic and it was difficult to understand where to go to get information about a direct boat to the Maldives. Fortunately, at that time, there were no planes that flew to these secluded islands. Nowadays there are regular flights, carrying millions of tourists there to live an unreal dream for a week, to drop into a made-to-order fictitious paradise that encourages them to spend money and gives them the illusion of relaxation.

Today the secluded paradise is one of the most polluted regions in the Indian Ocean, thanks to the stupidity of human greed, thanks to this human machine that manages to destroy everything because it wants to own everything.

At the port we learned that the maritime service provided trips to the Maldives only once a month, and the ship had left a few days ago. Had we arrived a week earlier, my life would have gone in an entirely different direction. Again, an unexpected, chance event had altered my life, just as a month ago a coin landing heads up had sent us toward the Orient. One month after spinning the coin, a boat missed by a few days finally brought us toward the real goal of our trip, toward the only real oasis that I have found.

Missing that ship made possible my meeting the being I have loved the most and still love. And I wouldn't miss that meeting even if I had to return to this form and this earth many times again. A series of apparent coincidences had brought me to the real purpose of my life. Still unaware, I saw all of these difficulties as obstacles and not as help coming to send me in the right direction, which is toward the Master.

In those days, I was always distressed by what I now call destiny, by the apparent sticks that fate continued to jam in my wheels, coming between me and what my mind had decided was the right thing to do. Living as machines, humans pursue goals that are not existential. So they pass their lives trying to reach outcomes they do not need. They exhaust all their energy and persist against all difficulties to get their own way, because they absolutely want to reach a particular status, or manifest a specific desire that, once realized, leaves them with a more bitter taste in their mouths than before.

If the person reading this page, in this moment, is sincere with himself and looks inside, he can only confirm what I am writing. We push against enormous difficulties that only dishearten us and rob us of our vital energy. In society, in our education and understanding, nothing helps us to follow the flow of life. Instead, we are subject to the conditioning of ambition; we have been trained to swim against the current in order to reach fixed ideals that really don't belong to us. These are the ideals of the society, the unrealized ideals of our parents. These, too, are the pseudo-religious ideals that are programmed in us from the moment we are born, like the little statue of Christ on the cross, hanging above the bed of every Catholic child – ideals that invade the mind with the concept of 'suffering,' if you're not suffering, you're not on the straight and narrow path.

Nothing, absolutely nothing and no one in the West comes to us saying: **Life is not suffering and if we let go into the flow of energy in which we live everything will go well.**

So, arriving in Mumbai, I was also fighting to go in a direction that was completely wrong for me, but which I thought was the right thing to do. Events, however, were too big to fight them, and anyway by now my ego was shattered.

6   Meeting the Master

    I had no desire to stay another month in Mumbai, waiting for the next boat, and nor did Donatella. Instead, we thought about going to a nearby beach, or perhaps to some local hill country where the heat would be more tolerable.

    Then I remembered receiving an intriguing postcard from India about six or seven months earlier, from an old friend called Maria Pia. She was a feminist, an adventurer and a rebel; she'd rejected every social structure, every social game, and was travelling the world in search of new ways of living.

    I'd received her strange postcard while living in Palermo and at first assumed she was staying with an international community of hippies, somewhere in India, as she'd done in London where we'd met.

    Her postcard had this message for me: "Here, everything is orange, even the soap for washing your hands. I have never been so happy in my whole life. Kisses. Maria Pia."

    At the time, I'd assumed she was exaggerating her happiness, but still I kept the postcard with her address… just in case. This, surely, was the moment to take out her card and see in which part of India she was living.

    The address read: "17 Koregaon Park, Poona." We looked in our guidebooks for the location of this city of Poona, which has since changed it's spelling to 'Pune,' and were surprised to discover it was on the Deccan Plateau, 600 metres higher than Mumbai, and only 120 miles away. Wow!

Our decision was made. We would spend the next three weeks with Maria Pia, then return to Mumbai to take the ship to our final destination, our oasis. In my mind, the oasis was still the goal, still beckoning on the horizon... a place where finally I would be able to relax and rest.

We left with the first available train, which arrived in Pune well after midnight at the end of a six-hour journey that included a long, slow climb up the Western Ghats onto the Deccan Plateau. It was night and we couldn't see much through the train windows, but as we climbed higher we sensed we were heading for a cooler, more civilised location than Dante's Inferno, back down on the coastal plain.

Coming out of Pune station, we decided to go straight to Maria Pia's house, knowing she would welcome us with open arms even though it was by now one o'clock in the morning. I showed Maria's postcard, complete with address, to a waiting rickshaw driver, who wagged his head from side to side in the classic Indian-style expression of assent – meaning, in this case, "Yes, I know where it is and I can take you there."

In the sleepiness of our early morning arrival, I'd forgotten that almost all *rickshaw wallahs* – especially those lingering outside railway stations after midnight – are members of a 'circle of greed' designed to extract the maximum amount of money from ignorant tourists like ourselves. I trusted the guy and he duly arrived at the address an hour later. Next day, we discovered the distance between Pune train station and Koregaon Park can be covered in ten minutes. The greedy one had taken us on a long detour around town in order to inflate the fare.

Koregaon Park was clean and quiet, its avenues lined with huge trees. However, as we entered one of these avenues, our way was blocked by a foreigner with an accent I recognised as German. He was wearing an orange robe, with long hair spilling down over his shoulders, and sported an impressive beard that gave his face a surly, unwelcoming look. Shining a bright flashlight into our eyes, he ordered us to backup.

"Who could this be?" I wondered. The last thing I expected to find in this city suburb was a tall, grumpy German, dressed in bright

64 | MY LIFE WITH OSHO

orange, acting like a traffic policeman. We explained we were on our way to my friend's house, which apparently was located on this street, but our pleas had no effect. The German informed us we could proceed only after six o'clock in the morning and continued to block our way with such authority that we had no choice but to turn around.

The incident certainly fitted with our experiences of the past few days: always more obstacles, always more exhaustion. Now we urgently needed a hotel, which our *rickshaw wallah* found for us after another half-hour of circum navigating Koregaon Park, even though, in reality, the hotel was no more than 300 yards from where we'd been stopped. We slept deeply, with no intention of waking up at six o'clock. Eventually, we left the hotel around 10 o'clock in the morning, on foot, as the hotel manager told us we were close to our destination.

Even though we were bleary-eyed and only half-awake, we immediately sensed the energy in Koregaon Park was completely different from Mumbai. It was inviting, fresh and somehow mysterious. We entered the street where the German had stopped us the night before and this time there were no obstacles. Rather, we felt this avenue opening up before us like a passage to the soul…

There was a silence in the street that seemed almost mystical, broken only by the singing of birds that fluttered from one enormous tree to another, and there was peace… yes, there was no other way to describe it… a sense of absolute peace. Two rows of flowering bougainvillea bushes, flourishing beneath the giant trees, gave colour to both sides of the street. Colonial English villas, a hangover from the days of the Raj, followed one after the other, with plenty of space between them for lavish gardens.

We arrived at a giant gate made of solid teak, painted black and decorated with gold studs. The gate comprised two sections that met in the middle when rolled together on small wheels. This, I later learned, was the so-called 'gateless gate' that separated the ashram from the world. Two big Germans were pushing the gate open as a stream of angelic-looking beings exited the ashram, all dressed in orange clothes. They were very beautiful. Almost all of the men had flowing, virile-looking beards, while the women, to my delight, wore soft, loose garments that revealed their marvellous curves.

I was very exhausted from the trip, but all of a sudden I felt like a black fly on a stupendous orange flower. I was dressed in black Pakistani pants, tied by a string at the waist, and a black t-shirt. My hair was closely cropped to cope with the excessive Indian heat and my face was decorated with a pair of Lenin-style glasses stolen from my father for the purpose of looking as intellectual and politically radical as possible. Here, however, I experienced my entire image as hard and heavy.

Some event had evidently just finished within the gate. Participants were streaming out and milling around the entrance, while others were heading in the opposite direction into the ashram. Those travelling in both directions took every opportunity to hug each other. These hugs had the quality of tender embraces, sweet and sensual, as if everyone was in love with everyone else.

Where was I? Where had I ended up?

I tried to ask some of these ethereal beings where I could find the house of Maria Pia, but it felt awkward to be so practical and mundane amid this ocean of love and sweetness. One of the two bearded Germans brought two chairs and calmly told us to sit outside the gate and wait. I studied his face and noticed that this was a being with beautiful blue eyes that seemed full of light.

So Donatella and I sat outside the gates of paradise, waiting...maybe for half an hour. Time became elastic and seemed to expand, while my mind and body gradually relaxed, as I watched these people who'd come from all over the world hugging and appreciating each other without any inhibition, without any prejudice, in a simple, natural and loving way.

Inside the ashram, I saw a wide path about one hundred metres long, stretching from the main gate to another gate that was more simple in design and made of metal. This was obviously the ashram's main thoroughfare, but people were also walking in different directions, using other paths hidden from my field of vision.

Suddenly, at the far end of the main path, I saw an old woman with white hair, dressed fully in orange, come running towards the main gate. It was a marvellous sight. She must have been at least 70 years old and yet she was running in a light and happy way with an ecstatic smile on her face. She looked so sweet and relaxed as she ran that I also became ecstatic just watching her.

I didn't think I could be the reason for this very beautiful and feminine run, but when she arrived at the main gate she hugged me, squeezing me between her warm and maternal breasts like a mother that was seeing her son after years and years of waiting and hoping. She looked at me and said, "Finally you arrived!" Still the memory of that moment makes me cry, even now, more than 30 years later.

Finally you arrived!

She looked at me with more love than I have ever felt in my life. I began to cry. In fact, I cried and cried for many days, so unexpected and pure was that loving welcome. Bhakti was the spiritual name that had been given to her by Osho. She was here with her daughter, who in the coming months was destined to be my 'Zen Master' – the ashram's favourite term for 'boss' – as head of the commune kitchen where I would work for part of my stay.

Why did Bhakti's welcome touch me so deeply? I understood it almost immediately: she was conveying to me the welcome of the Master himself. She was pouring his love and his energy into me, and it went straight to my heart. From that day on, I looked for Bhakti every day in order to give her a hug, exchange a few words and then continue on my way.

And so, on that first morning, it dawned on me: I hadn't simply arrived in the house where Maria Pia lived. I'd arrived in an experimental community founded by a very controversial spiritual Master. I had arrived... Or, to say it better, the flow of life had brought me here... Or, to say it even more profoundly, the Master had welcomed me to his commune.

In those days, the Master was called Bhagwan Shree Rajneesh. This name was given to him by his beloved Indian disciples. 'Bhagwan' is Sanskrit and indicates the divine, while 'Rajneesh' means 'Lord of the Full Moon.' Many gurus in India are called 'Bhagwan' by their disciples, but as far as I was concerned this man was much more than a guru. As I came to know him more and more deeply, I understood he was nothing less than a new Gautama

Buddha. He was the Christ of the 20th century who was bringing a new spiritual message for the next two thousand years. Many years later, Bhagwan was to change his name to 'Osho' and this is the name I prefer to use when referring to him.

Meanwhile, I had arrived in the cradle of this open-minded Master, the only one who had the power to dismantle the old religions that had dominated humanity up to now, as well as the political systems that went hand-in-hand with them.

In addition, he was the only one to have the courage to demolish the deeply ingrained hypocrisy that is inherent in all religious and political systems. He incarnated in order to bring a new concept of religiousness, disconnected from any organisation and any power structure. This religiousness is innate to the human spirit of every single individual but until now has been crushed by a collective hypnosis of church and state that has lasted for millennia.

But let us go back to the moment of my arrival. I was still crying in the arms of Bhakti as she took me inside paradise and introduced me to other Italians whose ships had already sailed into this spiritual haven. I was like a new-born baby, completely open and vulnerable, without the least resistance, feeling so much love that I no longer needed to protect myself from anything.

Around me was nothing but joy and love. This ashram was teeming with happy beings. It was stunning... the joy in all their faces. They looked at me and laughed as they welcomed me. They could understand, simply through exchanging a glance, the effort I had made to arrive here. It was as if I had suddenly become part of a single organism made of thousands of orange people, a piece of the puzzle that was now fitting together in the grand vision of the Master... and all the other pieces of this puzzle were now welcoming me with open arms.

Among the band of Italians growing around me that first morning, I recognised Maria Pia, who in the meantime had become Renu. When she saw me, she literally rolled on the ground laughing and her mood was so infectious that we all burst out laughing together. Joy was making a path to my soul. Unbeknown to me, gaping holes had been made in the defensive shell of my ego by the sheer fatigue of the trip, by the hardships and disappointments of the past. So the way was open for a new influx of vital energy to flow directly into my being.

The work of the Master could begin... was, in fact, already beginning, right now, as I stepped inside the gate. I was ready for a rebirth. The past could die peacefully and it seemed as though my long personal life-story had been created solely for the purpose of bringing me here. When the seed of a new tree sprouts, the pod that contained it needs to be left behind so that the tree's young roots can begin to grow in fertile soil. In my case, the fertile soil was the love and awareness of the Master, which I absorbed through my skin the moment I entered the 'gateless gate.'

Eventually we were escorted to a villa some distance away from the ashram, in which we would be living with other Italian disciples. The street was called Tadiwalla Road and was located behind the central railway station where we'd arrived the night before. There, we found a dozen Italians who all welcomed us in friendly fashion. The house was crowded, with two persons to every room, but Donatella wanted to live separately in this new world, so I shared a room with an Italian from Milano who was a veteran follower of Osho.

I think Donatella already felt that our love-story was coming to an end. Once we arrived in Pune, we saw less and less of each other and if it had not been for events that compelled me to return to Palermo two years later I would not have seen my family again either. From the moment I met the Master my life was, and still is, dedicated to him and his teachings. However, as one can imagine, I needed a few days to adapt to this new climate of joy and love that was flowing like a river through the ashram – or 'commune' as many people called it. Because of restricted space, not many people could live inside the ashram itself. Those that did so were mostly intimate disciples of the Master and working in essential functions in the commune. The rest of us lived outside in apartments, colonial bungalows, disused servants' quarters, or in bamboo huts constructed along the huge river that flowed behind the ashram.

This area of the city, known as Koregaon Park, was teeming with European and Indian disciples, who came inside the ashram every day to participate in a daily programme of meditations, the first one beginning at six o'clock in the morning. This timing explained the instructions given by the German guard during our nocturnal encounter to come back at six, when the gates swung open to admit the first meditators of the day. Dynamic Meditation lasted one hour, from six until seven, then breakfast was served at the rear of the ashram and people prepared for the Master's discourse, which started at eight o'clock in the morning, every morning. He was speaking for about two hours each time.

But his speaking was the most superficial aspect of what was happening. Simultaneously, at a deeper level, he was taking us by the hand, bringing us to a silent space at the centre of our consciousness. To say it another way, he was helping us experience something which already belonged to us, but to which we had paid no attention until now. At the same time, he was deprogramming us from the mass hypnosis to which all human beings are subjected by the societies in which they live. He was removing layers and layers of ignorance, accumulated over centuries by the human mind, in order to help us expand into the silent emptiness of existence.

I later heard Osho explain that there was another, far deeper level that the Master drew on, known in Hinduism as the Akashic Records, a kind of etheric collective memory bank where all the events of this and of other planets are registered. Osho was introducing new data, or information, that could be used for the transformation of human consciousness, now and far into the future.

The morning after my arrival, I rose early, showered, put on an orange robe borrowed from my friend Renu, and headed towards the ashram. I got in line for discourse, together with about 3000 other people, and left my shoes outside 'Buddha Hall' – the enclosed space where the master would be speaking and where all daily meditations took place. The hall was open on all sides and the roof was a temporary affair of corrugated steel sheets supported by wooden poles, covered on the underside by colourful Indian cloth. At the front of the hall was a small marble platform that hosted the armchair on which Osho was to sit.

I sat down, pressed between thousands of people who had come from all over the world, waiting for him – the Master. Everybody was now inside the hall, including the guards who took care of ashram security. Thousands of people were closing their eyes and going into meditation, their consciousness expanding.... The silence was intense, broken only by bird song from the trees surrounding the hall, with the occasional distant, mournful train whistle from the railway tracks at the far end of Koregaon Park.

He arrived in a Mercedes, driven by a disciple, accompanied by a woman who, I later learned, was his caretaker and companion. From somewhere on the other side of the hall, I could hear the sound of his car approaching, slowly and meditatively, like everything else in this place. Seated a good distance from the platform, I opened my eyes and watched as his car arrived behind the podium. Everything stopped. Time became very subjective, no longer the same for everyone. I was open and ready, yet I didn't expect anything. Nor did I think anything. I was simply here.

Silent, like a wild animal, he suddenly appeared, walking towards the podium with a very slow gait that seemed to take an infinite amount of time, as if in slow motion....*And at the time I no longer saw only the man but also an intense dazzling light around his physical body, extending several metres in all directions. Light, so much light, like the white colour of the moon shining like the noon day sun.*

Standing on the podium, greeting us all with a traditional Indian 'Namaste,' he turned his face in my direction and my heart literally exploded. Suddenly, all mechanisms of control were lost and my body convulsed in a centuries-old cry. My mind disappeared and I found myself curled up on the floor, crying in a foetal position. I felt as though I was coming out of a very ancient tunnel, like the babies I'd helped to birth as they passed through the narrow passage of the maternal pelvis. Now I was going through the birth canal of my previous existence, strewn with pain and suffering, and was entering a new world that was my home.

I didn't understand anything. Although he had begun to speak, the words didn't reach me. Instead, the heat of a pure energy radiated out to me, an enveloping energy like the embrace of a mother, with so much warmth and love that I could allow myself to fully let go into this amazing feeling of having arrived home. This being was my home. He was what I had been searching for, for so many lives. He was the goal that had been sought from time immemorial. He was the pure essence of love. What I had always felt in the depths of my soul had suddenly appeared before my eyes. I cried throughout the entire discourse.

At a certain point, I was aware that people were getting up and leaving Buddha Hall. Space was being created around me. Other companions on this journey were moving towards the 'outside.' The Master had been talking for two hours, then stood up and left. Many others headed for the exit, but I was still here, wrapped inside myself, savouring the deep emotions of having arrived in the place I'd always been looking for: the home of the Master, the home that we share with the divine inside us.

I don't remember the details. What I do remember is the extraordinary feeling that came to me as I stood up. I will remember it forever. With slow movements, like someone coming out of a long and exhausting illness, I walked out of the hall with the clear feeling that I was no longer the same person. It was as if the past had disappeared. I no longer remembered where I had come from, or how I'd arrived here. The people I'd known in my life until this moment disappeared. Parents, friends, acquaintances... all had vanished. There existed only pure warmth inside me, blending with the Indian air around me. Everything seemed very colourful this morning, the air filled with soft light as I moved slowly toward the exit.

In this moment, the only people who existed for me were those who were now leaving the hall after savouring the warm embrace of the Master. As I walked, I was still wrapped in an embrace of intense love, something that nourished me so completely that I didn't need to search outside myself for anything. I could simply stay within myself, inside myself, filled with this energy.

Emerging through the gateless gate, I set out along the avenue, heading away from the ashram. It was strange. I'd been here just one day and yet this street was already so familiar, as if I had always lived here. Seeing the state of grace that had descended on me, my new friends embraced me with laughter and joy. We were all drunk on love. We were immersed in the Master's 'Buddhafield' – the name given to the energy field that is created by the presence of a living Buddha.

From this profound experience, I understood that a Master, a real Master, never moves towards you. He is like the sun shining, giving life to everything. He does not choose. He is not someone who decides, "I will give my light to this person, but not to that person." His sun shines unconditionally on everyone. It depends on us whether we wish to expose ourselves to the light of his sun, or close ourselves and remain in darkness. I had exposed myself. I was open to the light without any opinion about what should be happening. Since I didn't know anything whatsoever about esoteric and spiritual phenomena, I was innocent and therefore completely open.

Many intellectuals and students of esoteric spirituality came to see Osho during this time, but they were unable to feel anything because of their expectations, assumptions and prejudices. In their own minds, they already knew how a Being of Light should be...how he should behave...what he should say. As soon as Osho said something that didn't agree with their preconceived ideas, they would become disillusioned and leave, saying they hadn't heard anything of significance.

As news about Osho spread, as his sun shone more and more brightly in Europe and the rest of the world, many different types of people were attracted to his light. But those who were able to remain at his side – heedless of the absurd and contradictory conditions he created – were those who could open their hearts to him and to his energy of love and awareness. In one of his morning discourses, Osho talked in detail about this phenomenon. He explained there are three circles of people around an Enlightened One: the student, the disciple and the devotee.

At the periphery is the great mass of human beings who are so unconscious and hypnotized by the collective mind that they cannot hear or see anything. Nevertheless, among these masses are people who have some understanding on an intellectual plane, and can recognize the unusual qualities a mystic possesses. They read his written words, noting his concepts, agreeing with some and refuting others. They may also be curious enough to visit him, but usually cling to their preconceptions. They see him through the window of a knowledgeable mind and cannot manage to open their hearts.

People of this type are drawn to the philosophical concepts of the Enlightened One and can do valuable work for the Master in the social world, since they can make his name known to other people. P.D. Ouspensky did this for George Gurdjieff. Vivekananda did it for Ramakrishna. But they themselves remain spectators. They don't transform their lives according to his teaching. They don't allow themselves to experience the techniques the Master creates to break the armour of the ego. Rather, they keep their ego structures intact, not risking anything of themselves. Osho defined this category as 'students.' They constitute the outer circle, most distant from the Master.

Next, there is a category of people who have the courage to jump into the unknown, beyond reason and intellect, and put their personalities at risk. These people change their lives and freely enter into a situation that will transform their consciousness. They start to work on themselves. They begin to take responsibility for their own lives, instead of following the dictates and norms of mainstream society.

To help this change in direction, both inside and outside, Osho invited us to become initiated as his *sannyasins*. Initiation consisted of exchanging our name for a new one given by him, dressing in orange clothes, wearing a necklace of 108 wooden beads – known as a 'mala' – with a picture of his face hanging from it, and by committing ourselves to meditate for at least one hour a day. The people who were initiated in this way by Osho joined his movement of *Neo-Sannyas*.

Why 'Neo'? Because India has a long tradition, dating back centuries, whereby people who dedicate themselves to a life of spiritual enquiry give up everything they possess, including their families and homes. They literally turn their backs on the world. They become wandering ascetics, sadhus, monks, and are known collectively as *sannyasins*. Osho wanted to make it clear that he was breaking away from the old tradition. In his view, there was no need to abandon family, work and worldly life in order to pursue spiritual attainment. There was no need to withdraw to a temple, or isolate oneself from the world.

His new movement didn't require any of these things. Instead, Osho asked us to take responsibility for enquiring within ourselves, searching for the divine principle at the very centre of our being. Nothing need be abandoned. On the contrary, a commitment was needed to explore spirituality while continuing with our normal, day-to-day lives. "Don't renounce the material world and social life!" he used to say to us. "Better to remain in the world without being part of it." He reminded us that a lotus flower, resting on the still surface of a lake, grows out of dirty mud at the bottom of the lake. But it is not part of the mud. And it is one of the most beautiful flowers in the world.

So he encouraged us to continue to be part of society, without getting lost in its chaos and its unconsciousness, keeping the flame of meditative awareness burning inside us while confronting the challenges daily life brings. Osho called this second category of people 'disciples.' Every day, more and more people eager to become disciples were arriving in Pune from all over the world. I was one of these. When a new disciple arrived, it was a celebration for everyone. Our family of sannyasins was growing bigger. The community was expanding and acquiring new colours.

Each new arrival would be met by one of the women who worked in the ashram's front office. Women were in charge of every department, at Osho's request, giving the organisation a feminine and heart-warming flavour. Newcomers would be encouraged to listen to Osho's discourses and explore his meditation techniques before becoming sannyasins. Some people were asked to do therapy groups, while others were asked to meditate for 21 days before asking for initiation.

Initiation took place during *darshan* – the evening meeting with Osho, which happened in a small auditorium, built as an annex to his house. A secretary would call your name and you would walk forward and sit close to his feet, then close your eyes. Sensing your energy, seeing your potential, the Master would then write your new name and its translation in English on a piece of paper that announced your rebirth, your entry into neo-sannyas.

Generally, Osho chose names from the Sanskrit language, or from the Sufi tradition. He then spoke to you directly, face-to-face, explaining the significance of your name and giving hints as to the direction of your spiritual path. He placed the beaded necklace around your neck and gently touched your third eye, giving a transmission of energy from which you tended to emerge so drunkenly that other sannyasins might well need to support you as you stood up, or even carry you back to your seat.

As I've already mentioned, people were arriving in increasing numbers, asking to become his disciples, expanding the circle of seekers. In fact, this process still goes on. Even now, more than 20 years after Osho's physical death – or, to say it rightly, from the time he decided to leave his physical body – the neo-sannyas movement continues to grow. There must be millions of us around the planet.

Now we come to the third circle of people, the ones closest to an enlightened mystic. Osho has called them 'devotees.' This refers to people who are totally in tune with the Master. This does not necessarily mean they are close to him physically, or that they have important roles within the organizational structure of his ashram – not at all. At this level, physical closeness has no relevance; function has no relevance. Rather, it is an energetic rapport that endures beyond time and space. The heart of the devotee beats in synchronicity with that of the Master. At the level of pure consciousness, they are one.

Devotion is a supreme form of love and few are the disciples who reach this degree of intimacy with the Master. But in Pune this made no difference to the welcome everyone received from Osho and his community of fellow travellers. Nor did it prevent people from being initiated as sannyasins. We were all devotees in potential, in essence.

Osho explained that his time on earth was limited and, unlike Gautama Buddha's approach with his followers, he didn't want us to meditate for two years before being initiated. Rather, he offered sannyas freely to all who asked for it, no matter what their spiritual status, knowing full well that some of us would be lost in the fog of the ordinary world, not understanding the precious key to awakening that was being given to us.

In this very practical and generous way, Osho gave everyone the same opportunity – an opportunity that continues today – to take their first step on the path of spiritual enquiry, as his disciple. He made it clear that it is up to each one of us to decide whether to continue or not. He said a person could become a true disciple – even a devotee – immediately, if his understanding goes deep enough. Or, it can take eleven years or more before real initiation happens. The intervening years would serve as preparation for the moment when inner search would deepen and begin.

I have seen many people give up before 11 years have passed. I have seen many people give up after 20 years. But I've also seen people return to the path after years of being lost in the world. In fact, the path is always available, for everyone. The work of giving up the ego is torturous and arduous, because it is rather like voluntarily seeking your own death. Our identification with the ego is incredibly strong and no ego wants to die.

Osho used to say that sannyas is like scaling a Himalayan peak. As the journey begins, many are enthusiastic about the new landscapes they can see when they start to climb. Nevertheless, as the path gets steeper, some of the group splits off. The higher one goes, the more people leave, until, when you finally arrive at the top, you find yourself alone. It is a solitary path and few overcome its challenges. It's a path that goes against the gravity of the mass of humanity, which continually exerts a downward pull. But the soul is pure fire, a fire that all of us have within us. It's a fire that needs to be fed continuously so that one day it can rise into the sky.

7   The Alchemy of Transformation

According to Chinese medicine, our bodies are made up of elements that combine with each other to create various functions, emotions and organs. In this system, there are five basic elements: earth, water, air, wood, and fire. Our bodies are composed of 73% water. Water, according to its nature, flows to the lowest point and disperses itself in the earth.

This, as I see it, is the main reason why 90% of human beings live a life identified with values that are worldly and material. The fire of spirituality never gets fed. They follow the simplest life, dominated by the energy of water and earth.

If there is no effort to become more aware, no aspiration for more consciousness, the water element continues to flow to the lowest level, following the law of gravity: we are born, we grow up, we have children, we grow old, we die...a cycle that, according to the theory of reincarnation, repeats itself life after life.

Applying Chinese medical principles to our own European history, the process developed by alchemists in mediaeval times was really about transforming water into fire, or, as they put it, turning base metal into gold – two metaphors for the same principle of inner transformation. If we also introduce spiritual terminology used in India, we can say that transformation of water into fire, fuelled by the Chinese element wood (will) is the same task as awakening the sleeping energy of *kundalini* in the pelvis and raising it until it reaches the higher chakras. Unfortunately, the destiny of the overwhelming majority of human beings is to get lost in the swirling waters of personal desires and emotions, and ignore the path that leads upward to the spirit.

To become a disciple of a Master like Osho is to voluntarily undergo an enormous karmic cleaning process for the soul. It is also a movement upward toward the final destiny of all human beings, which is to reconnect with the divine that surrounds us. This process takes time. So, for me, it wasn't a question of sitting in meditation with the Master once or twice, thereby receiving everything he had to offer. I meditated with him for twelve long years until he decided to leave the body and, of course, continue to meditate even today.

I am a medical man, a doctor by training, so the relationship between mind, body and spirit has always fascinated me. For example, at a biological level, the human body functions at only 10-12 per cent of its potential. Every human cell and tissue conforms to this functional percentage. Similarly, our DNA, the long chain of amino acids in which all cellular information is registered, functions at exactly 10 per cent of its potential. DNA chains are stored in the nucleus of a cell and act as the 'hard drive' of the cell's system.

Only a small proportion of these chains function during our lifetime. It has been calculated that if our DNA suddenly decided to function at a higher level – let's say another 10-20 per cent more – every cell in our body would explode like an atomic bomb. So, we can say that 90 per cent of the potential energy that has been put in us by nature is on standby. The brain also contains a large quantity of energy that is kept in reserve and not used. But in moments of necessity, our cells can produce huge quantities of metabolic energy.

We can observe the same phenomenon in our sexuality. Nature has created an enormous abundance in the mechanism of reproduction. In one square centimetre of semen there are about 40 million spermatozoa, only one of which is needed to reach the destination of the female egg and procreate.

The process of transformation, or meditation, is similar to these biological processes. When we begin the adventure of spiritual enquiry, we start to draw on new resources of the body-mind system, which have until this moment been dormant, on standby.

From the outside, when we see someone sitting in meditation, it looks like the simplest thing in the world. After all, he's not 'doing anything.' He's just 'sitting around, doing nothing.' However, maintaining a high level of awareness, or consciousness, for any length of time requires a significant effort. To look inside ourselves and embark upon an inner journey therefore needs a very high level of energy.

It is for this reason that few people take up the spiritual path, because they are continuously dissipating their energy in so many other activities. The energy supply is exhausted just by day-to-day living. A meditator, on the other hand, gathers all of his energy within himself and, over time, begins to use new cellular energy that allows consciousness to grow and expand. When kundalini energy begins to move upward, the body is deeply affected. Spiritual revolution brings with it a profound change in the body's chemistry. In my opinion, it isn't possible to have real spiritual growth without changes in cellular matter.

Osho was very thin, fragile and weak in his youth. After his experience of self-realisation as a being of light, his body started to get bigger and fill out with *prana,* or pure energy. Pictures of him taken before and after his awakening are like photos of two different beings. If this seems implausible, perhaps it will help to examine the different sources of nourishment for the physical, mental, emotional and subtle bodies that make up our being. It's not just about food. The body and its cellular components draw energy from many sources. Or, to say it another way, human beings receive energy from four very different types of 'food.'

1. The first source is our normal food that is eaten and digested. Most human beings focus primarily on this resource. Although it is our main source of nourishment, almost all of us in the 'advanced' countries eat badly, without awareness, so our primary source of energy also becomes one of the major causes of our sickness.
2. The second source of nourishment is water. Here, too, the

majority of us have little awareness about what we're drinking and the quality of the water we absorb from various sources, including soft drinks, tea, coffee and alcoholic beverages. Rarely do we stop to consider how precious is this liquid, without which we will die within a few days.

3. The third source of nourishment is more subtle and of great significance. It is our breath. Few people think of breathing as a way of nourishing the body, mind and spirit, yet it is through breath that we receive *prana*. Hence the importance given to the ancient Indian technique of 'prana breathing,' whereby energy and breath are absorbed as one. And we all know that if we stop breathing, we will die even more quickly than if we stop drinking water.

4. The fourth source of nourishment for the body-mind is sensory input. It consists of the vast range of impressions and sensations we experience every moment of our lives, including emotions, feelings, sentiments and all kinds of data from the world around us. Every moment, each one of us receives and registers impressions in staggering quantities: the air, the temperature, the wind, the heat, the sounds, the light, the multi-dimensional relationships with people and objects... and so on. Thousands of sensations are continuously nourishing the body at a subliminal level.

When we begin the spiritual journey, when a process of gaining more awareness commences inside us, we start to receive new energy precisely because we are becoming more conscious. In other words, fresh energy is drawn from 'the awareness of each act in the present moment.' For example, as we become more conscious of the food we are eating and the way in which we eat it, we are able to receive nourishment from the *prana* contained in our food. The same is true, as I've just mentioned, of our breathing, and also our water and sensory input. In the same way we are able to absorb light energy – an even subtler component in all of these sources.

Other changes may occur on a physical level. I once met an enlightened mystic in India who could not be touched because his body would begin to develop intense fever as soon as another person came in physical contact with him. Or, as another example, the body of an awakened being may undergo a process of early ageing.

Because of the global interest in spiritual guidance that has developed over the past few decades, many people have declared themselves as self-realised beings. It is, after all, a good business for opportunistic entrepreneurs, who follow the law of supply and demand. For those with little experience on the spiritual path, it is easy to fall prey to pseudo-gurus who pretend to offer spiritual awakening. So, the question arises: how to tell the true from the false?

Often, it is enough to observe the physical bodies and gestures of such impostors to realise this is nothing but a state of deliberate deception or self-delusion. At best, 'enlightenment' is merely a thought that has insinuated itself into the mind, not an alchemical transformation.

When kundalini energy is really activated and moves upwards, there is no logical mind remaining. It is like a fire that suddenly consumes you, filling your whole body. The mind, as we know it, no longer exists. Our ordinary time-space functions are so radically changed that one can never be the same after such an experience.

The way of walking changes, the way of eating changes, the way of talking changes and it becomes impossible to be with the majority of people. You enter into a state of absolute bliss in which the external world disappears and there exists only your inner world, which no longer has any individuality. Rather, it is an experience of oneness with the light that pervades everything, both outside and inside us.

When this process stabilises and becomes continuous – a state known in Sanskrit as *samadhi* – the ego dissolves completely. To say it another way, your identification with yourself disappears. The only thing that remains is the immense emptiness of enlightened consciousness. It happened to Gautama Buddha about 2500 years ago, one morning sitting under the bodhi tree. As night faded, as the sun rose and the last star in the sky disappeared, the last speck of his ego also dissolved.

It happened to Osho in 1953 at the age of twenty-one. One night, his consciousness expanded to the point that he felt suffocated within his house and was forced to spend the rest of the night sitting under a tree in a nearby park. By morning, he was still sitting there, but his ego was gone.

Osho has said that 90% of those who attain to *samadhi* leave the body immediately, because it is so difficult to maintain matter and light together. Of the ten per cent who are able to remain, only one per cent decide to speak and share the experience with others. The rest choose to stay in a state of silent bliss, knowing the task of communicating with ignorant people is enormously difficult and their words will be misinterpreted by the majority of those who listen to them.

According to legend, when Gautama Buddha attained enlightenment, he decided not to speak because he saw the futility of trying to convey his profound experience to others. Then the gods in heaven became worried, descended to earth and tried to persuade him, arguing that even if only one human being will be able to understand him it will be worth it.

Compassion prevailed. For the next 40 years, Gautama Buddha travelled on foot around northern India, sharing his wisdom with anyone who cared to listen, until his final *mahaparinirvana samadhi* – the moment of his death and leaving the body. No one can deny that his effort was worthwhile. Dozens of Buddha's disciples realised enlightenment in his lifetime and even today his message is still spreading, carrying seeds of awareness to the four corners of the earth.

The same thing happened to Osho after his realisation. He decided to remain silent. Only after a long time was he persuaded to speak by another enlightened being – a man who'd remained silent for his whole life. This was a very simple man known as Maggababa, because he would eat any kind of food that people put into his only possession, his mug. Magga means mug in Hindi. The two men used to meet late in the evening, when Maggababa's disciples had gone, sitting together without speaking, sharing a space of infinite bliss. One evening, Maggababa interrupted their meditation, saying that silence can be misunderstood by people just as much as words – his own silence had, indeed, been misunderstood by his followers. It was not helping any of them. Maggababa urged Osho to speak, knowing this young man had the capacity to spread the message throughout the world.

Osho understood the point. Soon he started giving discourses and experimenting with meditation techniques to see which would be of benefit to other seekers. Like Buddha, he spoke for almost 40 years, attracting thousands of people, offering a vision for present and future generations.

Now, here was I, in Pune with the Master; an accidental arrival, a newcomer, gate-crashing Osho's spiritual party, catapulted by life into what would become the most discussed community on the planet. Yet, at the time, I was ignorant of the enormity of what was happening. I was content simply to relax in the joy of being with new friends.

I stayed for many months in the villa on Tadiwalla Road with my group of Italians. Every day, I went to Koregaon Park to listen to the Master and afterwards felt free to do whatever appealed to me in the moment. Socializing was easy and natural in this community. I became friends with diverse individuals arriving in Pune, each with his or her unique story to tell. It was like magic: finding ourselves together in our love for the Master who was guiding us, one step after another, into our inner world.

On the night following my arrival, there was a communal meeting in our house, an event that – I later discovered – happened quite regularly. There was a lot of joy and lightness shared by the sannyasins, with jokes coming one after the other. It was all very different from the meetings of my old communist friends. They were sober and serious people, seeking to understand how to change the world. Here, no one wanted to change anything. They enjoyed being together without rules or structures.

At first I was uncomfortable seeing these orange people sitting on the floor, laughing and joking. I felt like a new-born chick that didn't know how to behave. But this didn't last long. One of them called me over and asked me to sit next to him. He was older than me, with a long beard and short hair. I soon learned that, before taking sannyas, he'd been a *sadhu* who'd travelled around India on foot.

Sadhus make up a vast spiritual movement on the subcontinent, characterised by the fact that – like traditional sannyasins – they possess nothing. They ask people in the street for food, they smoke a lot of hashish and they don't cut or wash their hair, so their appearance is rather like that of a Rastafarian, with one small difference – they have the habit of keeping their few personal possessions in their hair. Over the years, I met some incredible characters among these *sadhus*, who sometimes gather in millions at specific dates and places – usually close to the sacred River Ganges – to participate in a spiritual extravaganza known as 'Kumbh Mela.'

My new acquaintance, Chid, had been one of them. In order to become Osho's disciple, he'd agreed to cut off his thick mass of hair, which hadn't been washed in years. Unwashed hair gives off a strong odour and Osho was allergic to many different kinds of smells.

Chid had asked me sit down next to him, picked up two tambourines, one of which he gave to me, and asked me to play with him. I'd never played any kind of musical instrument in my whole life, let alone a tambourine, which to me was all rhythm and no melody. I excused myself, saying it was impossible for me to play a tambourine, adding politely that I would willingly listen to Chid. But he insisted, looking steadily at me with his deep black eyes as if I was his chosen prey, saying that I should simply let go of my inhibitions and play along with him.

"It's enough if you follow me," he said, beginning to beat a strange tribal rhythm that didn't resemble anything I knew. Slowly and timidly, I started to tap my own tambourine until gradually my fears vanished. Soon, to my surprise, I found myself playing in sync with Chid. Before long, the other sannyasins were dancing around us, while the two of us, like old shamans, banged out a rhythm that became ever more attractive and frenetic.

We played our tambourines for hours. Or, to speak for myself, my body was playing, because my mind was no longer there. Through our music, Chid gave me my first taste of an out-of-body experience. I learned later that he was already capable of going out of his body and making astral travels, a talent of his which I would experience personally on the evening of my initiation.

A few days after my arrival, I went to the ashram's office to ask to 'take sannyas.' I still felt like a baby chick, but sensed that I was completely protected in this environment and that whatever happened to me would be the right thing. So I went to Krishna House, to an office full of beautiful women loaded with energy and totally committed to supporting Osho's vision. The woman whose job it was to receive new requests for sannyas was Dutch, tall with blue eyes and square features. She was an assistant to Osho's secretary, a tiny Gujarati woman called Laxmi.

Laxmi was dark and very short, with eyes that seemed like bottomless pools. She had an incredibly charismatic power that made it possible for her to oversee the growth of the most controversial spiritual community in India.

The offices had glass doors, marble floors and marble walls. They were air-conditioned all day long, so that even during India's torrid 'hot season' – when temperatures soared above 40°C – the minds and bodies of these hard-working women were protected from the heat. I couldn't help but notice they were more feminine, powerful and committed than the women with whom I'd shared the revolutionary days of 1968.

Laxmi was seated in an armchair with an enormous back that made her look even smaller than she already was, but it didn't really matter because, as an energy phenomenon, she was huge. Her gestures and her eyes were pure totality. Every day, she passed on Osho's instructions and guidance, aided by the Dutch woman, Arup, who was her right hand support.

Arup asked me to sit next to her and we spoke in French. She asked me how long I'd been in the ashram and what therapy groups I'd done up to now. I looked at her blankly. I didn't even know what therapy was! I told her I'd been in Pune only for a few days and wanted to become like all those around me...orange people wearing Osho's mala. She asked me which meditations I'd done and if I'd been meditating in Italy before travelling to India. Again, I looked at her with the innocence of the baby, repeating my story of arriving a few days ago, seeing Osho and understanding that this was my home – this was all I knew.

Arup gave me a beautiful smile, hugged me, felt my innocent

heart and said that after three days I could see Osho personally and take sannyas from him. It was all so simple, the heart had spoken its truth and the person who heard my words had responded from her own heart.

Through the following years, through all the ups and downs with Osho, I always had the greatest respect for Arup. Time and again, she showed herself to be devoted to the Master, a woman of unshakeable commitment who lived through three successive communes in positions of authority. Her mother, father and brother all became sannyasins.

The night of my initiation, I was really emotional and excited. Toward sunset, the people who had appointments to meet Osho that evening lined up in front of the metal gate that I'd seen from the main gate on my arrival. This was the entrance to his house, which he'd named after Lao Tzu. He lived here with his companion, his doctor, his dentist, his Indian cook, his secretary, a household cleaner, a laundry woman and one or two editors who prepared sutras and questions for his discourses.

Among these women, I remember Mukta, who always stayed near Osho. She had purchased Lao Tzu House for him and spent most of her time caring for the gardens and trees surrounding the building. Mukta came from a wealthy Greek family that had homes in Europe and the USA, but she'd willingly abandoned the comforts of her former lifestyle to be with Osho, with whom she always remained in devoted harmony.

I also came to know Asheesh, an Italian engineer from Milan, who acted as a sort of handyman for his Master, doing odd jobs around the house. He was always a part of the mystic's personal retinue. He also ran the 'mala shop' where our necklaces of wooden beads were made.

Apart from one Italian and one Greek, most of the other people who were close to Osho in order to take care of his physical needs were English. I suppose, in a way, it was a kind of karmic justice: a reversal of the recently-departed British Raj. In the colonial days, the Indians had served the English. Now it was payback time!

In true English fashion, Lao Tzu House had many rules and

regulations, overseen with precision and rigidity, determining who could enter the house, at what times, and where they were permitted to go. Many years later, in 1987, another Italian would be called by the Master to come and live in Lao Tzu House. That was me, but that tale comes later.

Anyway, on the night of my initiation, a group of about 50-60 people were waiting to meet Osho. It included those taking sannyas, those wanting to say goodbye to him before leaving for the West, those who had just finished participating in therapy groups, or who were working in the ashram and wanted to ask a question about some personal issue.

Because of Osho's enormous sensitivity to smell, every single person, before entering *darshan* ('meeting with the Master'), was carefully sniffed from head to toe by two women who, on the basis of your odours – or, hopefully, your lack of them – could decide to let you in, or not. To avoid the trauma of being sent away, we all took great care to use neutral shampoo and non-smelly soap while showering, cleaning ourselves thoroughly before approaching the gate. Passing between these two women was like taking an examination.

Once through the gate, you walked along a tree-lined path that led to Chuang Tzu Auditorium, a beautiful little addition to Lao Tzu House with a marbled floor, high roof and semi-circular design that was open to the lush gardens surrounding it. Osho loved wild nature and told his gardeners not to cut anything, but simply to plant and then maintain what was growing. The local bird population was delighted and lived freely among the bushes and trees of this little paradise.

We entered Chuang Tzu, sat down on the cool marble and waited in silence for Osho to enter. The solitary song of a night bird, the rustle of leaves in the breeze, the soft creaking of bamboos, a lonely train whistle in the distance...all sounds became sacred in the intense silence of our waiting. Suddenly, in the garden beside me, among the shrubbery, Chid appeared. His face was very clear before me, an enormous face that seemed as big as the trees themselves, resting like a cloud of fog that had somehow shaped itself into his form.

Next moment, a door opened at the front of the auditorium, from which the Master emerged, calm as always, slow as always, beautiful as always...three ways to describe his style and manner that could be repeated eternally, in all circumstances. Months later, when a fanatic Hindu threw a knife at him during discourse, he would exhibit the same calmness, not even bothering to get out of his seat or stop talking. Even when he was arrested at gunpoint in the United States in 1985 and dragged around in chains, he exuded the same grace. Even when he was mistreated in the meanest way by federal officials, he looked beautiful.

He was always the same. Always, in every circumstance, he emanated peace, love and consciousness. Just the harmony of his movements as he walked into Chuang Tzu was enough to calm my mind. Just the grace of his greeting us with a *namaste* was enough to communicate his love. When he sat down, just his presence was enough to invite us all to spontaneously enter into meditation.

Sitting beside his chair, on the floor, Mukta invited us, one by one, to approach Osho and be initiated into sannyas. The scenes that followed were similar and yet completely different. During some meetings between the Master and a new initiate there was much silence. During others, Osho made jokes that made everyone laugh. Yet he himself remained imperturbable, with just a hint of a playful smile under his thick beard. Sometimes his eyes would open incredibly wide as he was speaking, as he emphasised a particular point in his guidance. Sometimes those same eyes would almost close in blissful peace, as he gave someone his blessing.

Mukta called my name. I stood up and went towards the Master. I sat at his feet and looked him in the eyes, already entranced by his inner emptiness. He smiled at me, wrote my new name on a piece of paper, signed it and handed it over to me, then explained the meaning. I'd told them in the office that I didn't understand English very well, so an Italian woman was whispering a translation of Osho's words in my ear.

"Your name is Swami Prem Azima," Osho explained. "A swami is one who sets out on the spiritual path and abandons the exterior world. Prem means Love. Azima means Great. So your name is: the

Man of Great Love." Osho then spoke to me of a river that is small at its origin but, little by little, as it continues its journey, it grows bigger and bigger, until one day it arrives at the sea and disperses itself in the great ocean of the universe.

He told me that there are two kinds of love: one is the small love that exists between a man and a woman; the other, the love between a man and the divine. My path, he explained, was that of the 'great love.' Even the most beautiful love stories, such as the one between Romeo and Juliet, would never satisfy me. My destiny was to rejoin the ocean in order to lose myself in eternity.

Then he leaned closer to me, stared more intensely into my eyes and said, "From now on, Azima, you completely forget politics, psychology and sociology." In that instant, I had the clear sensation that he knew me very well, with a most intimate understanding of my personality – much better than I did myself. Then he started talking again about love for the divine.

As he finished speaking, he placed the mala around my neck, asked me to close my eyes and touched my third eye. My body emptied itself, my mind also. When it was over, I stood up and returned to my seat in a state of ecstatic confusion. Darshan continued. When initiation was finished, Osho spoke to those sannyasins who were leaving for their own countries, then he gave a series of energy transmissions that involved the whole audience.

We were all gaga by the time we left, intoxicated by his energy and the love showering from him. Outside, friends were waiting to hug us and share the energy we'd received. Sitting on a low stone wall, just beyond the gate, were Bhakti, Renu, Chid and his companion Jyoti. When I'd recovered sufficiently to be able to speak, I told Chid I'd seen him in the bushes just before Osho entered the auditorium. Laughing, Chid replied that he'd been with me the whole time in his astral body. This sounded so mysterious to me and yet so matter-of-fact, as if I'd entered another world in which material reality was only a small part of the many dimensions surrounding us.

Such was the magic and mystery of this commune.

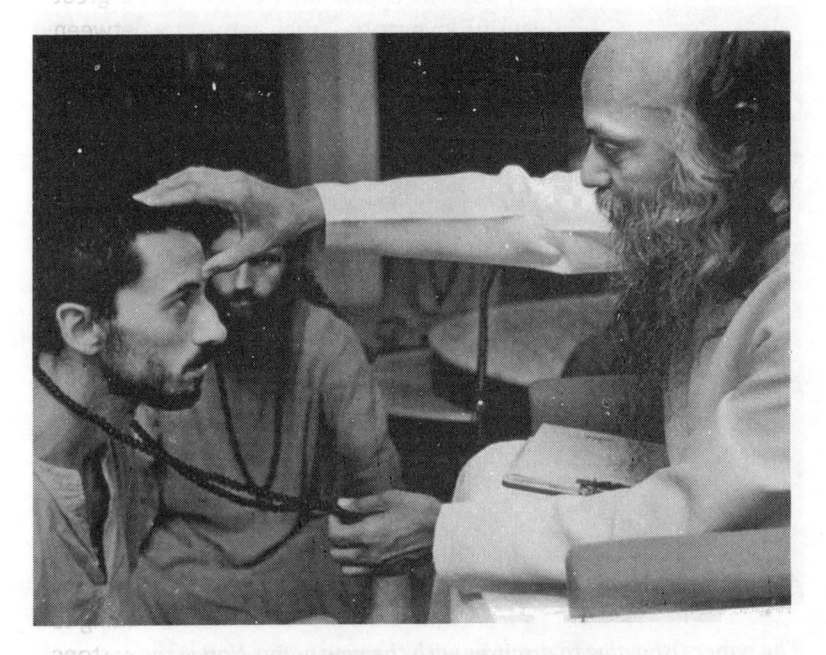

1978 Azima the day of his initiation to Sannyas

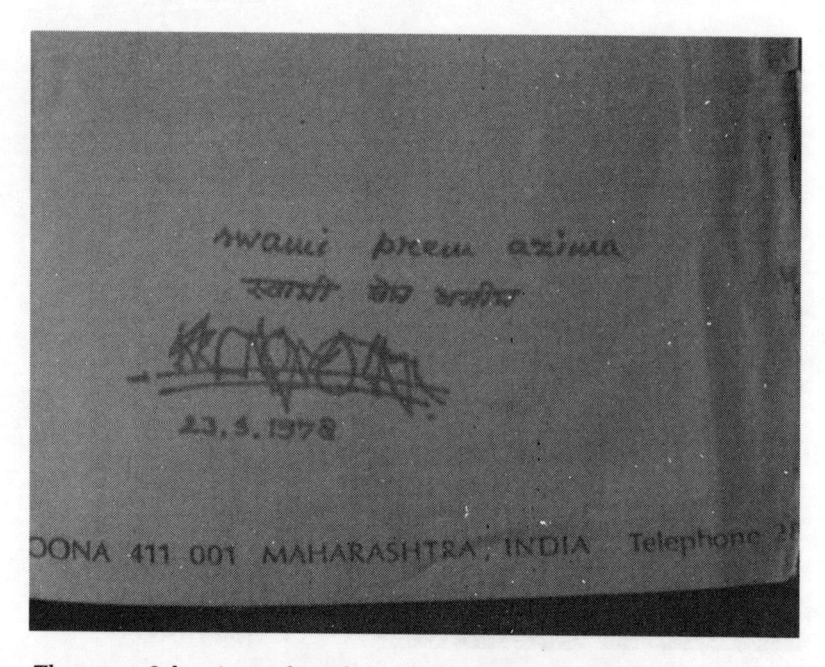

The paper Osho give to disciples with the new name. Notice the amazing calligraphy out of which many paintings had being publish later on

8   Deconditioning

I had been in Pune only a few days and already couldn't remember my past. Life in the commune was so intense, being with the Master such a total experience, that it seemed as though a day here corresponded to at least a month of life in the West. For this fellow now called 'Azima,' the next step was to participate in the therapy groups suggested to him by the Master. In this way, I began to confront my ego structure and the system of defences created by my personality.

Osho asked me to do four individual sessions of Rebirthing, a breathing technique that gently yet firmly put me in contact with my primal childhood emotions. On one hand, these sessions helped me to become more conscious of my breath and, on the other, to relive and release experiences of suffering created in the very first years of my life – sometimes even at the moment of my birth. Some of these sessions left me dazed and stunned for hours, often needing to remain lying down, alone in a corner, where it was possible to absorb the experience of the meeting with my 'inner child.'

After that, I went into a group called *Enlightenment Intensive* (later called *Awareness Intensive: Who Is In?*) that Osho used as a standard greeting from the commune. Almost every newcomer was directed toward this experience, which consisted of continuously asking yourself: 'Who am I?' These groups were large. In my group, I think there were 130-150 people from all over the world who found themselves assembled on a huge covered terrace. The structure was simple: two persons sat opposite each other. One asked the other,

"Tell me who you are." The other responded for five minutes, then a bell rang and they changed roles. After four rounds of this, they found new partners and began again. In this way, all participants conducted an investigation of their inner world for three days and nights.

I emerged from each session confused, with only one certainty: *I didn't know who I was*. Nevertheless, I realized these were ideal conditions for allowing time and space for my real essence to make inroads into my ego-image. From every session, I came out more real, more soft and light, more available to the dimension of 'living the present moment,' less engaged in future plans, abstract ideas, past memories.

Next came a massage group, in the course of which we all became naked, sharing our bodies with impressive naturalness. All groups allowed time for the ashram's two main daily meditations: Dynamic in the morning and Kundalini in the afternoon. These both were active meditations, and the sensations I experienced during them were intense and deep. Sometimes I felt as if a mild electric current was washing through my whole body, emptying it out and refilling it with fresh energy.

I began to understand that ordinary matter has more subtle dimensions and this showed me something about my ego attachments. It was easy to become identified with the physical world, such as the look and shape of my body, because it was solid and obvious. But with energetic experiences my ego wasn't involved. I just observed there was an inner world that I didn't know, part of a system more vast than my small physical body.

I made a special point of attending an evening meditation called Music Group, where many of us danced and sang to sweet music performed live by a group of sannyasins. These were devotional songs, choral music in which I let myself dissolve into the love I felt inside, like an old Sufi. At the end of these evenings, with my heart wide open, I usually met someone with whom I would end up spending the night.

The ashram was a paradise on earth. Osho had brought together all the spiritual traditions and a wide variety of therapy techniques in an enormous experimental cauldron in which every person could be transformed according to his nature. In a short time, I found I'd become a more joyful being. My hair grew longer, my beard too, and my new vision of life was also growing day by day.

I did two more groups suggested by the Master and these made profound changes in my personality. One was called *Tantra*, led by an American woman of Cuban origin, who was considered to be one of the most skilled therapists in the commune. She'd already been working in therapy prior to coming to Osho. As she worked, she was aware of each hint of emotion, each subtle mood, each attempt to hide or avoid looking at personal issues. She pushed us beyond our limits, helping us explore our sexuality, freeing us from inhibitions, encouraging us to meet and merge with each other in sensuality and love-making.

There were no taboos. Everything was permitted. The *Tantra* group went on for three days and nights and when I came out my Catholic conditioning and my former attitudes towards sex were no longer part of me. I was liberated from my old skin like a snake that had been rubbing himself against a rock, giving his sheath back to the earth, then slipping quietly away, his new skin shining in the rays of the sun. I felt free, as if I'd let go of a huge weight, as if I'd dropped a heavy load I'd been dragging behind me for years, a burden that I'd received from society but which, in reality, had never been mine.

After this group, my relations with women improved and my fear of sexual intimacy started to disappear. I began to feel more ease in my relationships – what liberation! Freedom to explore the many aspects of male-female relationships was one of the characteristics of 'Pune One' – the name given to our time in the ashram before Osho moved to the USA. The Master gave us freedom to experiment with each other in a free and spontaneous way, without structure. It was obvious that a big part of his work at the time was focused on sexual energy and destroying our negative attitudes associated with it.

Seen from a distance of 30 years, it seems the grand design of the Master was to work on our first and second chakras in order to liberate us from the gross energies that keep billions of people enslaved.

Here, I want to say something about the way the human body is structured, in order to better understand the chakras. I will focus on the spinal column, which is a continuation of the brain. At the top of the spine, in the occipital area, this column brings together many bundles of nerves that go all the way down the spine to the coccyx. Inside this pathway of nerve bundles there is an energetic channel that distinguishes humans from the other mammals, and it is along this channel that the seven chakras are located, from the *muladhar* at the base of the spine to the crown chakra at the top of the cranium.

Through this channel, passing from chakra to chakra, flows the potential energy of enlightenment. The obstacle to its realization is traditionally referred to as 'ignorance,' an energy that the Tibetans also call 'poisonous.' Ignorance of what? Ignorance of the fact that we are beings of light, ignorance of our divine being, of our true nature, since we don't know 'who we are.' When this ignorance is dissolved by the light of awareness, the way is open for energy to rise and for enlightenment to happen.

On either side of the spinal column flows a left and right channel that the Hindus call *Pingala* and *Ida*. These two channels maintain the balance of male and female energy or, as the Hindus say, the solar and lunar energy. The channels run parallel to the central channel, the *Sushumna*, crossing each other at each chakra. Within these two channels are the so-called 'poisons' that impede realization. In the left channel is the poison of attachment, connected with female sexual energy. In the right channel is anger, connected with male sexual energy.

In those years, Osho was doing a specific work on these two energies. Since, in this effort, he was trampling on ancient taboos, he was opposed and criticized both by the West, which labelled him the 'sex guru,' and by his own countrymen who, after millennia of sexual repression, were alarmed to discover a Tantric Master in their house who was dismantling their social hypocrisy.

Indian has a Tantric tradition, shown in various temples that dot the continent, most famously those at Khajuraho, where the outer surfaces of many temples are covered with sculptures showing all possible sexual positions. But this tradition has existed mainly underground, hidden to avoid condemnation and persecution by mainstream Indian attitudes, which in recent centuries have become more and more repressive – so much so that, until very recently, men and women did not even hold hands in the street. Kissing in public? Impossible!

Face to face with a Tantra Master in flesh and blood, the vast majority of people recoiled in horror and hindered his work as much as possible, threatening the very survival of the commune. But Osho was determined to share his vision and refused to be intimidated. "Just be grateful they don't kill you," he told us and continued with his work.

It needs to be said that in Pune One, sannyasins of Indian and Japanese origin were excluded from therapy. Osho explained that these cultures had given shape to a different type of mind than Westerners and would not understand therapeutic processes such as Primal. For them, it was enough to recognize the Master and meditate in his presence.

For Indians, especially, the devotional element was also very important and it was natural for them to bow down and touch the Master's feet. We Westerners, on the other hand, lacked a devotional element in our tradition. The Western mind is pervaded by scepticism and doubt, which are good for scientific investigation, but which inhibit the heart and its capacity to love.

In those early years, therapeutic and energetic work focused on the two lowest chakras. In the next commune, in Oregon, Osho worked primarily with the third chakra – known as the 'power chakra' – through which human beings may express the energy of pure power, or, more likely, its perverted forms such as the desire for dominance and control. This is power with all its shades of hypocrisy, jealousy, abuse, lack of respect for others, lies, control and also the shadow side – the unconscious desire to play the victim. All of this, in our case, was camouflaged on the Ranch by the astute feminine energy of Sheela, who by that time had replaced Laxmi as Osho's secretary.

In Pune One, Sheela arrived as a good-looking Indian woman, born in Gujarat but living and working in the USA with her American husband. She was keen to take Osho back to the States with her, and circumstances were in her favour. By 1979, the little ashram in Koregaon Park was becoming way too small for the huge influx of people arriving from all over the world. Osho asked Laxmi to find a bigger site in the north of India, where everyone could be accommodated inside the commune without spilling out into city suburbs.

At one point we came close to shifting to the coast of Gujarat; some people even paid for the train journey, while those with wealth could choose what type of room they wanted in the new place. All attempts to find a new home in India failed, however, and Sheela became convinced that our entire orange community should move to America, starting something entirely new, no longer associated with India's sprawling and chaotic spiritual scene, with its countless ashrams and gurus.

The bureaucratic details have little importance, but the fact is that Sheela succeeded in taking Osho to America, bringing him to a mansion in New Jersey, then soon afterwards buying an enormous ranch in Oregon where our commune was transferred. Having done that, she felt free to show off like a peacock opening its multi-coloured fantail, displaying all her feminine power. She was astute and provocative, with an abrasive personal style that irritated and alienated most Americans and eventually the majority of sannyasins as well.

After Oregon, a third commune was created when we all moved back to Pune, and this became known as 'Pune Two.' Here, Osho worked with the fourth chakra, the energy of the heart, in all its manifestations of love, compassion and devotion. After leaving his body, Osho gave us the opportunity to finish this work individually. And even now his consciousness resonates with thousands of human beings, helping them to create more awareness.

Historically, it almost always happens that the work of a Master begins to be recognized only many years after his physical death, because he is always ahead of his time. Likewise, disciples understand many things only after time has brought into manifestation what the Master, with his enlightened consciousness, had seen far in advance. Meanwhile, the vast majority of people don't notice anything, being firmly in the grip of their ordinary, everyday problems.

The last group Osho suggested for me was called *Leela*. Here, the group structure had no importance; what really counted was to spend time with the group leader, a disciple considered to be among those closest to realization. At that time, Somendra was about 40-45 years old, with a long beard, thick and black, giving the impression you were in front of one of those ancient warriors from Central Asia portrayed in etchings at archaeological sites.

His eyes were pure fire and the groups he led were filled with 'in the moment' presence. Nothing was structured or planned; everything was based on what happened in the moment. And, in the moment, so many things happened that no one ever forgot a group with Somendra. It was like finding yourself in another dimension.

On the first morning, Somendra got to know the people in our group by calling out our names, asking where we'd come from and what experience we'd had with therapy. When it was my turn, he looked at me and asked why I'd wanted to see Osho. I didn't understand English very well and even when someone translated for me, nothing made sense. So I was left dumb, with my mouth hanging open. Somendra laughed and went on with the group.

The early stages of the group were filled with emotional catharsis. In Somendra's presence, emotions just poured out. It was enough for him to touch someone to unblock old energetic knots that had lain dormant for years. He was an *energymagician*, a wizard, playing with us like a jester who could open doors in us that had been closed for a lifetime. He felt the thoughts in our minds, and could see people's past experiences and even previous lives in their auras.

One day, he said that two persons in the group already had the experience of going out of the physical body and moving on the astral plane. One was a Dutch woman who'd practiced yoga for many

Second energy meeting Azima receive in 1978

100 | MY LIFE WITH OSHO

years. The other, he informed the group, was me, adding that I'd left the body during an illness. How he could see all this seemed magical at the time. *Leela* certainly opened my mind to new energetic horizons.

Almost all the groups, including participants and therapists, met with Osho at some point during the process or after it ended. Usually, Osho would ask the therapist who'd been leading the group if he had some question, or something to report. Individual participants might also ask guidance from Osho about specific personal issues that had been triggered.

At the end of our *Leela* group, Somendra told us we would all go to *darshan* the next evening. Wow! We were already buzzing with so much energy it seemed impossible to absorb any more. Next evening, we entered Chuang Tzu with our whole group sitting together in the back. Osho entered in his customary way, sat down and gave sannyas, welcomed sannyasins returning from the West, bidding farewell to those who were leaving, and then began a series of energy transmissions. As usual, there was a huge wave of energy affecting all of us.

At the end, Osho looked as though he was about to stand up, then turned toward Mukta and told her there was someone in the audience that wanted to see him. To my surprise, Mukta called out my name. I was astonished. Me? Really? As far as I could remember, I hadn't asked for anything! I stood up, and went past several people already lying melted on the floor and arrived at his feet.

We looked at each other. He smiled and told me to close my eyes. I did so and he touched me on the third eye. Intense music began and my body was filled with a wave of pure electrical energy. It was like an orgasm that kept growing and growing without limits.

When it was over, my body was lying on the floor completely limp, so much so that a couple of strong male caretakers had to lift me up and move me to the side in order to give space for the Master to stand up, say goodbye and leave. I regained my strength after a long time. My body was shaking inside and it was difficult to walk, so I had to remain in the ashram for many hours before I could go home.

In the three years I stayed in the commune, I experienced seven of these energy events. I never went to darshan to talk with Osho. Even if there had been the possibility of doing that, I always chose silent or energetic meetings with the Master.

So, that's how I spent my first few months in the commune, doing therapy and meditating regularly. In the meantime, I had many relationships with women and my circle of friends also increased. The energy was high and there were always more people arriving from all over the world in order to meet Osho and be initiated by him.

I started to fall in love with India, a new and fantastic world so very different from the one I knew. Often, I would go into the city to buy material for robes and vests. I liked Indians and their friendly manner, sitting with them, chatting and drinking *chai*. I came from Sicily and the knack of doing business by barter was instinctive in me. Some Westerners were never comfortable with the process of bargaining, but for me it was enjoyable and easy to spend a long time chiselling away, trying to the lower the price of some object or garment that interested me – if only for the pleasure of being in a bartering game with a friendly Indian shop owner.

Tadiwalla, where I was living, became ever more chaotic, filled with people who were making love freely and frequently, and with music that continued far into the night. It was all I could desire. In order to learn English, I started studying the texts of Osho's discourses. Love relationships with foreign women, using broken English as the only means of communication, also helped. Between the women and the books, I started speaking the new language fairly quickly.

In the commune, there were people from everywhere with every imaginable history. Germans and Americans were the most numerous. Then, between 1978 and 1981, more and more Italians started to arrive, until they became the third most numerous foreign nationality. There were also many people from Spain, England, Holland, Brazil, Japan but surprisingly few French people – few but very refined. And of course there were many Indians in the commune, but many of these were coming for brief periods from other cities, whereas we Westerners had a tendency to stay much longer.

We were an educated lot. A majority of sannyasins arriving from America and Europe had university degrees. Osho used to joke that people with Ph.Ds. would immediately be sent to clean the bathrooms! There were therapists, psychologists, teachers, journalists, artists...people searching for a way of living that was different from the rules and constraints of their societies back home. It was a micro-world where all cultures were interwoven, dissolving in the unique energy of celebration and joy that Osho continued to spread.

I finished my groups and wrote to Osho, who said I was ready to work in the commune. But I wasn't in a hurry to start. For several months I lazed around, occasionally meditating, smoking hashish and travelling to Goa, a small state on west coast of India, south of Mumbai, where Western hippies had discovered a paradise of palm trees and clean beaches, with local people who spoke Portuguese – it had once been a colony of Portugal – and who also made very good food.

I went to Goa with friends from Tadiwalla Road. We rented a beautiful old Portuguese villa, employing locals who were happy to serve us – cooking, cleaning and doing laundry – for a few rupees while we swam and sunbathed naked and organized parties on the beach.

Living in Pune was also very pleasant. It was a city of hills, known as a command centre for the Indian military, and a place for spending healthy vacations far from the hell of Mumbai. By the time we returned from Oregon in 1987, however, it had developed into a major city, expanding in every way – in population, traffic, new apartment buildings and above all business. Right through the turn-of-the-century, Pune kept on growing as one of the main beneficiaries of India's booming economy. It is now, unfortunately, almost unliveable, a city packed with seven or eight million inhabitants. The streets are hellish, jammed with traffic and noise, and the resulting pollution is almost intolerable.

Nothing remains of that relaxed, easy-going, idyllic little city filled with gently decaying English villas and elegant parks full of trees. In a way, I guess I was lucky. Pune in the 1970s still reflected the old India with its lovable traditions and local customs. We used to travel around on bicycles, enjoying streets that were relatively free of traffic. Most of the time, we were relaxed with the Indian population and they were easy with us. Scores of parrots and other colourful birds would chatter in the trees around us, enjoying a healthy, uncontaminated atmosphere. Progress doesn't always mean a higher quality of life.

I was happy in India. One of my favourite activities was to hang out at the burning *ghats* by the river, where Hindu families brought the dead bodies of their relatives to be burned on a funeral pyre. There were many such ghats in the city, along the riverbanks, and I often went to meditate at a *ghat* located just beyond the city centre, situated under a huge bridge.

It had a magnificent banyan tree – a 'walking tree' – by the side of the river that was filled with fruit bats who would hang motionless all day, upside down, wrapped in their large wings, until sunset when they would wake up and start to fly around. Some of them were so big one might mistake them for flying dogs. Fortunately, they fed on fruit, not on people. During the day, the banyan tree looked as if it was filled with black fruit rocking in the wind.

Sunset was my favourite time. The light was majestic, the sky sketched in beautiful pastel colours, and there was a little hill near the river where I could sit and meditate. I would close my eyes, filling myself with the energy of the place, absorbing the sounds and odours, letting my body expand beyond its physical dimensions, basking in a profound sense of peace.

In India death is more easily accepted than in the West. The places where the corpses are burned are filled with sacred energy. Imagine trying to sit cross-legged and meditate in an Italian cemetery! I don't think it would be allowed for long. In my experience, meditating on death and the decomposition of matter is one of the most effective ways to realize dis-identification with your own ego. Many of the meditation techniques that Osho taught were based on the death process. And it was no accident that

Gautama Buddha used to send new initiates to live at the burning ghats for three months in order to deeply understand the transient nature of our lives on this planet.

Meditation practices based on death are powerful techniques and should be done with caution. If you are unprepared for the sense of emptiness that results from them, then it is better to begin with other meditations. Several Tibetan techniques are based on the practice of seeing yourself dying, identifying with death instead of the life flowing in your veins. More than in any other culture, Tibetans have dedicated themselves to investigating the complex phenomenon of what happens before, during and after death.

The most famous text is *The Tibetan Book of the Dead*, which describes the preparations needed for accompanying the soul on its journey through death. The first edition of this text in English was published in London by Oxford University Press in 1927. In the fourth edition, published in 1960, there is an introduction by C. G. Jung. The text is also called *Bardo Thodol*.

According to this book, the Bardo is a state of passing from one level of consciousness to another. There are six Bardo states:
1) The Bardo when we are in the womb waiting to be born.
2) The Bardo when in life we dream at night.
3) The Bardo when we are in deep meditation, in a state of ecstasy.
4) The Bardo when we experience our material life.
5) The Bardo when we are at the moment of death.
6) The Bardo of when consciousness seeks another incarnation.

Bardo Thodol is a detailed explanation of the transfer of energy during the death process, and the practice of the Bardo helps the soul of a dying person to reincarnate in its next life at a higher level, with more awareness. If the dying person is a practitioner and closely follows the instructions of a monk who sits close to him while he is dying and also after his death, this person may also gain full realization without any further reincarnation.

Some of Osho's meditations have their roots in Buddhist practices. Others are based on the wisdom of thousands of years of Hinduism. Osho himself, in a previous life, had been a Buddhist

Master and his radical vision, offering a new kind of religiousness, is both a continuation and a departure from those days.

Details are not clear, but it is said that several hundred years ago Osho was a Master with many disciples, living somewhere in the Himalayas. He didn't indicate the place in which he lived, but there is a legend that his body, along with the bodies of other great Masters, is preserved in a hidden chamber in the Potala Palace, formerly the winter residence of the Dalai Lama, in the Tibetan capital of Lhasa.

The last days of his previous life on earth were spent in one the most intense spiritual practices, through which it is possible to realize oneself as a pure body of light, but without the possibility of ever taking on another physical body. I believe he was practicing the 'Rainbow Body Meditation.'

This technique has been practiced by a few Tibetan Masters who decided to re-join the light for eternity. They close themselves in a quiet place and make arrangements that they are not disturbed for any reason. Only after 21 days can the door be opened. What the disciples find at the end of the 21 days are only the hair and nails of the Master, which are regarded as excretions of the body. The rest of the physical body disappears. Not surprisingly, this practice has been completed by very few beings.

It is said that Osho was completing that practice, after which there would be no possibility of further reincarnation. However, three days before the conclusion, out of compassion, he asked one of his disciples to kill his body so that he could reincarnate one more time – in our time. From a nonmaterial dimension, deprived of the normal time-space coordinates in which we generally move, he marked the passage of time on earth by observing the cycles of incarnation of those beings already familiar to him.

When he understood that 700-750 years had passed, he entered a physical body again in order to share his enlightened perspective with the people of the twentieth century and beyond. Seven years were needed for every day missing from the Rainbow Body Meditation, so that at the age of twenty-one he became enlightened, bringing to a conclusion a practice commenced almost eight centuries earlier.

This is the gist of what he told us. Osho was usually reluctant to 'gossip' about his own past lives and esoteric experiences because he did not want to nourish our spiritual egos. Indeed, in the later years, he avoided the subject almost entirely. But once in a while in earlier days he would make remarks, or drop hints, which together make up the story I have just related.

◻︎◻︎◻︎

9 The Past Revived

The monsoon started in Pune in June, beginning three long months of tropical rains. I'd never been in contact with Indian seasons before. I soon discovered that weather patterns in the East are much more extreme and powerful than what I was used to. In comparison, the climate in Italy is like a small child sheltered and protected by the surrounding European lands.

In this part of India, there are three types of monsoons, coming one after the other, spanning the period from June until September. The first is known as the 'ant' monsoon that is characterized by a light, steady drizzle that continues day and night until it penetrates to your very bones and makes all your clothing and bedding smell of mould.

Then the 'elephant' rains arrive, which in some coastal regions cause real disasters, floods that can carry everything away, even entire villages. The last type of monsoon that manifests at this latitude is the 'monkey' monsoon. In this case, it rains intermittently, with long dry spells in which the land has time to absorb the water, nourishing it even more.

During my first monsoon I decided to go to Goa for a week, alone, because I'd been put through so many experiences in such a short time that I wanted some days to myself in order to absorb them. I left Pune on a daytime bus, because I wanted to see and experience the changes the rains had caused in the countryside.

On board, I found myself remembering the ancient transport vehicles I'd taken when arriving in India. Now, in addition to the rundown quality of our bus, we also had the effects of the monsoon to cope with. We went charging into huge potholes filled with water, some of them long enough to qualify as streams, emerging miraculously at the other end, alive but soaking wet, splashed through the open windows on both sides. My Indian fellow travellers were laughing, taking the monsoon as fun.

Reaching the coast, a panoramic view opened up in front of me, a green vista as far as the eye could see. The vegetation was dense and the old abandoned Portuguese villas we passed were full of frisky monkeys. My eyes were inundated with green – trees, bushes, shrubs and creepers were everywhere – while pungent odours from the wet, fertile earth invaded my nostrils.

I stayed in a hotel in Panjim, Goa's capital city, enjoying the effects of the monsoon and the luxurious sense of being surrounded by rapidly growing vegetation. A good deal of the time I stayed in my room, passing the days peacefully in meditation. I returned to Pune in a calm mood with the clear impression that the first phase of being with the Master was completed.

The first days of September arrived and the rains began to diminish. The sun was shining brightly and the earth began to dry out. Blooming flowers were inundating the streets with captivating smells and colourful birds were flying everywhere. Osho continued to speak every day and the number of sannyasins continued to grow like plants in a monsoon, while the commune also grew bigger and, as a result, became more organized. Six months had passed and I realized I now considered myself to be an 'old sannyasin' compared to the newcomers.

The Master had told me I was ready to start working in the commune, but for some reason this scared me and I continued to postpone. I was now aware of the stages developed by Osho for people who wanted to live at his ashram: having become a disciple, it was necessary to participate in therapy groups in order to clean yourself of negative emotions and release suppressed energy. This made it easier to sit silently in meditation and was supported by the techniques devised by the Master and, of course, by his daily discourse. Finally came the invitation to work in the commune, which was considered in those days to be the ultimate relationship with the Master.

But I could already sense that work would a real challenge for me, as indeed it was for everyone. Work in the commune was pretty much all-consuming, a full-time commitment. Your work was assigned to you by women in the main office. The heads of the different departments were also women and the art, especially for men, consisted in voluntarily surrendering, letting go of your own ideas and doing whatever your 'boss' asked you to do.

The purpose was not only to work effectively, but also to watch and notice when your ego felt offended or hurt by the process. This game unleashed a series of dynamics that were absolutely unique, like working in a hall of mirrors, in which everyone played their part as totally as possible. Indeed, the motto of the commune was: totality in everything – above all in work. So, although my Master had already told me I was ready, I felt a need to prolong my enjoyment of a free and easy life, which for a while kept me away from work.

In the meantime, at Tadiwalla Road, Italians continued to arrive, to be welcomed, and then to disappear into the flux of the commune, just as it had happened to me. Our villa became a kind of transfer station for Italians. We were always helping each other, especially the newcomers, explaining how to settle into India and the commune. The floor was our furniture. As was the custom in many Indian houses, shoes remained outside the door and people mostly sat on mats on the floor. Our cooking stoves were located on the floor of the terrace.

For men, especially, the fundamental things for living in India were a good mat to sit on and a *lunghi* to wear – a piece of material about two metres long that you wound around your waist. Clothing for the upper body was optional, although another *lunghi* might be used as a shawl, or to sit on while meditating.

Western women also enjoyed wearing the *lunghi*, covering their hips with it from behind then criss-crossing it in front, with the two ends tied behind the neck. It did little to hide their bodies, but nobody seemed to care.

I'd heard no news from Italy, nor had I told my family my

whereabouts. But after the monsoon, a sannyasin from Palermo arrived, telling me my mother was out of her mind with worry, not having heard from me. Seeing that this same friend was returning right away, I entrusted him with a long letter to my family.

I know it may sound harsh, but it was as if the Western world no longer existed for me, including my family, Italy, political problems, old friends... everything from the past had disappeared, as if it had never existed. It was an effort to remember who I'd been before and what had interested me.

I wasn't sure how long this new state of mind would last, and I was determined to enjoy it while it did, without clinging to old ties, without being weighed down by old memories. The bonds I had with my parents seemed much less important than the love I now felt for the Master. The idea that my family was worried about me didn't touch me at all. So I continued to stay in Pune, knowing I was on the right track, understanding that my real family was now here.

After the monsoon, a woman from Milan arrived. She was upper-middle-class and in the beginning very tight and rigid in her personality. Nevertheless, she quickly opened to the energy of the place, leaving her past behind with great happiness. There was something different about her that immediately attracted me. I was impressed by her courage to leave behind a marriage to a German engineer and a comfortable life in Milan. Unlike me and many others in the commune, she didn't come from a revolutionary or alternative background. But within a few days her energy became as fresh, spontaneous, playful and fragile as a young teenager. She was very open to me, and I to her, so we fell in love and began to live together.

Almost a year after my arrival in Pune, a telegram from my father reached me. With typical clarity and very few words, he informed me of something I'd completely forgotten – something that fell on my head like a heavy shower during the elephant rains. He said, "The police are looking for you to take you to trial. You have to come back to Italy and turn over your passport."

The trial was, of course, related to my political activities, to charges which had been pending since an arrest many years ago with other revolutionary companions.

Now, with my new sannyasin perspective and the passing of time, I found myself in completely different circumstances, but this thunderbolt from a seemingly tranquil blue sky brought me back to my old world and all its follies. To go back or not? I had to make a decision but it was too difficult for me alone, so I decided to write to Osho and ask him about it. His answer was, "Come for darshan."

It hadn't occurred to me that I would sit in front of him and personally receive the answer, so I waited for a written response, such as "stay with us," or "go, I will be with you." No such response came and it became clear to me that this was going to be a personal meeting. By now, I'd been in a stable relationship with Prem, my new girlfriend, for some time and so she decided to follow me to darshan and be present at the meeting with Osho.

At the appointed time, Osho entered, calm, peaceful and natural as usual. After greeting everyone, he followed his customary pattern of initiating new sannyasins, then calling up those who'd asked to see him. Prem and I were ready to sit together in front of him, but then Mukta called only Prem's name. We were taken by surprise and for a moment Prem didn't move. Mukta called her name again and so, rather hesitantly, she stood up and went forward while I resigned myself to having been forgotten.

After Prem, Osho continued with a series of meetings with other people, but just when I was convinced everything was finished, Mukta called my name. I stood up, feeling happy that the Master had not forgotten me. I sat at his feet, looking into his eyes, and the meeting was sweeter than ever, reassuring and tender at the same time. Just being in his presence instantly communicated a sense of profound inner peace.

"Close your eyes," he said and touched me on the third eye. Again, I was overwhelmed by the feeling of sweetness, rather like a father coming to save his son from danger. I began to feel that everything would be okay. After a while, he put a small wooden box – shaped in the form of a heart – on my forehead, which seemed to fit perfectly with the contours of my face. The sensation added to the feelings of serenity and peace that I'd been experiencing since the meeting began.

When the energy transmission was over he gave me the box as

a gift, with a smile so big that it promised to fill my heart for months and months, saying: "Okay, Azima, now you can leave!"

At those words, my heart opened. I returned to my place and sat down, confident that whatever might happen in Italy would be for the best. The Master was with me, along with his magnificent smile, which I would never forget.

Once again, we had met in silence in a nonverbal sharing of energy. It was as if we were talking at a much deeper level, through our eyes, in a language that communicated essence-to-essence, leaving the mind far behind. It was the language of looks, gestures, sensations, energy and heartfelt emotions – silent transmissions that went beyond the barriers of ego and remained over time.

Once d*arshan* was over, we came out of the Lao Tzu gate and met our closest friends, who were waiting for us. Prem couldn't manage to restrain herself any longer and burst out crying. She felt the Master had separated us. He'd given me his blessing for the trip, but called her separately and did not mention anything about leaving. To her, his message was clear: it was better to remain in Pune. In the course of the past year, this was the second time that Osho had separated me from a partner. Nevertheless, after interminable crying and soul searching, she decided to ignore his advice and follow me.

It was a little more than a year since I'd taken sannyas and now I was preparing to return to Italy, not knowing how long I would stay.

Once more, I was faced with the practical tasks so necessary to move through the 'outside' world, including plane tickets, passports, visas and other practical things, all of which seemed alien to me after dissolving into the ashram. Moreover, I'd been living with such intensity it seemed that at least seven years had passed in Pune during these twelve months.

I felt completely changed inside, so very different from the man who'd left Italy. But it wasn't just a question of inner transformation. My exterior features had also changed dramatically. My beard had grown very long and my hair was full of curls that hung down over my shoulders. I was dressed in a bright orange robe and wore Osho's mala around my neck.

MY LIFE WITH OSHO | 113

Prem's personal crisis lasted not only during our time of preparation for departure, but also throughout the trip itself, during our whole time in Italy. I think her turbulence was created by her decision to go against Osho's message. But there was something more, a feminine intuition perhaps, hidden in some corner of her mind, as to what would happen a few months later.

As for me, I felt that I was being flung into an abyss without any certainty of the outcome, and yet I also carried within me the absolute conviction that everything would turn out well. The predominant feeling was of total trust in the Master and an understanding that this adventure in Italy was an opportunity to put trust into action. To me, it had the flavour of devotion: total trust in a man whom I recognised as belonging to other spheres of consciousness and awareness.

I never asked myself the question whether or not Osho was an enlightened being. Nor do I ask it today. The question itself contains a contradiction: not being enlightened myself, how can I judge if someone else is? Still, today, people sometimes say to me: "I have been with this enlightened guru, or that enlightened spiritual teacher," as if it is the most obvious thing in the world. But as I understand it, only a fully realised being can recognise another.

When I first saw him, I simply burst out crying, feeling that I had arrived home –a tremendously powerful sensation that is still with me today. The trust that I have experienced with Osho is always present. It was only because Osho had told me to go that I could manage to do so without fear, anxiety and all the other emotions that tend to arise when facing a serious situation.

The flight was exciting and unpredictable. We found ourselves on a plane with hundreds of people who were all wearing normal clothes, unlike ourselves, who were dressed in orange robes with malas around our necks. It was only when we boarded the plane that I became aware of the implications. What passed almost unnoticed in India would not only appear extravagant in Europe, but might be judged as absolutely crazy by a police officer, a court judge, or a psychiatrist – the more so in a conservative city like Palermo, capital of conformity and rigid traditions.

In India, ordinary citizens did notice us as different, but no more picturesque or unusual than the whole gamut of sadhus and sannyasins that were part of their society. In Europe, of course, it wasn't like that. Even on the plane, people were looking at us with distrust and suspicion. This in turn, made me more aware of the revolutionary spiritual process to which I had committed myself.

Arriving at Rome airport and then again in Palermo, I understood the game of the Master. We had become aliens, extra-terrestrials who'd just landed from another planet. In broad daylight, we had to walk off the plane, through airport controls and into a world into which we would never again be able to melt, merge and disappear.

In Palermo, hundreds of astonished looks greeted us, accompanied by ironic comments and cutting remarks that made us feel even more alien. Nevertheless, these comments did nothing except reinforce my centeredness, which I could feel more forcefully now I'd become so very different from everyone else.

How easy life had been in India! Even thousands of Westerners dressed in the colours of the rising sun were somehow accepted as part of the country's long tradition of spirituality that went back thousands of years and spanned hundreds of different approaches to religion.

But in Sicily, these bright clothes and the necklace could signify only a few things:
1. You were a circus clown.
2. You were crazy.
3. You were something to laugh at, either in your face or behind your back.

When we arrived at my parent's house, my mother opened the door and, gazing upon the son she no longer recognised, immediately fainted and fell to the floor. My sister, who was also present, started crying – more out of dismay than out of pleasure for seeing me. In fact, from that day on, my sister no longer wanted to go out in the street with me because she was so ashamed!

It was difficult to be with my family after being in paradise with the Master, but the energy we'd accumulated in the commune gave us strength and courage to deal with the situations and people that confronted us. I announced to everyone that my name was now Azima and asked them not to use my old name. Predictably, they didn't respect my request. The only ones who used my new name were my young nephew and niece, who were still innocent and therefore curious about this 'orange uncle.'

Both of them often stayed with me at night in order to ask many things about India, sannyas and Osho. Open and available to life, they were the only ones who could share my joy and understand something of the significance of having met a living Buddha.

With all the other family members, it was a hands-on experience of what we sannyasins call 'social conditioning' – the tendency of each society to program all its citizens with the same ideas, attitudes and beliefs, allowing no space for dissent. This is what the Master meant when he said the ordinary masses are under a 'collective hypnosis.'

The significance of taking another name is really to sanction another birth, this time a conscious one, embracing a new life that evolves at the spiritual level and is no longer preoccupied with material possessions and social relationships. To change your name is a 'psycho-magical' act that smashes identification with your family and social environment in which your ego was shaped.

My relatives were living in a separate world. My family of origin was not at all interested in me – the new me – or in my spiritual choices in life. Rather, ignoring the bright orange clothes and the picture of Osho swinging from my neck, they continued to treat me as if nothing had happened. From my perspective, on the other hand, my family now seemed like part of a giant insane asylum in which madness was perfectly normal and acceptable, and where attempts to step out of that world were looked upon at best with indifference, at worst as dangerous.

After being in the *Buddhafield* of the Master and having experienced what love and caring for others can really mean, it was obvious to me that the rest of humanity shared a total disinterest in such matters. By sending us to the West, Osho made us live inside the skin of normal social hypnosis, giving us a taste of identification with this state, which consists mainly of suffering.

For example, we have been educated to believe that it is quite normal to spend almost all our lives working in offices and factories, merely in order to earn enough money to live. We don't think of it as suffering. We don't see that we are sacrificing ourselves for work. We just put up with it and think this is normal.

So you can imagine the contrast we experienced when coming from Pune, filled up with exuberant vitality, with joy, with a desire to live passionately. The seriousness of the world now surrounding us was a shocking contrast to the lightness of the world we had left.

It wasn't possible for us to share our energy with others, although we tried. Their mistrust created an impassable wall of suspicion and denial. They didn't understand us and they didn't *want* to understand us. Those who were intelligent enough to intuitively understand the revolutionary and completely destabilizing potential of the message we were carrying, pulled away from us as if we were carrying a pernicious virus. To us, the name of the virus was simply 'awareness.'

Nevertheless, the neo-sannyas movement was growing and spreading. Beginning in 1974, Osho encouraged his sannyasins to create many meditation centres around the world. A few of these became really big, bringing thousands of disciples to the Master, spreading his message in the West. Predictably, many of these centres also experienced difficulties with the world, especially because of the cathartic element in some of Osho's meditations.

The modern mind is in a state of chronic stress and repressed emotions. It does not know the experience of silence, and has no idea about inner emptiness.

For Westerners, priority is given to activity, to action. In other words, if we can't find anything to do, we tend to become restless, irritated and feel at a loss. It almost feels as if we are dying.

From babyhood, we are taught to be active: the family, the school, everything around us is pulsating with the message for us to 'do something' and achieve results.

Knowing our mind well, Osho created an active meditation technique that was to become known – or rather, notorious – around the world. He called it Dynamic Meditation. At many of his meditation camps in the early 1970s, Osho guided this meditation personally. Later, he appointed sannyasins to lead it for him. It was created specifically to deal with the stress of modern living and immediately became controversial, first in India and later in the rest of the world.

Dynamic Meditation lasts one hour and has five stages.

The first stage, ten minutes, consists of deep, fast, chaotic breathing through the nose, emphasising the exhale. When you're doing it, you feel as if you've become an old steam engine, puffing along a railway track, slowly building up speed. Done properly, it creates a lot of emotional pressure inside and this is needed for the second stage.

Stage two, also ten minutes, consists of catharsis, intense emotional release and expression. People are encouraged to let out whatever is boiling inside. They may scream with anger, cry and weep, roll around on the floor, laughing insanely... everything is allowed and supported. This is how the pressure inside the modern mind is discharged.

In stage three, which also lasts ten minutes, participants jump up and down, their arms raised in the air, shouting the mantra "Hoo! Hoo! Hoo!" This mantra acts as a hammer on the sex centre, as does the jumping, releasing energy coiled at the base of the spine.

After these thirty minutes of intense activity, a voice cries "Stop!" Immediately, everyone stops as if frozen, doing nothing, remaining unmoving for fifteen minutes. This is the time when, having emptied the mind and exhausted the body, one can experience the emptiness and silence of meditation. The meditation ends with fifteen minutes of freestyle dancing and celebration.

Naturally, public attention focused on the screaming, and Dynamic Meditation was criticised for exposing the anger and suppressed feelings we all carry. In fact, it takes a real act of courage to dig into the deep emotional magma buried inside us, which is at the root of all social violence and aggression.

In 1974, Osho asked a German sannyasin and well-known musician, Georg Deuter, to compose music for Dynamic Meditation and other meditation techniques. These were published on audiotapes and CDs and sold around the world. They are still available today as a precious tool for people to begin the inward journey.

Among Osho's meditation methods, Dynamic has remained the best known and is used by thousands of therapists all over the world. It has even been used in prisons and institutions of re-education. It is my personal hope that one day it might even be introduced in our schools.

Osho explained that when you start using this technique many 'psychic toxins' begin to be released, not to mention all the uncomfortable aches and pains created by using the body in this unusual way. He also warned us that, during the first few days, one might not feel very well as the intense work of emotional cleaning begins. For this reason, he added, it is important to continue the meditation once a day for 21 days. Only then we will experience the desired benefits.

Dynamic Meditation also has the effect of freeing all seven chakras from energy blocks. With normal methods of Western therapy, it might take years to get rid of old feelings and emotions that kept us in misery.

Dynamic Meditation offers a short cut. It is my personal belief that three months of daily Dynamic will help you more than three years of psychological work.

10   The Only Alternative

When we practice various active techniques for a long time, only then, when the mind has started to calm down, can we sit and meditate, observing our breath, our body, our thoughts, and our emotions. A mind that is too active will always find something on which to chew, will always be thinking, will always be in a state of anxiety and will miss the real purpose of life.

In Tibetan, mind is called *lhun,* but *lhun* also means 'wind.' What connects these two concepts? The primary quality of the mind is continual movement, without a pause, as if agitated by a constant wind. If we don't learn to take distance, with our inner observer, then we will be in the grip of emotions and thoughts that toss us around from one experience to the other, without any destination and without any centre—just like a piece of paper being swept away by the wind.

Seen from this perspective, you may become aware of one of the mind's basic characteristics: a chronic underlying anxiety that pervades almost every activity: getting involved in a relationship, buying a house, having children, pursuing a career, even playing a game of sport or going on holiday... Inside, like a hidden river flowing just below the surface of the conscious mind – and sometimes above the surface – you will notice a perennial state of uncertainty and anxiety. This is so habitual that it appears to us as normal.

Why do we live in this chronic state? It is because, at some deep level that we do our best to ignore, we know that our security is precarious. We know we are building castles in the sand. The things we deem so important have no permanence. They are 'dreams tied to a cloud' and can disappear at any moment, leaving us in despair.

Human beings are under the hypnosis of the logical mind, which is fundamentally a bio-computer whose main function is to help us live in, and relate with, the outside world. But this rational mind is not the most important part of our lives, even though we persuade ourselves it is so.

Meditation techniques, little by little, help us experience states of consciousness beyond the logical mind, introducing us to the emptiness of mind and the state of pure awareness. This is the emptiness of which Gautama Buddha, Osho and other mystics have spoken. It sounds scary, but only because we're not familiar with it. Rightly understood, it is our true nature as conscious beings. If we are to live a life of inner peace, bliss and joy, moving ever closer towards the divine, then we need to become more and more familiar with the emptiness within us. A full container cannot receive anything. Only an empty container can be filled. In fact, the basic requirement for receiving bliss and other gifts from the divine is to be empty and silent inside.

A busy mind keeps us from relaxing and disappearing into this emptiness. Nevertheless, mind itself remains an integral part of the silence that is our nature. Just as a wave is a part of the ocean beneath, so a mind in movement remains part of a bigger, empty mind beneath it. The substance of the wave is the same as the ocean surrounding it. However, when we apply this metaphor to our own condition as human beings, we realize that no one has ever taught us to see the wave in terms of the whole ocean – no one except the great Masters.

One of the characteristics of modern man is our enthusiasm for technology that enables us to do things faster and more efficiently. But, rather than using this convenience to create and enjoy a more relaxed lifestyle, we simply find ourselves being carried along at a more and more frantic pace, that can easily bring humanity to self-destruction.

The fact is, only an empty mind can bring peace to mankind, allowing us to come into contact with our true self. Until we recognise allowing us to come into contact with our true self. Until we recognise this and make the effort to connect with the space of empty mind, we will continue to be ruled by a bio-mechanism that keeps us helplessly adrift on the surface of the ocean.

The Fourth Door
Empty Mind

Only by entering into regular contact with the inner space of empty mind can man live a life of joy and respect for himself and for other beings.

The fourth door introduces us to the consciousness of our essence. Emptiness is the substratum of all manifestations in this life, from the biggest stars to the smallest atom. Entering this door orients our life toward inner fulfilment, as part of one organic whole that consists of the stuff we call 'existence.' The empty mind enables us, without effort, to overcome every obstacle. It brings us gently towards our ultimate goal, which is nothing less than the dissolution of our personality into the light that surrounds us.

Normally, when we talk about the mind, we are referring to the thinking process and its stream of thoughts. However, I want to introduce you to a more complex model, in which the thinking process is merely one of seven layers of cognition and awareness. Three of these layers exist below our so-called 'normal mind' and three of them above.

The three lower layers:
○ The personal unconscious.
○ The collective unconscious.
○ The cosmic unconscious.

Opposite to these layers, like a mirror, there are the three upper layers:
○ The personal superconscious.
○ The collective superconscious.
○ The cosmic superconscious.

Let's begin our exploration of these layers by looking at the three below the normal mind.

Our personal unconscious is made up of memories, traumas and experiences gathered during the life we have lived. Sigmund Freud studied this layer in an effective way, developing the technique of psychoanalysis that sought to eliminate adult neurosis by bringing awareness to emotions, impulses and desires suppressed in childhood.

Freud discovered that a major part of our ego structure, which is created during childhood, revolves around the issue of suppressed sexual energy and traumas associated with it. He studied many symbols that existed in the personal unconscious and managed to construct keys for reading emotional repression. He did this mainly through analysing dreams.

His student and closest colleague, Carl Gustav Jung, went further in his research. Through studying many different traditions, including Indian philosophy, he concluded that below the level of the personal unconscious mind there is a deeper layer, a collective unconscious that gathers experiences and taboos from our cultural and social groups. In the last years of his work, Jung also began to talk about the cosmic unconscious that gathers symbols that pertain to our entire planet and perhaps beyond.

In this way, three mental layers came to be defined, levels that function as unconscious driving forces in the lives of all human beings. These forces are not only generated by childhood experiences of a single individual, but by ancient collective memories recorded in the body-mind system from our ethnic and racial origins, and, indeed, from the universe itself.

This shows us that men are not islands living in isolation from each other, but are connected below the surface through the unconscious mind, sharing common roots in a hidden, submerged landscape. We all belong to the same essential matrix. Unfortunately, Jung died with his studies of the cosmic unconscious incomplete.

These three levels are, as I have said, the driving engine of our lives and are valid for all human beings. When a person voluntarily undertakes a spiritual path, he begins the process of detaching himself from these unconscious forces and orienting himself superconscious. The path of meditation and increasing awareness brings us to the door of the personal superconscious, then to the collective superconscious and finally to the enlightenment of the cosmic superconscious, where we experience ourselves as separate from the mind-body mechanism and one with the light of universal consciousness.

Almost all Western studies of psychoanalysis, psychology and cognitive theories of personality are oriented toward the study of the mind in terms of the personal unconscious. Studies of the superconscious have been rare, although Osho has mentioned the work of the Italian psychologist, Roberto Assagioli, in this context.

Most scientific research focuses on a small fragment of consciousness – the normal mind and the personal unconscious – with no understanding that this fragment is part of a greater sphere of awareness. The healing effort of the great majority of psychological schools is to find ways to bring a sick mind back to the realm of so-called 'normal reality' so that it can again function efficiently in society. In other words, it is utilitarian, focusing on what is useful to the individual in terms of conforming to the behaviour, ethics and values of the social group in which he lives.

Only with the development of humanistic psychology in the 1960s and 1970s did people become interested in studying the nature of a healthy mind and its potential for growth and more awareness.

The same attitudes can be found in the camp of traditional medicine, where studies are oriented toward helping the patient to become 'normally healthy.' It does not pay much attention to the study of healthy subjects with the aim of discovering higher potentials. The concept of health in the West is basically a negative concept. If you're not sick, you must be healthy. We commonly define health as the 'absence of disease.' As yet, there has been no systematic attempt to define health in positive terms.

Until very recently, science has either ignored or dismissed mysticism. This is understandable, because science demands material proof in an objective way, whereas mysticism offers an experience of pure subjectivity. Fortunately, a few scientific researchers, especially in the realm of physics, have started collaborating with mystics like His Holiness the Dalai Lama. Together, they seek to find common ground between the nature of matter and experiences of meditative states of consciousness.

But these experiments and collaborations are exceptions, not the rule. Ninety-nine per cent of human beings identify with the so-called 'normal mind' and its relatively low level. In this state, they believe they are conscious, but in reality almost all of their actions and behaviours are determined by whatever has been locked away in the personal unconscious. Trusting the rational mind, they believe they can manage their lives by thinking, analysing and reflecting, but the force that powers this mind is minimal compared with the enormous energy that exists as a latent force under the surface.

Man suffers unnecessarily because he thinks he needs to move the great mass of the ocean with the energy of his single wave. If he could understand the nature of the ocean, he would allow his single wave to move in harmony with it. Struggling to live 'his own life,' he will easily feel isolated, separated from other people and from the existence surrounding him. He does not know that the mind, the total mind with its seven layers of unconsciousness, consciousness, and superconsciousness, is one.

Mind is one. There are not many minds for many beings. There is one mind that manifests as different waves. As a separate wave, life looks like an uphill struggle that does not last long. As the ocean, we are connected not only to each other but also to eternal life.

So, let me repeat: mind is a much more complex phenomenon than most people believe, including scientists. The brain is studied as if it is a map showing only the life of a single individual. In fact, the brain contains the collective memory of all other brains that have ever existed.

Information and data stored in each mind is, of course, different, as is our uniqueness as individual human beings. But the mind itself is one. Looked at another way, there aren't billions of minds —one mind for each body that lives on the planet. Rather, there are billions of bodies that have the same mind, the same essential matrix, the same conditioning, hypnosis, dreams, ideals, fantasies, and desires. If we could begin to live this radical understanding, it would change the *gestalt* of our lives, of society and of the whole planet.

At a very practical and individual level, as we have seen, it would eliminate the chronic states of stress and anxiety from which humans routinely suffer because they consider themselves as separate and disconnected from everything around them. Understanding our connectedness would automatically bring respect for others and for all living beings that share this planet with us. Understanding our connectedness means that we can begin to feel part of a great design, of an enormous family, part of a single organism that has one mind, that lives and breathes together in each moment of eternity.

To kill another being is equivalent to killing part of ourselves, to do harm to others means to do harm to ourselves, to destroy nature is to destroy ourselves. Only by deeply living this truth can we hope that our Mother Earth will survive the crisis that we have created.

The Fifth Door
Mind Is One

The mind of man is one. It is composed of various levels of consciousness that develop in seven strata. These layers belong to every individual on earth. A personal, individual mind does not really exist.

Only through meditation, an individual can start to experiencing the one mind that we share. Only through meditation can he begin to have experiences of 'No Mind.' In the process of meditation, when we first sit down and close our eyes, the rational layer of our mind continues to be very active. Then, after a certain period of time, which will vary from person to person, the thinking mind begins to slow down.

According to Osho, it takes about forty minutes before the mind enters a relaxed state and the production of thoughts starts to diminish. When this happens, if we remain centred in the observer, or witness, we begin to observe the space of inner emptiness that brings peace. We become less aware of the body, more detached from our emotions, less preoccupied by thought.

It is an interesting fact that the chattering mind cannot easily exist in the present moment. It needs to focus on either past memories or future expectations in order to continue. When we enter meditation, the present moment begins to manifest, allowing us to experience that it is beyond both time and space.

The physical location of the meditator begins to lose its boundaries and it becomes easier to access images and dimensions which are beyond the current time-space continuum. From this perspective, people who engage in channelling are simply connecting with these other levels and allowing themselves to be used as vehicles to bring news and messages from these dimensions.

When we speak of No Mind it indicates a state of consciousness in which the intermediate layer, the thinking mind, is no longer so active – or is altogether absent. This allows us to experience higher levels of mind, gaining confidence in spaces and dimensions to which we are not accustomed and which might otherwise scare us.

In meditation, the normal mind is no longer in control. This can be scary, because throughout our upbringing, society has repeatedly told us to control our emotions, control our minds, and even control our destiny. The more a person seems to be in control of his life, the more he is praised by others.

The spread of social media over recent years, including mobile phones, SMS, internet, Facebook, Twitter, computer games, YouTube and, of course, television have all become useful tools in the effort to control people – especially young people. New digital systems influence everything in our lives and as Marshall McLuhan once said, way back in the 1960s, "the medium is the message." In other words, the media control our tastes, attitudes, social interactions and beliefs.

Meditation creates the opposite effect. The more we let go of the ego and the identity we have borrowed from society, the closer we come to our centre and our authentic self. It's a paradox. The ego promises to give us a clear sense of who we are, but fails because everything it claims for itself is borrowed. The dissolution of the ego looks like the end of the 'I' but in reality gives us a deeper more authentic sense of who we really are.

If there is an effort to control, then the state of No Mind is absent. If No Mind manifests, there is no control; we simply keep the flame of the observer burning without choice, ready to reflect whatever experience manifests before us. This attitude of non-interference is a far cry from conventional Western culture, which is based on self-determination, making plans, creating change and generally trying to manipulate the world that surrounds us as much as possible.

Science doesn't help. Its inventions are put in the service of our culture and it tries to make miracles happen by manipulating the chemical and atomic building blocks of the material world. It ignores the fact that a world of miracles already exists inside us, with no need for any manipulation or control.

No one teaches us to relax and accept what life offers us. This doesn't mean we need to be always passive, but it does require us to open ourselves to the abundant dance of energy that is continually surrounding us, inviting us to enjoy life – just the way it is, right now, in the present moment.

You may have noticed that life doesn't move along straight lines. It is unpredictable, full of surprises. If we allow ourselves to move with the flow of events, without creating hindrances, then we can live in a state of acceptance and harmony with life, not constantly preoccupied with manipulating things to be the way we want them.

By now, you will have seen that meditation takes us through enormous transformations of consciousness. Change becomes our way of life. There is a continual invitation to let go of the past and embrace the new, the present, the unfamiliar. Unfortunately, most of us seek security by trying to fix things, keeping them the way they are. We have a deep fear of letting go. But the plain fact is that, as long as we try to control our lives we will always be unhappy, always in a state of stress, and will never experience the simple joy of living.

The bottom line is: the more we seek to control, the unhappier we will be. The more we seek for certainty, the more distressed we will be by the mysterious flux of life swirling around us.

A person who meditates must have the mental strength and the courage of a samurai, living totally in the moment without any fixed ideas about the future.

To decide to begin a spiritual journey of self-discovery is to go against the current of our mainstream culture. It is a journey that few initiate and even fewer pursue to a conclusion. The path of dis-identification is arduous, not least because our families, our friends, our teachers, our priests and politicians are all dedicated to the task of keeping us identified with the values of the society in which we find ourselves. They don't want us to change because this might cause them to question their own values and this, in turn, creates fear. So we are, in fact, swimming against the current of the collective mind of all human beings that surround us.

On the path of meditation, initially it is important to clean the layers of the normal mind and the personal unconscious, so that repressed emotions and negative attitudes don't block the flow of energy. When the mind is relatively clean, the second stage starts. This is the true state of meditation in which we begin to enter the space of No Mind. After experiencing short gaps – moments in which the thinking process stops – we gradually find that we can spend longer and longer periods in the state of meditation and its accompanying states of bliss and peace.

According to Osho, these spaces of awareness can be of two kinds: implosive or explosive. In the first, we begin to feel the body getting smaller and smaller, finally disappearing and dissolving into nothingness, imploding into an experience of emptiness. In the second case, we experience the body expanding in space and continuing to spread and grow until it loses all definition, melting and dissolving into a vast emptiness. These are two ways of experiencing the same thing. Either way, emptiness is the final destination.

I don't want to seem discouraging, but the possibilities and opportunities for giving up on the path of meditation are infinite. The ego, the personality structure with which we are identified, will do everything in its power to divert our consciousness from the path that leads inside to our being.

that leads inside to our being.

In these 35 years that I have continued to walk the path of inner exploration, I have seen thousands of people abandon the path with a wide range of excuses. For example, many who become curious about meditation are not open to changing their lives. They cling to the security of a steady job or a settled love relationship. The problem is that, sooner or later, spiritual growth requires radical change, often in the spheres of work and relationships. This is not always the case, but as a general rule it's true.

There is also a kind of 'pseudo spirituality' that focuses on feel-good processes such as self-actualisation, raising self-esteem, increasing personal power, employing awareness techniques in the workplace, manifesting better jobs and higher incomes...and so on. There is nothing necessarily wrong with any of this. But it's important to remember that authentic spirituality doesn't focus on decorating your life with floral embellishments.

The true spiritual path is a path of death; death of the person whom we think ourselves to be; death of the ego structure that seems to protect us but in reality keeps us insulated from life; death of all that is false as it burns in the flame of consciousness; death of relationships to which we cling when love has gone, out of a fear of being alone; death of the past and future as we embrace the present moment.

Death of the ego and the rebirth of the 'I,' the real 'I,' the 'I' that none of us yet knows because we haven't asked the fundamental question in this life: "Who am I?"

❏❏❏

11   Home Again

An Osho meditation centre was just opening in Palermo and, joining with other sannyasins, we did our best to recreate the energy of the Pune ashram, organising daily meditations as well as groups and retreats held during the weekends. It was during one of these retreats that a breakthrough occurred in my situation with the police and the courts. As requested, I had turned over my passport and was, in a sense, held prisoner in Italy, unable to travel.

Then, during one retreat, I met a woman, who I would never see again in my life, who helped me quickly resolve the stalemate situation in my pending legal case. Her father was the head of the Palermo Court and through him I was able to receive a new passport in a very short time, with the promise that I would return to Italy if I needed to appear in court.

To me, it seemed this woman was channelling the energy of the Master in helping me return to India as quickly as possible. Really, it was a miracle. Such things happen sometimes in our lives –a situation that seems unresolvable gets solved in the most unpredictable and unforeseeable way.

However, I must add that during this period, when Osho was alive, such miraculous events were happening to his sannyasins on an almost daily basis. We accepted them with grateful innocence, like small children running naked in the streets, indifferent to the glances of serious and rational adults who warned us that life was difficult and hard. We knew better!

But there was a sting in the tail. While I had managed to favourably resolve my difficulties in Palermo, Prem remained stuck in Milan with legal problems that had nothing to do with her. An innocent phone call to an acquaintance was enough to get her involved in a roundup of suspected drug traffickers. She was the last person in the world to be involved in that kind of thing, but one phone call, misunderstood by the police, was enough to keep her stuck in Milan for two years.

So while I was free to return to Pune, she was not. I couldn't help reflecting on her *darshan* with Osho, when he surprised her by not giving his blessings to her trip with me to Italy. The words that Osho had addressed to me, "You can go!" translated into a speedy round-trip ticket. The silence with which Osho had greeted Prem, on the other hand, ended in a one-way ticket. Reluctantly, we said goodbye to each other, not knowing when we would meet again.

I returned to Pune profoundly changed. Even though I went back to live in Tadiwalla Road with my old friends, I no longer felt the same lightness. It was as if I was moving into a deeper, more profound and more intimate relationship with Osho than before. When I arrived in Pune the first time, everything was a surprise. I was thrown headfirst into this paradise, without knowing anything about the commune, the Master and the Master-disciple relationship. Now I was returning after being in contact with my old world and the contrast added depth to my being.

I wanted to live and work in the commune, near my Master – this was now my choice. I'd had enough of lazing around. Moreover the shock of living in the West had given me a deeper understanding of what it meant to live in India, beyond the grip of Western values, and to have the precious opportunity of participating in a spiritual adventure with Osho.

The commune was now bursting at the seams, filled with extravagant characters arriving from all over the planet. In his discourses, Osho started talking about expansion, explaining that we would need to construct a new commune, as big as a city, to accommodate everybody who would be coming.

The idea seemed extraordinary to me. Leaving aside the fact that he loved to exaggerate, especially with numbers, I realised that Osho was serious about the new project. A little while later, I learned that he had sent Laxmi, his Indian secretary, on a trip to northern India to find a property big enough to accommodate us all.

Meanwhile, the energy of the ashram was becoming palpably more intense. To spend time behind its walls was like being in a cocoon filled with joy, love, laughter and consciousness... all the positive human values that have been crushed by normal society.

And so my second monsoon season began with the understanding that it was time for me to enter the commune as a worker and become an integral part of the Master's project. As usual, the monsoon brought a lot of rain, but for me personally it also brought a new realisation about my habitual attitudes, especially my rebellious side and my desire to see myself as separate from the masses through smoking dope.

Initially, it was through dope smoking that I'd discovered my inner world and also a different way of making friends and an alternative lifestyle. All my years of being part of the student revolution were marked by the symbol of the 'free joint.' Once I was in India, I joined the cannabis culture, in which smoking was considered a spiritual path.

Smoking meant being with others, sharing, playing music and passing the night together. But this monsoon brought with it an infection that took my body temperature above 104 degrees Fahrenheit. I couldn't do anything but stay in bed because the moment I moved the pain in my bones became unbearable.

Friends at Tadiwalla went to the city to call a doctor who was famous among sannyasins, first because he was a very good ayurvedic doctor and second because he was disciple of J. Krishnamurti, whom most of us regarded as the only other living enlightened Master. He was a meditator and knew that inner space of which most medical doctors are unaware.

I already knew Dr Lad, whom I'd visited once before and who'd prescribed remedies to give me strength, seeing as the Indian climate, and above all the food, had weakened my body. So Dr Lad came to Tadiwalla Road. I was in my bed on the floor, immobile, with a very high temperature. He sat down next to me, closed his eyes and stayed in meditation a long time, I think about 30-40 minutes.

After that he took my pulse. When his examination of the pulses finished, he took some white pills out of his bag and told me to take two twice a day. Then he asked me to fast for five days and to do Vipassana meditation two hours a day. For the rest, he asked me stay quietly in bed and assured me that on the fifth day the fever would be gone and I would slowly get better.

He said goodbye to me with the Indian *namaste* gesture, a *mudra* that means: "I honour the divine that dwells within you." It was the most beautiful medical visit I'd ever had in my life. The space of meditation and silence were as clear as a lake and his eyes were very deep. I didn't see Dr Lad again because a short while later he went to America, where he became famous, authoring several books that were interesting from both a medical and spiritual point of view.

On the fifth day, as predicted, the fever broke and I was completely exhausted. Already naturally skinny, after the fever and the fasting I'd become like those razor-thin *fakirs* seen on the streets in India. The only thing missing was a bed of nails and then I could have opened a magic show in Tadiwalla Road.

During my recovery, however, not only did I not open a magic show, I also did not open any packet of cigarettes, or even *bidis*, those small Indian cigarettes made of neem leaves with tobacco inside. Even less did I consider smoking hashish. From then on, my body completely rejected drugs, which I never used again for the rest of my life. The fever had carried away part of my old personality, but I also acknowledged to myself that drugs had been necessary to help me discover a world that was not merely materialistic.

Osho was never against drugs. To tell the truth, he was never against anything. He was a Master who taught totality in life. In his vision there was nothing that could be defined as negative or contrary to meditation. He accepted all the experiences of his own life, making them part of himself and his immense inner world. He was a door that was always open, allowing every type of experience.

When sharing his wisdom with his disciples, he didn't say, "Do this" or "Don't do that." He didn't like commandments; rather, he encouraged people to respond spontaneously to each situation with awareness. As far as drugs were concerned, he said they could be useful to open people to inner spaces that might otherwise be unreachable through the ordinary, rational mind.

On another occasion, he proposed that young people should be allowed to take drugs under the guidance of a teacher who could help students travel inside themselves, without getting lost or confused, which can happen with drugs such as LSD. But he also explained that drugs could only offer a glimpse. They cannot bring us permanently to a state of meditation – that work has to be done through the effort of a drug-free consciousness.

I need to add that when Osho talked about drugs as being helpful, he was referring to hashish and LSD. He never advocated heroin or other heavy drugs that destroy awareness. Many people in the early days of Pune continued with the experience of smoking hashish and were never involved with work in the ashram. This was understood and accepted, precisely because the Master never mapped out a single road to follow.

Rather, he left it up to each disciple to follow the road he considered right for himself. He showed us the path in various ways and from different perspectives, but he never imposed anything on anyone. He reminded us that he was with us to share his being, which was more like an absence that a substantial image.

During his whole life he fought against the rigid structures of religion and taught a new concept of religiousness, free of duties, commandments and precepts to follow. To him, spirituality was an open door through which to fly into the inner sky, free of any structures or conditionings. His teaching was both Tantric and Taoist in the sense that it accepted every aspect of life.

All conventional religions teach us to struggle against some kind of enemy, either inside or outside – there is always something or someone to fight against. There is always the need for victory or defeat. Muslims embrace the sacred cause of the *jihad*, the holy war against the unbeliever. Christians divide the universe into two conflicting sides, good and evil, and teach us to fight against the devil who represents evil. The Jews worship an unforgiving God who strictly imposes his commandments and punishes those who fail to obey.

Even though we may think that we are free of these faiths, the truth is that every form of religion exists in the collective unconscious, the second level below the conscious mind. From this hidden place, it exerts a powerful grip on us all. Many of us, arriving in Pune for the first time and listening to Osho's discourses, wondered why he spent so much time talking about religion and its impact on our psyche. Slowly, we realised the significance of what he was doing: exposing the unconscious, pointing toward the superconscious, bringing new visions of spiritual freedom that will one day surely be embraced by all mankind.

It's my understanding that Osho initiated a new vision of our world that will gradually take shape in the coming decades. I'm not saying that everyone will become his disciples. But my feeling is that many people will eventually accept his views with respect to religion, family, education, science, the true liberation of both women and men, and the acceptance of sexual energy and transformation of our negative attitudes towards it.

Rarely did Osho predict what would happen on Planet Earth. He wasn't so much interested in details. He was more concerned with imprinting on our collective psyche a new and positive basis for a life of religiousness and love. In 'Pune One,' during the 1970s, he did talk about religious fanaticism as one of the unconscious forces that would drive mankind into global conflict. He also said that life-negative attitudes propagated by all the major religions had brought mankind to a point where we are unconsciously preparing for a collective suicide. This, he said, was one of the biggest dangers facing humanity, this deeply ingrained hatred for life that might push us into extinction.

More specifically, he foresaw the kind of warfare we are now experiencing between the major Western powers and all kinds of small, fanatic terrorist groups that wish to break our grip on the global culture. All this is now in front of our eyes as the West struggles to defend itself against these terrorist attacks, especially those by suicide bombers who willingly embrace death as the price for destroying the enemy.

I don't want to paint a picture of doom and gloom, but I think I also ought to mention Osho's early prediction of rising sea levels from global warming that may threaten so many of the great city ports through which our commerce occurs.

At the root of it all is a basic flaw: man has denied his own nature; man is at war with himself; man has no peace. It is inevitable therefore that he will externalise his inner conflict and make war against both his own brothers and sisters and the planet on which he lives.

On the positive side, Osho also said that whatever portion of mankind survives the consequences of its own follies, will have the opportunity to let go of superstitions and construct a society based on respect for nature, centred in the heart. In short, Osho spoke for other people, not only for those who were with him, constructing foundations of a new thinking that can help humanity in the near future.

Our materialistic attitudes will have to change. The idea that we can have everything we want, in terms of possessions, has created a culture of consumer greed which we thought could continue indefinitely, our foot firmly pressed on the gas pedal in order to reach our idealized goals before anyone else.

It's easy to blame America for propagating this kind of materialistic frenzy, but the truth is we all have the same hunger. Our desires have no limit, but real happiness seems as elusive as ever. It takes a profound revolution in consciousness to understand that the contentment, fulfilment and peace we are mistakenly seeking outside ourselves has really been with us all the time...inside.

This, I believe, is the basic reason why Osho was so critical of conventional religion – because it has pretended to give man the peace he seeks but in reality has done everything to prevent us from discovering it. The cure that religion offered was in reality part of the same disease. And the elite controlling each religion has been far more concerned with consolidating its power over the masses than examining its own fundamental flaws.

As Osho sees it, religious and political leaders are in a deep conspiracy to keep man drugged, unconscious, so that they can continue to rule over the societies they control. Osho's work is that of deprogramming the human mind from its religious and social conditioning. But, and this is most important, he has no interest in reprogramming the mind. According to him, consciousness needs to be free of all unconscious forces, all programs, all belief systems. In this deprogrammed state, men and women are free to naturally experience and respect qualities like mystery, religiousness, silence, creativity and meditation.

Osho's prophetic descriptions of what may happen to us in the years to come were uttered sporadically, both in the early Pune years, the Oregon years and after his return to India. But I would not like to give you the impression that it was a constant theme. It was not.

His main concern was us, the people who were sitting in front of him. He focused his efforts on teaching us the path of meditation and consciousness. He pointed toward the state of enlightenment, which, he emphasised, was the birthright and essential nature of all individual human beings.

I was always profoundly touched when I understood the freedom from slavery that Osho was offering. He genuinely wanted each individual to be as free as he was himself. And this included freedom for his disciples to choose whatever they wanted to do in life, even if it meant staying away from the Pune ashram.

As for myself, I trusted that when change was needed in my life, it would be obvious, and so it proved to be. My illness proved a turning point, as did my decision to quit smoking. Not smoking had social consequences. It set me apart from my friends in Tadiwalla, thereby helping me make the transition to working in the commune. I was finally ready to do what my Master had suggested a year earlier. So I went to live in Koregaon Park, close to the ashram, ready to throw my energy full-time into 'work meditation.'

Koregaon Park, as I've already mentioned, was made up of a series of English villas with gardens so large the whole area really did look like a park. The ashram was nothing more than a few of these villas put together, since we'd purchased several properties adjacent to each other. In this rarefied atmosphere, we didn't feel as if we were in a city, with all its noise, odours, crowded streets and native Indian elements. We lived in a magic bubble and now I was determined to spend as much time inside that bubble as possible.

It was my choice, a decision taken of my own free will. By the way, I have never known a single disciple of Osho to ever feel guilty for his choices in life, even if they were completely different from the rest of us. The same sense of freedom was also alive in the commune. Freedom to choose your own destiny was the supreme ideal of the Master.

When I went to Arup to ask for work, she didn't do anything that would make me feel guilty for the year I took off, even though she'd been the one who'd brought me the invitation from the Master to be part of the commune – an invitation I ignored for twelve months. Both Arup and the other women in the office welcomed me with affection and joy.

After a short interview, they sent me to the kitchen that supplied the ashram's main canteen with three meals a day, feeding hundreds of people, including those who came in each day from outside. There was a smaller kitchen that prepared food for residential workers, who received their meals gratis. But I went to the main one.

And so I started to work in the commune, a voluntary commitment that didn't end until a year after Osho's death in January 1990.

◻◻◻

12   The Conscious Beehive

In the morning, the Master's discourse began at 8:00 am and usually lasted between ninety minutes and two hours; then the working day in the ashram began. It didn't end until six o'clock in the evening. I was sent to the kitchen, which Osho himself called the 'Zen department', because it was headed by an Italian woman who was strong, stubborn, irritable and unpredictable, capable of inventing new dramas at any moment during the day.

To be assigned work with the explosive Deeksha was considered by many to be a terrible fate. It was like working in a monastery where the abbot would try to upset your equilibrium by frequently changing your assignments, giving contradictory orders, and so on. Osho knew this perfectly well. On several occasions, he stated that working with Deeksha would speed up the dismantling of any ego and that those working in the kitchen should consider themselves fortunate.

My first job was to clean the kitchen workers' toilets, passing whole days mopping white floor tiles that usually became dirty again the moment someone entered, it being the Indian monsoon season. The mud on people's shoes made sure my efforts were in vain. It was illogical and absurd, but I accepted the situation because I knew the game didn't stop after reaching a certain level of cleanliness in the toilets but continued with cleaning inside of me, the Italian doctor and leftist intellectual who until a few years ago wanted to change the whole world and who now was unable to keep even a small Indian bathroom dirt-free.

My working tools were a hard bristly brush, a water bucket, a broom, a sponge, a floor rag and an endless supply of water that I wallowed in all day. Sometimes, when I'd just finished cleaning the entire bathroom, one of Deeksha's female coordinators would meticulously inspect all the tiles, as if it was a state affair, as if Osho himself was about to drive up in his Mercedes and stop for a pee. Predictably, she would always find something wrong and then I had to redo the whole thing with my little brush and soap.

In a way, it was a bit like doing Zazen meditation in which you stare at a blank wall all day. The white walls and white tiles of the bathroom offered the same opportunity to watch my mind in action.

One day, however, after some weeks of bathroom cleaning, they called me to the kitchen and told me I had to help cutting vegetables. In this way, I started working in an enormous open space, covered only by strips of waterproof cloth, which was the kitchen itself. About 150 people were working there. Various tables were used, each one specialising in a particular phase of food preparation.

At one of these tables there were about a dozen people standing cutting vegetables. Naturally, there was a female coordinator who acted as a link between our table and the female bosses of the other tables. Every day, for the lunchtime and dinnertime meals, we had to prepare food for between 2-3000 people. So I entered into a new kind of meditation – working with others. No longer was I alone in my bathroom, staring at walls.

To me, this was certainly a more attractive proposition. For one thing, instead of holding a dead brush, I had an alive and colourful vegetable in my hand and I learned a lot about how to cut every type of vegetable according to the daily menu. In addition, I was now with other sannyasins all day, many of them young and attractive women, chatting, playing, laughing and gossiping about everything that happened in the kitchen and in the ashram.

It was easy to make friends and to relate with the women at your table. Problems occurred, however, when interesting new prey arrived to be seduced, because the women I'd already been with were standing right next to me. It was a goldfish bowl in which everyone could see everything that happened. Fortunately, playfulness and joy were the basis of our being together and so everything was easy. It was enough that you didn't become attached to anyone, otherwise it would have been difficult to survive in that climate of absolute freedom.

After a little while in the kitchen I discovered that Deeksha, the big boss, was none other than the daughter of Bhakti, the woman who'd welcomed me like a prodigal son the day I arrived at the commune. It really surprised me, because they were as different from each other as two people could be.

The mother was so detached, warm-hearted and peaceful that she spent her days meditating and chatting with other women while sitting on the little walls of commune. With white hair and big blue eyes, Bhakti was a woman from a well-to-do family. From the moment she met Osho, she never left the commune and I guessed she also donated substantial sums of money to be able to live inside without working. It was as if she was beyond the personal ego games that we young people were playing every day and her sole interest was to meditate and be near the Master.

Her daughter, on the other hand, was completely involved in the organization of the kitchen and the commune; she was yelling and screaming the whole day, going from one meeting to another, giving orders like a general on the battlefield. She was in continuous movement and always had a swarm of women around her, as in a beehive with its workers attending the queen. She was respected by many, feared by some and a challenge and a provocation to all.

Often, during her meetings, a woman would be giving her a foot massage or a manicure – scenes I would never have imagined witnessing, but the presence of the Master enabled me to go beyond my left-wing attitudes and enjoy the absurdity of this 'royal' situation.

Working at the food tables, I made friends from many different countries, discovering worlds I never knew existed, with different kinds of social attitudes and behaviour. Tadiwalla Road seemed so far away and so provincial with its exclusively Italian atmosphere. It was already disappearing on the horizon of my memories. Instead, I was feeling more and more part of an international commune and movement that was being created around Osho. English was the language of communication and my use of it improved day by day. A big bonus from learning English was the fact that I could understand Osho's discourses better and better.

It was becoming clear to me what Osho had meant when he said working in his commune was the biggest commitment a disciple could make. In doing so, individuals like me became part of his grand design, in which he was working simultaneously on various levels, from the growth of a single individual, to that of a whole commune, to the societies from which these people had come. The ripples of his work spread far and wide around the globe.

Osho used to say that he was creating a Buddhafield, promoting new values that were clearly in opposition to existing religious and spiritual organisations. In one discourse he said, "I am here to provoke God," a remarkable and powerful statement with different meanings depending on one's perspective. For me, the most important meaning was that of provoking the divine inside us and in the whole world.

Certainly, in the kitchen we felt a continuous provocation to our individual egos. The women who were put in charge seemed to have been chosen especially for their talents in being absurd in their demands, slavish in their desire to please Deeksha, quarrelsome in their nature and tremendously adept at 'pushing your buttons,' which was commune slang for being able to find the weak points in your ego armour.

Many of them were beautiful, physically and energetically, and they had absolutely no hesitation in carrying out Deeksha's orders, manifesting her desires and implementing her decisions. Men were definitely in second place in the life of the commune that Osho created – and deliberately so. The Master explained many times that he wanted to redress the imbalance caused by man's domination of women for thousands of years.

Women arriving in the Koregaon Park commune revelled in the fact that they were finally free to express their energy without hesitation and without compromise. Of course, along with this freedom came responsibility, but most of them embraced that, too, without a problem.

For us men, it was a challenging situation. Seeing all of these women freely expressing their energy and taking charge of the daily management of the commune was, to say the least, intimidating. The only option the Master left us was to surrender and then use our awareness to notice what was provoked in our personalities and ego structures. I've already used the beehive image. Well, men were definitely in the category of worker bees, the manual labourers. Female energy was in the ascendant, exploding and expanding in every way: physically, sexually, mentally and definitely emotionally. In the commune we were living and breathing female energy, at every level.

Osho had shuffled the cards of the game and was making us see how society could be if women were given absolute power. Every little emotion came out in the open and was expressed. During the work day there were often conflicts between women bosses that were almost always resolved with intense crying, followed by hugs.

Watching these female-to-female conflicts, I couldn't help imagining how similar situations had been resolved by men in the past. If it had been between kings, whole countries would have gone to war. If it had been between two cowboys in the Wild West, there would have been a gunfight in which only one would have survived.

Conflicts between men and women in the ashram were almost non-existent because all of us men understood the game. We were being invited by the Master to experience what it meant to no longer be in charge, to no longer have the decision-making process on our own shoulders. As a result, many of us spontaneously began a process of male deprogramming, letting go into the hands of the women and through them into the hands of existence itself.

It was no accident that Osho guided us in this direction, because the path of a disciple is a feminine path. The only way to be with a living Master is to surrender to him, which necessarily means that the masculine aspect of your ego structure has to give way, yielding to the feminine principle.

Practically speaking, it just wasn't possible to stay in the ashram if you developed an attitude of resistance towards Osho. The few people who found themselves in this unenviable situation eventually had to leave, emerging from the commune like warriors from battle, looking weary and sad, with faces as taut as the strings of a violin.

Such people isolated themselves and were no longer available for hugs and cuddles, which were the norm between sannyasins, day and night. So it quickly became clear who was keeping themselves from melting into the warm soup inside the Master's energy field.

An aggressive male mind had no chance to survive in this atmosphere. It was a clear choice: either melt or find some excuse or some reason to leave. Osho always wanted his work in the hands of women, even after the experience in Oregon showed us how greed, ambition, jealousy and cruelty were also part of the female world.

So I passed my days in the ashram, meditating with the Master in the morning, working the rest of the day. Life moved quickly and intensely, rich with events every moment of the day, unpredictable and sublime. All of us who were working felt united in this project of transformation, in this alchemy to which Osho was always adding new elements. Ordinary daily life had become magical and things happened so easily that there was no longer any need to make effort. On the contrary, if you did things with effort, everything would go wrong.

Deeksha was more and more a hurricane of energy and I didn't stay long cutting vegetables – everything was changing constantly. For a while, I was given the task of cleaning the cutlery – forks and spoons – which I found to be one of the most difficult jobs because of the need to continuously transport utensils from the dishwashing area to the kitchen counters. After a few weeks I was transferred to the pot-washing room. It was one of the jobs I liked best. It was really Zen. The pots that the cooks used were arriving continuously, dumped at my door, in urgent need of being scrubbed and cleaned in order to be used again. There were small pots, with a capacity no bigger than for two or three cups of tea, and enormous pots that contained the main dish of the day for thousands of people. There were no moments of rest as pots continued to arrive throughout the day, along with pot covers as big as sombreros.

There was no space for the mind in the 'pot room,' also known as the commune's 'Zen Room.' You didn't have time to stop and think because, if you did, you would be flooded with pots. Cleaning the big ones demanded hard physical work. You had to find your own personal style that allowed you to overcome all the obstacles that accompanied cleaning a pot that was big enough to hold your own body inside it.

Then you had to lift it, placing it carefully on the appropriate drying rack. In the meantime, your only human contact was with the cooks, who came to reclaim the various pots. But pot-washing had one special advantage: the various bosses of the kitchen almost never entered that small space to check if things were going well. It was as if they acknowledged the strong male energy needed to do that work and knew better than to mess with it.

While pot-washing, I was the only person in the entire kitchen who wasn't subjected to the emotional catharses of various female coordinators who continually went around, making sure things were going according to what they thought was right. The interesting thing was that the criteria for what these women considered to be correct were liable to change at any time. They would give you instructions for a particular task, then return an hour or two later to announce you were doing everything wrong and had to do it all over again in an entirely different way. Only the plot-washing room remained inviolate, a zone free of female influence.

I stayed in the 'Zen Room' with my pots for many weeks, until one day the women from the main office called me in and asked me to do a completely different kind of work. Osho had asked us to construct an enormous boutique, almost the length of the main street of the ashram, where clothes, hats, socks, soap, assorted India *kitsch* and, above all, his books would be sold.

Like every new project in the ashram, it was urgent and had to be completed right away. For this reason, they needed to increase the size of the existing construction crews because their manpower was clearly insufficient for the task. So, in an act of generosity, Deeksha decided to add some of her workers to those of the construction department. Goodbye pots, hello hammer and nails.

From one day to the next, I found myself out of the Zen Room and into the boutique project, standing with a hammer in my hand and a bunch of nails stuck in my leather belt. For the first time since joining the commune workforce, I found myself only in the company of men for the whole day. We newcomers worked hard and learned many things about how to erect wooden posts and lintels for doors.

The monsoon was finishing and all at once the heat became so intense that women from the kitchen were regularly bringing us drinks to quench our thirst. It was a kind of role reversal and the sense of camaraderie on this all-male construction crew was great. I can't remember any friction between us. Almost all of my new colleagues possessed a good sense of humour and a lot of irony.

We discovered that male sannyasins worked well together. During that job, I heard the life stories of many men with very different pasts: men who had been fighting in Vietnam, men who'd participated in the social upheavals in America in the 1960s, who started the famous movement of the hippies; men who were physicists and professors at different universities around the world, and others who'd rejected Western culture and lived in different countries like natives in incredible ways, with fascinating stories to tell.

This was a whole male world of courageous and adventurous men who now found themselves, all together, in an esoteric school that was crazier than anything any of us had ever experienced. Working together with these men was a pleasure for me and I made many beautiful friendships during this time.

We finished the basic structure of the boutique in a few months and, with only detailed carpentry work to finish, many of us were called back to our departments. I came back to the kitchen and was greeted with promotion. May be because the bosses had seen my devotion to work, or may be because it was just the right moment, they asked me to be one of three regular cooks.

The cook was clearly the most important position in the kitchen, as far as food preparation was concerned. I had a direct relationship with the bosses in Deeksha's office and responsibility for feeding two or three thousand people a day. So I found myself at the gas cookers, which were actually old kerosene stoves placed on the floor with big pots on them. Pots I had washed. Pots that were now being cleaned by an aristocratic friend of mine from Palermo.

It was he who had given his villa in Sicily for use as an Osho meditation centre and it was there I'd met the young woman – make that 'angel' – who'd managed to persuade her father to give me a new passport. Osho's work moved in ways that were strange and inconceivable, but extremely effective.

All those who went to work in our kitchen of wild women would come out changed – more centered, with an air of quiet inner strength, with an ego much softened and smoothed.

I stayed at the stoves for the rest of my stay in Pune One. Every day, I prepared the menu for lunch and dinner with two other cooks, who were also Italian and who stayed at the stoves with me till the end of the first commune. Cooking was not easy. First you had to learn the proportions of vegetables required for each recipe, then the cooking times, then the right quantities of spices to add to the pots before they went to the food counters. Above all, a cook needed to learn how not to hurt his back when pouring from heavy pots containing various sauces being prepared during the day.

The work was tiring and I would end the day with very little energy remaining. So instead of taking part in the ashram's evening activities I would find myself returning to my room in Koregaon Park where, in the meantime, I'd started a new relationship with a Swiss woman who spoke perfect Italian, English, German and French.

Bhavana was very sweet and extremely sensitive to nature. Before becoming an Osho disciple she had been an assistant to Konrad Lorenz, a Nobel laureate in the field of biology, who'd studied the behaviour of animals in his whole life. She told me how she and Lorenz would pass their nights, perched on a tree branch, or immersed up to their necks in a lake, watching ducks and other wild birds.

She'd been a disciple for more years than I, and this I could feel in her energy. She had a quality and depth that helped me to go 'inside.' So I went from life in Tadiwalla – always with friends, going from one party to another, from one lover to another, from joint to *chillum* – to a deeper, more intimate life, lived between my work in the ashram and my relationship with Bhavana.

Often I spent evenings on the terrace of our villa, surrounded by trees that were full of birds, practising on my recently purchased sitar – a delightful and complex Indian string instrument – with Bhavana meditating beside me. I felt that my body was cleaning itself from the drugs I'd used in the past and my mind was relaxing more and more. The routine of my new life as a commune worker somehow added to its depth, as did my settled life with Bhavana.

In the ashram, everyone was free to choose the lifestyle they wanted because there were no limitations or guidelines laid down for us. Many spent those years having a good time, going from one party to another, and some, like me in my new incarnation as cook and boyfriend, preferred a more quiet existence.

From my new perspective, it seemed ironic that Osho was being heralded by the international media as 'the sex guru.' According to this lascivious image, his disciples should be engaged perpetually in sexual intercourse, perhaps pausing only very briefly to eat and sleep. The meditative component that constituted the primary activity of the commune was put in second place by much of the media, which became fixated on describing the erotic aspect of the neo-sannyas movement.

They wanted scandal and they got it. Eva Renzi, a well-known German movie actress, signed up for the ashram's Encounter Group and got her face slapped by another participant. Upset and indignant, she informed a German news agency and this made us even more notorious. German newspapers went on for years with this story, endlessly embellishing their articles.

For us, inside the commune, it was like a grain of sand that disappeared after the first article in *Bild Zeitung*. There was too much distance between us and a world that lived within the prison of its own fixed attitudes and sexual obsessions.

Nevertheless, during these years, some journalists arrived in Pune, initially expecting to be critical and cynical about Osho, but then experiencing the space of love and joy in which we lived and feeling personally attracted to the energy of the Master. Many of these journalists became disciples, sending out articles that were more realistic about the commune. Predictably, however, such articles were rarely published because it was more sensational and commercially appealing to present Osho as a 'sex guru' rather than an 'enlightened Master.' Sex sells newspapers. Meditation doesn't.

I felt myself becoming more and more involved in the commune and its projects, which continued to develop at a frantic pace. The new 'city-commune' Osho was talking about had yet to manifest but Laxmi, his Indian secretary, spent a lot of time out of the ashram searching the length and breadth of northern India to find land for it.

Laxmi's prolonged absences from the ashram gradually changed the balance of power within it, and Deeksha was becoming the new point of reference for the organisation. Only one other person had a status that seemed equal to hers – a young Indian woman named Sheela who up to now was serving Laxmi as one of her assistants. She was also a fervent supporter of the commune project, but in her view the best place to build it was in the United States, not India. She was determined to take Osho to America.

In the summer of 1981, just as the monsoon was beginning, we looked up from our work one day to see Osho's car being driven out through the ashram's 'gateless gate.' He was accompanied by his female companion, Vivek, as well as Sheela and a small entourage. None of us knew anything about this departure of the Master, nor about the mansion in New Jersey that had been hastily refurbished to receive him upon his arrival in the USA. We didn't know where he was going. We were astonished, having no idea what was going on or what would happen to Osho or to us.

The first explanation we heard was that the Master was ill and had been taken to the West for treatment of a back problem. There was some truth in it but, of course, it wasn't the whole story. Meetings were held to avoid spreading panic among sannyasins. The commune workers were asked to continue their jobs with a sense of responsibility and peacefulness, staying focused on the task in front of them. In fact, to me, this seemed the only practical thing to do, so I continued to prepare the food every day while watching to see what would happen next.

Everything began to change. Many of the sannyasins who didn't work in the ashram began to leave for the West or for other destinations. It was as if our protective cocoon was broken and the energy held together by the presence of the Master was pouring out into the world without any certainty about where it might come together again. Nevertheless, the commune in Pune and all our other communes, wherever they were, faithfully continued their work as meditation and therapy centres, spreading the message of the Master.

Weeks passed and it became known that Osho had gone to America. The explanation given by ashram officials was always the same: treatment for a chronic back problem. But many of us sensed that something else was going on, something bigger and more exciting, something that was being kept secret for the moment. Our uncertainty was filled not so much with anxiety as with humour. Marlon Brando was making headlines in the West in a controversial movie called 'Last Tango in Paris,' and some witty sannyasin managed to print orange T-shirts for us declaring 'Last Mango in Pune.'

It was funny, but it was also a sign of the times. More and more, we felt the commune in Pune was finishing. I continued to cook, but the ashram was pulsating with the sounds of demolition. The temporary wooden houses we'd constructed were brought down and other illegal structures demolished. Some departments were closed as workers started leaving, most of them heading for their own countries or to Osho meditation centres and communes in Europe.

We said goodbye to each other without really knowing what would happen. It seemed like the dream was over, shattered by a Mercedes that took away our queen bee – make that 'king bee' – to an unknown destination. But I wasn't in a hurry to go anywhere. I continued to cook and started making myself useful around the ashram wherever there was a need.

The boutique had to go. We'd built it without planning permission and it was completely illegal. I joined in the demolition because it seemed important to me to destroy the structure I'd built with so much effort and love only a short time earlier. I was learning that with Osho you couldn't remain attached to anything, neither to objects nor to people.

During his whole adult life, he seemed to continuously create and abandon organisations, communes and other structures. They weren't important. His only goal was to help people transform themselves spiritually. His effort was to help us drop the ego and make us aware of the reality that exists beyond the mind, beyond the barriers and projections we produce when clinging to a social identity.

This is an important point to understand, because later on some people got very upset when the Oregon commune fell apart. They didn't understand that Osho wasn't interested in building a city so that we could live 'happily ever after'– as they say in fairy stories. He was even less interested in creating a social alternative to the *modus vivendi* of communist or capitalist societies.

He wanted people to wake up. He wanted people to become more conscious. He wanted to demonstrate to the whole world that it's possible to live together in personal freedom, love and harmony without any violence. For him, this was true religiousness and was one of the foundation stones of his teaching, along with his invitation to live as an integrated human being, which he called 'Zorba the Buddha'.

In this meeting of Zorba the Greek and Gautama Buddha, Osho was offering us a union of West and East, bringing together the material and spiritual reality in a new man who lived both of these dimensions with totality.

To him, one of the greatest crimes committed by all the major religions has been to divide the material from the spiritual, separating the body from the soul, setting worldly pleasures against spiritual aspirations. In the past, any sincere seeker in search of the divine was automatically expected to abandon the world, either by entering a monastery and taking vows of celibacy, or in India becoming a sannyasin and giving up all worldly possessions.

Osho taught us not to abandon the material for the spiritual, but to live both dimensions simultaneously. This holistic approach to life he saw as the future path for a healthy humanity. With penetrating insight into human psychology, Osho showed us that when we try to renounce something – such as sex, for example – we do not really get rid of it. Rather, we repress it in the unconscious mind, where it gathers energy and takes revenge in perverted and indirect ways.

Today, we see this manifesting in the many scandals concerning Catholic priests who, all over the world, have been exposed for their sexual perversions with young children. They all took vows of celibacy when they were initiated as priests, not knowing what harm this would do to both themselves and others.

On the other side, people who focus entirely on acquiring possessions and enjoying material pleasures – ignoring any kind of spirituality – often end up feeling alienated, lonely and shallow, knowing that whatever they have acquired will prove futile in the face of old age, sickness and death.

Live both! This was Osho's message. This was the new vision we were living and celebrating in the first Pune commune, living two dimensions simultaneously. We received the message in his discourses, in his books and then through our experiences when we applied it to our own lives.

As I have said, the most controversial element of his vision concerned his acceptance and transformation of sexual energy. Like unrefined oil, it provides the raw power that drives the lives of human beings and for this reason needs to be fully lived with innocence and without perversion.

Only by living sex naturally can we elevate our consciousness to the most divine dimension of love, he explained. Sex cannot be ignored. Sex cannot be pushed aside. Sex cannot be denied or suppressed. We have to face it, live it and only then can it be transformed.

This, from my perspective, was the strongest message that Osho directed at the collective mind in those years. He was addressing the unconscious and sleepy masses that, predictably, were unable to hear or understand him. It was really for this reason, during and after Pune One, that he was called 'the sex guru'.

For years he carried this label with him, until, after the foundation of the new commune in America, they saddled him with 'the Rolls Royce Guru'.

13   Switzerland

So the first commune of the Master was created in 1974 and ended in 1981. During these seven years, the Westerners, who at the beginning of the experiment were a small minority in the midst of masses of Indian disciples, became the absolute majority. It would be their job to spread the word of Osho throughout Europe and America in the following years.

From the time the shell was broken and the sannyasins left Pune, Osho's message flowed through them to other continents, like a surging river.

Many sannyasins who returned to their country of origin, or transferred elsewhere, opened meditation centres, following the suggestions of Osho given during the ashram years. The physical commune in Koregaon Park stayed in the hands of the Indians, who found themselves alone after all the foreigners had left. I stayed till the end of the year and continued to work, helping wherever I was needed, contributing mostly to the work of dismantling the commune.

We took apart everything that had been added as an 'extra,' not touching the original villas, which soon emerged in their original form – as if they'd been the only buildings that had ever existed on the site. Around the site of Buddha Hall, where the Master had spoken every morning for seven long years and where all the meditations took place, there were now cattle grazing, imported from a small farm about two hours' drive from Pune.

In the end, the ashram was unrecognizable, empty of objects and people, a skeleton of what only a few months before had been the most dynamic and exciting community of the twentieth century. **The centre moved** and, as happens at all levels when the centre moves or is missing, everything around it either shifts or vanishes.

Each sannyasin followed his own intuition and his gut feeling for moving into the world, going in the direction he believed to be right. Osho didn't give any specific indications – not then and not later. He told us to respect our feelings and to follow our heart wherever it took us. Unlike other religions in the world that taught commandments to follow, Osho never ever gave us any commandment. The only principle to follow was absolute respect of individuality, absolute respect for the choices of each person in his private life.

As far as I know, no Master before or since has given such a total *carte blanche* to his disciples, leaving them free to make mistakes and to learn from those mistakes. Because this attitude was so revolutionary, Osho was attacked from every direction. The churches, the politicians, the international organizations, the philosophers and, of course, all families at every social level were lined up against him, precisely because Osho was the first Master to teach total freedom.

In doing this, one of his primary concerns was to make it extremely difficult – in fact impossible – for any organised religion or power structure to be created around his teachings after his death. He meant what he said. He genuinely wanted every individual to be free, to make his or her own choices without following any dogma or belief structure. Still today, over twenty years after the disappearance of his physical body, no religious structure has been created. That's a remarkable achievement.

The ashram was dismantled. Some Westerners stayed on to do office work, but that was not where my talents lay, so I decided to leave, letting go of what had once been paradise on earth for me and for thousands of others.

I decided to head for Switzerland, going to Lausanne, on Lake Geneva, where I would meet up with Bhavana. Her mother's house faced the lake and everything was peaceful, clean and well organized, quite the opposite of my lifestyle in India, where chaos reigned supreme over all people and every household. Here, nature had been tamed and tailored to human dimensions and Swiss people were like the nature: composed, kind, efficient...so everything functioned perfectly.

Bhavana had recently lost her mother, whose death she took with quiet composure and without the typical emotional outpouring that characterises Italians, which I'd experienced during my upbringing in Sicily. She had a natural innocence that I gradually came to experience as a healing balm for my angry and rebellious leftist past. In addition, her French accent, for me, made her more lovable and more feminine – two aspects that I have always loved in her.

After a few weeks, however, I began to feel a hunger to meet other sannyasins and for this reason I went to Geneva, where there was a small meditation centre in the heart of the city, in front of the *jet d'eau* of the lake. It was a one-storey house with a garden, belonging to a Swiss sannyasin who worked as a therapist and sometimes held Osho mediations there. The house had a messy look, typical of a single man thinking of his own work more than domestic matters and food.

Nevertheless, he welcomed me in a friendly way, together with a Canadian sannyasin, also shipwrecked by the demise of Pune, who didn't yet know where to go. Mark and I were full of energy and we soon got busy decorating the house, painting the walls and organizing evenings of meditation. Slowly, like mushrooms in the forest, a few Swiss sannyasins began to appear in the centre. This was remarkable, because everybody knows how suspicious the Swiss are when it comes to practicing the principles of community.

A few weeks later, Bhavana joined our little group, which gradually became more stable and reliable. We sent invitations to all French-speaking sannyasins, announcing there was finally an Osho centre where they could come and meditate and celebrate together. For the first time, an Osho centre had been created in which French-speaking sannyasins could feel at home.

Someone took care of the kitchen, while others organized

therapy, meditations, tarot evenings, events and other activities that would acquaint the bourgeois population of Geneva with the work of Osho.

The only thing we knew about Osho himself was that he was in America and that his physical condition was not better. Living without the physical presence of the Master was not easy for me, but creating an Osho centre and pouring my energy into its activities served to keep the flame of devotion burning in me. In this way, circumstances were teaching me how to live in the pure energy of the Master in his absence.

With her inherent maternal instinct, Bhavana proved to be a very sweet 'mama' and many people started to trust in her. I worked more as a therapist and doctor, practising acupuncture and keeping busy with people's physical problems. Everything was going well and, after about a year, our activities had expanded so much that it pushed us to begin looking for a larger villa along the shores of the lake to make a bigger centre.

But I was in for a surprise. As our project got bigger and more complicated, many Swiss sannyasins started to pull back with their energy, returning to their private worlds and disconnecting from our meditation centre in the city. Through a series of meetings we tried to understand what we really wanted to do together, but the Swiss have a personality that tends to be very conservative, cautious and closed. This makes it difficult for them to push ahead into uncertain territory, preferring, in the long run, the cosy certainty of a peaceful life. After some weeks of discussions, we decided to close the centre in the city, seeing there was no prospect of future growth.

One of the lessons I'd learned during those years of the Pune commune was that if a decision arises from the heart and is sincere, then all the doors of life open and more and more beautiful gifts arrive. In contrast, if a decision is only mental, everything becomes complex and laborious.

The human mind has a great tendency to get lost in endless deliberations about what is the right thing to do at a certain moment in life. But the right way is not a *choice*, nor does it have doubts. It doesn't say, "Leave this work or continue it... change the house or wait... this is the right man or not...' and so on. Whenever the mind doesn't know whether to choose left or right, then one thing is certain: we are on a level of reality that belongs to the logical, rational mind, which is thousands of miles from the existential reality.

The superficial mind, the first level of mind, is like a radio that is receiving many frequencies at the same time. Different transmissions are overlapping each other in a chaos of words, concepts and ideas that belong to thousands of influences, some going back as far as childhood. This creates a cloud of confusion without any direction. However, our tendency is still to think we can sort it all out and make a correct decision. Mostly, it never happens. We remain at the mercy of a hodgepodge of ideas continuously revolving in our brains.

This seems to be a global phenomenon. Whether we are white, black, or Chinese... whether we are academic intellectuals or farmers... whether we are men or women, old or young, rich or poor... we all have this tendency to be blinded by a mental process that is crowded with thoughts, accepting and rejecting them in an effort to make our way through the world and the decisions required of us.

The brave new world of computers, laptops, mobile phones and pads has greatly increased the amount of ideas and information flowing towards us, creating more confusion and distancing us even further from reality. But the digital age is not the problem. As usual, it's us. Like all the gifts of science and technology, the tools we have developed are neutral. It is our own level of consciousness that determines whether they are used to help us live a happy and joyful life, in harmony with other people and our surroundings, or whether they simply accentuate the problems we are already facing.

Unfortunately, many human beings are attracted to the Internet and other social media because they are incapable of having genuine relationships, preferring to chat with people on the other side of the planet rather than risking an intimate conversation with the girl or boy next door. The computer screen becomes a substitute and also an outlet for unexpressed emotions and even perversions. For example, becoming dissatisfied or sexually frustrated with a real-life partner, it is tempting – particularly for men – to stimulate themselves through the prodigious amount of pornography freely available on the world wide web. In this way, we are distancing ourselves so much from nature that we are losing contact with our own roots.

The day after our decision to close the meditation centre in Geneva, we called Arup to inform her about what had happened. In response, without making any comment on our local problems, she spontaneously invited us to join the 'new commune' that was taking birth in Oregon. Our eyes turned towards America.

◻◻◻

14   America

The Master had been staying in New Jersey for a few months, where his disciples had bought an old mansion in the shape of a castle. Deeksha and a handful of sannyasins were taking care of him while Sheela looked urgently for a place to create a big new international commune. She found what she was looking for in a 64,000 acre former cattle ranch in central Oregon. A few weeks later, Osho was flown to a nearby airport in Oregon and then driven to the Ranch.

Slowly, disciples began to arrive from every part of the world, helping to put in basic facilities such as roads, housing, power and water supplies. To stay there was more difficult than in Pune, especially in that first year, when one needed a special invitation to join the Oregon commune.

Residential capacity was growing daily but still very limited. Visas, work permits and Green Cards (residential permits) were all very sensitive issues, as the new community was attracting a lot of attention from state and federal authorities. The region was semi-desert range land and the climate was severe, with many cold months and a short summer. In fact, the locals used to joke, "Central Oregon has two seasons, winter... and July and August."

The Big Muddy Ranch, as it had been called until then, was certainly big enough for us to build a big city, if that is what living with Osho now required, with 120 square miles of territory and a beautiful river that flowed along the eastern boundary of the property.

Personally, I never saw all the borders of the enormous ranch that was re-baptized with the name *Rancho Rajneesh*. It was a remote region with sparse population and few roads. Hours of driving were needed to get to the property from Portland, which had the nearest international airport.

Our little group from Switzerland arrived about six months after the first work had begun to build basic necessities needed to receive Osho and the hordes of sannyasins waiting to be invited. A beautiful trailer was created for the Master in a small side valley, to which other structures were joined over the years, surrounded by lots of newly-planted trees that he loved.

We landed in Portland, where Sheela had bought a hotel as a kind of transit station for those coming to the ranch from around the world. We spent two days in the 'Rajneesh Hotel' and there we began to meet old friends we hadn't seen since India. Our collective image had been radically transformed. Gone were the orange clothes, long hair and beards. Now people were well groomed, with short hair, wearing stylish European clothes that might be mistaken for normal if they hadn't all been in shades of red. We'd switched from the orange colours of the rising sun to the red colours of the setting sun and the change was so drastic we had trouble recognising each other.

We found ourselves in a big American city with very intense rhythms and sounds that seemed strange and uncomfortable after the silent spaces in India and the bird song of Koregaon Park. But the energy among us was high and loving. We passed these two days hugging old friends and catching up on what had happened since we said goodbye in India.

Some had returned to their families, many had taken jobs while waiting to see where the new commune would be created. It was a trademark of sannyasins that we picked up employment and then dropped it again in a very short time. With Osho, everything was happening so fast that we couldn't settle anywhere, and yet we somehow managed daily necessities with astonishing speed and ease, based on the innocent assumption that if we were meant to live this crazy life we'd be sure to get the help we needed from existence. Almost always, we would find the right connections to resolve various practical problems in order to be with him.

And whenever obstacles were there, they too seemed part of our destiny or dance. But most of the time, for almost all of Osho's disciples, unexpected gifts, or opportunities, or invitations, manifested at just the right time, in the right place, to enable them to settle their affairs and go to where he was living.

It was interesting to feel the difference among sannyasins between the happy-go-lucky majority and those who are not so connected to the Master. It almost always happened that those who were unable to let go of their need for security, or possessions, or relationships, remained on the periphery of the movement and were not able to throw themselves into the creative vortex that whirled around his presence.

In this new situation in Oregon, where not everyone was able to live and work on the Ranch, thousands of people would come from all over the world to celebrate together during four annual festivals, then depart as they had come. Thousands more gave away everything in order to be with him and become part of the project. Being part of this dance, sharing it with friends, was an amazing experience.

On the second day of our stay at Rajneesh Hotel, a big bus filled with about 50 of us made its way out of Portland and up the Columbia River toward the Cascade Mountains and eventually to the Big Muddy Ranch. During the trip, which lasted many hours, I enjoyed watching the American countryside, rich with pine forests and fertile valleys, all of which made a magnificent preamble to the desert-like conditions we encountered once we'd crossed the mountains and entered 'the dry side.' All of us were excited by this new adventure, a classical Wild West pioneering adventure story in which a handful of men and women build a city in the middle of this typical Western rangeland.

Bhavana and I felt as if we were in a special state of grace due to this unexpected invitation to join the commune, because up to now the people arriving at the Big Muddy were mostly Americans. Foreigners were very few. By now, we knew enough not to ask what might happen next, because we'd learned the script of the Master: throw yourself head first into life without expecting anything; be total in what you are doing without a purpose or a final destination. We were simply in a state of wonder for everything we were experiencing with our eyes and our emotions.

Then, little by little, looking out at the American landscape through which we were passing, there arose inside of me a silent feeling of 'not belonging,' a very different sensation from what I'd experienced in India as I arrived at the ashram. In Pune, I quickly felt at home. Ancient memories, perhaps from previous lives, helped me identify with the rhythm of Indian life, with its colours, it smells and its way of living. Paradoxically, amid the chaos of India I felt peace and acceptance of life and death, whereas in the silence of these magnificent areas of North America's nature I felt the human mind that shapes nature to its own uses and consumption.

Here, as in Switzerland, you felt the hand of man in everything. Wide and well-constructed highways had been carved through completely wild mountains. Wooden houses, prefabricated buildings, service stations and shopping centres appeared and disappeared from view, one after the other, in an incessant rhythm, as we passed. These places did not resonate with my being.

I don't want to seem jaded or communistic, but everything seemed to be constructed and designed around the principle of circulating money. There was no sign of spirituality in the air, no indication there was anything in the minds of these men that went beyond their material interests.

Many hours before we arrived at our destination we passed through scenery that reminded me of the Native Americans and their struggle to cope with the arrival of the white man and his totally different way of living. Enormous boulders scattered among juniper bushes in a rocky terrain reminded me of other heroes before the coming of so-called 'civilisation.'

Then we passed an American Indian reservation and I understood why those images had filled my mind only minutes before. It was a different energy, a different approach to nature, with more sense of interiority – you could also call it 'soul' – than the rest of the country we'd been through. But when I saw the poverty of the reservation and the dismal-looking faces of its Native American inhabitants, completely destroyed by Western culture and all its perversions, images of diabolical invasions came to me, carried out by the white man as he ventured into Indian lands.

No! In this part of the world, I certainly didn't feel my heart opening, my mind relaxing or my spirits soaring as had happened when I walked the ordinary streets of India. But, like it or not, the Master had chosen this place to play out the next instalment of our spiritual drama. I don't know if he chose the 'land of the invaders' on purpose. I don't know the motivations that prompted Osho to agree to come to America. Indeed, it took me many years to understand even some of the reasons why others had pushed him to come to a place that was so hostile to the spiritual dimension.

Many of the old sannyasins who'd been deeply connected with India would never come to America, remaining tied to memories of the old days of Pune One. But, as far as my own relationship with the Master was concerned, I would have gone to any part of the world if he'd invited me. So, now, here we were, in this land that he himself had described as the most advanced democracy on the planet.

We arrived at the Ranch late in the morning. We'd travelled for many hours and, when the bus driver told us that from this point on it was all commune land, we were overwhelmed by its enormous dimensions. I don't think any of us expected such a grandiose thing. The bus kept going for many miles, following winding dirt roads over a sequence of hills full of junipers, sage, rocks and wild animals that jumped out of the bushes.

Already, in my imagination, I was seeing before me an adventure film, set around the mid-1800s, in which men, women and children, travelling in horse-drawn wagons along the Oregon Trail, were dreaming of establishing new homes, new towns, new cities.

We arrived in the Ranch's main valley at a place where two creeks formed a 'Y-shaped' neck of land. Here we saw the old ranch house which, together with a couple of barns, must have been the only building on the property when Sheela first arrived. Her main office and living accommodation were located just behind the old ranch house in a modern, newly-erected trailer home.

Sheela's secretaries welcomed us, explained the basic layout of the community – the whereabouts of the canteen, sleeping places, and so on – then assigned each of us to a female coordinator who would oversee our work and be a contact person in the commune. We were not housed in finished buildings but rather in big tents, along with many other people. About 100 yards away stood trailers where we could shower and use the toilets.

Bhavana and I were soon separated. The message was clear: here the work is hard and there is no time to lose in personal relationships. We had to build a city as quickly as possible. Unlike Pune, where emotions, personal feelings and our inner world in general were the most important things, there was no space here for such subjective issues. We were here to work, to build and to do it in a hurry.

My tent was located a few miles from the so-called centre. There were old yellow buses, formerly used for transporting American schoolchildren, circulating continuously through the Ranch carrying people to their different destinations.

I found myself in a small isolated valley where there were a hundred or so tents. The weather was dry, but sudden changes in temperature were extreme and my Mediterranean body wasn't used to it. On those rare occasions when it started to rain, everything was quickly transformed into an enormous quagmire of mud, graphically illustrating why this property had been named the 'Big Muddy Ranch.'

I met with Bhavana at mealtimes. We rarely slept together at night because we were pretty exhausted by the work. Relationships selected themselves automatically because you spent time only with those people with whom you worked during the day. I found myself working in a big tent in a small valley, a long distance from the centre, with a couple of dozen men and women. Strangely, the coordinator was a man, an American whom I didn't know but who was an expert in construction with wood.

Our task was to build out-houses: very basic, non-flushing toilets that could be used wherever the main plumbing had not yet reached. Essentially, it was a small wooden hut placed over a hole, dug deep in the ground, with a raised wooden toilet seat covering the top of the hole. Each user was obliged to scatter disinfectant powder down the hole, after use, to eradicate the smell.

Our crew, which included several beautiful, young and innocent American women, built about 50 of these out-houses in three months. Had this been Pune, many of us would have quickly ended up in bed together. Here, however, during the whole time we were working together, nothing like that happened.

We greeted each other affectionately in the morning and then started to work. The coordinator explained what to do and then left. He was busy with another urgent project and other members of our team, building wooden platforms for tents to be used during the upcoming 'First Annual World Celebration' – Osho's invitation for sannyasins from all over the world to come and celebrate and meditate in his presence.

Early in 1981, before leaving Pune, Osho had stopped giving discourses and his policy of remaining in silence continued after he arrived on the Ranch. He met daily with Sheela, his secretary, and any messages he wanted to give – either to us or to his worldwide movement – were passed through her. Generally speaking, however, he was content to give us responsibility for building this new great commune.

Osho wasn't a Master who did special things. As far as is possible for an enlightened being, he lived a normal life. He didn't pretend to perform miracles, or try to impress us with demonstrations of esoteric skills. The greatest miracle performed by Osho was to make us live with so much intensity that we had to be more aware of what we were doing. He often said he acted as a catalyst and his presence was like an enzyme that accelerated the processes of growth.

In any case, Osho didn't try to direct the course of events to his own liking. His trust in existence was so strong that he went along with the general direction in which things were going. His silence lasted from 1981 through 1984, covering about three-fourths of the time he spent on the Ranch. We saw him very briefly each day, lining the road to greet him as he passed in a Rolls-Royce on his daily drive. Other than that, we would see him at festivals in a vast newly-constructed hall, sitting on a podium that seemed much further away than he had been in the Buddha Hall in Pune. Together with his silence, this further served to add distance between us.

Now let me say something about Osho's health. When Osho became enlightened at the age of 21, his body was weak and fragile and his eyes full of stupor, like those of a new-born baby, soft, black and deep. He decided that it would be helpful to continue an academic career and so, after receiving his degree in philosophy, he held several university posts and eventually became a professor.

Recognition of his enlightened state was beginning to spread, however, not to mention his brilliance as a speaker, so he started travelling and teaching, making hundreds of train journeys to different cities, and meanwhile transforming himself into a man who was strong and powerful, capable of withstanding the gruelling demands of his new lifestyle.

His body, sometimes clothed only in a simple white *lunghi* around his hips that left his torso naked, became more powerful and more handsome. He became an enchanter who fascinated hundreds of thousands of listeners. In his talks there could be 50-80,000 people who were often possessed by a real mystical delirium generated by the *pranic* energy that emanated from his presence, a potent transmission of pure *shakti* energy.

This initial phase of transformation is known as the *Raja Guna* – the Phase of the Sun. Like the sun, his body emanated the pure light of *prana*, or divine energy.

In 1974, when Osho arrived in Pune and founded the first commune, after years of travelling all across India, he looked strong and healthy. His beard was black and his warrior chest manifested the same strength that emanated from the magnetic light in his eyes. Those eyes were incredible. It was difficult, almost impossible, to stand looking into them for long.

Nevertheless, he'd been suffering from allergies, diabetes and other physical problems while living in Mumbai prior to 1974, which is why his disciples invited him to live in Pune, where the climate was less extreme. But his health problems continued. He became thinner and more fragile. His hair and beard thinned out.

After a few weeks, another transformation happened. Osho entered into the most intimate phase of his evolution, which he called the lunar essence, the Chandra Guna. His *shakti* energy was at its most powerful and total, even more intense because the fiery Raja Guna was still present in his body, complimenting and alternating with the Chandra Guna. By the time he went into silence at the end of Pune One, he had clearly left the Raja Guna behind. At the ranch he continued with his silence, no longer giving either discourses or *shakti* to his disciples.

He came to sit with us during festivals, but remained in silence, as if the night had now sent away the sun. In this phase, words were no longer necessary to connect us to him, or to his philosophy of life and his revolutionary mystical vision.

Those who could relate to him only through his words were no longer able to follow him. His silence threw us into an absolutely existential dimension, where the mind no longer had a hold on us, where thoughts no longer existed, a space in which you were forced to abandon any sense of security in order to enter an unknown dimension. Thousands of people sitting with their Master in silence in a desert valley in Oregon, under an enormous roof that did its best to protect us from the cold, was one of the strongest experiences I lived as a sannyasin.

Many things have been written about Osho's saga in the United States, and of these many focused more on his secretary, Sheela, rather than on Osho himself. In a way, it was inevitable, because of her provocative confrontations with an American government that tried in every way to get us out of the Ranch, out of America, by both legal and illegal methods.

For a long time, Osho gave no discourses and conducted no interviews with journalists. Once he went into silence, very little could be said about him, so media attention focused on his secretary, who acquired the position of sole interlocutor with the government, with journalists, with the American legal system and with everything regarding the public life of the commune. As a result, Sheela quickly became notorious as a kind of antagonistic, spiritual Don Quixote who fought against any kind of obstacle, real or imagined, that she saw in front of her.

Osho's global image also began to change. The man who'd been labelled 'the sex guru' in India now became known as a money guru, mainly because of his growing fleet of Rolls-Royces and the commune's seemingly limitless financial resources.

In India, as I've said, sexual energy had been repressed for hundreds of years. Even so-called 'modern-minded'-women in sophisticated cities like Mumbai had little or no experience of orgasm, while in rural areas women still occasionally burned themselves alive on their husband's funeral pyre is as a demonstration of undying fidelity and love. Meanwhile, child marriages between boys and girls no older than puberty – sometimes even younger – continued on a wide scale.

This was an India impregnated with authentic spirituality, but with enormous holes in social awareness, including all kinds of taboos surrounding the issue of sex. Only now, in the last decade, has India started to emancipate itself and come slowly closer to Western values regarding sex education and the liberation of women.

A sexually repressed Indian public found it difficult to receive anything in Osho's vision that didn't relate to sex, as demonstrated by the controversy surrounding one of Osho's first books, titled *From Sex to Superconsciousness*. Ninety-nine per cent of people stopped at the word sex. They never managed to get beyond it to superconsciousness.

Something similar happened in America, which, hiding its greed behind a veil of hypocrisy, nevertheless raised the sacred dollar to divine status, and the drive towards profit and the accumulation of wealth as sacred commandments. It was inevitable, therefore, that when viewing a Master who mostly sat in his room in silence, what captured their imagination and headlines was his rapidly growing fleet of Rolls-Royces and the ability of his disciples to purchase anything they wanted – including, most controversially, a small town called Antelope, which they took over, filling all the council seats with sannyasins.

As I stated previously, Osho said, "I am here to provoke God," a concept containing many implications, most of which escape the ordinary mind. Osho loved to be provocative and did it at many levels. All his life, he provoked people and institutions in order to unmask the hypocrisy ingrained in us for centuries. Seen from this perspective, the Rolls-Royces were a stroke of genius. "With 93 Rolls-Royces I shattered the pride of America," he commented after the Ranch ended.

But the cars weren't just for show. Osho loved to drive, especially when the cars were beautiful and fast, and he loved to push beyond the legal speed limit every time he drove – in other words, he drove like hell.

Another Master, also living in the 20th century, shared his love of speed. It was George Gurdjieff, who in the last stages of his life engineered a crash while driving his motorcar – a crash that would have been fatal for anyone else. After the 'accident,' in which many bones in his body were fractured, Gurdjieff was found leaning against a tree, far from the mangled wreck of his car, looking completely relaxed and at ease. It was there, leaning against the tree – according to Osho – that Gurdjieff had his final experience of becoming a Buddha.

Osho's driving record was a little different. He never had an accident, but he acquired a number of speeding tickets from Oregon's traffic cops; the fines were willingly paid by his disciples. On the Ranch, Osho received his first Rolls Royce from a group of his American disciples. One afternoon, he went out with his companion for a drive that lasted many hours, leaving the Ranch and travelling the local highways. From then on, he made daily excursions to local towns and back again, small journeys that constituted a big provocation to the American public and later to the world.

When someone wanted to give him a gift, he asked for a Rolls-Royce and within a very short time his personal garage was packed with a grand total of 93 Rolls-Royces. A skilled sannyasin, an expert with airbrushing paint on cars, was given the task of making colourful designs on these handsome vehicles, including flying swans,

Azima and Bhavanaat drive by in the Ranch Rajneesh in Oregon –USA in 1982

MY LIFE WITH OSHO | 171

rainbows and weather patterns that began as thunderstorms at one end of the car, transforming into sunshine at the other end.

Predictably, inevitably, journalists around the world fell into his trap and began calling him 'the guru with the Rolls-Royces.' When they came to the Ranch, they insisted on visiting the garage where the cars were kept. One American television network even hired a helicopter to make sure they got footage of his private house and the legendary garage. As far as Osho was concerned, the important thing was to have his name spread through the international media, attracting people's attention, making them curious to know more about him and through this free publicity making it possible for more people to become his disciples.

By his actions, Osho was saying, "If you value appearances – how fancy is the car, or the house you live in, how expensive are the designer clothes you wear – then here are the Rolls-Royces as my business card." This was the approach of the most provocative Master who ever visited this planet, the most impudent, rebellious, eccentric, excessive and lovable Master.

But apart from his daily drive in the car, Osho didn't come out of his room or participate directly in the life of the commune. He was content to withdraw into his private silence. Personally, I thought there were several reasons for him to choose silence right at the time when we were building the biggest commune America had ever seen.

One level was surely private: The Master had entered into a phase of his evolution that didn't permit him to spend a lot energy on the outer reality. As he'd said in the past, the majority of people who realize their fully enlightened consciousness leave the physical body immediately, while a few manage to stay anchored in the physical body. Of these, only one in a thousand decides to speak and share with the world their experience of the 'light of being.'

I imagine that, nearly thirty years after his realisation, which happened in March 1953, and after upsetting half the world with his revolutionary teachings, he needed to recharge his energy. This could only be done by going inside himself, to his space of bliss. There is also another level: ninety per cent of the 'Ranch experience' unfolded on a material level, with rapid construction of the physical structures, and the meditative aspect was put aside.

In Pune, his daily presence at morning discourses brought the whole commune to an energetic level of heartfelt sweetness and play, of hugs and continuous sharing. Yes, we worked, but the ashram was relatively small and the work often seemed to be created more for us to be together than for any objective necessity.

Building the Ranch, on the other hand, was an enormous challenge because there really was a huge amount of work to do, from laying pipelines to building houses to paving roads, not to mention all the cooking and cleaning. Out of necessity, all the energy had to be concentrated on the experience of manual physicality.

Apart from the festivals, when we meditated with Osho, I can't remember ever having the time and space to meditate. Nor did I ever see a single sannyasin sitting somewhere on the Ranch with his eyes closed, meditating, whereas in Pune, in almost every corner of the ashram, someone could be seen sitting and 'going inside.'

However, Osho's decision to stay in his room and be separate from the commune, did not mean that he had isolated himself. Many times he told us that the authentic connection with the Master happens on the astral plane rather than physical. This made sense to me. I felt Osho was still working on us, but not so much in a personal way, so that the largest possible number of people could participate in his great experiment.

Osho had shuffled his deck of cards one more time and then gave us the whole deck to play with, seemingly without his direct control, in an intense situation in which the most powerful nation on the planet had become our adversary.

As I see it, America has the noblest Constitution so far written by human beings and the most open democracy in existence. The very fact that today we see an African American for the first time in the White House speaks volumes for the openness and flexibility of the social structure created in the United States. And yet, as we shall see as my tale continues, this very same country became our persecutor and destroyer.

Meanwhile, back on the Ranch, I was in ignorance of anything happening outside my personal world. During that first year in Oregon I found myself in a small valley constructing hundreds of out-houses made out of wood. There were very few of us available and there was always work to do.

Predictably, in such circumstances my relationship with Bhavana became weaker from day to day, even though there was no personal antagonism between us. Events were taking us further and further apart, until one day I was called into the office by one of Sheela's secretaries, who told me, with a big smile: "The commune needs money to construct the city. We thought that you, as a medical doctor, could give more by working in Europe and sending money here than by doing manual labour."

From long personal experience, I knew that negotiation with the secretaries wasn't an option, nevertheless, speaking my own truth, I told her I would prefer to stay and work rather than return to Europe and become a doctor again. It was hopeless. What I was hearing was not a proposal but a decision already taken. All possible means of creating money had to be exploited to pay for this enormous project of constructing the city.

So the idea was communicated to me again in clearer words: "You have to leave the commune. Make money and send it here. Full stop. That's all. You will leave in a few days."

So continued my up-and-down relationship with the Oregon commune, which for me was always somehow a goal to be reached and not an experience to be lived totally like the other two communes. To me, this 'request' felt more like expulsion because, in my own eyes, I'd been invited to participate in this great pioneering project of founding a new city and being with the Master. Now I was being kicked out.

Ironically, at this very moment, Osho was coming closer to us again through a spontaneous change in the 'drive-by' event which happened every lunch time, when we lined the Ranch roads to greet him as he went out for his daily drive. One day, a group of sannyasins brought guitars and sang a song as he passed. To their astonishment and delight, he slowed down, stopped and waved his hands in time to the music, encouraging them and making eye contact with them for several minutes before driving on.

This triggered an explosion in small musical bands that flourished by the roadside. Guitars, drums and other instruments were quickly found or purchased in order to form these bands and to play and sing for Osho. From then on, he frequently stopped and gave energy to the music, while everyone in the line danced with joy, joining in the celebration.

Drive-by was transformed. Instead of standing quietly, as we'd done before, we were dancing, playing music and singing at the top of our voices in order to celebrate with the Master, who was clearly enjoying the new situation as much as we were. In this way, it was possible to feel the energy of the Master again in an upbeat and joyful way, very similar to our experiences back in Pune.

For this alone I would have wanted to stay on the Ranch, but I had no choice. I had to leave. This also meant that once again, I would be separated from my love partner who, in marked contrast, had been invited to stay. Bhavana was the third woman I had to leave behind during my on-going adventure with the Master.

In the normal world of social organisations, most decisions coming from above are discussed, challenged, and sometimes even resisted, before being carried out. Not so in the energy field of a Master.

Already in the first commune it had become clear to me that the concept of 'letting go' was also a valuable door for experiencing something entirely new, beyond my own limited ideas and preconceptions, taking everything as an adventure.

For example, it wasn't easy for me as a doctor, with a briiiiant career in front of me, to find myself cleaning toilets and cutting vegetables all day. After a year of slogging away in the kitchen I became really tired of smelling the odours of food cooking on the stoves, so I wrote Osho requesting a change of work. I reminded him that I was a fully qualified doctor and could be useful in the ashram's medical centre, where sick sannyasins were treated.

His answer was given to me by Arup, who on many occasions acted as an intermediary between me and the Master in the first commune. She called me to the main office and communicated Osho's answer to my request:

"The Master reminds you that this is not normal society where you choose what to do. This is spiritual community and the rules here are completely different. Go back to work in the kitchen!" The message was clear... So clear that from then on I didn't ask anything. Instead, I took everything that happened to me as a new teaching. So in Oregon I did not try to fight the decision. I didn't react or blame anyone for it.

In society, especially in the dimension of working and earning a living, we can easily find ourselves adrift in a sea of opportunism, greed, mistrust, arrogance, exploitation and uncertainty, all of which may very well cause us to shut down our more vulnerable, sensitive feelings and trust no one. With Osho, however, I found the centre of my life, and from then on I did not feel that anyone could take it away from me. It's very difficult to describe what this means, this feeling of having total trust in the Master, but it has something to do with recognising the essence of spirituality – something I'd always felt inside me, as a potential, from the time I was a child.

With the Master, I was willing to throw myself into any adventure, no matter how disappointing it might initially seem, trusting that I would emerge from it happier and more conscious. To give one example, I'd arrived in Pune with less than a thousand euros, given to me as a loan by my friend Silvio. This sum of money could last a long time, considering how cheap it was for Westerners to live in India in those days. But it wasn't enough to last for the whole time I ended up staying there.

One day, an old sannyasin who'd been in India a long time and had all kinds of connections in Mumbai, asked me to help him change money on the black market. At the time, the official exchange rate available through India's banks was very low compared to the high rates you could obtain on the black market. So the whole subcontinent was swarming with unofficial dealers who changed foreign currency.

The risky part of this particular financial transaction was that we needed to visit a dangerous part of Mumbai where foreigners never went, a kind of Indian version of the Bronx, where the local mafia ruled, along with criminals, smugglers, drug dealers, prostitutes and the people who live at the very margin of society.

Well, I decided that the Master was with me in this venture, so I faced the expedition with remarkable tranquillity. We arrived in Mumbai in the afternoon, taking a beautiful room in a good hotel in a wealthy part of the city, and the next day made our way to the black market. We entered a very small alley and then a series of tangled streets that were loaded with shops as small as closets. Besides humans, there were animals of every kind...dogs, cats, rats, donkeys and buffaloes.

Bicycles grazed you as they passed closely, cows were sitting comfortably in the streets and a wide variety of intense odours assaulted our senses – perfume, incense, necklaces of jasmine, rotting food, dead dogs and people relieving themselves one very corner. We had decided not to carry a knife or other means of defence. If something happened, we could never have escaped in this neighbourhood, so it was better to move calmly and confidently, without provoking anyone.

We walked deeper into this neighbourhood for about fifteen minutes, finally arriving at a tiny little shop, entirely anonymous amid dozens of others on the street, announcing itself as a jewellery store. Inside the door was a small corridor, about two yards long, with a glass showcase in which lay four or five pieces of jewellery that clearly had no value.

A small man was sitting on a stool near the showcase. Seeing us, he pushed a button that sounded a small alarm behind the door at the end of the corridor. His face showed no emotion, completely expressionless, his brown eyes mirroring the emptiness of the small room. He had a typical Indian face and could have been a postal employee, a fruit vendor, a merchant, a family man, or a criminal, which, in this case, was perhaps his true profession.

In response to his push of a button, a small window opened and two fat hands came out to take the cash. We counted the foreign money entrusted to us by different friends from different countries, while they counted the equivalent in rupees. In a few moments, the transaction was over and the little window closed, accompanied by a faint "goodbye."

We said goodbye respectfully to the man on the stool and exited the shop, our bright orange tunics stuffed with Indian money, our malas with Osho's picture waving around our necks. As we walked back down that street, we were acutely aware that everyone in the neighbourhood knew we were loaded with money. But no one lifted a finger against us, nor did we suffer the slightest provocation from either thieves or poor people.

For years, this type of trust pushed me to do things that were well outside the usual norms of society, and always without dire consequences. In my opinion, men need to have this quality. They need to develop trust in themselves, trust in life, trust in the grand design of the cosmos. Although we are a very small part of that design, even microscopic, we can feel connected to it, we can participate in it, and we are forever part of it.

It's not blind faith. It's not an idealisation of the Master-disciple relationship. It is simply the understanding that our minds tend to limit us, keeping us in a safe little box, not daring to experience that there is a vast, pulsating, dynamic life outside it. The development of human consciousness necessarily passes through this experience of the Sixth Door.

The Sixth Door
Trust

Trust is an inner state that is cultivated by the awareness of being an integral part of an organism to which every single entity in this universe belongs.

❏❏❏

15   The Return of the Doctor

I had to return to Europe, without any plan and with a clear request to make money for the commune. If I'd stopped to think about it, to try and work it out, I would have become paralysed with insecurity and fear. But the energy of the Master and his commune had given me the strength to jump without a parachute. Bhavana and I had a friendly separation and we have remained friends ever since. She stayed a lot longer at the Ranch.

Focusing on Switzerland, I asked Pratibha, a Swiss Italian friend, if I could stay in her big house while looking for work. She agreed. So I found myself in a kind of castle near a lake within a private park, where I stayed for several weeks, living with her. One of the levers that lifted apparently insurmountable obstacles among sannyasins was a widespread sense of belonging and friendship that distinguished the neo-sannyas movement. You could, and still can, travel from one end of the world to another, always finding yourself in the home of a new friend who is willing to give you a hand.

Pratibha was a therapist and also an architect, from a well-to-do family. She had the distinction of being the first sannyasin woman to give birth to a child in Pune. She was a seeker of truth and before coming to Osho had travelled to South America in order to study spiritual and shamanistic traditions on that continent.

During the next few weeks, I made several requests to be employed as an assistant doctor in Switzerland's Italian hospitals, and was waiting for an answer. In the meantime, thanks to Pratibha, I was introduced to the head doctor of a hospital in Locarno, who invited me to his house a few days later. We spent a pleasant evening together with his family and I was delighted to realise that I could begin to develop a close friendship with these people. But, even so, I never imagined that this beautiful family would soon become disciples of Osho.

One morning, this doctor – I will refer to him as 'Dr P' – called me, asking if I was still available to work as an assistant. The doctor who was scheduled to fill the position as his assistant had unexpectedly withdrawn and the position could not be left unfilled. They needed a doctor immediately and there was no time to organise interviews or conduct more screening processes. I agreed, he asked me to begin next day, and before I knew it I was hired.

Once more, challenging events and apparent difficulties had dissolved with disarming spontaneity. Once more, life with Osho was proving rich and full of surprises. The next day, I went to the paediatrics department of the Locarno hospital where Dr P introduced me to the rest of his staff, explained the basic setup, and then handed me over to one of his assistants who'd been part of his team for several years. It was he who introduced me to the details of my daily routine.

Apart from interning in paediatrics at university, I had no experience with babies, so I needed to make a big effort to learn as much as possible in a very short time. But the atmosphere in the ward had the same friendly quality as Dr P had shown to me in his private home: relaxed, simple, without the usual inflated egos you were likely to run into in the medical world. The team members worked with the best of their ability and they were always happy to collaborate. Dr P, as the 'father' of this paediatric group, was always ready to explain his therapeutic decisions and was very gentle in his approach to babies and their mothers.

One day he called me into his office and asked me if I was meditating, because he was interested in experiencing a variety of meditation techniques. I was happy to introduce him to Osho's active methods, and so that afternoon we arranged to do Kundalini Meditation, together with his wife and a friend who'd rented me a small apartment in the countryside.

Perhaps I should mention that as soon as I began working in the hospital, I left Pratibha's house and moved to an apartment in one of the valleys near Locarno. The apartment was on the property of a villa belonging to a divorced woman who had a child called Noa. Surprisingly, it was this young child who showed himself to be most open to the energy of Osho.

We started meeting in the afternoons, in my room, where we began to meditate and share personal feelings. After a few weeks, I proposed doing Dynamic Meditation each morning, specifying that we needed to do it for at least 21 days. My companions agreed, so the four of us started to greet each new day with Dynamic, among the chestnut trees surrounding the villa.

One afternoon, entering my room, I saw Noa, the child, seated in front of a photo of Osho. His mother and I stood silently at the door, watching. Seeing him kneeling before a photo of the Master and looking intensely into his eyes was a fantastic experience for me. There was something very pure in this connection between an innocent child and the Master happening before us. After about ten minutes, he stood up, walked toward his mother and put his arms around her legs, saying with simple innocence: "Mama, I also want to be with him and have a necklace like Azima...." Osho had another disciple.

Osho loved children. He initiated many children in Pune One, speaking to them at length and giving them a lot of respect and energy. On one occasion, he told us many of them had been with him in another life and that through their innocence, the little ones recognized his presence more easily than adults. He followed the progress of some of them step-by-step, especially children of sannyasins who'd been with him a long time, offering suggestions as to what the parents should do as their children grew up.

Many of these children, like the daughter of Pratibha, grew up in a variety of communes. When they became teenagers, we found ourselves among adolescents who were intelligent and also very aware, having experienced an education so open they seemed to be at least ten to fifteen years older than they really were.

Seeing Noa kneeling before the photo of the Master, who was not physically present but thousands of miles away, was something that filled my heart with joy, helping me understand that in a relationship with a being like Osho, separation by time and space doesn't exist.

In that moment, I felt as if I was actually in the Oregon commune with him and my other friends. I understood that the Master was inside of me and that the dimensions of his spiritual commune were vaster than I'd ever imagined. Osho was working beyond the physical world and this became even clearer to me after he left his body in January 1990.

Noa's mother was an intelligent woman and accepted her son's decision with warmth and joy. So we decided to contact an Osho centre that had just opened in Lugano in order to ask for initiation for Noa. The Lugano Centre was run by an old sannyasin – old, not in the sense of age, but in the sense of being a disciple for many years. She was a strong, charismatic woman, speaking at least five languages. An astrologer and therapist, with good business sense, she created in a very short time the only centre that ever existed in the Italian-speaking region of Switzerland.

The centre was in a big villa on a hill outside Lugano. The house had two separate levels as well as a large garden, so there was lots of space and an all-pervasive sense of harmony. Anugatha had the dynamic energy of women on the Ranch, strong, decisive, sure of herself, maternal, not only with her son who was about eight years old, but with all the people who worked in the centre as well as the guests who came. And, as I discovered some time later, she was much sweeter in private than she appeared in public.

Noa was initiated as a sannyasin on a Saturday, along with many other people. He was the only child. We arrived with his mother and two other friends from Locarno. Before the celebration, however, we couldn't find Noa. We searched everywhere without success until we decided to go into the meditation hall. There we found Noa, stretched out in front of the photo of Osho, sleeping innocently like a new-born puppy. Noa's initiation was followed in time by that of his mother, Dr P and his wife, his children, his lover and two other friends.

In the meantime, my relationship with the head physician became more and more a relationship of friendship than of work. We were spending a lot of time together outside the hospital. I discovered he had been my son in another life, so it was inevitable that I would take care of him, spiritually speaking, while working at the same time as his assistant.

The feeling he'd been my son in a past life started shortly after I began working with him. I was astonished at how much care I gave to meeting his needs. Outside the hospital, we were simply two friends sharing our lives and it was he who continued to ask me, directly or indirectly, for help. In response, I found myself giving him a lot of attention.

When Dr P later separated from his wife, his children and his big house, he went to live in a small place in the countryside, in the valley where I had my apartment, and there we spent many evenings together. I cooked and put his house in order – it was very messy, seeing as he spent most of his time reading. There, I started to feel a strong maternal love towards him, something I've never experienced with anyone.

At the time, I was experimenting with third eye meditations, done in the darkness of night, and began to see myself as a woman and him as my child. The emotions were strongly maternal, but at a certain point I saw visions in which this mother would have to abandon her child, against her will. Then I understood why I felt this familiar connection, beginning almost as soon as we met, and understood why coming to Locarno would serve to close a circle that had remained incomplete for a long time.

During this period, I learned a lot as a physician from Dr P and through him had the opportunity to meet a man whom I'd idolised and followed for years. Dr P was, in fact, a friend of Dr Frederick Leboyer, the famous French doctor who developed a new way of delivering babies without stress and suffering. Even though he was very busy, Dr Leboyer came to Locarno every year to visit his friend in the hospital's paediatric section, where he also gave a conference or demonstrated his latest work with newly born babies.

So I was fortunate enough to spend a weekend with Leboyer, the father of 'nonviolent birth,' a pioneering work that became admired and accepted by open-minded gynaecologists and doctors throughout the world. For the first time in the Western world, Leboyer had proposed spontaneous and natural childbirth, with a few fundamental principles:

1) Not cutting the umbilical cord right away, but letting the infant rest on the belly of the mother with the whole placenta.
2) Not having noise or loud music in the delivery room.
3) Keeping the lighting soft and creating a relaxed atmosphere to help the mother feel good.
4) Not weighing the baby right away, or taking it away from the mother, but leaving the baby with her. After the child has had time to adapt, weighing the child on a scale that is not cold and not metal.
5) Preparing the mother for childbirth with yoga exercises, breathing and music, which were the new elements introduced in the seminar in which I participated that year.

The seminar was exceptional and so was the film Dr Leboyer had made. Then he had us listen to the sounds he played for the women, which were none other than Indian music and mantras. It was clear that Leboyer had spent time in India, where he'd become aware of the therapeutic potential of sound.

That evening, the three of us had dinner together. I discovered that Dr Leboyer was a disciple of Krishnamurti and had been to India many times. During one of these trips, an Indian woman had introduced him to pre-birth songs.

In our evening together, I experienced Leboyer as an introverted Frenchman of medium build, with very controlled gestures, acute and penetrating eyes, who talked little about his private life, focusing instead on the subject of work. It was as if his private life was non-existent. He was a typical disciple of J. Krishnamurti, an intellectual with a sharp mind, a sincere seeker of the truth, who approached the spiritual path with seriousness and determination. But, from my perspective, the component of celebrating life that I discovered with Osho was missing. Intimate, personal sharing was also excluded. As a result, we didn't succeed in having a deep meeting, neither that night nor during the following evenings.

On the positive side, these meetings with Dr Leboyer reinforced the conviction that I developed as a doctor and disciple of Osho, namely that the basic requirement of good therapy is love for the patient. I didn't see Leboyer again, but he remained a source of inspiration in my medical work, just like Dr Lad many years before, when he'd helped me stop using hashish by treating me with Ayurveda and meditation. Dr Lad was also a disciple of Krishnamurti. These two doctors were a fountain of inspiration and, without knowing each other, shared the same Master.

Many years later, in 1993, I met my third source of medical inspiration and followed him for years in order to learn the art of Homeopathic Medicine. This was George Vithoulkas, who'd also been in India, was also a disciple of Krishnamurti and became his own Master's private doctor in the last years of his life.

Life is an energy field made of magical spirals and extraordinary connections. If we let ourselves go into the constant flow of mysteries that stream before our eyes we will develop a sense of wonder. In this way, my harsh expulsion from the Ranch transformed itself into a rich and beautiful experience in Switzerland.

□□□

16   J. Krishnamurti

In 1978, a few months after I arrived in Pune, I heard Osho talk frequently about another enlightened Master who was alive on this planet. This was J. Krishnamurti, who at that time must have been in his early eighties.

As a young boy, Krishnamurti had been chosen by Annie Besant and C. W. Leadbeater, the founders of the Theosophical Society, who considered him to be a 'vehicle' for Lord Maitreya, the expected World Teacher. Besant and Leadbeater had been searching for the right 'vehicle' for some time, and surely could not have expected to find him on their own doorstep.

Krishnamurti's father worked as a clerk for the Theosophical Society, at its headquarters in Adyar, close to Chennai (formerly Madras) in India. In 1909, his son Krishna was spotted by Charles Leadbeater, who claimed that the boy possessed an amazing 'aura' and was destined to be a great spiritual teacher.

Together with his younger brother Nityananda, Krishnamurti was carefully tutored by members of the Theosophical Society, with a strict regimen that included both a British education and intense spiritual instruction. The brothers were very close and, as they grew up, both became more and more involved with the Order of the Star, an organization specially created by the Theosophists to support the coming World Teacher.

In 1922, Krishnamurti went through a number of spontaneous, deep, life-changing spiritual experiences while residing at Ojai in

California. This gave him the insight that the development of his inner being had nothing to do with organisations like the Theosophists and the Order of the Star.

In 1925, Nityananda died from tuberculosis, robbing Krishnamurti of his only real friend. According to eyewitness accounts, the news shattered Krishnamurti and 'broke him completely' but twelve days after Nitya's death he was 'immensely quiet, radiant, and free of all sentiment.'

Four years later, in 1929, when the Theosophical Society brought thousands of people together in Holland to present the new Master, Krishnamurti shocked the organizers and the entire movement by publicly dissolving the Order of the Star. He declared that henceforth his lifelong purpose would be to speak against all organized belief, the notion of gurus, and the teacher-follower relationship, vowing instead to work in setting people 'absolutely, unconditionally free.'

From that moment on, Krishnamurti became a real Master and taught continuously throughout the world until his death in 1986, at the age of 90. Osho encouraged us to go and see him, so when we knew he was in Mumbai giving a series of teachings, about 20 of us decided to go, curious to see what it would be like to sit in the presence of another living Master.

Krishnamurti's discourses were scheduled to be held at night in a park in the centre of Mumbai. We arrived in the morning aboard the famous 'Deccan Queen' train that travelled between Pune and Mumbai. I say 'famous' because the 'Queen' was the main means of transport for sannyasins between the two cities.

Pune is about 600 metres above sea level and the road to Mumbai descends through various hills in an arduous, torturous route that, to the eyes of Westerners, seemed more like a roller coaster than a highway. Traffic accidents and breakdowns, especially on the hilly sections, were frequent and could more than double the time of the trip.

India's trains were quicker, but also an adventure. You never knew when, or if, the trains were going to leave. Moreover, you had no idea when they would arrive at your chosen destination. In marked contrast, the Deccan Queen was the only train at the time that bragged about being on time – which, give or take half an hour, it usually was – and also having an air-conditioned passenger car. We all loved it.

We arrived at the park at sunset – and sunsets in India are undeniably spectacular. Even in the bedlam of Mumbai, we managed to enjoy the chorus of bird song that announced the fading light and growing darkness. As night fell, the sultry weather eased up and a fresh sea breeze was softening the heat and drying the sweat of the day.

Having arrived early, we naturally seated ourselves in the front row, but soon a crowd of about one thousand local people gathered to hear Krishnamurti speak. The stage in front of us was made of wood and on it stood a simple wooden chair, with the whole stage situated under a beautiful banyan tree.

The simplicity and austerity of the preparations were already an indication of the character of Krishnamurti. It was difficult to find elements in common with Osho, who arrived at our meditation hall in a Mercedes – and later, in a Rolls-Royce – and seated himself in a special armchair constructed by the engineer from Milan.

It was a question of two Masters, two unique beings, so very different in their appearance and their individual characters. It helped me understand that every enlightened person maintains his unique characteristics. Osho was treated like a king and over time he, in turn, treated us like so many kings and queens. In his communes, the search for beauty and comfort was tangible and evident, even in simple household objects.

Here, I found myself in front of a stage that was modest and sloppy, yet when Krishnamurti arrived, all the people and things surrounding him lost their importance. What appeared, in my eyes, was a bright yellow light around him, like a small sun that was shining… It felt like love.

With Osho the light was infinite, intense and white, and the feeling it triggered in me was to have arrived home after millennia of searching. With Krishnamurti these sensations were not so intense, but the love that emanated from him – and above all the compassion – were irresistible. Tender and warm, my tears fell and my heart was also filled with compassion, the supreme form of love.

Krishnamurti was thin, fragile and he trembled slightly due to Parkinson's disease. But his presence was spectacular in its physical beauty. In fact, he was one of the most beautiful men I have ever seen in this fortunate incarnation.

His face had occidental features, with straight hair that was long and greying, and deep black eyes that seemed intensely directed toward his own interiority. He had long hands and a long-limbed body. Elegant, dressed in sober Western clothes, simple and modest, but at the same time refined, he was the image of an old aristocrat from the eighteenth century. He greeted us by making the Indian *namaste* gesture, as Osho did in his discourses.

I saw Krishnamurti again on other evenings of the retreat in Mumbai and many years later in Switzerland, at Saanen, where he had an annual gathering. In his talks he discussed the experience of being 'the observer' and elaborated on complex concepts in extremely simple terms. He also often expounded his view that no one can help another on the spiritual path —we have to walk completely alone. For him, spiritual masters were misleading and dangerous because they didn't leave the disciples free.

Still, even today, reading the works of Krishnamurti gives me a sense of my heart opening in a way that only a real Master can give you. He had an excellent facility with language and for dealing with his subjects in great depth, qualities that brought him very close to Osho. Yet he lacked the joy and the jokes with which Osho used to bring us back down to earth, with our feet on the ground, after a discourse that had taken us on the highest flights of our being. He lacked celebration. Being with him was like eating a meal made of only one dish. With Osho we had hundreds of hors d'oeuvres and another ten or twelve courses from different sources and traditions around the world.

The sense I had with Krishnamurti was of a path undertaken by a single man, who was sharing his life like a solitary flower, luminous and amazing, but always alone. I never had this feeling with Osho. With my own Master, I felt the oneness of a big spiritual family that faced a difficult path, and who were supporting each other in order to succeed.

All of Krishnamurti's disciples that I knew, such as Leboyer and others, had this characteristic of seeming like solitary men, but without the negative connotation of being isolated. They could be social and communicate with others, but they were alone in confronting life, whether it was at the social periphery or within their own interiority.

However, these differences are fundamentally superficial. For me, it was extremely important to see another living Master who was enlightened, another being who had reached the heights of human consciousness, who had reached the peak of evolution, beyond which you become one with the light. The meeting with Krishnamurti helped me understand the differences between Masters, their different approaches to teaching and to life, and how they choose to live their experience of bliss and meditation.

Osho was a meditator 'in action.' He was a light that was reflected in millions of dewdrops, creating infinite rainbows simply for the pleasure of enjoying life. He was the leader of the pack who brought his followers to pathways never reached before, paths that were difficult but fascinating and profoundly nourishing to the soul.

Osho was also the creator of a new spiritual path that didn't separate spirit from matter, physical pleasure from the bliss of consciousness, that didn't separate Gautama Buddha from Zorba the Greek, that no longer separated races according to colour and religious beliefs, that no longer separated male from female, life from death.

J. Krishnamurti was a meditator who seemed to sit silently by himself, observing the river of life as it flowed by him. Over the years, many people sat with him on those riverbanks – the banks of awareness – and each one interpreted in his or her way what they saw, according to their own personal experience.

None of this is intended to detract from the fact that Krishnamurti was one of the most evolved souls of the past century. For me, it was a great honour to be with him on two occasions in my life, two experiences in which I again saw reflected in the eyes of another human being the light of the divine that flows silently inside each of us.

17   The Visit

After about six months of work, a possibility of returning to the Ranch opened up. There was a festival coming up and the dates corresponded to a period in which I could get away from work at the hospital. I suggested to Dr P, the head doctor, to come with me to the Ranch for 15 days – he could meet Osho, see the big commune that was being built and be able to form a better idea of what it would mean to be a disciple.

He accepted, rearranged his schedule at the hospital and we left together. I was looking forward to greet the Master again and curious to see what had been constructed since my last visit. The trip was simple and fun. Dr P was always relaxed and easy-going, his emotions very subtle, almost non-existent. Since the first time we met I always found him in this mental state.

We arrived first in Portland. We spent the night in the Rajneesh Hotel and the next day found ourselves in a long line of people waiting to be taken to the Ranch. This year there were many more people. As we arrived at the Ranch, it was obvious that everything had been multiplied and energised. It was now the size of a small European village. There was a post office, a bank and even a police force that acted more or less like the traffic police in Italy. So many houses were under construction that it just left me astonished. From where had it come, all this energy and all this money? It was a miracle, a miracle that Osho perpetuated as long as necessary for his visionary project.

The embraces, at least in the beginning, were continuous and the joy of seeing the Master again was out of this world. The energy more interior than in Pune, more rarefied, as if a dense cloud full of rain was slowly opening in order to allow a glimpse of open sky. Often he had told us that, in meditation, the state of watching one's thoughts is like watching a sky in which clouds pass quickly, running after each other without a pause, but the state of pure consciousness and awareness is like a completely empty sky – full of empty space, without any more clouds. Now it seemed as if Osho's physical body itself was thinning out like the clouds.

Those two weeks were magnificent on many levels. We came back to Switzerland, to our little Locarno, full of joy and energy and then found ourselves charged up again by the effect of sharing our experience with friends. I returned to work, but this time my intention was directed to the aim of returning to the Oregon commune as soon as possible. I had seen the Master again. I felt he had entered a new phase of his teaching. I'd seen the happiness of the sannyasins participating in this enormous project of constructing the City of Rajneeshpuram and I wanted to be there too, in this common undertaking.

On my return, I went to live in the old city of Locarno, very near the hospital, in an apartment with two floors that was occupied by a colleague from the hospital, who was also connected to the circle of friends of Neeresh, the new name of Dr P, my chief physician.

The year and a half I spent in Switzerland, plus my six months in the emergency ward in Palermo, were the only hospital experience I have ever had. For the rest of the time, as a doctor, I've always worked alone, taking all the responsibility on myself. I've never felt comfortable submitting to a health care system that was sick in its roots, sick from corruption, power trips and a logical mind that had brought the medical profession to the extreme of seeing man only as a machine.

Nevertheless, I was grateful for this paediatric experience that brought me in contact with different kinds of births. If a birth was expected to be difficult, there had to be a paediatrician in the delivery room to take care of the new-born baby. The gynaecologists were responsible for taking care of the mothers. So I found myself in the delivery room dozens of times.

Often the father came to the delivery room to be near the woman.

But often when the labour was difficult and pain was written on the face of the mother, the father would leave, unable to watch his woman in such pain. It was obvious to me that the body of a woman is stronger and more able to withstand pain than that of a man, just as she also tends to be more decisive and more open-minded.

The 'weaker sex' has been put down for centuries because men fear the strength of women. Moreover, the fact that a woman is capable of creating new life, giving birth to a new human being, gives most men a deep-seated feeling of inferiority, provoking them to try to show the rest of the world how powerful and secure they really are.

To care for a new-born child is a magical experience. Everybody, at least once, should have the experience of holding a just-born baby in his or her arms. I guarantee you will not forget such an experience for the rest of your life. The quality of the newborn was what I saw when I looked into Osho's eyes – his eyes were empty, deep as a sky in the night. Paradoxically, he also looked like a wild lion from the jungle that could kill you with a single blow. It was this combination of new-born innocence and exploding energy that made Osho a magnet, attracting people to him from all over the world.

Unfortunately, the natural innocence of children is gradually destroyed as they start to interact with the social environment around them. By the age of five or six, they have learned to be cunning, to try and manipulate the parents and experiment with many other political strategies which will form the basis of personality and ego. This 'fall from paradise' happens to every child.

By the time adolescence comes along, the child and all other family members have forgotten the fragility inherent in the human soul, present in the very early stages of life, when consciousness first explores the experience of having a new physical body. Every child instinctively tries to cover up his own fragility with ego strategies of one kind and another, according to both his environment and the karmic baggage he brings with him into this life from his previous incarnation.

Ego is the armour we construct in order to be able to protect ourselves from the world, with its apparent cruelties and difficulties. Without this ego we wouldn't be able to walk the streets, because we would be crushed immediately by other armoured egos. Only a real Master can one day look into our eyes, bypass the ego, see inside our soul and commune with us in the silence of his gaze. In the silence of the emptiness that surrounds him, we can let go and relax, knowing that existence is our mother and cannot do us harm, knowing that evil is only a shadow of the fact that we are identifying with our mental conditioning.

***

Only a real Master unmasks your ego and leaves you naked so that you can return to the innocence of a new-born child. All the other false gurus that circulate in the streets of the world reinforce it, and they make you feel more secure in yourself, with an ego that is even more armoured – the spiritual ego.

***

The experience of the fragility of new-born babies has always stayed with me, reminding me that if we had the courage to set aside the ego and face life from a space of vulnerability and insecurity, the world would be changed into paradise in an instant. The spiritual path is a process of stripping ourselves of all this armour and having the courage to face life without arrogance, without fear, without the need to defend ourselves against others or to attack them – remaining naked under the sun and embracing life with all the mystery that it holds.

**The Seventh Door
The Master**

A real Master is not one who gives you something but one who strips away all your systems of defence, leaving you naked and alone before the immensity of existence.

18   The Second Try

From the time of my return to Locarno, my mind was in America with the Master. As soon as I had completed my second contract with the hospital and put money aside – as I'd been told to do in order to be able to stay in the Oregon commune – I left for the Ranch. Bidding farewell to Locarno, I was convinced that this time I would remain at the Ranch for a long time. But when I arrived at our hotel in Portland, I realised the situation had altered during my absence. The sannyasin community had experienced many changes, including new problems and lots of new people.

I hardly knew anyone at the hotel and the atmosphere was more business-like, more sterile, with fewer hugs and kisses exchanged between the hotel staff and those of us arriving. Now it seemed more like a normal hotel, with usual check-in procedures and a brisk, business-like vibe. I was not accustomed to such a cool atmosphere between sannyasins. Up to now, arriving at any Osho centre was like arriving home after a long time and being welcomed by the members of an extended family. In the hotel, however, I found myself among disciples, mostly Americans, who worked efficiently and seriously.

Next day, I arrived on the Ranch during a festival. This transformed my mood into cheerfulness and joy when meeting others who, like myself, were visiting from around the world. But with those who were living and working on the Ranch itself, contact was minimal. At the end of the festival, when most visitors had left, I asked for a meeting with the women who ran the commune's administration. I waited a long time, during which I filled out a form explaining the reasons for my request to stay.

The main Ranch office was located in a trailer home, the kind of portable unit that could be trucked to any location in two halves then banged together. It seemed to be made largely of plastic. Smaller units had been added to the central office space, leading to rooms occupied mainly by women who had important functions in running the commune.

I began to feel uneasy. I didn't like the smiles painted on these women's faces. They seemed to convey the classic image of a phony American welcome: "Hi, nice to see you...everything is fine...life is great...so, hey, how can we help you...?" and so on. In my case, though, it had the reverse effect: instead of opening up, I found myself contracting my aura to protect myself from this weird behaviour.

Truth be told, I'd never felt at home in America, or on the Ranch. On the contrary, it felt like I was millions of light years away from my 'Indian home,' where there weren't any fake smiles or phony masks to make you believe people were taking care of you. Yet here I was, in a commune filled with new American sannyasins, who seemed to work as if employed in any retail store in the country. Later, I came to understand how Sheela had given this new flavour to the commune's way of functioning. And the more she developed it, the less I liked it.

I waited and waited. After almost two hours, someone from Sheela's staff approached me, a hollow smile stretched across her big lips, inquiring why I had come to the office. I hadn't known this person in Pune and I don't think she knew me, but she did her very best to make me feel like an insignificant and irrelevant visitor.

It was a very different feeling from those times in Pune when I went to the office to speak with Arup. She also held responsibility and power, but she'd always made me feel at ease, even kissing me while handing me the Master's answer, when I'd asked to work in the medical centre. Even on that occasion, notwithstanding the tough hit I was receiving, I felt like someone was taking care, that I was an integral part of the commune and the medical project. I didn't get what I asked for, but still I belonged. I was no less valued as a member of the community, just because I didn't get to play doctor.

But in this context, on the Ranch, I felt like a stranger. Briefly, I told my story: I'd been asked to leave the Ranch in order to make money, which I done by working in Switzerland for more than a year. Now I'd returned to the commune to stay for a long time. She looked at me with eyes that already conveyed her answer. Producing an exquisitely forced smile, she asked if I was American. Now, leaving aside the fact that I spoke English poorly and with a heavy accent, this woman knew from the form I'd just completed that I was Italian. Her question was rhetorical, masking the truth she wanted me to understand on my own, without having to explain it.

"If you aren't a legal resident, how are you going to stay in America?" She inquired condescendingly.

"Are you telling me that in order to stay in this commune I need to have a Green Card?" I retorted.

She practically jumped out of her seat. "I haven't said anything about a Green Card," she replied, nervously. "But it's obvious that in order to stay in America you need to be an American or have a residence permit, otherwise you cannot remain for long. We don't need money, but we do need people who can live and work here legally."

The situation was clear. On the first occasion, I'd been sent away from the Ranch because they needed money and I didn't have any. Now they didn't want money. They wanted Americans, or foreigners with official permission to stay in the country, holders of the precious Green Card that permits you to work and allows you to become an American citizen after a few years.

But I had no intention of returning to Europe empty handed, or giving up the idea of living on the Ranch. I certainly didn't want to go back to Switzerland and continue working as a doctor while the City of Rajneeshpuram was being constructed over here in Oregon. I might not like the place, but this was where Osho was living and therefore where I needed to be. So, at the very least, I was determined to remain in the USA in the hope that, sooner or later, I could find my way back onto the Ranch.

After staying a few more days, I came in contact with several people who'd been living at an Osho centre in New Jersey, on the East Coast. As I already knew, Osho had stopped in New Jersey for several weeks on his way from India to Oregon, living in a mansion on a hilltop, with a wonderful view of the Manhattan skyline from his bedroom window. The mansion was known affectionately by sannyasins as 'the castle' and was still functioning as a centre.

When I was informed that it was a beautiful place that needed sannyasins to help out, the idea immediately appealed to me. On previous visits, New York had affected me strongly. It was the most chaotic place I'd ever seen. Manhattan was a fascinating mix of huge skyscrapers and tiny shops that sold everything from books to fruit to the most obscure objects.

In New York, luxury was thrown in your face by all its major stores in a completely uninhibited and haphazard way. Its restaurants offered an astonishing variety of cuisine from every ethnic source, while music from around the globe could be heard live in the streets, piped into the shops, or broadcast at deafening levels by black guys in local parks holding enormous ghetto blasters on their shoulders with the volume cranked up. It boasted such a wide variety of nationalities and races that, as a white European, I clearly felt in the minority.

In the past, I hadn't stayed long in New York, but I'd returned often. It was a place where I loved to spend a few days amid the chaos and madness of the most frenetic consumerism I've ever seen. But this time, after arriving from Oregon and spending a few days in the city, I made my way out to 'the castle' in New Jersey, which had been purchased for the sole purpose of housing Osho, while Sheela looked hastily around the 'States for a property big enough to begin building his new commune. It was here he'd rested after his first trip out of India.

The mansion really was a miniature version of an old Renaissance castle, with many turrets and balconies, plus windows stained with coloured glass in shades of orange and yellow. The entrance was a large rectangular space, leading to a magnificent winding staircase that led to the upper floors, reminiscent of any chateau on the Loire river. Osho, by the way, never used the stairs. He preferred the elevator.

On the ground floor, the reception area branched out into corridors that led to rooms where different centre activities were conducted. There was an office for day-to-day business, two massage rooms and a big room where meditations were organised from time to time. Another beautiful room was used for meetings with guests staying in the castle. On the upper floor, the suite used by Osho during his stay was not inhabited – presumably, in case the Master ever decided to return this way and needed to stay over. Other rooms on this level were occupied by the centre leader and two women who'd been part of the team for a long time.

I was permitted to visit Osho's room on the second floor and to my surprise was told I could sleep there for one night. It was a big room, with little in the way of furniture, giving it an empty feeling. But the bathroom was more lavish. Prior to his departure from Pune, Osho had let it be known that he wanted a bathroom tiled in marble, which was duly built by Deeksha and her construction team. They'd also restored the small service elevator that Osho used to avoid the stairs.

Towards the end of his stay in Pune, the Master had begun to suffer intensely from lower back pain and sciatica... problems exacerbated by his preferred lifestyle of doing nothing, remaining seated for long periods of time without moving his body, except when coming to discourse, or to darshan, or during infrequent walks in the gardens of Lao Tzu house.

The bathroom was really beautiful. On the floor and walls there were scintillating reflections of light and colour, emanating from deep green marble tiles that gave a relaxed effect to the whole atmosphere. There was marble everywhere and an enormous mirror about ten feet wide and seven feet high. The bathroom window was relatively small, however, when compared to the enormous window in his bedroom that allowed him to see the lights of Manhattan at night.

As you can imagine, I didn't sleep much during the night I passed there. It was like being in space, or in a vacuum, as if my body was floating in a void. The place seemed to defy gravity. My mind stayed lucid and alert the whole night, even while my body was relaxed and drowsy.

I soon discovered this castle was no ordinary meditation centre. In Europe, such centres offered a regular programme of meditations that continued throughout the day, similar to the ashram in Pune, with busy work schedules for all commune members. The bigger centres also offered therapy groups. All the centres, big and small alike, offered a video of one of Osho's discourses every evening.

There was nothing like that here. In fact, there was no real schedule. The centre leader was a volcano that erupted each morning, creating a hot lava flow that gave us sufficient energy to move ahead with whatever immediate projects were at hand. Niro was a big woman from Belgium...big and tall, but you couldn't say she was fat. She had an explosive energy that was untypical of her body type. She was about five feet nine inches in height with enormous breasts that tried desperately to free themselves from the low-cut blouses she wore, presumably in an effort to enjoy the fresh air of the New Jersey hills.

With big blue eyes, short blonde hair, a strong round face, Niro was the type of woman who could have been director of a circus, manager of an apartment building, an actress in a Fellini film, an organiser of several different kinds of black-market business...but surely not a spiritual seeker.

She had the energy of an avalanche, rather like Deeksha in Pune, and each morning materialised in dramatic fashion, descending the great winding staircase like a Hollywood diva, singing and screaming her joy with her powerful voice. Her first command to guests in this 'grand hotel'– she ran it like an aristocratic matron on vacation – was to sit with her in the big meeting room and choose a card from her Tarot deck. The card you chose would indicate the flavour of your day ahead, and Niro interpreted one card for each guest, suggesting how they should behave in response to its illustrated message.

After the Tarot readings, breakfast was made and then, after breakfast, everyone was free to do what he or she wanted. This, indeed, was a radical departure from life on the Ranch, where hard work, instantly obeyed orders and long hours had come to be enshrined as the chief commandments of Sheela's new religion. Free choice? Free time? Unbelievable!

I told Niro about my woes with the Ranch administration, adding that I wanted to stay for a while in New Jersey to get used to being in America again, and to see what life had in store for me. She welcomed me with open arms and soon became a good friend, so much so that, after a few weeks, I became her *confidant*, lending a sympathetic ear to her relationship problems and the difficulties of running a centre. After all, I'd lived in Pune and therefore had a great deal more experience with the running of communes than she did.

Seeing I had experience in cooking for large numbers of people, she asked me to take care of the kitchen and meals, to which I readily agreed. She gave me a big American car, which seemed more like a boat than an automobile, plus the keys to the storeroom and money for purchasing food. Now, as we all know, food is dear to everyone's heart, or, rather, to the stomach and is also – one might argue – a substitute for an absent mother's love. Very soon, I was offering regular meals with fixed hours and, as a result, the volatile and haphazard mood of the centre began to settle down, losing its former ambience as a temporary campsite set up inside a hotel.

Niro rarely left the mansion, so in the afternoons, when most people were outside or busy, she and I started to share a lot about ourselves. I came to admire her strength of character and her courage, qualities the rest of the world would recognize several years later, when she wrote a book that made her famous: she was the first person to go from HIV-positive back to negative in tests and clinical results. Niro had been lovers with a Dutch dancer who had a past history of drug dependency and was a homosexual for the greater part of his life. She believed it was from him she'd contracted the AIDS virus – he died of the disease a few years later.

As we became friends, we agreed to make a mutual effort to transform the energy of the castle, which until now had been more like a residence than a centre. With steady resolve, we introduced the elements of meditation and celebration that Osho wanted in all his centres. The high point of these changes was a 'musical meditative meeting' that we arranged on Sunday afternoons, with live music in a nearby park followed by a big buffet at the castle when the meditation was over.

As word got around, many people from the New York area started coming to these Sunday meetings. New Yorkers, as a species, tend to be a reclusive bunch of workaholics and our NYC sannyasins proved no exception. This was a totally different kind of disciple than I'd encountered so far. Usually, these people never visited communes and rarely ventured outside their home city. But when news spread that our Sunday parties were beautiful and fun, more and more people managed to set aside their busy schedules and travel to the New Jersey suburbs in time to celebrate with us.

In addition, more people started coming to stay for the weekends with us, and two disciples began working full-time with me. One of these was a guy I'd worked with before. He was German, but his facial features made him look Tibetan. He was physically very strong and had big, dark bags under his sky-blue eyes. His mind was really strange. Each time we talked, no matter what the subject, he would eventually lead the discussion around to concepts of transcendental spirituality. Maybe he'd been a Tibetan monk in a past life – he certainly looked the part – because it was obvious to me that his ego was identified with being a very special person in contact with a high circle of disembodied spiritual Masters. I never cared to contradict him in his delusion, but I declined to join him with tales of my own.

One of the things Osho taught us was not to brag about esoteric experiences that might occur during meditation, because the ego would eagerly jump on them as evidence of spiritual progress, thereby blocking the path to deeper experiences that might be waiting to manifest. Hence, I've always had a built-in tendency to avoid speaking about such things. But, seeing that I am now at a point in my narrative where I feel more intimate with my readers, I will recount my first mystical experience in Pune, which happened in 1980 while working in the ashram kitchen.

However, let me first repeat that Osho never gave much importance to such experiences. His advice to us was to keep moving along the spiritual path without clinging to special moments of bliss, revelation, or visionary insights. Such attachments would only weigh us down, he warned, and prevent us from investigating further, as we continued to scale the heights of consciousness.

Nearly all the therapy offered at his ashram in Pune One was oriented towards unburdening us of emotional negativity and releasing suppressed energy. But this was intended only as a bridge to meditation. At much more profound level, Osho worked on us in a mystical way that sometimes produced unexpected and unusual experiences.

One evening, I was working in the kitchen, cleaning the tables outside the ashram's canteen, which were now empty because *darshan* with the Master was happening just a few yards away, inside the little auditorium attached to his house. Osho gave *darshan* every evening, initiating new disciples, welcoming old disciples returning from the West, saying farewell to those who were leaving and sometimes giving *energy darshan* by touching people on the third eye as a way of transmitting his energy.

Up to this point, *energy darshan* had been given mostly to one person at a time, called up to sit in front of Osho, supported by one or two female mediums, who would sit behind the individual and help him receive Osho's energy by putting their hands on his back, head, or heart. Later Osho began to invite three or four people at a time – sometimes even six or seven – surrounding them with a host of female mediums. As a result, about thirty people, most of them women, went into trance as soon as he initiated the energy transmission.

Other sannyasins present in *darshan* would participate by raising their arms, closing their eyes, then humming and swaying for as long as each session lasted. At the same time, a group of musicians would play fast, dramatic music.

When he touched his disciples, Osho simultaneously turned off the lights by pressing a button with his foot, plunging the entire ashram in darkness. In that instant, wherever you found yourself, you had to sit down and remain immobile until the lights came back on. This was similar to an exercise George Gurdjieff designed for his disciples in his commune at Fontainebleau in France, which he called his 'Stop Exercise.'

In Pune, a grand total of about a thousand sannyasins were participating in this experiment, either inside or outside the little auditorium where Osho was sitting, including people like myself who were working in various jobs while *darshan* was happening.

That night, as I've already mentioned, I found myself in the garden of the restaurant, cleaning tables so they would be ready for breakfast next morning. When the lights went off, I sat on the nearest table, crossing my legs and closing my eyes, relaxing into stillness in order to receive the intense energy that was radiating from Lao Tzu House, a few yards away, where Osho was giving *energy darshan*.

My body started to tremble, with the tremors becoming more and more violent, together with a pronounced shaking that swiftly grew in intensity and frequency. In short, my whole body was in the grip of a potent energy that was comparable to what one might experience by placing two wet fingers in an electric socket. Except, in my case, it wasn't just two fingers but my whole body that was being invaded by an uncontainable electric current, as if a dam had opened inside me and a cascade of water was crashing down with all its force.

With the benefit of hindsight, I could say that my body was wracked by a series of spasms that reminded me of an epileptic fit. The difference was that I remained fully conscious through the entire experience, observing my body as an external object. This continued the whole time that Osho was giving *energy darshan*...and beyond it.

After about an hour, the lights returned. Slowly, people went back to their jobs around the ashram. Sannyasins were also coming out of *darshan*, overflowing with love and sweetness, but my body continued to be inundated with an energy that didn't diminish. I remained sitting on the table, continuing to shake and lurch without pause. My mind was helpless and could do nothing but observe my body, which was no longer responding to my will.

After a long time, one of the women responsible for the kitchen approached me. When she was about three or four yards distant from my body, I could see that she seemed to emanate a dense 'fluid' that I perceived as the energy of her consciousness. This consciousness, I sensed immediately, had been completely deprived of love. Perhaps to mask her insecurity, the woman acted in a tough manner, telling me to stop whatever I was doing, stand up and go back to work. She didn't understand that my normal 'I' no longer inhabited this physical shell and my body was possessed by an indomitable force, creating this electrifying dance.

She stayed for a while, repeating her order for me to move, then gave up and left. My body continued to shake like a harpooned tuna that had been pulled out of the sea and thrown into a net. After some time – I don't know exactly when because normal time had ceased to exist – an Italian sannyasin arrived who'd been given a name similar to my own. He was called Asimo, one of many Sufi names that Osho was giving in this period.

We knew each other, although we had no great friendship. Asimo didn't say a single word. He simply hugged me and stayed with me, making me feel his body and his male strength, which slowly brought me back to a condition more acceptable for survival. I think we must have remained hugging for 20 or 30 minutes, after which I made an effort to get off the table. I noticed that my will was once more trying to take control of my body. My physical form was trying to do what my mind wanted – with varying degrees of success.

Asimo helped me stand on my feet and then, still holding me, walked me slowly to the main gate of the ashram, which at that hour was almost deserted, because, by the time we got there, *darshan* was long ago finished. Walking was difficult. The 'orgasms' of energy that had been passing through my body were less frequent, but still continued in an erratic, unpredictable way. When they became too strong, I needed to stop.

Asimo managed to get me into a rickshaw that took us to where I lived. The ride was an interesting experience. Those who've been to India know what it means to go flying through the streets at full throttle in these flimsy little tin cans. The roads are full of potholes and when you hit one at speed in a rickshaw you literally jump out of your seat. The roof is made of plastic, but you need pay attention to the single iron bar that supports the soft hood, otherwise you can suffer a nasty bang on the head.

Fortunately, it was night and the traffic situation was relatively calm. But, just to be sure, Asimo passed the whole journey chanting "Shanti, baba! Shanti, baba! Shanti, baba!" This was our common sannyasin formula for slowing down the fervour of rickshaw drivers. 'Shanti' means peace, or, in this case, a plea to take it easy. 'Baba' means father, uncle, grandpa, or, more generally, any guy with whom you happen to be talking.

For me, every shake was like a wound opening up inside me. I felt I had just emerged from a hospital operating room, where they had stitched up my skin – I was so sensitive. Nevertheless, we managed to arrive safely at my house. Asimo took me to my room, laid me down on a mattress on the floor, and then arranged himself on another mattress in front of me.

That night, Asimo was my guardian angel. He stayed with me the whole night, watching over me, without disturbing me with words, just giving me the reassuring feeling he was present and available. If I needed something, I was not alone. I owe a lot to this man who, by his presence, helped me pass through one of my most intense experiences with Osho, an experience that was beyond words, beyond both mind and feelings.

The experience continued throughout the night, until dawn, but in a sporadic and discontinuous way, with diminishing intensity. Several times during the night I got up and walked around the house in order to feel my body. For this reason, I went to the bathroom many times, which was located at the end of the villa's main corridor. It was a small bathroom, but decently equipped and had a mirror.

When I gazed into the mirror, I saw my image without being able to recognise it. Staring at the face reflected to me, I did my best to remember who this might be, but, however hard I tried, *I didn't know to whom this face belonged, or what his name might be*. It didn't scare me, but it certainly surprised me. I was astonished to see this face in front of me, without any idea who it was. As a matter of fact, I didn't even know where I was in the world and in what historical period I was currently living. I had lost not only my personal and physical identity, but also my temporal and spatial identity.

I was totally empty inside. There was no memory of me, nor of the time-space continuum that I occupied. The only thing I recognised was the face of Asimo, who was now sleeping serenely on the mattress next to mine. But I recognised him as a friend, without knowing who he was, or where we were.

At dawn, I began to hear birdsong and smell the odours of India. The sense of smell has always been important to me. In India, there is a vast range of different scents, from intoxicating flowers, to passing herds of buffalo, to spices being mixed in a cooking pot.... They were part of my life and I was delighted by them. When I went on bicycle rides, when I walked in Koregaon Park, when I went to the old city among amorphous crowds of thousands of Indians, I nourished myself with the abundance of different smells this country offered.

And so it was that, as dawn broke and daylight returned, the odours of the surrounding neighbourhood slowly brought me back to something vaguely resembling normality. Little by little, I realised that I was in India and knew that I'd been living here for some time. Then, with the rising sun and the brightening of a thousand different colours – the blankets in my room, the trees outside my window, the pictures on the walls – my memory gradually returned. My mind reconstructed the elements of my actual life, reminding me I was a disciple of Osho who, during the previous night, had undergone an intense energetic experience and had emerged from it, safe and sound, in the light of day.

Still, I had to be careful. My mind and body remained very sensitive, all day long, so I passed the time in my house, doing nothing. After many days, I started working in the ashram again. After a week or so, when everything was 'normal,' I wrote to Osho to let him know about the experience and ask if I needed to do anything about it.

At that time, the Master was answering personal written questions, sending his replies on small yellow sheets of paper. His answers were usually telegraphic. When they required more detail, he sent verbal responses through his secretary, Laxmi, who would either deliver them herself or pass them via her own secretaries, Arup and Sheela.

You would find Osho's answer to a written question in the main office in a small rosewood box, made by our carpentry shop. Sometimes his message would simply be "See Laxmi" or "Go find Arup." Mostly, his answers were typewritten by the secretaries, but on this occasion there were two lines written in the incredible handwriting of my Master, which was small and very precise, almost like Arabic script cut in marble. The characters were rounded and completely symmetrical, written in a perfectly straight line, even though there were no lines on the yellow paper.

Looking at his writing, I could tell he was totally present with each word he wrote. It was the same when he initiated me. When he began to write my new name and its meaning on a piece of cream-coloured paper, he gave his total attention to the act of writing. It was as if neither I, nor the other people in *darshan*, existed any more. There was nothing but the paper and the moving pen, as if he was alone in his room, completely immersed in the act of writing. Even with the passing of time, I still have a vivid sense of his totality in the act of writing.

This time, his words said: "The first time you meet God you feel fear, but from that time on you will always be more familiar with him. Go find Paritosh."

Paritosh was a long-time Osho disciple who had once been a Jesuit priest and a student of Carl Gustav Jung, the famous psychologist. Now Paritosh was in his 70s, living inside the ashram. His function was that of a therapist, but unlike most of the other therapists he didn't lead groups. Osho used him more as a private counsellor, an old commune sage who could help you when there were difficult moments to face. My meeting with him did, indeed, relieve me of the fear provoked by my intense experience of 'cosmic orgasm.'

Now, having told my tale, I need to say something about sharing spiritual experiences. Over the years, I've seen friends and acquaintances moving from one spiritual teacher to another, from one type of spiritual training to the next, from a course on self-esteem to a seminar on past lives to a course on the esoteric messages of Jesus Christ...and so on.

Each new discovery is greeted with great enthusiasm and many of these people talk freely about their experiences as if they have discovered the ultimate truth. But, after a few months, these same people may well be found talking about new truths. Not surprisingly, on a spiritual level, there is great confusion today as all kinds of experiences are described in books and shared between friends and acquaintances.

As I see it, life is a mystery that needs to be live to the fullest, not a problem to be solved or destination to be reached. The mind can never understand or manipulate the higher levels of consciousness, which belong to a reality that is utterly different from the one we normally inhabit. Mystical experiences, when they are real, are not something that belongs to us, nor can they be claimed as 'mine' by the individual ego. Rather, they are passages that open up to the sacred universe that surrounds and pervades us, to which every small atom of this existence naturally belongs. There is no separation, no division and therefore no 'I.'

Seen from this perspective, the individual, with all his personal experience, is only an illusion of the mind, which projects its distorted images on the universal consciousness, losing sight of reality. Experiences, whether big or small, can be viewed as pearls of energy that accumulate inside us, waiting until there are enough to make a necklace of understanding and ultimate liberation. And we have no idea how many pearls are needed to make that necklace. All we can do is maintain the fire inside us, without dispersing it, then the alchemy of transformation can do it secret work.

In other words, you can't really talk about it. So, when people develop the habit of sharing inner experiences, it is usually the by-product of an ego seeking appreciation and gratification from others. Certainly, my German friend in New Jersey had an enormous need for recognition as a spiritually advanced being.

❏❏❏

1978 Darshan together with Vivek, Osho care taker

The last Energy Darshan Azima receive on 1980, after that period Osho stop doing the energy work with his disciples

Energy Darshan in 1979, on the back of Azima again Vivek, crying of bliss

19   Trust

One weekend we organized our usual musical event with meditation and buffet, and this time were rewarded with many new people coming from New York. It was a magnificent spring day and in the late afternoon light you could clearly see the 'Big Apple' with the glare created by its downtown lights. After sunset, there was a unique sight as all the planes and helicopters that flew in and around this sea of light that was New York became suddenly visible. It looked like a scene from a science fiction film, very evocative.

After the meditation was over, I made contact with an American woman who was visiting us for the first time and who seemed quite introverted and yet at the same time very radiant. She seemed to be a person who was satisfied with her life. She had a mature female physique with wide hips, typical of women who have given birth.

We introduced ourselves and spent the rest of the day together, talking while walking around the magnificent park in which our little 'Renaissance castle' was situated. As I suspected, Elizabeth was a mother, with a grown son, and was separated from her husband, as indeed were many American women whom I met in those days. She had dark hair and big black eyes that reminded me more of a Latino than a Caucasian.

We talked a lot. She wanted to know everything about the Master and how it was to live near him in the commune. She'd never seen him but planned to go to the next Ranch festival in order to meet him. Many people were taking sannyas by correspondence at that time and had never actually seen their Master. Elizabeth was one of these people, who continued with their day-to-day lives and were not yet connected to the commune.

We spent a pleasant day together and the party went on till late in the evening. I asked her if she would like to spend the night at the castle, partly because it was late and for a woman to travel alone to New York at night was not without risk. She happily agreed. There was no great passion between us that night but the energy was warm and friendly. Our conversation and acts of love were all somehow hinged on our mutual love for the Master.

She was a like a sponge, soaking up water in desperate need of quenching her thirst. She'd lived a life that had not been easy and her marriage had started to fall apart very early, leaving her alone with a son. She worked, she took care of her son...she had what many Americans would describe as 'a normal routine.'

Then one day she read a book by Osho and was hooked by it. She located a small meditation centre near where she lived, listened to Osho's discourses and after a short time took sannyas by mail. Like a flower barely open, her sincerity and her innocence really touched me, so our relationship continued.

After that evening, she frequently came back to the castle to meditate and be with me. During one of our evenings together I asked how it would be for her to marry me, so I could stay in America. After that, we would be free to spend long periods at the Ranch with the Master. She was surprised and delighted. The way it was all happening seemed so natural and easy that we both felt it was the right thing to do. We were good together. We knew there wasn't an overwhelming passion between us, but we also knew that we were adults, she was alone with a son and it would help her to have a man in her life to give her support.

For my part, I wanted to settle in America in order to be able to stay near the Master. At the time, it seemed as though Osho would be staying in the US for the rest of his life. The enormous effort that was being put into building a city around him in Oregon gave me the impression that it would all last a very long time, requiring me to settle their for years.

Anyway, the Ranch 'moms' – as its female administrators were humorously called – had clearly told me they needed people who could stay there as residents, not as visitors. So I decided to throw myself into the unknown again and take a step that up to now I'd never even considered. I left the castle and went to live with Elizabeth in her house in New York's suburbs, a typical little American house with a little garden, next to many other houses that looked exactly the same.

After a few days we got married, in an atmosphere that was so degraded that it took away any nuance of sweetness or grace from the ceremony. The local registry office was an anonymous-looking building with big rooms connected by enormous corridors leading to other government functions. The marriage line was long and there wasn't a single couple that was American. It seemed like a border post full of immigrants who came from all over the world and were waiting for entry visas.

The atmosphere in that building was sordid; it really disgusted me. Maybe it was for that reason that, many years later, I needed to have a real wedding ceremony with my second wife. More and more, I was becoming disillusioned with the so-called 'American Dream.' The difference between the myth and reality was becoming wider and wider.

To the rest of the world, particularly the developing world, America seems like a magical paradise, full of wealth and opportunity where anyone might, with hard work and a little luck, become successful and enjoy a fabulous standard of living. What I saw while living in America was a big country with an economy based on the law of the jungle, where the strongest reigned supreme and where the majority of the population lived well below the social level most of us enjoy in Europe.

Wealth is concentrated mainly on the coasts, East and West, but the rest of America, through which I travelled from one end to the other in Greyhound buses, showed me a land of agricultural semi-poverty and survival, with plastic houses, mobile homes, pickup trucks and gas stations everywhere. Even on the coasts, in places such as these government offices, I got the feeling not of abundance but of a daily grind of low paid work, where bored officials administered and enforced a host of impersonal rules and regulations. These offices had nothing human about them, or anything that indicated respect for human beings. Bloated bureaucracies were carrying out their functions with arrogance and false smiles.

One good thing: we didn't have to wait long. The usual procedures for marriage were speeded up with an unimaginable superficiality, and in the space of ten minutes everything was finished and we heard the magic word, "Next!"

We were happy and spent some nice days together. Then I had to leave in order to obtain the documents required for residency in the United States. So I went back to Italy, completed all the formalities for immigrating, and after a month came back to America to re-join my wife. Then I just had to wait.

One day, as promised, the famous Green Card arrived. This was the magic passport with which I could stay on the Ranch. In that moment, Elizabeth was busy with her son and asked me to go ahead of her and she would join me at the next festival. It was the first time I'd been with a woman who was also a mother, and it took me only a short time to realize that, for a woman with children, the child is the main priority, and the man is always second in importance.

The biological drive to care for her children is really strong for a mother, stronger than any other experience in life. So Elizabeth stayed with her son, who, like most children of separated couples, had big problems in school and didn't appreciate the presence of an unfamiliar man in his mother's house.

Again, I was heading for Oregon with the hope of being admitted to the commune as a resident, this time *forever*. There was a festival and people were coming from all over Europe. If, during the early phase of his teachings, Osho's disciples were mainly Indian, by the end of the first commune in Pune they were primarily European. The phase of the Ranch drew an enormous number of new American disciples. But when the Ranch ended in chaos and Osho was deported, most of them stayed in their own country from then onwards. They didn't come to Pune Two for the next cycle of teachings, between 1986 and '90.

After Osho left the body, more and more people came from all over the world, and this movement continues up to now. Disciples arrive from surprising places – Iranians, Palestinians, Africans and many Russians. These are the people who approach the teachings of the Master in recent times, but in the time of the Ranch it was mainly Americans who came to settle in the commune. Most Europeans came only for the festivals.

So again I had the opportunity to meet old friends and meditate with the Master, who in the meantime had become even more spectacular and theatrical in his choice of clothes. The Ranch was continually expanding and assuming more and more the dimensions of a real city. They had constructed a dam and big lake where it was possible to swim. So in the middle of the Oregon desert there was a nice little beach with umbrellas where we could dive into cool water.

Along with the expansion of the commune, the number of rules had also increased and a police force of sannyasins followed Osho's car, carrying weapons and walkie-talkies, ready to identify and deal with any threat to the Master. The energy of joy was always present, but the presence of weapons disturbed most of us who came from outside. Personally, it didn't please me at all to see the Master escorted by armed guards, even though these guards were sannyasins and many of them people I knew well.

In fact, the whole organization Sheela had created pleased me less and less, but the Master was here, so that's where I wanted to be. Those who complained about the new 'military' aspect of the organization were told that the situation was much more dangerous than it had been in India, with much more risk to Osho. "We are doing this to protect Osho," was the answer you heard if you went to the offices to complain.

After fifteen days of being there, I was expecting Elizabeth to come for the start of the festival. Late in the morning, I received a call from the office and was told to go to a checkpoint at the entrance to the property, about five miles away, because there was a problem with my wife. I took a yellow bus that was part of the Ranch's free transit system in order to get to the checkpoint. It was a prefabricated house converted into an office, like a customs office in the desert, where new arrivals were welcomed and received instructions on how to move around the commune.

Before being admitted, all visitors were checked for drugs because, understandably, they didn't want any type of illegal drug entering the community. After receiving a medical-style wrist bracelet that was to be worn at all times – with different colours according to the length of each person's stay – the new arrivals were conducted to the centre of the commune.

When I arrived Elizabeth was upset, confused and crying, as if she had been struck by an attack of hysteria, something that was not at all like her. She explained to me how the 'welcome team' had rummaged through her luggage and found some medicine without a label that they'd taken for illegal drugs, confiscating it and prohibiting her from entering the Ranch.

I was shocked. They were worse than real customs agents! I spoke with the woman who was in charge, explaining to her our story. I made it clear that neither Elizabeth nor I used drugs of any type and that this was the first chance for Elizabeth to see the Master. It was really important for her to see Osho and that she had left her son and everything else in order to meet him.

The woman was tall, with a heavy build, short hair, square face and few feminine attributes. She really looked like a policewoman, with a heavy energy and distinctly uncooperative attitude. She didn't want to know. She said that in the pre-festival information folder it was clearly written that you couldn't bring any drugs or medicine without a medical certificate authorizing the use of those pharmaceuticals for reasons of health.

There was nothing we could do. It was like hitting our heads against a wall. I turned to Elizabeth, who continued to cry, and hugged her without a word. After about an hour, a car arrived to take her to the local town where she could organize her return home.

I was in shock. I didn't understand how this could happen in the Master's commune, how it had become so rigid and bureaucratic. Maybe in order to find a plausible justification for what I had seen, I continued to think of the necessity of protecting the Master. Maybe I didn't know about many things that were happening? Surely there must be an explanation for this ugly behaviour, for the police, the weapons...and all the rest.

Certainly I knew about the ill feeling directed against the Ranch by many of the locals, who didn't want anything to do with the 'Rajneeshees'– as the newspapers termed us. I also knew there were many legal battles involving the Ranch management, and our team of sannyasin lawyers was growing larger every day. About 20 lawyers worked to defend the commune from outside attacks and by the end of the Ranch this had become one of the most important departments. Nevertheless, this inhuman display against one of our own sannyasins could not be justified.

I stayed in contact with Elizabeth by phone almost every day, and she kept telling me that everything was ok, but I could tell by her voice something major had shifted inside her.

As usual, the festival was marvellous and the Master continued his majestic silence with an audience that was always increasing in size. He seemed to belong to another sphere of existence now and the small problems of the Ranch didn't seem to touch him. With hindsight, I understood that the Master was cutting us loose in order to make us more aware of the mechanisms of our monstrous egos. He left us free to make mistakes, letting the situation develop, becoming more and more extreme, until 1984 when he again took control of the commune by coming out of silence and speaking to us once more.

I participated in the festival with all my heart, but the rigidity that was growing ever stronger in the organization and the memory of what had happened to Elizabeth prevented me from completely letting go into the celebration.

A few days after the end of the festival, I went again to the office to speak with the women who'd already sent me away from the commune twice. As usual, I waited in the hall, watching with growing scepticism the frenetic work that was going on around me. Then, out came one of Sheela's women who greeted me with the customary, "Hi beloved. What can I do for you?"

We had started badly. This phony phrase, delivered with a forced smile, typified the energy I didn't like at the Ranch. Anyway, I explained my story – from the end of Pune One until now – and concluded with pride that I was now an American resident and could stay as long as I wanted to in the States.

She looked at me as if I were in the wrong office, as if my whole story didn't interest her at all and she was busy with other things. "My dear, we are at the height of our expansion," she explained. "We don't need people to stay here forever, we need money, only money... Do you have money?"

I had spent most of my money going back and forth to Italy and getting together the documents needed for the Green Card. Now I had just enough money to stay on the Ranch for a few weeks. I told her about the message I'd been given the last time about the need for workers who had official residency in the US.

"I'm sorry but if you don't have money you can't stay here," came the reply. "Go away, make some money and come back. Then you'll be welcome!" It was the third time I was being thrown out of what I thought was my commune.

I stayed a few days, then left to re-join Elizabeth. But her reaction to the incident had been much stronger than I imagined. She didn't want to hear anything more about Osho, nor of the commune. She felt she'd been unjustly attacked, unfairly rejected, and she didn't want any more experiences with the Master. Her traumatic 'welcome' at the Ranch had become her litmus test for the whole neo-sannyas movement and the work with Osho.

Elizabeth wouldn't listen to me when I started to talk about the Master-disciple relationship, which is essentially a relationship of trust and letting go. She didn't listen when I told her about the beautiful experiences in India, when the commune was completely different from this new city in the American desert. She wasn't listening any more... and that was all. From this one negative experience, she closed herself in a way that I could understand, but could not do myself.

There was so much I wanted to share with her, in the way of my own experience when facing such challenges. I had known Osho and had lived three years in the Pune commune. I had met him personally and had been in seven *energy darshans* with him that had alchemized my whole body/mind for the rest of this incarnation.

But for Elizabeth, the time for sharing was over. For her, sannyas had been an attempt to find a solution to her unhappiness, to her difficult life of being a single mother with a difficult child. Maybe it was more from a space of need than an existential search for spiritual fulfilment.

I remember Osho saying that some disciples arrived because he called them, while others were simply attracted by his teachings. Elizabeth, like many Americans, was attracted by the pioneering dream – so strong in their collective mind – of heading West, living together and constructing a city with her own hands and her own strength.

It would be unfair of me to typify all Americans as flaky and half-hearted. But I did notice, on many occasions, when American sannyasins encountered difficulties inside the commune, they had a strong tendency to quit, as if their precious ideals had been sullied, leaving with rancour and disappointment, exactly as Elizabeth was now doing.

Our brief story together, which began in a Renaissance castle, now crumbled like a sand castle. We had built our relationship on the idea that we wanted to live together in the commune, with her son. But this *tableau* of an alternative family lifestyle had not been supported by the existential flow of events, or by the Master.

Years later, when Osho started to give me hits and systematically destroy everything with which I had become identified, I understood that he is interested only in bringing about the death of the inflated ego, so that the divine can manifest in our physical form.

I stayed with Elizabeth for about two more weeks, trying to soften the blow by staying close to her. But her son became more and more hostile and she continued to close herself in an impenetrable shell. We'd created a dream that perhaps did not belong to her or to me, and which melted in record time.

With no possibility of repairing the damage, I told Elizabeth I would go somewhere and look for work, since my money was practically finished, and that after some months I would contact her to see what we wanted to do. She was the fourth woman from whom Osho had separated me.

As I left, I remembered the initiation Osho had given me in 1978, when he told me that my way was the path of 'Great Love, Love for the Divine.' No matter how beautiful the love story with a woman, like that of Romeo with Juliet, it would never satisfy my yearning to merge with the Whole.

Almost six years had passed since then and my fourth significant relationship was finished. It would not be the last. Now, however, my own sense of certainty about wanting to live and work in the Oregon commune was wavering. The story of the Ranch was testing my trust in Osho and, through him, in existence itself. I understood that the teaching of the Master was one thing, the organization something entirely different, but what he was allowing to be created around him was for me at least questionable.

All these super-efficient women were cutting my ties with my Master. I felt more and more fragile and insecure. If it hadn't been for those three years in Pune with him and his commune, I don't think I could have kept running around America trying to remain close to that fountain of love and of awareness, incarnated in that beautiful oriental body.

The contrast was astonishing. The first commune in Pune had welcomed me with open arms from the start, more than my own family. The second commune gave me exactly the opposite experience: pushing me away continuously and leaving me cast on the seashore like an empty shell.

I didn't have any more money. I'd worked hard for three years to be able to stay on the Ranch and I'd achieved nothing. The commune's doors were always closed to me and my desires continuously castrated. Nevertheless, I didn't feel rancour in my relations with the Master, nor did I blame him for anything.

Inside myself, I knew for sure that I needed to go forward with my life. I needed to be ready for the time when I would be welcomed again to live in the presence of the biggest fountain of love I had ever experienced in my life.

20   Lake Tahoe

Lake Tahoe, as any guidebook will tell you, is the largest mountain lake in America and the second largest mountain lake in the world. It's situated in the Sierra Nevada Mountains, between Nevada and California, at an altitude of 6225 feet above sea level. Its water is cobalt blue and crystalline cold, flowing from the snow-capped peaks that surround it.

The Native Americans had lived for centuries in those rich valleys. In modern times, however, well-to-do Californians have colonised it, building homes and cabins in order to ski, spend money in the casinos and live freely their sexual pleasures, thanks to Nevada's permissive laws regarding gambling and prostitution. It wasn't too far from the Ranch, about ten hours by car, but the atmosphere was so different it felt like being on another continent.

When I drove to the mountains for the first time, to a place called Incline Village, it struck me how suddenly the landscape had changed. Almost without any transition, the vast Nevada desert that had accompanied me for hundreds of miles transformed itself into a pleasant and verdant Alpine countryside surrounded by mountains and woods that extended as far as the eye could see.

I stopped the car to get a sweater from my luggage because the burning sun of the desert had given way to the colder climate of the mountains. More appropriately dressed, I bought a cup of hot tea in a local cafe. While in the United States, I never managed to drink coffee, which in my opinion was just hot water with very little taste and a lot of caffeine. Then I called my friend Russell, an American I'd met on the Ranch, with whom I'd stayed in touch.

When Elizabeth left the Ranch, I had called him, told him I had a Green Card, wanted to stay in America for a long time and was looking for work. He invited me to join a group of sannyasins, almost all of them Americans, who were living together and had formed a small company through which they provided service jobs for wealthy customers with big houses.

When I arrived at Incline it was late in the afternoon and the area was covered in snow. I found the house, a two-storey residence that was to be my home during my stay. After a few days, I started doing small jobs. I shovelled snow around houses that were due to be occupied on the weekend, took care of gardens and did many small maintenance jobs that were needed.

In my free time I started making carrot muffins with organic ingredients, delivering them to various health food stores that were popular in the area. I didn't make much money with the muffins but the activity kept me busy in slow times and gave me the opportunity to meet a lot people.

Russell had put together a kind of small commune. He was a very practical man and had taken part in many communes during the '70s, when the idea of creating a new social structure had first surfaced. He was used to living with others and was very charismatic. But neither he nor the other sannyasins tried to create a space of meditation in the house. And this, I missed. Even though they were all Osho sannyasins and very likeable, they never ventured outside the limits of jovial, conventional communal living.

After a month or so, I called Elizabeth in order to check on how she was feeling and to suggest a meeting. It was not any easy call. She was still very angry about how she had been treated and, as I'd already experienced, this turned her against everything. She lumped everything together: the Ranch, Osho, life in the commune and our relationship.

Like dry wood she piled it all together into one big bonfire on which she wanted to burn the whole experience. She felt deeply betrayed and my attempts to heal the wounds and see her again proved fruitless. I was sorry for how things had gone and wanted to heal the rift, but she asked me not to call for a long period. She would let me know when her wounds were healed. I agreed, not knowing what else to do.

From any normal social or moral perspective, she was right to feel betrayed. But I was standing on other side of a 'grand canyon' and couldn't communicate my advice not to close off from Osho just because of one isolated event. A Master always puts his disciples to the test before bringing them closer. Gautama Buddha asked people who wanted to be his disciples to wait two years, and if after two years they still wanted to be initiated, then he might accept them. But Elizabeth had never met Osho and had never felt his love; this made it difficult for her to understand.

Meanwhile, I continued to do odd jobs, while maintaining my small production of muffins. One afternoon, my friends in Incline told me there would be a party about an hour's drive from our house, where other sannyasins were living. So, five of us left for an evening that would change my future once more.

We arrived late in afternoon when there was still light and the sunset colours were intense. The house was located in the high mountains, even higher than ours. It was spacious and had large windows that allowed you to admire the spectacle of forests and distant valleys.

The owner was an American sannyasin who lived there with his wife, an English woman who had taken sannyas in London. She had an accent that was so English it seemed she was living more in England than America. They were a peaceful couple, living a quiet life. Everything was very organized and orderly, with simple wooden furniture. They'd decided to make a party, to bring together the many sannyasins living in the area. I had no idea there were so many sannyasins around, so I was very pleased.

Ghuen, the owner of the house, was a professor of sociology at the University of Reno. When he wasn't teaching, he spent most of his time in his house in the mountains, writing books. The people who came to the party were mostly well-educated and cultured, including my friend Russell, who was currently making money by doing service jobs but in fact had a university degree. I felt at home in this atmosphere and spent a very pleasant evening, enjoying dancing, drinks and food, then more dancing... all of which seemed to be closer to the energy of the Master than our little commune at Incline.

I talked a lot with Ghuen. He was interested in alternative healing and wanted to know everything about the kinds of therapy we'd been doing in Pune One. He himself had never been to India and had seen Osho only at the festivals, which had been a regular feature of the Ranch calendar over the last two years.

Ghuen had an attractive presence, calm and serene, with a shambling gait. I thought I was tall, especially when compared to most Sicilian men, but Ghuen towered above me at the dizzying height of 6'6". He had blue eyes, wavy hair, already with flecks of grey in it – although he was only a few years older than me – and in his manners seemed more English than American.

His hunger for knowledge was enormous and we spoke a lot about Osho. For him, it was a love that was just blossoming and we decided to meditate together at his house, since there was no meditation space with Russell. As for the rest of the evening, the party was simple and fun, and in addition to the strong rapport created with Ghuen I enjoyed meeting new sannyasins.

We met again after a few days, when I went again to their house to meditate. Besides Ghuen and his wife, there were two of their friends, so there were five of us. We did Kundalini Meditation together, followed by 40 minutes of Vipassana. Ghuen was not teaching during this period and we saw each other frequently, meditating and chatting at length about various healing techniques.

One day, he mentioned an acquaintance who lived in a nearby town, a very interesting man who was a retail dealer for all kinds of healing machines. We decided to visit him. After a brief drive through the forest, we arrived at his house. A man of about 35 opened the door, with long, straight blond hair and a smile on his face that showed little that was false and a lot that was joyful.

John was typically American in the way that he was living his alternative lifestyle, keeping up with all the latest inventions in the field of physical health. He had a full-on program: eating vegetarian health foods, going to the gym, doing yoga and drinking water from a filter system that later became famous but few knew about at the time – the reverse osmosis filter.

From that time in 1984 until today, I have always filtered my drinking water with this system, and have always recommended it to my patients. John told us about the studies of an engineer who had created a machine for testing the vitality of liquids, and this also later became one of the instruments used in my medical practice.

In short, John was a well of fascinating information and we stayed the whole afternoon and the evening with him. He explained all the systems he knew for maintaining good health, including organic farming. It was pleasure to meet him and share his enthusiasm for health.

When we entered his house, I was struck by the space he was living in. It was a large one-room space with big windows, full of light. Everything was arranged on tables in a careful way with many machines glittering and shining – some of them really strange ones – and every corner contained a different kind of equipment. I felt like I was in the house of a mad scientist from the future. It was really a pleasure to be with him, and both Ghuen and I were delighted to share John's enthusiasm.

"Now I want to show you a machine that I think will be a good business in the future," he announced.

He took us to the end of the big room. Situated on a platform was a beige armchair with an extension to support your out-stretched legs, permitting the body to extend itself in an almost horizontal position. It seemed like a simple armchair, but on one arm there was a control panel similar to a TV remote that put into action a mechanism contained in the back, consisting of two rotating rollers. These rollers would give a massage along the entire spinal column, from the neck to the lower back. It could also focus on any one area of the back for a more in-depth massage. The chair was known as a shiatsu chair, as the technique used in the massage was akin to that used in shiatsu, an ancient healing modality that has its roots in Chinese medicine.

Both Ghuen and I tested it out, fascinated by the idea of being massaged comfortably and effectively at home. After ten minutes in the chair, I did, indeed, feel significantly more relaxed.

John told us he wanted help in marketing the armchair because it wasn't well known and this – in his view – was the ideal time to conquer a new market and make good money. He offered us, if we wanted it, a regional sales territory stretching from California to Texas. He would give us 33 per cent of the sale price, which was $900.

The idea was exciting to us and we returned to Ghuen's house talking the whole time about profits, organization and advertising. At the time, there was no internet, no web pages through which to make something known in the whole world while staying at home. It was necessary to find another way to promote the chair.

Ghuen and I met several times over the next few days and finally decided to create a company in order to show the chair in exhibitions taking place on the West Coast that were promoting health, exercise equipment and so on. From there we would decide how to proceed with the sales.

Ghuen became the president of the company, which we called Health Promotion. I became the vice president. John would be our wholesale supplier, and the more chairs we sold the bigger the discount we would get. But first we needed to buy a chair for ourselves, for displaying at shows. We put up the money for the first chair and for incorporating the company, which meant going to an office and paying $30 to get a license. In a few hours, we had a real company with certificates, registrations and so on.

This experience went a long way to compensate for my previously negative view of America. I really liked the ease and speed with which things could be done, which was light years away from the complicated Italian bureaucracy. American society really offered the opportunity to make money without obstacles, without putting a stick in the spokes of your bicycle wheels. All you needed was the right attitude: "It's easy, just go for it!"

So Ghuen and I found ourselves in partnership, him a university professor, me a doctor, selling armchairs that massaged the back.

Wow! Moreover, we could legitimately write on our business cards, "Professor so-and-so...and Doctor so-and-so...." What a coup! The people who saw the chair immediately had confidence in our product. When asked if we were really a professor and a doctor, we explained that our chair was a work of art for self-healing and that it had convinced us to leave our professions in order to spread the wellbeing to others – and to make money, although we kept the latter motivation to ourselves.

So that was how I became an American businessman. After two or three months of cleaning houses, I now found myself with a product, a partner, a business plan and the possibility of making a lot of money in a short time. I left my friends at Incline, who continued with their jobs agency for several years to come. Ghuen and I became travelling salesmen. Ghuen's wife went back to England because she wanted to be close to her daughter from her first marriage, whom she hadn't seen for a long time. So their house served as our base, somewhere to go when we had a gap in our travels.

We arranged to participate in a series of shows and business fairs of various types in California, Nevada, Arizona and Texas. We travelled a lot and, for the first time in my life, I discovered the 'do-it-yourself' motel. When we had finished working in the evenings, we often went to these motels. All you had to do was put in your credit card and the door of the room opened automatically and you slept there and left in the morning without seeing another human being.

We started with health fairs, which in America were really popular, and we soon understood that our business would work. We were an odd couple and we had a lot of fun selling our chairs. From the competent and scientific answers we furnished, our prospective clients soon got the message that we were businessmen of a much higher quality than the average snake oil salesman or hawker of holy healing water.

We believed in our product and we enjoyed working together. So the success of our enterprise was guaranteed. In fact, we sold more than a hundred shiatsu chairs in the first six months. Ghuen never felt competitive with me, knowing that in a year's time I would leave the company, because my priority was to be with Osho as much as possible. He, on the other hand, was interested in developing an alternative income that would give him more free time to write books on health. His contract with the university was limited and a permanent teaching position would be possible only many years later.

We had some great adventures. We often passed through the Arizona desert in the evening, giving us the chance to see spectacular sunsets and the silent passage of the moon. In Los Angeles, near Disneyland, we stopped for ten days for a show featuring interior decoration. Working like crazy kids and inspired by Minnie and Mickey Mouse, we sold something like 22 chairs at this one show.

But it didn't always go like that. Sometimes we spent days sitting in squalid places, neon lights jarring the senses, without a single chair being sold. Sometimes we found ourselves in small theatres watching body builders show their muscles and women jumping around in aerobic dances. Other days, in enormous spaces packed with furniture, with thousands of people filing by in front of our booth.

Few were our days of rest in the house in the mountains. In time, we invested more, buying more chairs at a better price, to the delight of John, who was happy the business was going well. After many months, Ghuen's wife came back from England with her daughter; on a couple of occasions they accompanied us to fairs in California.

For almost a year, I lived in this dimension where everything seemed to be flowing and producing money. Ghuen was satisfied, but he started to feel sorry that he wasn't able to spend much time with his wife and he was worried this might ruin his relationship. So we slowed the pace of our travels, which in any case were bringing more income with less effort.

After about ten months of work, I counted my money and decided it was enough for me to go back to the Ranch. It wasn't easy for me to tell Ghuen that I was leaving the business we'd created with so much joy and enthusiasm. Nonetheless, I had to go; the pull was strong. So I went out of the business and left the Sierra Nevada mountains.

The calendar now announced that it was March, 1985, and I was returning to the Ranch for my fourth attempt to stay in the commune. This time I had a Green Card, money and even an American driver's license. I saw no obstacle ahead of me in my desire to be with the Master. I was wondering what things might be invented this time in order to put me out again.

❏❏❏

21 The Dream Ends

I went to the offices that had felt so unfriendly in the past. This time I talked with a very sweet young woman. I told her about my three tries that had failed when I'd been rejected by her 'colleagues' and explained that now I had all the prerequisites for staying which had been requested – money and all the documents.

There was no judgment in her eyes, neither about my story nor about the commune. She understood all the effort I'd made and welcomed me with a big smile to the permanent workers program of the Ranch. In addition, she said I would be accepted as an official resident after a few months. Once I became a resident, I would be protected as part of the commune.

Then I was sent to another woman who asked me what I would prefer to do; I told her I had an American driver's license and wouldn't mind driving a bus. After a few seconds of looking at my commune experience, she said it was better that I go into the kitchen to cook once more.

"You're Italian and you cooked for Deeksha in Pune; this is great, we need good cooks here."

So again I found myself in the commune kitchen, but this one was a far cry from the one in Pune. Here the rooms were large, spacious and well lit in every section of the kitchen –the cooking area, the pastry area, the potwashing and dishwashing sections, the vegetable cutting area and so on. Everything was gigantic in relation to Pune, where it all had to be crammed into a fairly small area.

Adjoining the kitchen was the dining area, a space that could seat a thousand people. In the other part of this great barn, behind the kitchen, there was a big room with modern ovens for making bread and pastries. This was one of the commune's specialties, with a steady production of croissants and confectionery from various countries that helped the workers forget their fatigue. Connected to this structure was another building with big rooms that served as the dishwashing area. They were all lit with bright lights and big windows on two sides.

I went to work immediately and after a few days they left me alone with two enormous pots. I was given *carte blanche* to cook as I wanted, unlike the Pune commune where there was always a controller...and someone to control the controllers...and so on.

I had to choose the menu, order the ingredients and be ready for the next day. I was not the only cook during the day, but when it was my turn to cook I had to organize everything by myself. This was made possible thanks to two gigantic electric pots, about five feet high and made of aluminium, which I could move electronically in any direction. There were stoves set against another wall where I could prepare the different kinds of grains that we cooked every day.

Basically, we had a daily menu of tofu, brown rice, unfertilized eggs from our own chickens, lots of fresh veggies and huge amounts of salad that we grew on our truck farm down by the river. In the big pots we cooked the main dish of the day. To the right of the great pots were racks that occupied about 13 feet of wall space, stacked with every imaginable spice, including all the Indian ones, which was to be expected given the presence of many Indian sannyasins on the Ranch.

The kitchen was called Magdalena and to me it seemed like a futuristic mega-space...everything was so modern...I'd never seen anything like it before. Cooking here was a lot less stressful than in India, but still, working in the kitchen was one of the toughest jobs in the commune because you were always under pressure. Breakfast, lunch and dinner were three fixed times in the daily work schedule that affected the whole commune and there was no respite or postponing. The food had to be ready on time.

I lived in a trailer far from the kitchen, at least six miles away on a partly paved road, and when I woke up to start work at five in the morning it was like finding myself on the moon at night. The desert was rich with the sounds of animals that were unknown to me, including snakes that had always lived there happily. The most dangerous were moccasin snakes that could be fatal, but more common was the rattle snake that made a sound like little bells with its tail.

There were scorpions as long as your index finger and many different birds that flew high and alone in these ancient desert skies. Often I had the chance to see deer or antelope running in the early morning or at sunset. With time, they were becoming friendlier toward these strange creatures arriving from all over the world, who were busy 24 hours a day constructing this city in the middle of the desert.

I decided to buy a mountain bike, dark blue with many gears – I never counted how many – which made it easy to go up and down the hills and arrive at the kitchen in a joyful way, in time for my shift. Thanks to my success as a massage-chair salesman, I was now a resident of the City of Rajneeshpuram, happily roaming around on a blue mountain bike in the Oregon desert.

The work was intense and it didn't leave me a lot of time to socialize. Besides, in that period I didn't have much interest in the opposite sex and spent my days happily between work and the 'drive-by,' in which I could see the Master in all his bliss and beauty, and the rest of the time I spent by myself.

In that time of living at Incline and then on the Ranch, after the separation from my wife, my sexual energy hid itself in the maze of my chakras. I entered more in contact with my 'inner woman', finding joy in taking care of myself in my free time and meditating in my room, among the wild sage bushes that surrounded my trailer home. It was a period of wellbeing – a feeling that kept expanding. It had taken me three-and-a-half years of continuous effort to become a resident at the Ranch, and now I was starting to relax deep inside myself.

I felt good alone. The nature that surrounded us at the Ranch was very nourishing. Nature in general, more or less wild, always was an energetic food for me from the time I was a child, when our family went to spend the month of September in the countryside at some property my father had in the middle of Sicily.

Every day at the drive-by, Osho lavished his disciples with more energy and stayed longer with the crowds that were dancing and playing music along the roads under the scorching sun. We were all happy to see our Master and delighted in seeing how much strength he had gained during his stay on the Ranch. Clinically speaking, I think his body was really nourished by the hot sunny days and the dry nights. His bones, the herniated disks and his breathing surely benefited from the desert climate in these years.

In the meantime, the Ranch continued to expand. The little airport was given a bigger runway and a terminal building. Construction was completed on the hotel, a disco, a nursery and a big two-story mall in the centre of town, which now held restaurants, boutiques, a bank, a travel agency, and many of the community's offices. The therapy groups were filled with people arriving from all over the world. And the legal department was also expanding at a frenetic pace, fighting lawsuits involving local ranchers, land-use watchdog groups, the county, the State of Oregon and the US Government itself.

County elections were coming and Sheela made a move that for me represented the beginning of her decline and the decline of the Ranch itself. She wanted to ensure the results of the election were in our favour, but a large percentage of us living on the Ranch were foreigners who couldn't vote.

So Sheela created a program which I call the 'harvest of the homeless', which totally upset the equilibrium of the Ranch. She sent sannyasins around America with buses to collect hundreds of homeless people – those living in the streets without any money, any home, or any property whatsoever. She called it the Share-a-Home program.

America is full of homeless people, especially in its big cities. When I was in New York the contrast was shocking to see: fancy cars and big limos in downtown Manhattan passing by the homeless rummaging through garbage bins on street corners, hoping to pick up something to eat, or sell.

So Sheela sent sannyasins to collect these people, offering them a roof over their heads in Rajneeshpuram. Many of them accepted, preferring to jump into the unknown rather than live a life of hardship on an empty stomach. So they started to arrive at the Ranch in busloads. They were washed, disinfected, given new clothes and medical care, and housed in large new trailers purchased just for them. For them it was as though they'd died and gone to heaven.

But obviously they were not meditators. The basis of our communal lifestyle was meditation, the spiritual search and our love for Osho, our Master and spiritual guide. We had already worked a lot on our sexuality and our anger, spending months or years working with our emotions, feelings and conditioning through different kinds of therapy.

Till the homeless people arrived, there was never a single crime committed in City of Rajneeshpuram. To journalists it seemed impossible that in three years there had never been a crime, small or large, never a rape, never a theft, never a mugging, nothing. This was our home, we were one big family of seekers. The doors to the houses were left open, the offices had no security, cars and machinery were left out in the open, women walked alone even in the middle of the night to get to their trailers.

It was difficult for these homeless people, carrying the weight of the rough lives they'd left behind, to integrate themselves into our community. With their arrival, the first problems arose in regard to the molestation of women, small thefts and the lack of respect for our meditation structures. As more of them arrived, the air of tranquillity at the Ranch was more and more disturbed.

About two thousand homeless were catapulted into the commune within just a few weeks. They wandered around in the streets without understanding what this place was about, or who these red-clothed people were, who lined up every day to wait for a Rolls Royce driven by a man with a long white beard – and then broke out into wild dancing at the sight of him.

A few of them adapted and established good relations with our women and with the rest of the commune, some even took initiation, but most were comparable to white flies in a hive of industrious bees – they didn't have any connection to us, or have any way to hook up with what we were really doing there.

It was at this time that Sheela lost it completely, as far as I was concerned. She lost control of her greed, and started to justify completely absurd actions to obtain not only control of the county through the elections, but also tighter and tighter control of the commune itself.

I wasn't part of the management team on the Ranch, so I don't know the details of the ugly manoeuvres Sheela used during that period, always with the justification to protect the Master. There was talk of attempts to poison the water supply in a neighbouring town, and of violent confrontations when she tried to isolate the most intimate members of Osho's circle, those living in Lao Tzu House. These were the people he wanted near him, the people who'd always been his real protectors.

But what I did see clearly was ruthless way that Sheela and her clan pushed away all those disciples who were not in agreement with them. For those who didn't like Sheela this was a very difficult time, when such people were either exiled to a remote job in a distant part of the commune, or simply ordered to leave, or refused admittance – as they'd done with me, assuming that since I'd been part of Deeksha's kitchen in Pune One, I was not to be trusted. Sheela and Deeksha never got along together.

In fact, Deeksha had left the Ranch early, soon after arriving from the castle in New Jersey, thinking she would be in charge or have a powerful position in the commune. Instead, she found a triumphant Sheela, who was beginning to build the great commune the Master wanted. In those circumstances, the egos of both women displayed all their greed, fighting for power until Deeksha left.

The Master has pointed out to us that it doesn't matter whether your body is male or female, the ego always has the same basic characteristics: wanting to possess, wanting to control and dominate others, by whatever means available. The means usually chosen by men is violence and force, while women usually resort to trickery; but the basic game is the same.

By the way, Sheela's attempt to take over the local county failed. Registration of new voters was blocked several days before the election, so that few of our new population of street people could vote. Shortly afterwards, a mass exodus of the once-again-homeless people began, as almost all of our new guests were encouraged to leave the Ranch.

To me, it was like being in a bad movie, a movie Sheela had dreamed up. This movie provoked inside many of us a sensation of shock, as if we'd been running happily along a magnificent tree-lined boulevard full of birds chirping, when all of a sudden we hit an invisible wall, a solid wall whose impact sent us into a deep state of confusion. That's how I felt when I entered the Ranch project in its last year, when it became more and more clear the organization was degenerating, elements of which could be seen from the very beginning, as I'd experienced first-hand with Elizabeth's unfortunate attempt to enter the commune.

In fact, Elizabeth didn't want to hear anything else about the Ranch or about Osho, and in the end she didn't want to hear anything more about me. Our phone conversations became more sporadic. And, of course, when news of the corruption and betrayal of the guru's secretary surfaced in the newspapers at the end of the Ranch, Elizabeth was even more convinced that her choice to abandon sannyas and Osho had been the right one.

Working in the kitchen, I didn't see what was happening around the commune, but during the meals I heard talk from sannyasins who were increasingly worried about what was going on. Rumours spread that some of the food at our annual summer festival had been contaminated, that a few people were seriously ill with intestinal infections, that all the departmental offices were bugged, with special operatives listening for subversive talk against Sheela...and a lot more gossip and speculation that started to make the atmosphere much heavier.

Nevertheless, the celebrations were beautiful and overflowing with people. I think the last festival had about 25,000 disciples in our big new meditation hall, sharing the silence of Osho, who didn't show any sign of concern about what was happening. The commune had become enormous, super-efficient, rich and densely populated. It was difficult to believe that behind all these achievements there were dark plots with roots deep inside the organization.

One day the Master decided to start speaking again, after nearly four years of silence. He began giving discourses every evening to a select group of disciples in Lao Tzu House. Videos of these discourses were then shown the following night to everyone in Buddha Hall, after work and dinner.

A few months later, Osho started giving morning discourses to the whole commune in Buddha Hall, and in the evenings agreed to give interviews to the press, using a room located in Jesus Grove, the cluster of trailer homes that was Sheela's headquarters. Many journalists from the American and foreign news media arrived soon afterwards, hungry for news coming directly from the guru. In this way, the centre of attention of the commune shifted from Sheela and began to revolve again around Osho, who little by little took upon himself the energy of guiding the whole commune.

Osho was beautiful during the press interviews, which we could watch on video. It seemed like the years of silence had changed his energy, refining it even more and making him more spacious and light, like a cloud in the sky. He made all the journalists laugh, even the most serious ones, who burst out in big belly laughs at the sharpness and subtlety of his reasoning. He caught them off guard, and helped them to laugh at themselves, with his jokes about their own beliefs and false morality.

The lion was taking back his tract of forest. The journalists were showing the whole world, through the interviews they were reporting to their news organizations, what the Rolls Royce Guru was really about.

When Osho started speaking to us all, in his daily discourses in Buddha Hall, his words were fire. He spoke a lot about doubt as a fundamental requirement for inner growth, saying that it is important to doubt everything because only with subjective experience can we create an energetic centre that will remain immutable over the years.

Then came the day when he roared like never before. He shouted that we were all behaving like sheep and that none of us had the courage to raise our voices against the vile things that were going on right before our eyes. He said that he no longer wanted sheep with him and, after having brought journalists from all over the world and put them in the front row, he denounced Sheela in a loud voice in public, exposing his secretary on whom he had bestowed so much power during his long period of silence. He said that she had betrayed the commune, manipulating the power she'd gathered by our consent, or to say it more accurately, our silence, manipulating the minds of his disciples for her personal enrichment.

He was pouring out lava for days and the lava was burning many of us, but above all it destroyed Sheela and her clan of greedy women who had been running the commune undisturbed, thanks to the silence into which the Master had withdrawn.

Osho publicly denounced his secretary and asked that her criminal acts be investigated. The flow of lava went through the whole commune and beyond, to the sannyasin communes around the world. The castle Sheela had built was dismantled and the joy, simplicity and happy celebration that were typical of Osho's neo-sannyas movement started to shine again.

Sheela and the women around her had already fled, taking with them a considerable amount of money. They left as soon as they had understood the Master was about to open the mouth of the volcano in order to sweep away human unconsciousness.

Osho continued to throw out fire and brimstone for days, giving interviews and public discourses in which he clarified what had happened in these years. He explained he had entered a state where it was impossible for him to communicate to the world and told us that the man we were seeing now with our own eyes was no longer the same person we had known in India.

His body was still alive, thanks to our love and our need to be with him, but he was in fact 'dead' and his body was now more an absence than a presence. He said that other enlightened ones had entered into silence and understood that if it persisted for more than 1000 days – I think that was the number – it wouldn't be possible to speak again, which was why he had interrupted his silence. And then, with all that we had done in those years, it was necessary for him to take the reins of the commune again.

Among other things, Sheela had tried to create the religion of Rajneeshism, publishing a red book with 'commandments' that were paraphrased sentences of the Master, spoken during his discourses. Her justification was that, in the United States, officially recognized religions enjoyed a lot of privileges, one of them being that we could remain undisturbed at the Ranch.

A few people believed this, but many of us remained sceptical. Osho had been speaking against organized religions his whole life, specifying that he'd done this in order to make sure there was no possibility of creating even the shadow of a religion after his death.

Instituting Rajneeshism was absurd; it was going to the opposite polarity of Osho's teaching. But the mind finds justifications for every malicious thing, as history has taught us millions of times with dictators, invaders and religious crusades. From time immemorial, man has killed his fellow man in the name of ideas that served to justify religion, false democracies, imposters and criminals of every kind, who used religious symbols and beliefs to manipulate the masses.

We had also fallen into this trap in order to justify acts that went against the teachings of Osho. We justified everything Sheela had done, saying that it served to defend us against our enemies, most notably the American government itself that didn't want us on its soil.

Of course, over the years there had been many sannyasins who rebelled against the excessive power of Sheela and her decisions, but they were systematically isolated and kicked out of the commune. In order to be near the Master, many of us had closed our eyes to all the absurdity that was going on right before our eyes. And now, in these very intense days, the Master was opening our eyes to the possibility that the mind had taken us on a path that was far from the existential truth.

The work in the commune continued as before and every department took care to keep moving forward, notwithstanding the fact that the big boss had left, along with her narrow-minded clan and many millions of dollars. Osho spoke and didn't stop, giving daily talks that shocked us because the words made us see our masks, our attachment to our personality. And still there was a lot of joy because our beloved Master had returned to guide the ship and we all felt calmer.

It was soon discovered that Sheela's people had installed listening devices in the bedrooms of people suspected of not being in agreement with her. Even Lao Tzu House was fully bugged, including Osho's room. Everything was in the control of the women in charge. As these things were exposed, we felt a sense of guilt for having put our lives in the hands of Sheela, who's paranoia had brought the commune to edge of the abyss.

Then one late-summer day they came in succession – the state police, the FBI, undercover agents and every other type of agency at the disposal of the government. In short, we found our commune full of cops who went around to the offices and houses investigating anything that was possible to investigate, and many things that were not. The once-fresh air of the high desert was getting heavier by the day.

I continued to pedal my blue bike every morning to the kitchen to prepare the daily meals. Meal times were when we could all meet and let off steam, talk about all that had happened in front of our eyes, and share the latest news and information. Meanwhile, Osho continued to throw gasoline on the fire as soon as it started to go out, as was his habit.

One afternoon in October, I was called to the main office, in a big building that was far from the kitchen. The energy was more frenetic than normal. It felt like the air was different, as if an event was waiting to happen. I had no idea why they'd called me, but when I was told that from this moment on I was an official resident of the Ranch, my heart jumped for joy. I hugged her and went to share the good news with my friends.

The office was on a little hill, overlooking the county road that went through the Ranch. From there you could see, along the length of the valley, the traffic of buses and cars coming and going from the Ranch. It was truly a beautiful city we had constructed in a few years.

But coming out of the office with my great news, there was no way to share anything because people were buzzing like bees flying around in every direction, both on the hill and down below. There was a big turmoil, people were running, people were calling on walky-talkies, cars were speeding down the road. Wherever I looked, there was a great frenzy. I'd never seen anything like it before; at the Ranch everything generally happened in a slow, calm way.

I spoke with a small group of sannyasins standing by the side of the road smoking, but no one had a clear idea of what was going on. Maybe it had something to do with the police? I got on my bike and started going toward the downtown area, following the flow of the crowd. Maybe I would understand something down in the city.

In the time it took for me to arrive, the situation was suddenly clear because everyone I met in the street was telling me only one thing: "Osho is leaving!"

Immediately, I started to pedal toward the airport, hoping to see the Master before he left. When I arrived, there were maybe a hundred people waiting for Osho. They confirmed he was leaving the commune for an unknown destination.

Then, in the distance, you could see one of his Rolls leaving a great cloud of dust along the road. It was him, he was arriving. Instruments materialized out of nowhere and everyone started to sing and celebrate for the pure and simple joy of seeing him, even though he was leaving. We didn't know anything about why he was leaving, but we burst out in spontaneous joy that was so strong that my heart broke into tears and I sang, sang and cried.

The crowd was making space so Osho could get out of his car and enter the privately hired jet aircraft, which in the meantime had arrived. Its cabin crew opened the door and lowered steps to the ground. In the confusion, amid the crying, pushing and singing, I found myself in front of the steps and saw Osho getting out of the car in front of me, less than a couple yards away – calm, serene, white beard waving in the wind, very slow, very beautiful, full of love, with a big smile.

He greeted us all with a long *namaste* and then slowly moved toward the steps of the plane, then turned towards us once more. We continued to dance wildly, happy to have been able to see him, even if only for a moment, before leaving. Before climbing the steps, he turned again and I was there, in front of him, a few feet away from his physical body which emanated an indescribable love, a big smile on his face, like a new-born baby finally receiving what he had asked for, enormous infinite eyes that emanated light in the form of pure love.

I looked at him, directly in the eyes. I cried, I cried for joy. I cried because he was going away. I cried because in the same instant they had made me a resident, after four long years of struggle, he was leaving. I cried because, beyond my personal story, that instant was worth a whole lifetime and I felt it with all my heart. That moment was everything and he looked at me and smiled and emanated pure love and I was completely there to receive it.

An instant, an eternity, an infinity of time, in which space no longer had any importance, in which everything I had lived before dissolved in a single atom of pure present – present filled with love, warm and nourishing, a moment totally alive. And again now, while I am writing, the same tears run down my face, the same tears still fill me with joy when I see him again inside of me, that fountain of love that was the Master.

He went up the steps slowly, like a lion that goes around his tree before sitting down, before taking his seat on that airplane that would take him on one of the most incredible stories of the twentieth century: *the arrest and imprisonment of the new Buddha*.

After two millennia, men would once again crucify Christ, without recognizing him, once again crucify him as a criminal in the midst of real criminals, exactly as they had done with Christ, with Socrates, with Mansur and with many other Masters who walked this planet, trying to raise the level of consciousness and transform human consciousness toward a more refined form of love and compassion.

The steps were retracted inside the plane. Osho stayed by the window watching us as we continued to dance and sing, drunk with love for this fortunate meeting, stolen from destiny and from life. Our eyes met again and again. And as in Pune, where we only spoke in silence, in the darshans I had in Chuang Tzu Auditorium, so it was now, after five years in which I had seen him only in a drive-by and only at a distance in the hall, our eyes met again and my heart melted in him and in his emptiness that was so full of love.

❑❑❑

22   Osho Arrested

The screen was gigantic, hanging at the back of the Buddha Hall. Every evening we met there after work in order to see the news. We were seated on the floor in a scattered away, astonished, watching American television giving information about our Master in jail, guilty of having spread love all over the world.

A few American sannyasins had suggested that Osho leave the Ranch until the waters calmed down, clearly not feeling safe with all the police, FBI and undercover investigators inside the Ranch. The idea was for Osho go to the house of a wealthy American disciple, far from the Ranch, in North Carolina on the eastern coast of America. There he could rest peacefully until the situation had calmed and justice had run its course. But the trip didn't go exactly the way these disciples thought it would.

As a matter of fact, once the plane had landed in Charlotte, North Carolina, dozens of police and agents were waiting with weapons pointed at him. *They chained his hands and feet* without any arrest warrant, arrested him and put him in jail. There was no reason for his arrest and our lawyers fought for days in order to stop this injustice, without succeeding. In the meantime, they had stripped him of his clothes and dressed him in a green shirt with blue jeans, all in very bad taste, and held him in jail for an indeterminate time.

The news media across America gave big headlines to the Rolls Royce Guru who'd been arrested so that his commune could be dismantled and the nightmare of the 'sex guru' brought to an end. The Puritan mind was happy to be rid of a man who could corrupt young people with terrible approaches to life like 'Love-Awareness-Joy-Celebration' and other teachings judged to be harmful to a society based on war and exploitation.

The first time we saw Osho dressed that way, chained and in prison, many of us burst out crying and Buddha Hall was transformed into one of those therapy groups held in the commune, where you let the sadness come out without holding back. It was unthinkable to see our Master-Superstar chained and in prison, and dressed so obscenely. We tried to understand how this could be our destiny, but above all, his destiny.

The police had used the illegalities carried out by his secretary in order to arrest Osho, as a way of cutting the roots of this beautiful international tree, from which grew the possibility of being able to live, men and women together, in a space of mutual respect and meditation. First they would arrest him, then find a criminal charge against him, and after poisoning him they would throw him out of America. In a word, they were simply saying, "No!"

Meanwhile, we continued our work in the commune at the same pace as before, and there was even more passion in the work, now that the Master was in prison. We were living in a state of suspense, as if in limbo. We didn't know anything and our lawyers didn't bring good news. We knew, however, that his cell was very small and that the lawyers had asked for a more decent one for him, but he had not yet been transferred.

We were informed that if he received gifts he would be legally obliged to keep them in his cell. Someone had the bright idea that, if we sent a lot of gifts, they would be forced to move him to a larger cell. So I and many other friends from all over the world sent flowers and other gifts to the prison in Charlotte for Osho. After a few days they moved him to the prison infirmary where there was more space and more care from the nurses, who really were very loving with him.

The situation, however, didn't get resolved and we continued our work, while the 'forces of law and order' continued their undisturbed investigations at the Ranch. The number of police personnel increased, while some sannyasins, stricken with panic, started to leave the commune.

One evening, we learned from a local TV station that Osho would be returned to Oregon to stand trial. From North Carolina our lawyers confirmed this, and said they hoped to get him released on bail as soon as he reached Portland.

To make the trip from coast to coast takes about five hours by plane. For Osho, however, this simple move lasted several long days in which he disappeared from public view. Not even his lawyers knew where he was much of that time.

They moved him at strange times, on unspecified days, taking him from one jail to another, without any trace of him being registered anywhere. We knew about it only when he reappeared in Portland – *thin, tired, exhausted and, as he himself told us much later, poisoned*. Then he told us they had intentionally caused difficulties and suffering during the moves, putting him in cells with disease-infected prisoners and others who could have done anything they wanted with him. Through all these days, his trip to Portland was intentionally and unnecessarily prolonged.

Later, when back in India, he told us that while being held in a jail in Oklahoma, they'd poisoned him with radiation that probably came from something contained in the mattress. In a short, when he reappeared in Oregon, his physical health was destroyed. Only then could his lawyers talk to him and learn of his mistreatment.

When he finally reached Portland, Osho was released on bail and returned to the Ranch. There his lawyers urged him to agree to a plea bargain to avoid prolonging the case. A protracted legal battle with the US government would surely put a huge strain on Osho's already weakened body.

There was no proof that Osho had committed a single crime. However, his lawyers knew there was no point in persisting with his claim of innocence. The federal authorities were determined to expel him from the United States and it was better for him to agree to a criminal charge, be convicted, pay the fine and leave America.

In the end Osho chose not to run the risk of further harm to his body by fighting the case. So, while clearly maintaining his innocence, he entered a plea to the charges of instigating and supporting illegal immigration into America. His lawyers made it clear that he was allowing the negotiation of a plea solely to end the case, so he could leave America. For this small charge he was found guilty, having to pay a fine of $400,000 dollars and leave the United States within 24 hours. Such a fine, for such a crime, had never been seen before.

We followed all these events sitting on the floor, in the evening in the Buddha Hall after work. Other details of this sad affair, including the poisoning, were recounted by Osho himself much later, when the effects started showing up in his body.

Initially, Osho returned to India, but when his own disciples were prevented from entering the country to see him, he embarked on a world tour, looking for somewhere new to start building another commune for his sannyasins. But wherever he went, no matter which country, pressure was applied from Washington to make sure he could not stay there.

In some cases, he was blocked right at the airport. For example, when his private jet landed at Heathrow in London, the pilot had to rest for the night, having flown the maximum number of hours permitted under international law for safety reasons. But Osho and the other passengers were not permitted to rest and wait in the first-class lounge. Instead, he was forced to spend the night in the airport jail.

This vagabond life went on for eight months during which Osho found respite in Nepal for a few weeks and then in Greece for less than three weeks. He was staying on the island of Crete, having just begun a series of new discourses to sannyasins who were quickly gathering around him, when one day the Greek police arrived to throw him out.

Since he was just a tourist, there was no need for a trial. They could just kick him out, using the accusation that "his talks were corrupting the minds of young Greeks!" It was the same accusation reserved for Socrates hundreds of years before. My congratulations to a country that obviously has not learned anything since then.

Finally, he was able to find a home in Uruguay, thanks mainly to President Julio Sanguinetti, who welcomed him and allowed his caretakers to rent a villa on the coast. There these 'inconvenient guests' could relax, while Osho's application for permanent residency was processed.

In this period, Osho gave a series of very beautiful discourses that are collected in three magnificent books on 'The Psychology of the Buddhas'. After two months, however, the American Government successfully forced the departure of Osho, by threatening to recall millions of dollars in loans to the Uruguayan Government if he was allowed to stay.

In July 1986, eight months after having left the Ranch and having meanwhile flown around half the world, he returned again to India, landing in Mumbai, where he was a guest in the villa of an Indian sannyasin near Juhu Beach. From that date, my personal connection with the Master started. From that date until he left the physical body it would be my honour, my good luck – something I deserved or that just happened – to be near him and live a few metres from his energy field for the four remaining years of his life. But I will talk about all that later.

I stayed at the Ranch until the last days of December 1985, until the New Year's Eve of my fractured American dream. For the whole time Osho was in prison, the commune went on smoothly without a pause, but the more weeks that passed the clearer it became that the American government wanted us out, just as they wanted Osho out.

I have to say that there were no acts of violence against us while we were at the Ranch. Once Osho had been arrested, the pressure came off us all; we were now a sideshow to the main event. The state and federal investigators did their job of investigating and discovering all the shady deals Sheela had done, without disturbing the activities of the Ranch and without committing any physical or psychological violence against us.

This needs to be acknowledged. But obviously, with all that was happening, the commune was closing. Many sannyasins started to leave, letting go of a dream of constructing a city with the Master, based on joy of life and meditation. By the beginning of December we were already few in number, with only a cold and icy snow to accompany the farewell to our American Dream.

The dining hall became a meeting point and there we organized ourselves, individually or with friends, to leave for some temporary destination in some part of the world, waiting to see what would develop from these tumultuous events.

Many Americans who'd arrived during the Ranch's expansion were now so shocked they weren't talking about going to another commune. Instead, they simply wanted to return to their homes. I learned one thing about Americans: they are much more attached to their cosy lifestyle and familiar traditions than appearances suggest. It's all free and easy up to a point, but then a nationalistic rigidity kicks in, beyond which they just aren't prepared to go.

Many Europeans organized themselves into groups that would return to the communes in Europe - in Germany, Italy, England and elsewhere. Some organised communal houses in other parts of the world where they could stay together...in Hawaii, Brazil and so on, wherever the mood of the moment took them.

If a sannyasin knew a good place to go, others joined and organized a trip in that direction. Many Europeans, for example, headed south to California, knowing they could meet their immediate survival needs by picking up service jobs in affluent areas. But I almost never saw American sannyasins planning a future for themselves in India, or in Europe, or anywhere outside the US, to stay within the energy field of the Master.

They were enthusiastic about building the dream in the 'promised land' and they'd arrived in thousands to lend a hand. But once the dream vanished the majority of them disappeared from the circle of disciples near the Master.

Looking back, it's clear the Ranch transformed itself into an experience of purification. It was a point of departure for those who were near the Master not out of love, but for their own personal interests, for their ideology, for their psychological motives, for the beauty of living together and building their own future with their own hands, for the pleasure of being with a group of people who were joyful and happy, where the energy flowed like a great river.

Or perhaps they'd been attracted by all the beautiful women in the commune...and who knows what other motivations drove thousands of people to come close to Osho during the American period.

Afterwards, many started to criticize Osho, finding mistakes he had committed and speculating about how things could have gone differently. And many started to judge the silence Osho had kept, suspecting that he knew everything that was going on during the years that Sheela was concocting things.

I didn't have an answer because I didn't have questions. If it all happened with Osho present, for me it was going well. I knew the limits of my own consciousness and the poor vision I could have in respect to the Master. I didn't trouble myself with finding alternatives to what was happening.

So I continued to work and to see others depart. I continued to see the Ranch empty out, not just of people and things, but also of energy, joy, celebration, music, silence created in meditations....

With the Ranch covered with snow, more and more federal agents arrived by helicopter. The Ranch was transformed into a kind of military base, a camp that was crisscrossed continually by jeeps and other vehicles. Many offices started to close, as did restaurants and shops, and many trailer homes were abandoned. The city that had been built in a few years was dismantled, taking apart the dream we had lived with Osho.

In those years, Sheela had spent a tremendous amount of money to buy the property and build the city. Many disciples, convinced this was the definitive project, or simply because they loved Osho, gave a major part of their wealth to the commune. Houses were sold all over the world by individual disciples in order to give the proceeds to the commune.

When the Ranch closed, many of those who had given huge sums of money to support this dream felt betrayed and robbed. And so they never came back to the Master and his next stage of work in India. It seems to me that their giving was not without expectations, and I am reminded of a story I once heard from Neelam, Osho's Indian secretary after Sheela. This is what I remember of her story:

Before Neelam became a disciple in the '60s, her husband knew Osho and participated in meditation retreats with him. After a while, he tried to persuade his wife to come and meet the guru with whom he was infatuated. She wasn't interested. She only wanted to be a wife and mother.

For Westerners who will read this account, it is worth mentioning that almost everyone in India has a guru to consult or worship. Whatever your caste or social status, rich or poor, businessman or farmer, you had access to some kind of guru. Even today, though India has evolved socially and economically, Indian families all have their guru, with whom they consult when it's time for the daughter to marry, or for advice on investment decisions or other important matters.

The First Door that I mentioned in this book, the door of devotion, is an experience grounded in centuries of understanding for Indians, who don't have a problem with kneeling on the ground and touching the feet of a person in whom they recognize a spiritual quality.

So Neelam assumed Osho was just one of the many gurus who went around India giving advice to people, with no special quality, and she didn't feel attracted to this world. But, after many months of persistence on the part of her husband, she agreed to go and see Osho.

At that time Osho used to lead meditation camps, experimenting with various meditation techniques that he subsequently developed and perfected, and which were ultimately used in the commune from 1974 onwards. During breaks between his discourses and the meditations, many Indians got in line to receive his blessings, including not only those participating in the meditation camp but also people passing by, who, realising a guru was available, would stop to touch his feet.

Neelam got in line with her husband. When it was her turn, she fell at Osho's feet, almost fainting, and remained there for a long time. She was utterly stunned by the force of the Master and from that moment stayed close to him. Even after Osho's death, Neelam stayed in the Pune commune for nine more years, then left to construct a new meditation centre close to Dharamshala, in the Himalayas.

In India, it is a tradition that when you find a Master you bring him a gift as a symbol of your recognition. Neelam and her husband spent days thinking what they could give him, and in the end they decided to bring him a diamond ring that had belonged to her mother and her mother's mother. It was the most valuable and precious thing she had, and she wanted to send a signal to Osho that her devotion was total.

So at the next meditation camp they brought the famous family diamond. Neelam got in line with the others and when her turn came she kneeled down to touch the feet of the Master, then gave him the box with the diamond in it. Osho looked at it, brought it near to him and blessed Neelam by touching her head. She moved away in order to give space to the next person in line, who was a passer-by, like many others who were taking advantage of the situation in order to receive blessings from the guru. This man was not one of his followers.

Osho also blessed him, and then gave him the diamond he had just received from Neelam! The man was there only by lucky coincidence, and he was given her precious diamond! Neelam was very shocked by this incident but nevertheless continued in her devotion to the Master.

About twenty years after the ring incident, Osho reminded Neelam of the gift of the diamond. He told her, "If you give an object to someone as a sign of love, you need to totally let go of it, otherwise it is just an attempt to tie that person to you." He had waited almost twenty years to make sure the teaching was understood, then closed the circle by explaining the message behind his act.

For thousands of people – whether they had money or not – the Ranch experience was one huge opportunity to see their attachments and their desires. It was another chance to be total in giving, in love, without expecting anything in return.

Real love is in fact a gesture that manifests naturally in the fullness of the heart – the heart full of nectar, full of joy in sharing, full of divine energy that isn't personal, a heart that overflows and shares with everyone without discrimination.

The Master, by the simple fact of his being, like the sun or the stars, lights the way for those who open their hearts to this light. His giving is not an intentional act; he's not thinking, "Now I will work on Tom, Dick and Harry because they need to change their attitude toward life, or because they need to open up to love." Osho simply let the energy flow, interfering in the stream of events as little as possible.

With this in mind, it becomes clear that all the criticisms that were levelled at Osho after the Ranch were just hollow words blowing in the wind. From the standpoint of the growth of human consciousness, it didn't matter that Osho committed practical errors, because, as he himself said: "I am not God! I am a human being with his limits."

This needs to be remembered, because many people expected Osho to be infallible, that he should have seen the future and interfered to save his commune. But all these ideas were just a projection of the mind of individual disciples who imagined that their Master was a special being like God, mainly because it satisfied their egos.

Osho perhaps made errors in calculating and anticipating events, but this doesn't take anything away from his message, his teachings and his energetic presence. The change that is experienced with a Master happens through work done by the individual, by the lone disciple, on himself. It is for this reason that the spiritual path is a solitary path, because it depends totally on us – how much energy and awareness we put into the process of transformation.

If the disciple is closed, a real Master cannot do anything, while a false master may try to persuade or push the student toward change according to the direction he thinks is right. Osho, Lao Tzu, Krishnamurti, Gurdjieff, Chuang Tzu, Socrates, Saint Francis, Buddha, Mahakashyapa and all authentic Masters have never forced anyone. They never promised anything to their disciples; they simply remained available, and whoever was alert enough could feel the fragrance of their spirit.

Of course, disciples who lived through the events that took place in the commune while remaining identified with their own vested interests, their own ego attachments, could only suffer feelings of betrayal. But the Master, in his compassion, never compromises.

In August, 1986 at Juhu Beach, Mumbai, when he started talking again, after having flown the skies of the planet and been in half-a-dozen jails, Osho declared: *"Now I finally have my disciples.* I have had to dirty my hands working in the mud for decades, looking for my real disciples. Now that the base of the temple has been built I will raise the temple for all my real disciples, those alive now and those coming in future generations. Like a fisherman who throws his net, I am now pulling it up, and I find myself with the people that remain with me because they are my real disciples."

When he pronounced these words we were crammed in the living room of the Indian disciple who offered his house to the Master. We were about forty people, of which only five or six were Westerners, and the rest Indians. In the following days, slowly, day after day, many old sannyasins arrived, and in the space of six months hundreds of devotees came back to the feet of the Buddha, having passed through one of the most intense spiritual devices ever to take place on such a scale.

On January 4th of 1987, we returned to the old commune in Pune in order to live with him the last three years of his stay in the physical body, constructing – as he himself said – a temple. But it wasn't a temple in Pune. It was far, far bigger than that. It was a temple where thousands of people continue to arrive every year, regardless of age, social class or nationality, in order to continue to construct:

"The first temple in history that doesn't have walls, that doesn't have a structure, that doesn't have hours for entering or leaving, that doesn't have priests, popes or spiritual leaders who indicate the 'right' path, manipulating your life and conditioning your expressive potential. The first temple that doesn't have ceremonies, that doesn't have limits of time and space, that doesn't assert anything, that leaves every single individual to grow on his own path, in his own time and with his own errors, respecting to the maximum

the life of every single disciple, without asserting any commandment or rule to follow, that doesn't have the excessive seriousness found in all the organized religions, but rather is based on the celebration of life in all its manifestations, including death.

The first non-religion that teaches the religiousness of life, of the mystery, of the magical and the divine that is inherent in every being, in every tree, in every grain of sand and in every galaxy that exists.

The first religious teaching that gives to its disciples a blank sheet, where everyone can write their own life, choosing the direction that suits them, respecting above all themselves, loving first of all themselves and exalting the inherent qualities of the individual.

The first Master that passed through this planet and left behind him a space that was absolutely empty, without any trace of organizational, religious or spiritual structure. "I am like a white cloud," he said one day and, "in this chair you see a body but inside there's only emptiness. I am a window from which you can see the divine, you can experience that the divine exists, you can know what's possible."

The first temple that doesn't have physical walls because it resides in the heart of men, in every single person that wants to raise himself from the quagmire of the mind in order to plough the skies of awareness and bliss."

▫▫▫

23 Leaving America

That final winter on the Ranch was hard and cold, the snow turning to ice in the night and the mercury going below zero. Every day the departments shrank in number. The lake was frozen, the airport wasn't functioning, and in the sky you only saw the police helicopters. The feeling was terrible. We felt invaded and violated and above all we felt alone without the Master, who in the meantime was experiencing harassment and abuse elsewhere.

In the space of about two or three weeks between November and December 1985, several thousand disciples left the Ranch. Those who stayed supervised selling off a great deal of what we'd gathered or built, while others did practical mechanical work, maintaining essential services, or were involved in collaborating with the police, who continued to find new intrigues on the part of Sheela.

By the end of November, I didn't know what had happened to my life. Many people thought that the whole story with Osho had now reached a definitive conclusion. For them, it was over. Not seeing any future organization, they organized themselves accordingly.

Among the people who remained was a middle-aged Italian woman who came to the kitchen every day to get some brown rice and a few raw vegetables. We'd known each other from the time of Pune One but had never become friends.

Pratiti had a powerful charisma and, leaving aside the fact that she didn't seem to care much about her appearance, she had a very refined energy, a presence that created an aura of respect around her. She had large black eyes that revealed a unique intelligence, a mixture of spiritual devotion and sharp scientific understanding.

Osho had spoken with her many times in private because she had created a big commune in Italy, and even today, after almost 30 years, it continues to expand. That is because of Pratiti. She died in 1986, not long after our meeting at the Ranch, but she created the Italian commune in such a solid way that Miasto is still one of the largest communes in the world.

After she approached me a few times in the cooking area, ignoring the self-service section, I understood she required special treatment. So, every day, I prepared a plate of rice the way she wanted it, with raw vegetables I chose especially for her. She walked slowly with her Birkenstock sandals open to the winter cold, taking her plate from the area where I worked and going to sit in the main eating area.

One day, she told me she wanted to speak to me. We had breakfast together in the big hall. Her eyes were very alive, as if a small light was coming from the pupils, illuminating an inner world that could manifest only through the long silences between her sentences. I liked her a lot. With her, I felt the space of meditation. I felt the emptiness of the Master had penetrated her.

The calm presence of this intelligent woman, above all when she was examining her own thoughts like a dissecting surgeon or Tibetan lama, reminded me more of the energy of Gurdjieff than that of an Osho disciple. She was definitely an explorer of the depths of the soul and had done a lot of work on herself. At a certain point, she told me calmly that she was on this diet because she had a tumour and didn't want to treat it with ordinary allopathic medicine. She was under the care of an Indian doctor in London, who was also a disciple of Osho, and who was treating her with alternative techniques. She thanked me for the care I gave without her asking for it.

Pratiti told me about a dream that she wanted to realize before she died. She wanted to create a 'holistic clinic' where healing was carried out through acupuncture, homeopathic medicine, Tibetan medicine and old-style traditional medical practices of which she was an avid student. Not being a doctor herself, she wanted to find a doctor to work with to realize her dream. She told me she felt I was the right person to help her. I was amazed, surprised and gratified by this proposal.

We talked a long time, finding a particular rapport between our minds, which she seemed to have guessed just by looking at me. In the end, she told me she would be leaving after a few days and she invited me to Miasto, her commune in Tuscany, where I would be welcomed as a permanent resident. We hugged like two old friends who had just met after a long time. Her eyes were still shining as we parted, having made an appointment to meet in Tuscany as soon I concluded my work in the commune.

Once again, my future had taken an unexpected twist right before my eyes, without my having done anything in particular to make it go in that direction. I was convinced, along with many other disciples, that a big new international commune with Osho wasn't going to happen any time soon and the idea of transferring to a commune in Italy appealed to me. Why? First, because I would return to my native country after seven years of travelling the world. Second, because I would remain in the energy of a commune and the meditative space I could find there, without divorcing myself from external society. And third, because I now had the opportunity to start a clinic where I could express my own scientific creativity and my medical vision, which had always been holistic.

When I announced I was going to Miasto, a German friend wanted to come with me. He was a bodyworker and wanted to see if it was possible for him to give sessions or groups in the commune that had been born in Italy. So we decided we would leave together. We would go to Germany first, to get his car and rest for a few days in his mother's house, then drive to Tuscany.

A rumour was circulating that those leaving the Ranch had to have their names and nationalities recorded by the police who were stationed at the boundary of the commune. This didn't please us, so we looked for other friends with whom we could leave the Ranch at night without being disturbed.

One evening, some American friends told me they would be

leaving in a few days and would go to San Francisco, where one of them lived. They had one of those old Volkswagen vans that typified transport for young people in the hippie era.

I asked if we could join them in leaving the Ranch. They agreed and we made our plan: we would meet at the downtown shopping area around three in the morning a few days hence, and from there go on foot to the airport, where the van was parked. From there we would head for the snow-covered hills of the Ranch in order to reach the highway that would take us from Oregon to California. We hoped we wouldn't meet any roadblocks before leaving the land that had been ours up to now.

As we walked to the airport in the middle of the night, the deserted icy roads and closed offices gave the Ranch a very gloomy demeanour. We loaded our bags into the indestructible van. After a few tries it started, the sound of the old motor echoing through the valley.

We left slowly, full of emotion, soon reaching the Ranch boundary where the federal police might be waiting. But there were no living creatures to be seen. Everything was silent; nature was sleeping undisturbed in a deep dream of the night. We passed through the town of Antelope without any problems and by the evening of the next day we were in an apartment on the outskirts of San Francisco, all of us safe and snug in our sleeping bags.

I slept the whole night and when I woke up the big commune had disappeared. Before my eyes was a simple American suburb, with its houses and streets in good condition. We didn't lose time, my German friend and I, because the six of us couldn't stay together in this little house very long. So we started to look for tickets.

In less than a week we found ourselves at the San Francisco airport, boarding a flight to Frankfurt. Arriving at our destination, we took a train to the town where his mother lived in a very clean house with a garden and everything necessary for living a quiet, boring life. We stayed with her for three days. We ate a lot, slept a lot, and on the third day got in the car, a red Golf, and headed toward Tuscany.

Until this adventure I'd never been in Tuscany in my life. The landscape was completely different from the barren high desert we'd left behind in central Oregon. In marked contrast, we were now surrounded by woods and cultivated fields. Cypresses and so much green, with few houses, made this countryside an idyllic picture.

Miasto is about 20 miles from Siena and about 40 miles from Florence, tucked in a forest of oak. We arrived there in the afternoon, after driving on a dirt road for four miles. At the entrance were two rows of big cypress trees, which opened up into a large old stone edifice with a meditation hall on the first floor and bedrooms on the upper floors. In front, about 50 yards away, was the stone house where Pratiti and her close associates lived. Beyond that was an even bigger and older building, with offices on the ground floor, a kitchen on the first floor and rooms for workers above.

The buildings and surrounding land were aesthetically beautiful and very harmonious. From the tallest building you had a spectacular view toward Siena, with the Tuscan hills crisscrossing each other like in a Chinese landscape painting, range after range, rich with old houses surrounded by olive groves and vineyards. I liked it immediately.

Nevertheless, as I discovered very soon, the mood was very austere and serious, resembling a Franciscan monastery more than other Osho centres I had known. It was totally different from the crazy centre in New Jersey, which was much more relaxed, with a handful of eccentric women and lots of space for everyone to express their creativity.

The reception we received on arrival wasn't exactly welcoming. The people looked as though they had just come out of a meditation retreat where they had been in silence for several weeks, but in fact this was just a by-product of the office work they'd been doing all day. At the time, there were about 20 sannyasins living and working at Miasto and they all behaved in a serious and severe way, like good spiritual seekers who were doing something very important.

I saw Pratiti the day after my arrival and found her very tired and stressed compared to our meetings on the Ranch a month earlier. She told me she couldn't support me much in this project because of her precarious health and I would have to present my plans to the people who were in charge of running Miasto. So that is what I did.

After a few meetings, we decide we had to find a location in a nearby city or town, partly because we would be working primarily with people outside the world of Osho. We choose Florence because the commune had more contacts in Florence than in Siena. I moved to the city after a month of this convent life, where at night I'd been forced to creep into the basement to steal pieces of wood to light the stove, which they did not want to use in order to save money – with the temperature outside below freezing. And I was obliged to say goodbye to my German friend who, seeing how things were going in this gloomy place, returned to Germany to look for a centre that met his needs better.

I found myself living in an apartment in a suburb of Florence, but I spent my weekends in Miasto, having one meeting after another. I don't know why all these meetings happened, but I think it was because of Pratiti, who was very therapeutically-oriented in her approach to the commune, so everything had to be shared, discussed and analysed, just to decide that it was better to have another meeting later where the subject could be discussed in greater depth and reworked again.

For two months these meetings went on, with decisions being taken and then changed again in later meetings. The original project transformed itself into a financial absurdity in which they asked me to take on all the expenses and all the legal risks, while they would take most of the profit. It was the same as if they were asking me for a donation for all the work I had done for nothing.

The final meeting lasted until two o'clock in the morning and was filled with bitter discussions between all of them and me. It was clear they had never wanted to jump into this project. The idea was too new and too far beyond their scope of activity. Besides, they had no legal credentials for doing it. It was clear that the project was only a desire of Pratiti, whose health was getting worse and who couldn't participate or give clear directives. So I decided to leave the commune and go my own way. Pratiti died a few months later, and the managers and almost all the people who'd been working there slowly left Miasto in succeeding years.

Today the commune has completely changed, now managed by people whose minds are more open. Personally, I am sorry I met Pratiti so late. She was close to death and her energy was necessarily oriented toward the inner world, not toward projects or organizations that were ultimately of little importance to her.

Death is the real Master of life. It puts us directly in front of the mirror where our false images of ourselves are reflected and burned in the light of the real. Pratiti rightly spent the last years of her life going inside herself and spending most of her time far from the busy life of the commune. It was difficult to ask more of her and I wanted to respect her space as much as possible.

Even though our meeting was too late for her dream of a holistic clinic to be realized near Miasto, her intuition about me was correct because, exactly nine months later, I found myself setting up a multi-disciplinary alternative medical centre, at the direct request of Osho, in the last commune in Pune.

❐❐❐

24 Turning Point

After that long meeting, I left Florence and went to Siena, where a German sannyasin acquaintance put me up in her house. I threw myself into the search for a place where I could open my own medical practice and it all happened in a few days. I registered with the local medical association and in less than ten days opened my first private medical practice, where I practiced Homeopathic Medicine and Acupuncture. I think I was the first doctor in Siena to offer acupuncture and alternative medicine.

The clients who arrived were a bit suspicious, but happy with the results I produced. Many sannyasins in the area started to contact me for their medical problems and slowly the practice grew. It was April '86 and Osho was still travelling the world, getting kicked out of different countries or refused at international airports.

I had opened my first medical office and was thinking of staying for a long time. I found myself alone in the small city of Siena, surrounded by a medieval wall; it felt like being in a big family whose life revolved around the Palio di Siena, the famous horse race that takes place twice each year in the Piazza del Campo. I bought a minimum of furniture and threw myself into working in a society I'd abandoned almost ten years before, disgusted by the bad habits of the public hospitals.

To say the least, it felt strange. Having been in two big international communes with the Master, having lived many amazingly rich and adventurous experiences, having been near a living Buddha, having seen another Buddha – J. Krishnamurti – and having absorbed the light in the depth of their eyes, I was now living in a small apartment in an ancient citadel city that was successfully defending its cultural heritage from the invasion of modernity. I found myself sitting behind a desk, meeting and treating people I didn't know, who were coming to me and expecting something like a miracle.

At that time I knew Dr Franz Morell, the German-born creator of Mora Therapy, who was giving courses in Florence. I studied with him for five days. He was already very old and limping, but blessed with a mind that was pleasant as well as razor-sharp; he approached the subjects of chemistry and physics with disarming simplicity.

He gave a seminar that definitively changed my way of looking at medicine. If my paediatric experiences, and above all my meeting with Dr Leboyer, had consolidated my intuitive feelings about what I wanted to offer as a doctor —a simple and human relationship with the patient, through the heart— my meeting with Dr Morell opened up a theoretical and therapeutic perspective that I have carried with me ever since.

I became totally involved in my work. I lived with my German friend and her son, and often went to meet friends who were living in a big old building full of sannyasins about 20 miles from Siena. This place was run by two American therapists, Satyarthi and Anubuddha, who were conducting trainings nearby in Rebalancing and Rolfing, techniques for working with the body. They were disciples from the old Pune days, and after the Ranch had organised a series of trainings in Europe.

I knew everyone there and felt at home with them. They had real creative intelligence and a playfulness that only people who had been around Osho managed to have - joy and irony that made life bubbly and light like just uncorked champagne. In fact, a lot of champagne was circulating because these two therapists represented the 'Zorba side' of the Master. Often they had parties in the evening and friends from outside were always welcome.

One day, a woman who was an assistant in their Rebalancing trainings called me in my office because she was suffering from migraines. I gave her an appointment without any idea that this woman would change my life.

When she entered my office, I immediately felt the energy of the commune and the Master. Even though she was in pain from the migraine, her smile and her presence were intoxicating. I felt as though I was in a meditation hall where Osho was holding his discourses, so strong was her presence.

We had never met personally, even though I had seen her many times on the Ranch, in a Rolls Royce with the Master on his drive. She had been one of Osho's mediums in Pune One, one of the few women who were around him every evening in energy darshan, through whom he transmitted energy to the whole commune. And in the end, she was sometimes his lover on the Ranch.

I invited her to sit down and after a brief conversation started to take notes on her symptoms, but I had to make a monumental effort to keep myself present and upright, and not lie down next to her on the examination table. I tried to be professional and help her as best I could. I think Nandi really enjoyed our first meeting too, and she was so cordial, simple and maternal that my embarrassment slowly dissolved.

Nandi was German, tall, the colour of cream, with a round face and short hair that was chestnut red and reminded me of those Russian dolls with the big eyes that one saw in history books about old Russia. She had a strong and gracious beauty, with fingers that were long and slender in relation to her extremely beautiful body, very much like that of Monica Bellucci, the beautiful Italian actress.

As a man, having her in front of me was disarming because of the energy she was radiating. Of course she knew it, like all beautiful women know it, but was not egotistical about it. In fact, she succeeded in putting me at ease with her simple smile that made her even more beautiful, along with a deep sense of relaxation and fulfilment that I could sense in her whole body. She emanated a sense of fullness that I had never felt in any woman until now. I had only seen women so full and so complete after they'd given birth, holding their babies.

I advised her to change her diet, gave her a cure for draining fluids from her body and invited her to come for a series of acupuncture sessions. When she left I was pretty dazed and even today I don't know exactly what happened. I only knew that I felt a strong intimacy with her while pretending to be a doctor.

The next step, to spend the night together, came very soon. A few days after we met, as soon as I finished work, I took my old green Citroen, which seemed more like a frog than a car, and drove like a madman to meet her, feeling happier than I'd ever felt.

Life was showering on me in abundance. I was doing work I enjoyed and which seemed to give me long-term possibilities as a therapist, healer and doctor. I lived in the Siena countryside surrounded by the most beautiful views I'd ever seen and I'd just met a female goddess that had filled my heart and my soul.

I continued to live and work in Siena but stayed with Nandi at every opportunity. I also spent lots of time with the old friends who were living close by. They were inviting many other people to stay with them, including Neelam, who, as I've already mentioned, was soon to become Osho's secretary. Neelam, for Nandi was like a sister. Those times were wonderful and, as always seems to happen around Osho, those few months that I lived so intensely seemed to me like years.

I ate with them whenever I could, went to their parties and, more importantly, stayed with Nandi, who little by little introduced me to the magical world of the Master's personal life, with small anecdotes, jokes and memories of the commune. In the evening, we were often in Nandi's apartment, which was in an old village not far from where the trainings were held. We got together in her garden with the rest of our friends, sharing what sannyasins love to do together most: gossip.

Nandi was a kind of queen bee around which all the others were buzzing, so I found myself in the middle of a central hive. We didn't know anything about Osho yet, and while awaiting news we were celebrating life, as he had taught us to do.

Meanwhile, my work was expanding. People from North Italy were calling and I didn't know how they'd heard of me. I participated in other seminars and met colleagues who had an approach similar

MY LIFE WITH OSHO

to mine and with some I developed a deeper understanding and friendship. It was a period that was very rich, even though it was short. The medical and scientific component, as well as the emotional and spiritual, took a direction in those months that were like an incubator for the rest of my life.

Nandi's maternal quality was nourishing me, helping my male side to grow and embody more of its natural authority. Our relationship got better by the day and we had a sexual connection that was wonderful and sweet at the same time. The nights spent together without sleeping made me walk through the following day as if I had wings on my feet, keeping me well above the ground. My mind emptied and my heart was overflowing.

Having Nandi near me was like having a goddess at my side, transmitting love to whoever was nearby. Everyone loved her and she returned love continuously. I never knew if she was really 'in love' with me. She was so centered in herself that she was never emotionally off balance. But I felt her respect for me and that gave me hope, knowing that for women this feeling of respect is one of the first signs of love toward a man.

She didn't let herself go into emotions and sentimentality. Besides, she wasn't Italian but from Teutonic roots, and gave her attention equally to all the people who surrounded her, without making me someone special in her life. Nevertheless, we often spent our evenings and nights together and as time passed I felt her respect for me was growing. For me, being with her was like being under the influence of a psychedelic drug; the whole world was shining and full of colours.

When Neelam arrived in the village it heightened even more the sensation of living near Osho. She had an energy similar to that of Nandi, but her female side was more devotional than maternal. When she was speaking about Osho we all remained in silence, whoever was there, listening to her soft Indian voice describe the events she had lived with him.

She was with Kamaal, a German man and a therapist from the commune who taught hypnosis. He and I developed a close relationship because of our two queens, who were considered to be spiritual sisters and for whom we were the favoured ones. He was really funny and each sentence he uttered was an ironic joke about something or someone. He had a sense of playfulness that made one feel he was eight or ten years old.

Kamaal was really beautiful, tall, blond, with long straight hair and sky blue eyes. His face was square and long, resembling one of the characters in the comic strips of 'Nathan Never,' half-human and half-bionic, with a perfect body and an angelic face. As soon as he entered the scene he brought lightness and joy, jumping from one corner to the other, ready to do anything in order to amuse us.

Slowly, being close to Neelam and Nandi became familiar and natural. The presence of Kamaal helped me relax and not take anything seriously. Being the only Italian in the little group, I willingly took the initiative in resolving small problems that appeared along the way, such as finding good restaurants in the area and other places to frequent.

Happy months passed, full of joy, full of colour, full of friendship, full of the energy of the Master, full of femininity, both in the body and in the mind, which opened a new inner space for me.

Amid this atmosphere of friendship, Neelam never gave us any details of where Osho was, or where he would go next. Not wishing to intrude, we asked her nothing in this regard, but it was known that she was waiting for a call from the Master.

May, June and July passed. It was very hot that year and this was good for us, because the winter had been particularly severe, reaching temperatures well below freezing and destroying all the olive trees in the region of Siena and Florence. The sight of these trees, now burned by the bright sun after being frozen to death, hurt your heart. At about this time, the newspapers were full of stories about the explosion at Russia's nuclear plant at Chernobyl and for a few days all we ate was the food we had in the house.

For the rest of it, I remember those months as the happiest moments of my life. The body and spirit of Nandi nourished me and healed a deep wound from my childhood, a wound inflicted on me by the seriousness and rigidity in which my family had lived for years, thanks mainly to the authoritarian attitude of my father.

I was now living a rich life from every point of view and the most surprising thing, for me, was that this was happening without being in the communes of the Master, protected and cared for by his community. For the first time I was independent, I was working and having a social and personal life that was exceptional and satisfying.

In the communes we'd all been protected and sustained by the energy of Osho and the *Buddhafield*, which is to say, the energy created by disciples around the Master. But in ordinary society you have to find the resources in yourself, and it was challenging to find them after spending so many years in another dimension.

One afternoon, I had just arrived at the hotel where the Rebalancing Training was taking place when Neelam received a telephone call from India. She didn't say anything, but by next morning she had left. We later learned that the Master had stopped in Mumbai. After months of trying to establish an ashram in another part of the world, he finally had no choice but to return to India where, as an Indian citizen, it was hoped he would not be pursued. He was staying in the home of an Indian sannyasin, who opened his door to the Master in spite of objections from his wife, who wasn't a disciple and didn't like this invasion. The house was in an upscale part of Mumbai called Juhu Beach, situated along an arm of the ocean that bathed the west side of this enormous city.

But at the time, no one knew anything about where Neelam had gone, not even intimate friends like ourselves. After three days she called Nandi and told her that she was with Osho in Mumbai and that he also wanted her and Kamaal to come. Clearly, they had to leave right away. Nandi asked me not to say anything to anyone. The Master was resting and he didn't want people to know where he was, knowing that within a matter of days half the world would descend on the house. So, suddenly the game was over. Osho had called this marvellous woman to his side and I found myself with a terrible emptiness around me.

I begged Nandi to ask Osho if I could also join them. We four had spent some beautiful months together and now the three of them had been called by Osho and I felt excluded. Thus I received the first in a long series of hits given to me by the Teutonic goddess from this moment onwards. From the sweetest maternal goddess she was transformed into an Amazon warrior without pity. She stared at me with cold eyes and, without the slightest visible emotion, told me in a sonorous voice with a strong German accent: "Remember that you never ask anything to a Master, everything that happens to you is a gift you receive when you are ready."

She didn't add anything more. She just turned and left because she was in a hurry to leave as soon as possible. She left me stunned. The hit had been strong and my ego was vibrating from the blow. I knew she felt that it had been beautiful to be together in these months, but now that the Master had finally called, she was saying: *"Au revoir mon chéri! Just continue on your way and thank existence for all that you have received up to now and do not ask for more."*

Nandi seemed totally indifferent to leaving me. When she turned away it was as if I had never existed in her life, that I was just something between parentheses. She didn't share any sad feelings of separation and passed the hours of preparation for her trip alone, or with Kamaal. I didn't exist any longer. I felt like I had been thrown in the garbage like an old toy.

The next day she was gone, leaving nothing behind except the memories in my mind. It all happened so fast that I was stunned by the energetic change and the void that was left behind, first by the departure of Neelam and then by Nandi and Kamaal. It was like the emptiness caused by the sudden death of a loved one in some accident. The sense of shock was total.

I was completely in love with a woman so marvellous I felt like I was living in a fairy tale, in a dimension that was beyond human. Now, without warning, the fairy tale had vanished in the emptiness of my heart, like fog in the morning when the sun breaks through with its brilliant reality. Everything around me seemed so mundane and superficial. I couldn't work or communicate with others. I spent days without energy to do anything. I stayed in my little office and thought about the sessions I'd given to Nandi and how beautiful she was, this goddess stretched out naked on the examination table.

For a few days I remained closed up in my office, without seeing anyone. Then I decided to go to the hotel where the Rebalancing Training was in progress in order to break the gloom, meet friends and see if there was any news about Osho. The energy of the training was flowing like before with trainers, participants and assistants all enjoying themselves.

But I was no longer able to share their joy. Nobody here knew about the reason for Nandi's departure and even less about Osho. Obviously, I kept my mouth shut, returning to Siena late in the afternoon and hoping against hope that some day, one day, I would hear something from Nandi.

A week later, while I was sipping tea in the hotel where the training was held, a friend from the staff came to me, lowered his head near my ear and told me in a low voice that Nandi had called, asking for me, and she would call again in the evening. I was so happy! Apparently she hadn't forgotten me, nor thrown me into the trashcan of her memories. Surely, if she weren't interested in me she wouldn't have called from Mumbai just to say, "Hello! How are you?" Evidently something strong had happened between us and it wasn't just my imagination.

I stayed for dinner, eating with my friends and noticing that somehow the world seemed brighter again. Colours had returned to the furnishings of the hotel and all the shades of green in the surrounding countryside started to shine again – just as they had when Nandi and I were together. People seemed lighter, happier. My heart ached for the ringing of the phone, the thought of which brought sweat to my brow.

After dinner, around nine o'clock, I was called to the hotel's reception. Nandi was on the phone. Her voice was very professional, and she didn't waste time talking to me in the way you would expect between lovers: "How are you? I miss you..." and other romantic sentimentality. She simply informed me that she'd asked Osho if I could join them and the answer was..."Yes!!!!"

She gave me details of my reservation at a hotel in Juhu Beach where she was living and added in a German tone, "I advise you to say absolutely nothing about where Osho is, or that you are leaving to meet him. Ciao."

I stood there, the receiver in my hand, my mouth open, my legs wobbly as if I had just run several miles, and my heart beating at its own rhythm. After a little while, I managed to sit down. It was dawning on me that, for the first time in my life as a disciple, the Master had called me personally and in secret to allow me to share with him a space of intimacy I had never imagined possible.

Apart from the seven energy darshans I had with him in Pune One and my initiation in May of 1978, the Master had been unreachable physically. I saw him from afar in meditations and in discourses. I never imagined, nor even hoped to be, one of the few people that were physically near to him.

Osho was so far from me that the idea of being near him left me surprised. I was expecting for Nandi to tell me that she was well, that everything was going well...and blah, blah, blah. At the most, I was thinking she might tell me how things were evolving around the Master. But no, nothing like that. Nandi had called for the sole purpose of letting me know that she had asked Osho about me and he had invited me to join a small group of intimate disciples. Full stop.

From the tone of the telephone conversation it was clear to me that her primary relationship was with the Master and that personal relationships were of secondary, if not tertiary importance. I understood that the people who were close to the Master had a different priority. Their private lives took a backseat and only he existed for them.

For the first time, I found myself entering the mind-set of those who for years took care of the physical health and needs of the Master. I started to feel an urgency that went beyond my small private life, appreciating the attitude of total dedication demonstrated by Nandi, Neelam and others around Osho.

I understood in that instant that I had become part of a very restricted number of people who took care of the Buddha. In the kitchen in Oregon, I'd been a nobody, one sannyasin among many, one of those silent disciples who'd struggled to stay in the Master's energyfield, who didn't have any interest in putting himself in the spotlight or being seen by the bosses in order to have a place near him during his discourses.

Now, out of the blue, came the news that the Buddha himself was welcoming me in the house where he was recovering from a terrible year that undermined his health. It was a year that changed the history of human consciousness, a year in which America took on the karma of prosecuting him, poisoning him and persecuting him, a karma for which America will have to pay, in many centuries to come, as happened to the Jewish people after they crucified the Messiah.

Human beings never realize how much their actions can affect the subtle energy that flows in the universe. Only after great upheavals, such as world wars and enormous natural disasters, do they come back to the energy of the heart and become more sensitive and aware of their actions.

The masses live like automatons that have absolutely no awareness of their actions. As the Master repeatedly stated in his discourses: "To destroy a flower is very easy, but to destroy a rock is more difficult. The rock falls on the flower, crushing it, while the flower leans on the rock, making it more beautiful and more harmonious."

Meditation and awareness make man more fragile, sensitive and harmonious, more like a flower and less like a rock – the condition closest to the masses. Unawareness is now destroying the planet and if more flowers don't grow soon on the Earth – flowers of consciousness and silence – the rock of ignorance will destroy most of the societies that live here.

In a way, we are fortunate. We live at a crucial time when the lies of institutionalized power can be seen by all, when the opportunity arises to turn our energy inwards and begin the spiritual journey towards the self, the self that enables man to live like a Buddha and no longer like a programmed machine.

25 Return to India

For five years, I hadn't taken a flight to India, the continent where my spirit felt at home, the place where something deeply relaxes in my mind, while my body becomes more fluid and flexible. Even my way of walking takes on a more conscious gait. If my first trip over land to India in 1978 had been guided by the Master in an astral way, this trip was undertaken as a direct result of a personal invitation from him.

I was no longer the same person. In those eight years I'd lived so many experiences with such intensity that I hardly remembered the young man who, shortly after graduation, had left Italy in desperation, not heading toward any particular destination, but running as far away as possible from his past.

Now I felt a centre inside of me, like a ball of fire that burned slowly, bringing clarity to the path I had discovered. In these eight years, I'd learned a very basic and important lesson: if you are total in whatever situation you find yourself, sooner or later life offers you gifts when you least expect it; if you let go into the flow of life, the gifts always arrive. And now what I'd received was probably the most beautiful gift of my life: being able to stay physically close to the Master – *at the feet of the Buddha*.

Unfortunately, contemporary man has completely lost the sense of devotion toward a being who can guide him along the torturous path of life. Today, human arrogance has reached its ultimate expansion and men are convinced they can do everything by themselves, thinking they know everything. The human mind today is based on egotism and arrogance and until we let go of these poisons, life will be in a battlefield with nothing but continuous wounding and suffering.

As soon as I learned I could join my beloved and my friends, I moved quickly to organize my trip. It was the end of July, which was a good time to close my office for a 'summer vacation.' I didn't know if my 'vacation' would be permanent. I didn't have a fixed plan. But in August most of Italy goes on holiday, so the timing was perfect to shut my shop. How was I to know that India would be Osho's final stop on Planet Earth and I would have the honour of being near him throughout the last years of his life?

A few months earlier, I'd tried to go to Crete to be with him during his brief stay there. In fact, I'd already booked my flight when I learned, a few days later, that he'd been expelled. This time, I booked an open ticket to Mumbai, valid for three months, having no idea what the future held for me. As always happens when you go with the flow of existence, everything went smoothly. I closed my office in a few days and booked my flight for the beginning of August...destination Mumbai.

In the meantime, in the afternoons, I continued to visit my sannyasin friends at the hotel and have dinner with them, without telling them that in a few days I was leaving in order to meet Osho. But our sannyasin bush telegraph was busy and news began to spread around the world that Osho had stopped travelling. Before I left, I went to a meeting, held at Miasto, at which Hasya, Osho's new international secretary, brought the latest official news about the situation. The hall was packed with sannyasins from all over Italy. There must have been about 500 people there and, as usual, it was an occasion to celebrate and party.

I met a lot of old friends that afternoon and the fact that I couldn't talk about my imminent departure created an intense excitement in me that got stronger when Hasya began to speak. She informed us that the Master had, indeed, stopped travelling, that he was well and that he would soon start to see his disciples again.

It was the first time I saw Hasya, a mature and elegant American woman from Los Angeles, who had the unenviable job of taking care of the organizations that had been tangled and muddied by the Sheela disaster. But Hasya inspired a lot of trust and was totally different from the arrogant Sheela.

She was simple, elegant, softly-spoken and her presence inspired calm. She had a distinguished bearing that emanated from the way she dressed and the way she moved; she was wealthy without being ostentatious. I would never have thought that, in a few months, we would become good friends sharing the honour of living in the house of the Master.

My plane was leaving early in the morning and I had to get up at dawn to fly the Indian skies, so I left Miasto while everyone was still celebrating in the hall, conscious of the fact that I alone was heading toward the Master. While others were celebrating the good news, I was moving toward the source of love that made all these people dance. It was a strange sensation I'd never felt before. Obviously, I felt favoured and privileged, but inside me there was no idea of being special.

Existence had given me a gift and I simply received it in my heart, knowing it could easily create a big fantasy for my ego, but it was definitely worth the risk. In any case, I'd always loved to take risks and this time the risk was great because I was coming closer to an intense source of light where, judging by the experience of Sheela and her gang, almost all the moths and butterflies were getting burned. Or were they, like Nandi and Neelam, happily immolating themselves? From the outside, it was hard to tell.

I reached Mumbai in the morning. As the door to the airplane was opening, a gust of wind filled the cabin with the smells of India, accompanied by a blast of heat so intense that I felt like I was in a pressurized spacesuit. Arriving at immigration, I found myself in a hall full of turbans, saris, colours, sounds, masses that were moving in every direction, which seemed surprising for a moment, until I realized that I had actually arrived in India.

India is a world apart, and after my five years' absence the country seemed even more contradictory and illogical than before. Those years spent in America and Europe had taken me so far away from the Indian collective mind that this time, even though I was already aware of its magic, it all seemed very unreal and I was even more shocked than when arriving the first time.

Maybe because then I'd arrived by land and had the opportunity to adapt myself gradually to the change of mentality between Occident and Orient, whereas this time I landed in a completely different world after few hours of flight. And yet I found myself moving with a certain confidence, following Nandi's instructions about what to do to reach my hotel.

Riding in the taxi, my eyes were filled with images that were so far from me that I understood even better how much I had changed in these years. On that first trip, seeing all those poor people in the streets of Mumbai was fascinating. I'd felt myself melting in the chaos and becoming one with that mass of human energy that surrounded me. This time, however, I was only interested in reaching my hotel and meeting Nandi and the Master. The dramas playing outside the taxi windows seemed far away. I felt a sense of detachment in my belly that grew stronger the more I moved through the traffic of this chaotic city.

I felt like I was coming home, and the sense of relaxation got stronger, little by little, as I got closer to Juhu Beach. I was thinking, "I will see her soon!" and I was very excited by the idea that we could embrace each other in India and live this adventure together.

The hotel was located near the Hare Krishna Hotel that everyone in Mumbai knows. I told the taxi driver to wait and walked in to the hotel's reception. The excitement was growing stronger and I tried to stay calm in order not to make any big mistakes, but disaster struck anyway. The woman who greeted me at reception knew nothing of this German woman. I told her Nandi's family name and described her. Then I asked her to look in her book. As all those who have been in India know, communicating with Indians is a challenge and you never know what the final result will be.

After fifteen minutes of discussion I succeeded in persuading her to open her guestbook, while she continued saying, "No *baba*, she is not here." Together we searched through the list of guests and I didn't find Nandi's family name on the list, but then I saw the name Nandi among the other Indian names. Finally, I understood she had given her disciple name instead of her German family name. I was relieved, feeling happy and light. I asked the woman for the room number so I could meet Nandi, but with an innocence that is typically Indian, she looked me in the eyes, smiled and said, "She's not here, she left two days ago." With a big smile on her face, she added, "I told you she wasn't here, *baba*."

I asked if she had left a message or said where she was going, but there was nothing. She hadn't left any trace, she had disappeared like a grey cloud carrying sad waters, and my heart fell into total desperation. I had no way to contact her. I had no telephone numbers. I didn't know where the house was where Osho was staying. I didn't have any trace of her. What to do?

I felt totally lost in this mass of chaotic humanity, this noisy illogical crowd, lost inside myself and lost in the world outside. I'd arrived from a long journey, full of hope and joy, convinced that I would soon embrace my beloved again. Instead, I was adrift in the streets of Juhu. I couldn't even call Italy because no one knew anything about my trip. I was here incognito and my last connection had disappeared in the hot wind of Mumbai.

How was it possible that Nandi could leave, knowing that I was arriving, without even leaving news of where she could be found? Had something happened to the Master that forced her to leave? Again, I felt abandoned by Nandi, who was obviously totally preoccupied by her life with Osho, considering me as little more than a disturbance or a pleasure, depending on her mood.

I paid the taxi, took my bag, and started walking aimlessly in Juhu, trying to lose myself in the river of Indian life. I didn't have a goal, didn't know where to go. I was just walking. I felt desperate. After many years without smoking, I bought a pack of *Ganesh bidis*. I sat down to smoke the small Indian cigarette and watched the world of India going by, in the most unimaginable scenes possible: a beggar with no legs, sitting on a little platform of wood, riding on tiny steel wheels, dragging himself along with his hands; women in saris carrying all kinds of things on their heads, pigs frolicking, traffic moving with a millimetre between the vehicles, horns and other sounds everywhere, children playing with anything that was around them, dead animals along the sidewalk, multi-coloured birds flitting among the leaves of the robust trees, serious-looking men walking at a brisk pace with their little plastic briefcases and their greasy hair full of coconut oil, cows lounging in the middle of the street and even an elephant passed nearby with a man in brightly coloured clothes sitting on top, guiding it through the traffic. It was relaxing to watch the life on these Indian streets – here everything is unexpected and everything is possible, without any limits of judgment or morality.

For several hours, I moved around in the streets of Juhu. It was early afternoon and I was hungry. I made my way toward one of the luxury hotels where I could leave my bag at reception and eat something in a good restaurant. I think it was the Jolly Hotel or some other enormous edifice with five stars stamped everywhere on it, with doormen in livery who opened gigantic doors and made you feel immediately important and rich even if you weren't.

I left my bag and went to the coffee shop that had a view of the ocean and the hotel swimming pool filled with Westerners playing around, happy to be in paradise. I sat down at a round table with an enormous window on my right – the ocean view – and a balcony of green marble that served as a bar on my left. I ordered a grilled vegetable sandwich and rice with dal, two dishes with which I hoped to avoid any dysentery. The toast wasn't that great, but the rice and dal were good and the spices were mild.

I ordered black tea, but before the tea arrived a vision appeared that opened up the path to the Master for the next three and a half years: Nandi and Maneesha entered the bar and they were both beautiful, luminous and joyful. Maneesha was an English woman, actually Australian, but very, very *English*. She read the questions to Osho during his discourses. She was a woman who'd been near the Master for a long time and whom I had always known from far away...very far away.

In that instant, my worries and my feelings of being lost vanished. I felt I had arrived. I had reached the oasis. Nandi seemed happy enough to see me, but she didn't display any signs of joy or affection. She sat down at my table, ordered a drink and explained to me how the situation was evolving. She hadn't left any message for me – she explained – because she had to get away from that hotel, but was sure we would meet in Juhu, or that I would find the house where Osho was staying.

I understood from what she was saying that Osho wanted to start speaking again as soon as possible and this was causing them quite a bit of turmoil about how to organize his discourses in the small space available. We didn't stay seated long. They were both in a hurry and wanted to leave quickly. I had entered this hotel desperate and alone. I left a little later with two beautiful women who would take me to the feet of the Buddha.

Maneesha went to the Sumila Building, the house where Osho was staying. Nandi and I headed toward her hotel. Nandi showed me the room and after resting for a little while she also went to the house where Osho was staying. We would see each other in the evening. When she came back in the evening, she told me that Osho would start talking again in a week. She would take care of giving out tickets to see him.

The room for discourse wasn't big and no more than about 40-50 people could attend at one time, so it was necessary to 'take turns,' creating a waiting list to give everyone the possibility of seeing him. In the meantime, Neelam had become his personal secretary and had asked Nandi to take on the job of organizing the rotation of people who wanted to attend. For this, we had to find a comfortable hotel that could serve as a meeting place for the sannyasins who would soon be arriving in droves.

In the morning I found myself already at work with Nandi, not losing any time, with all our energy concentrated on creating what the Master had asked. We talked with different managers of the various hotels in Juhu that were near the house where Osho was residing. Really, we were asking the hotel for an indefinite time frame, using the hotel as an office to receive people arriving from Europe and elsewhere.

In return, we guaranteed to fill the rooms with guests. Many refused. But one, the Golden Manor Hotel, a fairly nice hotel with a garden and a pool and without many stars, accepted this agreement.

So we moved in there, into a beautiful big room, at a heavily discounted price, and after a few days Nandi and I started to receive people in the garden, handing out tickets.

After a brief interview, Nandi gave people a weekly ticket if they were staying a long time. To those who were staying for a short time, she tried to reserve many daily meetings. Nandi, Kamaal and other staff would attend every discourse. And me? Later, in the evening, in our room, she told me that I could attend every other evening, without a ticket.

The first evening I would not be able to enter because Osho had invited many Indians from Mumbai. But from the next evening, I would attend on alternate days. Around Osho I quickly learned there was always a whirlwind of energy. Those years spent near him were so intense that I don't have words to describe the emotions and sensations I experienced – being near a Buddha who gave the most contradictory directions possible every day of the week. Only by being in a space of No Mind was it possible to remain near this intense fountain of energy. Only with enormous trust and a totally open heart is it possible to accept the hits that land on our little egos from a fountain that comes from other levels of awareness.

From the following day, I found myself so busy there was no way to think of myself or have a private space. Our room was filled with friends who were constantly coming and going, and, as I'd already seen in Tuscany, Nandi was good in this role of the big mama who took care of other people's problems. She was always available and tried to resolve every problem with intelligence and grace.

Meanwhile, I was going around doing practical things to prepare for the discourses to begin. At one point I even found myself being driven around the streets of Mumbai in a big blue jeep – provided by the hotel – in order to buy things needed by the organization.

I often met with Kamaal in the evening when everything was finished. Together with other friends, we went to eat in different restaurants in the area. Neelam rarely came with us because she was taking care of Osho personally, all day long. Kamaal was always jocular, enlivening the energy of the group. Even though his companion was completely absorbed by the Master, Kamaal was always in a good mood.

Finally it arrived, the first evening when the Master would begin speaking again. I couldn't enter, but I went to the house in order to be in the energy of joy and celebration that exploded when the Master decided to see us again. When everyone had entered, I stayed in the garden, under the window where Osho was speaking. I didn't want to miss this first discourse after the adventure of America, and besides, I really didn't feel like going back to the hotel. So I sat with my eyes closed under that window and listened to the whole discourse from outside. Even though I couldn't hear everything perfectly, I was in his energy field, gathering the subtle vibrations beyond the words, which became superfluous, and even beyond the silence, in that space where feelings are no longer linked to the sounds but to a dimension of the heart.

His beginning was incredibly dramatic. The question Maneesha asked was: "Beloved Master, what does it mean to be part of a mystery school?" After a long silence he slowly answered:

"My Beloveds, you are fortunate to be here today, because today is not only the beginning of a new series of discourses but also the beginning of a new phase and a day that will be recorded as a historical day. Today, Saturday, the 16th of August, 1986, here in the Sumila Building, at 7 o'clock in the evening, I declare that...."

He went on, speaking very slowly, saying that his big phase of preparation, begun at the end of the '60s, was finished and that now he had with him his real disciples. These were the disciples that had gone through all his devices in order to stay with him and who were now ready to create an energyfield of people connected with him through the heart and not the mind. From now on, he would initiate a phase in which the Master-disciple relationship would be direct and for this reason these discourses were entitled *The Osho Upanishad*; *upanishad* means "sitting at the feet of the Master." From this moment onward, he would be erecting the columns of an invisible temple where millions of people would take refuge in the future.

As he went on like this, I was sitting in the garden, crying uncontrollably. I was touched by how much love this being had lavished on others so they could know their inner Buddha, sharing with them his space of bliss so that we could experience what it means to be in harmony with existence. In order to do this, he had to take on enormous burdens and mammoth responsibilities. The compassion of a Buddha is infinite, because he navigates alone against the current, against the force of gravity that drags human beings downwards.

The tears rolled down my cheeks for the first part of his discourse, then the emotions disappeared and a great relaxation arrived that lasted the rest of his discourse – nearly two hours long.

At the end, I moved toward the gate where the ones who had been attending the event were starting slowly to come out, in a state of grace and meditation. When Nandi came out, we hugged a long time, intensely and very lovingly, maybe for the first time since I arrived.

I saw Osho the next night. Coming in through the main door of Sumila, you went up ten steps that lead into a corridor. Along the left side of the corridor were private rooms and to the right was a large rectangular room where Osho's chair was set up. Behind his chair was a tapestry with the design of a bamboo tree in Japanese style, occupying most of the wall. Sitting close together were about fifty people, most of whom were Indian.

Osho had a large number of Indian disciples. Before the Pune One commune, meaning before 1974, he used to speak in mass outdoor gatherings, addressing crowds of 50-70,000 people. The ones who were here now were intimate followers who had followed him everywhere and who were all very sweet with each other and, above all, with us Westerners, whom they respected a lot, knowing that for us it was not a tradition to have a Master or a guru, and therefore we found it more difficult to surrender.

They seated me near the window through which I'd heard the previous night's discourse. It was located to the right of Osho's chair. So many people were packed into that small place, there was barely room to sit on the floor with my legs crossed.

He entered, slowly, as usual. He seemed to have aged a lot. His beard was a lot whiter and longer than when I had seen him last on the Ranch, when he was going up the stairs of the airplane that had taken him directly to prison in North Carolina.

As usual, he entered with his *namaste* greeting and slowly came towards his chair, looking at us with careful attention. He sat down slowly and after a few seconds of silence, which seemed like hours, he started the discourse. I closed my eyes, relaxed the body and slipped into that empty inner space that expanded like clouds in an open blue sky.

I always noticed that, when he talked, my mind was receiving every one of his sentences and understood the subjects on which he was speaking, but soon afterwards I knew absolutely nothing about the things he had spoken. My mind continued to register the words and the sense of the sentences, but as soon as the sentence was finished, it vanished from my memory and my mind became as fresh and empty as before.

At the end of a discourse, which usually lasted two hours, it was difficult to remember what exactly he had said and my body was in a deep somnolence, in which moving and talking became almost impossible. Sometimes, I came back from this state in a few minutes, but at other times hours were needed in order to come back to what is called 'normal.'

In all those discourses at Sumila, the intensity of the meditation was so strong that time was needed to recover, after which, in slow motion, we left the building, heading toward the local restaurants in silence or at the most exchanging a few words, always in a space of suspended time. When we were seated at the table ready to order our food, our movements usually recovered their normal speed. It was a magical space.

When Nandi and I managed to have some intimacy in our room in the hotel, making love was even more beautiful than in Tuscany. We were both very sweet and peaceful, and the sexual energy was full of gratitude and tenderness. It was as if passion was transforming itself into an experience of opening the heart rather than remaining at the level of physical pleasure. We were also sharing our work and every afternoon we would sit in the garden and receive sannyasins, who arrived in larger and larger numbers. Nandi always tried to help everyone and she became sweeter and more maternal every day. You could feel the intensity of her love for the Master and her eyes reflected a state of constant bliss.

After we had been in Juhu for a little more than a month, we had almost run out of money. Mumbai is an expensive city and even though we had a discounted hotel, we were both coming to the end of our resources. For a woman like her, accustomed to living well, it was unthinkable that we could keep going with very limited funds.

So one day I went to the centre of town to look for a store that sold acupuncture needles so I could start giving sessions. It wasn't easy to find good needles, and the best Indian needles corresponded to the second level of Chinese and Japanese ones. Nevertheless, there was no alternative and I had to buy needles that were coarse but with which I could work. The next morning, after Nandi had gone to Osho's house, I gave my first acupuncture session in India. I soon became known as the doctor of the small community that gathered in Juhu in the five months Osho stayed there. I was the only medical doctor there and all the sannyasins who had any problem started coming to me.

Between me being the doctor and Nandi taking care of all the disciples who arrived, we became the ones to contact for all those arriving to meet the Master. A small 'ashram' developed around us, with many people spending the day on the grounds of our hotel, and often late into the night after the discourses of the Master. It was beautiful and strange at the same time to be at the centre of this small movement that was gathering around the Master. Strange because I wasn't used to being at the centre of the vortex of energy around Osho. Up to that moment, I had been an illustrious nobody that only a few people knew. Now, all those who arrived from different parts of the planet already knew they had to come to Nandi and to me because, as I said, gossip was the preferred social activity of sannyasins and our names had spread to Europe and beyond.

After a couple of months, Neelam, whom we saw rarely but with great joy, told us that Osho wanted a much bigger space and so they had told all the influential Indians to look for a place where they could build and where he could stay with his disciples. They were looking in the north, in the Himalayas, and also in and around Mumbai, but they didn't find a suitable place.

They needed a big building for him and for his staff and then a series of residences for the thousands of people who would arrive. In addition they would need money, which after the Ranch had become a difficult thing to manage, seeing that Sheela and her women had emptied almost all the pockets of the sannyasins and shocked those who, until that time, had been generous with donations.

People did whatever they could to find a place, but nothing showed up on the horizon and Osho continued to give discourses in Sumila. The weeks passed. Also passing was the patience of the wife of the sannyasin who'd opened his house to the Master, and the tension started to be felt.

In a few months, I think about 1500 people arrived from Europe, whereas we saw very few from America. Meanwhile, we learned that the Ranch had become a desert again; most of the movable structures had been sold. A few sannyasins were still there taking care of the remaining buildings, and the last one to leave the Ranch, in 1988, arrived in Pune Two only when absolutely everything had been closed. Of course he was German.

Our life became more and more intense, filled with disciples that revolved around us, either to have tickets to enter the discourses or because they wanted to know what was going to happen next and how they would be able to cope with it. We started to create strategies for disappearing, either Nandi or me, in order to have a bit of privacy. Otherwise we constantly had dozens of sannyasins around us, asking us questions. I continued to see the Master every other evening and Nandi every evening.

By October there were no longer any traces of my Siena medical office in my head. One day, like lightning in a peaceful sky, I suddenly remembered it, called my German friend where I'd been staying in Siena, explained the situation to her and asked her to take care of closing everything, selling what she could. She could keep whatever money she recovered. I didn't know when or if I would ever return, but the immediate future was now, here, near Osho, intensely involved in the latest phase of his work.

In November and December, the situation with the owner of the house in Juhu became more and more difficult and the Indian police started showing signs of impatience, seeing that the whole movement was congregating in this small area of Mumbai and was highly visible.

There was no sign of another place to go, but Osho's voice continued to be heard and the number of his disciples grew accordingly. Now, it was no longer a dozen people who followed us around. Hundreds were waiting to hear him, waiting in line, and we were the link between Osho and this ever-growing queue of his beloveds.

His discourses were like drops of divine essence that fell on us every evening, nourishing us and bringing us to a level of meditation that had not happened before.

One night, I was present at discourse when a letter written by an old Indian sannyasin was read out as a question to the Master. In his letter, the disciple described an experience during solitary meditation in his house, on a full moon night. He had left his physical body and had seen that Gautama, the Buddha, had entered Osho's body and that the two bodies had become one. The bliss he experienced was such that he remained in a state of total grace. He had written the letter in order to have the confirmation of the Master as to whether this experience was real or only an illusion of the mind.

Osho not only confirmed the union of consciousness between Gautama the Buddha and himself, but also confirmed the state of enlightenment of the man who'd written the letter. At the end of the discourse, as Osho was leaving, the man calmly stood up and went toward Osho, letting himself fall at the feet of the Master while the Master touched him on his head, giving him his blessings. Many of us burst out in tears of joy, seeing the Master bless an enlightened disciple.

It's important to remember that, in all the years that Osho had been speaking to us in Pune One and at the Ranch, no one had stood up and gone toward the Master when he was leaving or while he was talking. There were always guards ready to stop anyone who would make even a slight movement in that direction. This time, however, everything happened as if it was the most natural thing in the world and no one in the crowd stopped the man from going toward the Master. As far as I know, this episode was the only one like it in the history of the Master. Naturally, news that Osho had confirmed the enlightenment of one of his disciples spread quickly through the streets of Juhu, then into the rest of India, Europe and the rest of the sannyasin world.

In the mornings I gave sessions, and in the afternoons I helped Nandi distribute tickets in the garden of the hotel. In the evening, after the discourse, we stayed out late with the friends who were constantly arriving. In the evenings that I didn't attend the discourses I stayed alone in my room and meditated. Life was rich, intense and joyful.

Osho continued to move with disarming simplicity into what became the last phase of teaching. This was his swan song, which lasted from 16th August 1986 to 19th January 1990, the day he decided to depart forever from any physical manifestation in this earthly dimension.

From that day in August, Osho opened the doors of his 'mystery school,' which was not, as esoteric intellectuals think, a secret place where few arrive after having discovered secret maps, in order to find learned texts that describe the secret life of the soul. It is simply an energetic space that can be experienced when the heart of the disciple is open to the energy of the Master.

Thousands of people had found their way to him over the years through intellectual curiosity, especially about the so-called esoteric. Many of these 'curious disciples' drifted away after the Ranch and didn't ever return, lacking the capacity to open themselves and let go into love, and also because of a certain disappointment at not having their expectations met due to their own excessive ego-identification with 'the spiritual trip.'

In time, a few of them even wrote books criticizing Osho and his decisions. The mind functions like that. The mind is essentially a child that hasn't grown up and wants to imagine that all its expectations can be satisfied. The median mental age of human beings is fifteen or sixteen years old. Like many adolescents, they have difficulty with giving and receiving on anything but the most superficial level.

Dozens of books by ex-disciples have come out in these years after his departure. While a few describe with sincerity their relationship with the Master, others bitterly criticize his work, emphasizing the errors he committed. Instead of courageously admitting they could not go further on the path of investigating themselves, the path of transforming egoistic personality into mind, they find excuses for their actions by looking for weak points in the Master and criticizing the choices made by him.

Osho opened his mystery school without any structure and without any orders, because he felt that now there remained around him people who loved him unconditionally, independently of what had happened during the years of the different communes.

Without a spiritual guide, it is practically impossible to navigate beyond the stormy seas of the hypnotised mind, which remains convinced that No Mind can be experienced through the mind itself. But this is nonsense. To enter such spaces, the ego needs to dissolve. We need to die to our past totally and have the courage to stay alone in a dimension that is absolutely unknown.

Osho repeated many times that he was not interested in creating a perfect organization that could function smoothly and efficiently. He was only interested in his disciples being able to undertake the inner journey, in the search for their Buddha. He didn't want to change the world, nor even less give a message of peace to future nations. His teaching was, and is, to enable a few courageous ones to set forth on the journey to ego-death in order to explore the light of existence.

His message absolutely rejected all religions and spiritual structures that interpose themselves between us and the divine. As he used to say to us: "If you can be Christ, why be a Christian? If you can be a Buddha, why be a Buddhist?" Osho put all the responsibility for our lives in our own hands, without heaven or hell, without punishment or reward, but simply indicating the path of subjective development that leads to the realization of our inner Buddha, which depends mostly on the level of our totality.

From Juhu onwards, Osho no longer wanted a community around him; he didn't want people to leave everything behind and live parasitically on his energy. He simply wanted a space where disciples could share his energy and be with him as much as possible, then return to their own countries.

❐❐❐

26   The Close Encounter

In terms of climate, the best time to be in India is in December when the days are warm and the nights are cool. Walking at night on the streets of Juhu was a pleasure and Nandi and I often strolled there quietly, escaping for a while from the storm of chaos blowing around us. On a few occasions, Neelam came with us at night and it was delightful to be with her, soaked as she was with the energy of the Master. She had become so calm, happy and soft that I was frightened when I hugged her, feeling I might break something in her body because she was so soft.

When she went out with us she relaxed and we usually didn't speak about work, but sometimes she shared the latest news about the Master. In December, she told us the time was coming when Osho would move, even though the new place was still unknown. Meanwhile, of course, ever more disciples continued arriving in Juhu and the situation became more and more intense.

Toward the end of the year, Neelam informed Nandi that Osho would almost certainly move back to the old commune in Pune because they couldn't find a decent place anywhere else and the situation in the house had gone too far. She also told us not to say anything officially till the situation was clear.

Before New Year's Eve, Neelam asked Nandi to go to Pune with a few women in order to prepare Osho's room. She would follow with the Master as soon as everything was ready. Nandi asked me to stay in Juhu and continue to meet people without saying a word about what was going on. Mainly, I had to convince people not to rush to Pune. I would have to act as if Osho was intending to remain in Mumbai, but obviously Nandi's absence made everyone suspicious and they pestered me in my hotel room to find out what was going on.

For two days, I stayed in my room as much as possible. When I went out, I was immediately surrounded by sannyasins asking thousands of questions. It was an absurd and uncomfortable situation, but obviously people were curious and were dying to know what the next step in the saga would be. For three days it went on like this, then Nandi called me from Pune telling me I could come. It was now official that Osho would return to his old commune, but I could not make any kind of announcement. I had to simply pack up and move.

It was the 3rd of January 1987 and I was packing my suitcase in my hotel room with people knocking on the door. I left in the early afternoon, hoping that fewer people would be in the hotel at that time. But although I had taken precautions, when I went out into the street there were a dozen taxis full of sannyasins ready to follow me anywhere I went. So I left Juhu with a line of taxis following mine.

Halfway to Pune, when we were already up on the hills – after about a hundred hairpin bends overlooking the valley below, without any protection– I asked my taxi driver to stop in a village in order to drink *chai*. I got out and headed toward the other taxis that had also stopped. In many of them were old friends. We hugged each other and I explained to them, apologetically, that I couldn't have acted differently in Mumbai, but since we were clearly on the road to Pune, which many of them knew very well, it was obvious the Master was moving back to the old commune. We enjoyed *chai* together, laughing and hugging, happy that the Master was returning to Pune, which for many of us was the site of our favourite commune so far.

Among this group was my old friend Renu, from Palermo, who with her mysterious postcard, ten years before, had been the channel to me for the energy of the Master. Between us all, dozens of personal stories were exchanged, daring and adventurous stories that, together with the love all of us felt for Osho, united us deeply. We were now coming back to the old commune, something that nobody would have thought possible. More importantly, the Master, after being persecuted and subjected to violence in a hundred premeditated ways, was with us again.

We set off up the hills once more, reaching the Deccan Plateau, which, I noticed, had become more crowded since my last visit. As we started to approach Pune itself, the sprawl of the expanding city came out to meet us. Back in 1978, this sleepy old city had about one million inhabitants. Now that figure had more than doubled.

We arrived at the ashram in Koregaon Park in the late afternoon. I went toward Lao Tzu House, while the friends who had been following me went to find an apartment or hotel. When I arrived at Lao Tzu, I saw that many people had been trying to prepare the Master's abode in record time. However, the work still wasn't finished. I greeted Nandi, who was very busy and immediately asked me to give a hand in the garden in front of Osho's window.

Mukta, the Master's gardener, wanted him to see the fountain working, as it always used to when he was living here, so I dropped my luggage and went immediately to the garden where a German sannyasin was trying to repair it. The poor fountain hadn't been working for years and the engine was almost destroyed by the corrosive climate — especially by the humidity of the monsoon — but we did everything we could to get it working again.

After the first hour, we were up to our knees in water, our bodies dirty with grease, our hands oily like professional mechanics, but nothing happened. We needed new parts. With the equipment we had, we couldn't make the fountain start. Reluctantly, we surrendered to the inevitable and I went to clean myself up, change clothes, find Mukta and explain that her surprise for the master could not be realized.

In the house, many sannyasins were continuously moving around, busy with different tasks. Nandi told me Neelam had called to say that Osho was arriving shortly. It was already almost ten o'clock at night and we were working hard without stopping to eat, but the excitement that the Master was arriving warmed and nourished us.

By midnight, Neelam had already called three or four times, each time giving a different hour and even a different day for the arrival. We were tired. Those fortunate sannyasins who were going to live in the Master's house had already gone to rest in their beds. I couldn't work any longer and informed Nandi I was going out of the ashram to find a room in the nearest hotel, so that we, too, could rest.

Again, the Amazon inside her woke up, gazing at me with incredulity. In her best Teutonic voice she said, "Are you stupid? Don't you understand we are going to live in Lao Tzu?"

How could I understand it? To me, it was unthinkable to live in the Master's house. It was too far from my expectations, even in my most fantastic dreams I couldn't have seen myself living in Lao Tzu, but she told me in such a matter-of-fact way that it touched me deeply. Seeing my astonishment, she graciously left some space for my mind to catch up with the news, so that eventually I could croak, "Then where is our room?"

It was on the ground floor, two doors from Osho's room. Next to us, in the middle, there would be a room for Neelam and Kamaal. Good. I took my luggage into our room and went to lie down on a big bed in one of the upstairs rooms, where Nandi, Kamaal, and Devageet – Osho's dentist – were also resting.

We were all tired and didn't know when Osho would arrive. By midnight, we still didn't know anything, but we were taking turns to sleep. In one of those moments when I was awake, I went down to the garden for a little walk. Lao Tzu garden was always very wild and natural because Osho didn't like to cut plants, to prune and cultivate trees in a rational way. The gardeners mainly cleaned the garden and never interfered with the spontaneous growth of the plants.

Walking in that garden in the dark was like walking in a little tropical forest, animals and plants interlaced with each other, filling the place with a magic that was already sacred. Beyond the gate of Osho's house, the ashram revealed itself with its paths, houses and offices that most sannyasins had now abandoned because they were sleeping.

Finding myself there, inside the house that in Pune One had been an unreachable Shangri-La, where I entered only for a short time to meet the Master, I reflected on my good luck. The fact that I'd ended up there seemed unreal, yet another part of my mind took this dream as something exceptionally simple and natural, not special at all. It was just something that happened to me, without any effort on my part, and I was trying to live this moment in the most total way possible.

At two o'clock at night the ashram was calm, silent and very few people remained inside. In Lao Tzu, there were about a dozen people, many of them sleeping, waiting for his arrival. At three o'clock Neelam called and said they were close to Pune and would arrive within an hour. We all woke up, made sure everything was in order and waited for the Buddha to arrive at his old residence. At four o'clock Neelam arrived at Lao Tzu, telling us that Osho was immediately behind in another car with Vivek.

Suddenly the whole ashram was lit up and some sannyasins started to play music and sing, standing along the driveway from the main gate, ready to welcome their Master. We opened the gate of Lao Tzu, which was at the end of the long corridor from the ashram entrance. Neelam gave me a torch and told me to stay behind the car of the Master, making sure that nobody came near the vehicle.

I was walking slowly behind the Mercedes where his body was still resting. We passed through Lao Tzu Gate, which I closed behind me. Slowly the vehicle headed for the porch, and then stopped. The driver was Manu, an old sannyasin from Mumbai. Osho was in the back, lying down on his left side, with his hands under his head and his legs pulled up on the seat.

Vivek was seated in front and she came out first, then opened the door for the Master, who had continued sleeping – if you can say that of a Buddha – for the whole drive through the ashram, while his disciples were singing, happy for his arrival. Milarepa, an American sannyasin with a gift for spontaneous music, was playing his guitar, and about 10 or 11 people formed a semicircle on the side of the car from which Osho would emerge, jumping for joy and singing.

Vivek called him without receiving any answer, so she went to help him out. She took his legs and gently put both feet on the ground so that he would understand that he had to move. In that moment, his physical body came to life, suddenly he was there, totally present, whereas just a moment before his body seemed uninhabited, abandoned on the back seat of the car.

Nandi was like a wild child in ecstasy, screaming for joy and jumping like she was in the 'Hoo!' phase of Dynamic Meditation. I was singing happily, and yet one part of me was observing the scene from the outside, without any emotion, without involvement or judgment. I was one step away from him, never having been so intimate and never having dreamed to be so close.

Strangely, Osho seemed to be alone in our little crowd. It was almost as if he was already in his room, by himself. Nothing touched him, he was totally with himself, standing still by the side of the car, whereas all of us were in ecstasy at the sight of him. He caressed his long beard with his hands, slowly and softly, as if he wanted to comb it, fixed his moustache, and again softly touched his beard. After a minute of these 'beauty touches' he joined his hands in a *namaste*, looked at everyone, one by one, then joined in the dancing, moving his arms and hands to the rhythm of the music, sending energy toward us who were all plunged into a frenzy of joy.

After a few minutes of this celebration of happiness, he stopped, turned and started walking slowly toward the steps of the car porch in order to go to his room. His body, seen from close up, looked like that of an automaton, in some way used by an energy that didn't belong to his physical form. Something made him move, walk, go up the stairs, but his movements were more like those of a perfect bionic being than a normal human identified with his body.

Watching Osho from close up was impressive. When he stood up in front of the car it was as if an external source went into his body and started to make him move, but between the body and the energy that was activating it from inside there was a clear separation. I've never seen anything like that, not even Krishnamurti gave me that sensation of clear separation between body and energy.

In the presence of that phenomenon, my scientific mind didn't have anything to cling to. From a strictly medical point of view, his gestures, his movements, his way of walking were unexplainable unless you categorised them in a specific clinical picture: only catatonic patients I'd seen in psychiatric hospitals during my years at medical school came close to that condition of complete separation from the body.

The difference was that next to a catatonic schizophrenic I felt a kind of deadness, the total absence of human warmth, feelings and life in general, whereas with Osho the perception was completely opposite: all around that empty body there was an impressive presence of love, joy and awareness that were palpable. It was as if a halo of energy was penetrating into your own body so you could not do anything but choose: bursting out laughing, bursting out crying, or just bursting... and that was it. Your mind was in a total blackout, unable to interfere, obscured by the energy that his body emanated. After that experience, you felt stunned, like after an orgasm when you just want to relax and let yourself go with that sweet nectar you just tasted.

Dawn found us exhausted, full with the energy of the Master. We couldn't do anything else but go gently to our beds and sleep for a few hours. This day now dawning was the beginning of the last chapter of Osho's story and we had much to do.

Later, when we all woke up, Neelam explained the reason for all those contradictory phone calls. She knew that in Mumbai the police were getting heavy, even monitoring our telephones calls, so she wanted to avoid nasty encounters during the trip to Pune, or a police visit to Sumila before departure.

In fact, the local authorities were trying to interfere with Osho's teaching, both in Mumbai and in Pune. After learning that Osho had somehow slipped through the net and arrived in the city, the Pune police – who'd intended to prevent his entering the city – didn't waste much time before coming to knock on the door of Lao Tzu House.

The morning after Osho settled into his old house, senior police officers arrived to deliver a paper in which they ordered him to leave Pune "because his teachings would pollute the minds of young Indians."

Always the same old story of polluting young minds...as in Greece, as in America. The few men who were in Lao Tzu – I think there were six of us that morning – locked the doors of the house, barred the shutters and stayed ready to repel any policeman who should want to trouble Osho, who was resting. We were determined that nobody would come in, otherwise they would have to use force against us. The Master could not be disturbed!

Outside the house, we could hear the wrath of God being unleashed. Police officers were screaming to be allowed in and our Indian disciples were trying to convince them to go away. It went on like that for more than an hour. Inside, Vivek from time to time emerged from the Master's room to find out how the situation was developing.

After a long turmoil, with cries and quarrels that gave the impression all hell was breaking loose outside those doors, we heard Neelam knocking. She, too, was in the chaos trying to convince the police to leave. Calmly, she addressed us by our names, informing us we could open the door because they had arrived at an agreement. Before opening, we asked Neelam if everything was quiet, and when she quietly answered "yes" we took the bars away and opened the Lao Tzu doors.

Outside there were about thirty people, four of them Indian police officers. The rest were Indian sannyasins who had been trying to reach a compromise. The compromise was that these officers could enter in the Master's room, give him the documents to read and then go away, letting our lawyers and the Indian courts deal with the matter thereafter. We allowed two of them to come in and brought them in front of Osho's room. By this time, Vivek and Neelam had woken Osho, informing him of the situation.

I stayed outside his bedroom with the other men of Lao Tzu. The two officers entered and delivered the document andOsho read it with incredible calmness in front of them. When he'd finished reading it, he looked the officers in the eyes, tore up the paper in little pieces, threw it toward them and said: "I've read it. Now you can leave my room." He went back to bed and everybody went out of the room. We escorted the police officers out of Lao Tzu and locked the doors behind them. Everything calmed down. The lawyers took care of this latest trouble, which, in time, decayed and disappeared like many other stupid and provocative charges.

Meanwhile, the commune was taking shape again, but it wasn't the same as in years before. Now Osho wasn't asking us to build a great commune where we could all live. He simply gave public talks again and shared his energy with us. *The Osho Upanishad*, the name he'd given to the series begun in Mumbai, means exactly this: being in the presence of the Master.

Over the next days and weeks there was an explosion of old and new friends arriving. Within a few months, there were thousands of disciples gathered around him, most of them Europeans. He started to speak in Chuang Tzu Auditorium, which was the space where, years before, he initiated people into sannyas and also gave discourses before moving to Buddha Hall.

Now that I was living in Lao Tzu, I tended to spend a lot of time in the house without going out into the commune; Osho was giving two discourses a day for while, morning and evening, and we who were living there were the only ones who could attend both discourses, always seated in the first rows.

After we had settled in Lao Tzu, Neelam informed me that the Master wanted me to take care of the medical centre of the commune. Events happened so fast around Him that there was no time to think or to brood over the facts – we simply acted. I found myself alone, reopening the doors to the small medical office that was used in the early years of the ashram. The office was in Krishna House, in the central office building of the commune, really in the middle of everything. Now I was alone, opening those two rooms that had remained closed for years.

After a few brief meetings with disciples who were interested in working at the medical centre, I found myself with a team of two doctors, a woman from Argentina and a man from Switzerland. Two nurses arrived, then three, and in a few months a whole team was created.

Like a queen bee, Nandi now had at her disposition a big hive, with a lot of people buzzing around her. For me, it would have been nice for us to spend a few evenings together, but she always chose to be in the company of others. So I have to say that in Lao Tzu our intimate relating vanished like snow in the sun. In that house, only the Master existed and all the energy revolved around him. There weren't many living there: about twenty people, who made up his personal staff and took care of him. Two of his secretaries were also there, Neelam and Anando. Then there were a few new people like me, there because of our connection to one of the women on his staff.

Kamaal, Om, Nivedano, Milarepa and I were seen by the staff as the companions of our women. It was clear we were being treated like temporary residents of the house. This attitude affected me, not least because in the commune there were prejudices against Italians, according to the classical stereotypes of us being lazy, imprecise, emotionally unstable, with thoughts revolving mainly around women and spaghetti. Obviously, many of these judgments were well founded.

In fact, apart from the engineer from Milano, who was present for twelve years in Lao Tzu as a handyman and factotum, I was, as far I know, the only Italian living in the house at Osho's request.

For me, it wasn't easy, even though my character doesn't correspond to the stereotype of the average Italian, forever talking and gesticulating, but is closer to that of the silent Sicilian. I wasn't comfortable in this very English atmosphere, with its extreme reserve and a sense of sarcastic humour that I didn't understand.

In the meantime, the medical centre became one of the busiest departments in the commune. I also started to take care of the hygiene of the ashram, both for food and for water; this was one of my passions. I convinced Neelam that we needed to put water filters in the ashram so that sannyasins would be able to get unpolluted water that was good for their health. In a few months, good filtered water was available everywhere in the ashram, with a marked reduction in the cases of amoebic dysentery.

Osho hadn't given limits to my medical work, so I added acupuncture and then after a few months homeopathic and ayurvedic medicine. Pratiti's dream had come true in the commune of the Master one year after she had left her body.

In the two previous communes the medical centre had practiced allopathic medicine exclusively, meaning classical Western medicine, with a heavy reliance on chemical drugs. Eventually, on the Ranch, the medical centre became part of the long arm of Sheela's power, serving to control the rebels of the commune.

So people were happy with this more natural, less invasive medical approach. They trusted us more, contributing to the growth of the centre. Amrito, Osho's doctor, however, wasn't too pleased with this opening to alternative medicine and he started to interfere in the centre, trying to plug this naturalistic leak that had been created through me.

Amrito was a doctor, but in recent years he had had only one patient, namely Osho. He was the most rigid of the Anglo-Saxons in the house of the Master and there wasn't much point in talking to him because he always thought he was right. More than conversing, he was imposing decisions with which you couldn't argue. Even though I respected him for his work in taking care of the Master, there was no way for me to agree with Amrito about the practice of medicine. In fact, his whole approach to life was diametrically opposite to mine.

In the first months, all of us living in the house were almost always involved with the discourses that Osho was giving twice a day for a total of four hours minimum, plus one hour of preparation, which meant six hours a day we were inside the house. In this period, I went out only to go to the medical centre, which was a mere 50-60 metres from my room in Lao Tzu, for another six hours of work. I didn't see the front gate of the commune for many, many weeks. I was totally absorbed in my life in Lao Tzu and the medical centre.

Before each discourse, two sannyasins would bring into the hall the armchair Osho would sit in, and, once everyone was seated, one of them would open the door and wait for him to enter, closing the door as soon as he was seated. Neelam asked Kamaal, Milarepa and me to take turns with the other man who carried the chair and opened the door. Because the discourse happened twice a day, it was my turn about once a week. That was one of the most intense experiences of my life with him.

Carrying in the chair before he entered was an honour and a pleasure, but to open and close the door was a uniquely intense experience. The door opened into a room that Osho used only as a corridor between his own room and the discourse hall. Once he entered this corridor, it seemed to take an eternity for him to walk to the hall.

I would be seated in the hall, just in front of the open door, and I could see him walking…slow…calm and aware…like a panther moving with extreme awareness while hunting prey, silently and totally present.

By the time he arrived in the hall, my mind had already left. I felt my body completely empty, free from the pressure of thinking. Very slowly he moved to the front of his chair, all the while giving a *namaste*. Turning slowly, he continued to greet his disciples, from one side of the hall to the other. Then after a couple of minutes he sat down while I, or one of the other guards, headed for the door in order to close it.

A similar scene would take place at the end of the discourse. Before leaving, he gave energy to all the people in the hall, waving his arms and hands in time to live music. That intense wave of energy sent everybody into ecstasy. To stand and close the door at his back was really a big exercise in awareness; by that time my body could hardly stand on its feet and my heart was drunk with energy.

Seeing Osho's way of walking and moving from close up was a unique experience – I've never seen it in another human being.

Christ consciousness – or divine consciousness, or whatever you want to call it – manifests with an intense inner explosion that cannot be described with words – not even by the person who has realized that consciousness. It's from his daily acts, like eating, walking and moving, that you can feel and see the other worldly nature of an enlightened being – something you never imagined.

Even when Osho was arrested in North Carolina, his presence was that of an emperor, not of a recluse. Even when they were pointing guns at him in America his calmness was total. And when they took him by force in Greece, he didn't lose his composure at all and maintained intact his consciousness of being and light.

In recent years, I have seen many men who claim to have reached the same level of consciousness, but in private they behave just like any ordinary businessman. In their acts and in their way of being there's no trace of grace. The message of a Buddha passes to us through his silence and his gestures, bypassing the logical mind, penetrating and nourishing the consciousness of those who are around them. All the great Masters have had qualities of grace that have transformed the consciousness of their disciples more than the discourses they have uttered.

Meher Baba, who lived mainly in Pune and Ahmednagar between 1894 and 1969, was a great master of the last century. His name was given by his first disciples, who called him Meher Baba or 'sweet and good pastry.' He stayed in silence for more than 30 years, but, even so, transformed thousands of people and spread his message of love throughout the world, including America, where he was taken in the '40s to undergo scientific experiments – he wanted to show the academic world that in the sphere of consciousness the laws are not the same as on the material plane.

They performed many electro-encephalograms in order to see what was going on in his brain as he entered into spaces of meditation. Every time they were surprised to witness that the graph of the electro-encephalogram went completely flat, as if he was a corpse. Even his heart was stopping, while he was laughing with his wonderful big black eyes and his splendid long black hair.

Meher Baba was working with presence, as was Ramana Maharshi (1879-1950), who lived on the sacred mountain of Arunachala in southern India. Ramana even walked naked, but his presence was such that the best minds Europe and America bowed down at his feet. Without having studied, he conversed with the best known philosophers of those times and dismantled their arguments with a few simple words.

The same was true of Gautama Buddha who spoke and taught for 40 years, yet transmitted his most profound teachings through total silence. One morning, he appeared before his followers with only a rose in his hand and remained in silence, gazing at the rose. His disciples started to become restless because he had always spoken to them. He'd never behaved like that before, so they asked him what had happened, but Buddha remained silent with the rose in his hands. After a long time he said, "What I could communicate verbally to you I have transmitted, but today, with this rose, I have transmitted the essence of my message to Mahakashyapa."

While Mahakashyapa remained in deep meditation, Buddha gave him the rose and Mahakashyapa became the originator of Zen, the branch of Buddhism that has produced the greatest number of enlightened beings of any tradition on the planet. Everything was transmitted in the deepest silence with very few gestures, so that only the Master and the chosen disciple perceived it.

Spiritual life is so different from our day-to-day reality that it can only be understood from the acts of the Master, by those who have eyes to see and ears to hear. Unfortunately, the great majority of human beings have neither, being unable sense the spiritual world that constantly surrounds us and of which we are part.

Many who read this 'ship's log' may not feel a resonance inside with what I am reporting, rather like being unable to appreciate a certain kind of music. It's natural not to hear divine music if we've never let go totally into trust in a being who is more conscious than we are, and can show us the path towards spiritual fulfilment. But, sadly, modern society creates egoistic individuals who think they can do everything by themselves – who, in fact, are convinced they *have to* do everything by themselves.

It is exactly the opposite on the spiritual path, where there is no competition and no struggle. It's not a race. It simply focuses on the development of the divine consciousness that resides inside each one of us. In this development, it's difficult to make progress without letting go into the love of a Master who teaches us the magic of relaxation – of acceptance and trust in existence.

A Buddha is here to make us see that the evolution of human beings doesn't stop only at possession, at power, at violence, but can also evolve on other levels of consciousness with all the beautiful spiritual values inherent in humanity, such as acceptance, love, compassion, joy, creativity and intuitive intelligence.

The teaching of Osho is that 'Buddha nature' and the divine are inherent in every one of us, not reserved for a few chosen ones.

Today there is the need for a totally different vision than the one lived for the last 2000 years. It's a vision of the world where every individual is focused on both material and spiritual wellbeing. When these two dimensions are lived together without separation, the future years and decades will be years of cooperation rather than separation.

Separating and destroying are the infantile components of a mind that wants to discover everything and for this reason takes everything apart and analyses everything to understand its meaning. That's what science does today, that's what the world of capitalism has done up to now. Instead, we need to return to the understanding that reality is not separate, it is one.

It is time for man to grow up, to go beyond the stage of adolescence, in which he wants everything right away at any cost, to a stage of maturity in which the profound mechanisms of reality are understood. These are the principles of unity and coexistence, at the centre of which spirit and matter go hand-in-hand, and the two polarities, male and female, coexist inside each one of us, just as all opposites exist inside of us, like anger and compassion, sadism and masochism, light and dark.

I will tell a traditional Zen story that can clarify this concept.

One day a sumurai, a great warrior who had killed dozens of enemies and was feared in every district, decided to meet a Master who knew the secrets of existence. When the samurai arrived before the Master, he asked: "Tell me Master, do heaven and hell really exist?" "Why do you want to know, you who are so ignorant and sanctimonious?" said the Master, deliberately offending the samurai. Now for a samurai an insult is paid for only with death and so he instinctively drew his sword and was about to cut off the head of the monk. The monk looked him straight in the eyes, without a trace of fear, and said calmly: "This is hell." The samurai was paralyzed, his sword held in the air. In a moment of pure awareness, he had a clear vision and understanding of the Master's teaching. Slowly he put the sword back in its sheath. Then the Master said calmly: "This is heaven."

This story needs to be remembered constantly during our daily life. The awareness that we create for ourselves, our hell and our heaven, makes us take responsibility for events without blaming anyone else for our bad acts and our suffering. Only when we assume such responsibility can we grow and become mature men.

Without taking responsibility for the hell we create, we won't ever take the first step to initiate change, real change that takes us toward the light that is inside of us, toward the source of love that is in us and that is the fountain of life: the third door through which we need to pass.

◻◻◻

27 Out of Lao Tzu House

For five intense months my life was spent only in Lao Tzu House and in the medical centre, a mere 50 yards away. No longer were we asked to wear any particular colour. It was the first time in the commune that everyone went around in whatever colour she or he preferred.

Osho had disposed of every rule. Of the three pillars of sannyas in Pune One – wearing orange, wearing the mala and meditating daily – only meditation remained as a prerequisite. We meditated in the discourses with Osho at least two hours a day, then there was a whole daily programme of meditations which were optional, including Dynamic Meditation first thing in the morning and Kundalini Meditation in the evening.

The Master put all his energy into his discourses and their publication, reminding us that we were no longer a commune in which disciples would come and stay forever. Rather, this was a temple where disciples could come, sit and meditate with the Master, stay for a few weeks or months, before returning to their daily life wherever they were living in the world.

This new phase of his discourses began with several question-and-answer series and then, later on, he chose to focus almost exclusively on Zen, commenting on the sutras of Zen Masters and the experience of enlightenment that happens to individuals when they finally decide to bring all their energy inside, not outside.

In April of '87, Osho started a new cycle of work, devoted to the relationship of male and female. As usual, he began his work in an ironic and joking fashion, starting with the people who were physically close to him. One morning after the discourse, Nandi and I were still in our room and Maneesha, the woman who asked Osho questions during discourse, sat down with us and told us that she had just seen the Master, who told her he wanted written questions from all of us who lived in Lao Tzu.

Each one of us had to write three or four questions for him to use in the public discourses. Clearly, it wasn't something to do tomorrow, or in the evening, but now, in the immediate present, as was the Master's custom. When he asked for something, everything else became secondary. So Nandi and I, each of us on our own, wrote questions. I think I wrote three that day, but none of us knew what was going to happen.

We were happy that Osho had asked us to write the questions, but we were absolutely unaware that this would be the beginning of a cyclone that would hit Lao Tzu and its inhabitants, spreading to the whole commune and to sannyasins around the world, and many years later to society at large.

In Lao Tzu, nearly all of us were paired in couples. Only two or three people lived alone. So it was natural that we would write questions about problems in love relationships, and this was the subject on which he was about to start a major work of transformation.

In the following days, there were many questions from Neelam, Kamaal, Nandi and me. The question that was asked wasn't really important. What was important was that he took it as the starting point for his intention, which was to create a wave of awareness about the nature of relationships between men and women, male and female.

The first of my questions that he answered was: "How to grow together, in a couple relationship, in love and meditation?"

I was seated right at his feet, about two metres from his chair, blissfully unaware that my ego was about to be transformed, so to speak, into cream. He looked at me directly in the eyes and said to me: "First of all, Azima, you don't know anything about love, neither of meditation…." He went on like that for his whole answer, exposing my personality in front of the commune and, of course, in front of the global community of sannyasins who would be listening to these discourses shortly thereafter.

At the end of his discourse, after having given his *shaktipat* and sending the whole hall into ecstasy, the Master left and I was stunned, as if I'd received a big kick in the head. I didn't know if I needed urgent resuscitation, or if I was already dead.

Many people came and hugged me, giving me so much love that my body warmed up and my heart started to beat once more. Even Neelam came and hugged me. And in the end, Kamaal made a joke that got me laughing with him, which was a big relief. Nandi was luminous and looked at me with great affection, as if my having survived the avalanche of the Master had given her more joy.

But the avalanches from Osho were not finished. He never quit on his victims and went straight to the depth of the wounds, until he had exposed them to the healing light of consciousness. In the following days, he answered a question from Nandi, telling her that she should enjoy herself with other men and leave this "stupid Italian fellow," meaning me, who had done nothing but weigh her down.

He encouraged her to fly like a butterfly to the magnificent male flowers that were in the commune, reminding her to lock the door of her room because I would doubtless come looking for her. He ripped me apart, but put Nandi in the palm of his magnificent tapered hands, showing everyone how beautiful she was.

I don't remember exactly when, but one morning in those stormy days, after he had again massacred my ego, the Master pulled the carpet out from under my feet. After discourse I walked slowly and meditatively back to our room, which directly faced the discourse hall, so the journey required very little time.

When I entered our room, I saw that my things were no longer there, neither my clothes, nor my mattress. Nandi's things were still there, along with feminine objects that had replaced my things. I was dumbfounded, looking around the room and trying to understand what had happened to all my stuff and my clothes, of which there was not a trace.

Then Neelam entered, who had also just returned from the hall after the discourse. She hugged me and, with a lot of sweetness, told me: "Stay calm! The Master hasn't sent you away from the commune. He has only separated you and Nandi, and for this reason I have given you a room in Krishna House. You will go there right away and your personal effects have already been sent there and are already organized. The Master is working on you!"

She hugged me with so much love that I could do nothing more than let go into her soft arms. It had lasted less than six months, my life in the house of the Master, but what months! I had learned what it meant to live totally in love with another being, what is meant by devotion, the first door to go through in our inner temple, beyond which our personality begins to get worn away like a rock by the slow and inexorable dripping of water.

I was in strange state in which I knew what to do, knew how to be independent, but my mind seemed to be turned off, as if someone had turned down the volume so much that I could no longer hear the constant noise of thoughts nor the flow of emotions.

Making an account of that whole experience, in just a few days Osho had:
1) separated me from the woman I loved;
2) told her publicly to go with other men and have a good time;
3) thrown me out of his house, which for a sannyasin was like being expelled from paradise;
4) made fun of me and called me a 'stupid fellow;'
5) told me that in ten years of being a disciple I had understood less than nothing;
6) said that I wanted to possess women as if they were plastic flowers;
7) said that I was a sex maniac;
8) said that my body was so rigid that if I continued like that I would break all my bones (which, by the way, is what happened six years later in a serious car accident).

I didn't know what was left of me. I continued to work like an automaton and would need many months to come back to myself after that first hit, because his hammering on my ego didn't stop there; it went for about another two years, with direct blows to all the masks I had worn up to now in my life.

A few days after the impact of the avalanche I was so dazed and worn out by the work that, after taking care of a sannyasin who was ill one night, I fell asleep in my chair, then fell over, hitting my head on the floor. I had to be taken to the emergency ward of a nearby hospital.

The next day I was back in my room in Krishna House, when Nandi, whom I'd seen only from a distance recently, came to ask me to go to work without any 'unnecessary self-pity.' From then on I saw her walking in the ashram with many other men and every time my heart was jolted by an onrush of fantastic memories.

She was the fifth woman from whom the Master had separated me. Only this time there was a difference: he made the separation directly, in public, without any doubt about it, and with a big scalpel that didn't leave any room for interpretations of the ego. This time our separation was a public fact and in that period no one talked about anything but the hits the Master was giving to the couple in Lao Tzu.

Many people made jokes the situation, but fortunately my closer and more intelligent friends demonstrated a lot of sensitivity, and limited themselves to hugging me without comment. In the meantime, Osho was taking aim at other couples in Lao Tzu; his favourite targets soon became Latifa and Om, about whom he went on for months.

After me, he threw out Om, then Kamaal, then Milarepa and then Rafia. By the end of the year, only three men remained in Lao Tzu: Amrito, his private doctor, Devageet, his dentist and Asheesh, the Italian engineer who moved like a shadow that no one ever saw or heard about.

The Master had separated the couples and sent away the men, but I should not give the impression that women were spared the surgeon's knife. It wasn't easy for them to give up the cosy security of their partnerships and stand on their own feet. Shortly afterwards, Osho asked for the creation of a therapy group called 'Women's Liberation' to help women recognise their neediness, their demand to be loved, their dependence on men, their low sense of self-esteem. Many sannyasin women passed through this group, facing all their female conditioning, in order to restore their dignity, which had been robbed for centuries.

Soon afterwards, he also created a 'Men's Liberation' group, which would serve to uncover the natural masculinity inherent in men, provoking their male energy to manifest itself, then switching to the opposite extreme and giving them a deep experience of the feminine side suppressed within them.

Looking back, I can see that Osho wanted us all to be lions, men and women alike, strong in ourselves, content to be alone, not needing anyone else as a prop, coming together only out of friendliness and joy, afterwards departing gratefully without any sense of clinging, jealousy, anger or regret.

Not surprisingly, many couples in the commune began to separate. Women began to respect themselves more, compromising less and giving more importance to the balance of their own male and female energies. Osho had started a movement that would arrive in many places in Europe and America, involving thousands of men and women who started to see themselves with new eyes, respecting themselves for who they really were.

From then on, during the Pune years, work on male and female issues spread through all fields of therapy. Even outside the sannyasin world, the subject has become important in various branches of psychology and psychotherapy.

So I tried to recover from the hits and adjust to my new life in Krishna House, where I no longer felt the stress of being continually aware with every act I did, as in Lao Tzu. For example, when I was still living in the house of the Master, Anando and Vivek called me to an empty room, closed the door and hassled me – Anando more than Vivek – about smoking a *bidi* on the terrace roof of the house, the smell of which had reached Osho's room.

Osho, it was known, was allergic to odours; in fact, so sensitive that all who came close to him were sniffed beforehand. It was true that I had smoked a *bidi* on the terrace, trying to cope with these emotionally intense times, but it seemed unfair to single me out. The whole population of Lao Tzu went to the terrace to smoke. The smoking section of the terrace was a meeting place for inhabitants, under the enormous limbs of a banyan tree. It was as far as possible from Osho's room, a corner where people met and exchanged a few words, made jokes and smoked a *bidi* or a cigarette together, or simply relaxed for a moment.

But they were aiming at me, trying to squeeze me, like examining each clause of an unwritten contract, accusing me of being in the house only because I was Nandi's boyfriend, saying I had to be much more aware of every act because we were all guests of the Master and had to respect his requirements to the best of our ability. In short, many large and small episodes made the atmosphere of Lao Tzu increasingly ascetic and inhuman.

Now I found myself in an atmosphere that was free of watchdogs and guardians. I started to feel the rightness of this space, of the liberty of movement and the joy of being in a house where I could do what I wanted, within the limits of communal living. Krishna House was a building with about 25 rooms, which meant about 40 people were living there, workers in the commune who were giving their energy to advance the projects of the Master.

The medical office was right below my room, so I had to walk even less than before to get to work, which continued to expand, especially at night, because of the growing number of so-called 'cuckoos' who disturbed the sleep of those living in the ashram. In the avalanche of energy surrounding the Master, some people had lost control of their emotions. Any one of these 'cuckoos' might, for example, indulge in an orgy of loud crying, late in the night, disturbing the tired workers resting in their rooms.

The work of taking care of the 'cuckoos' got bigger with time. Within a year, I had a team comprising two experienced female therapists, three nurses and myself. I have to say that among all the sannyasins who worked in the commune there were no manifestations of mental illness. The cuckoos were people living outside the commune, usually alone, who after participating in the meditations withdrew to the privacy of their houses, far from the ashram.

They weren't really part of the commune but we felt we couldn't abandon them in a continent like India. Medically, their behaviour could be diagnosed as episodes of schizophrenia, or temporary dissociation, that can happen if you start a spiritual path alone, without support, or in the presence of psychological fragility, or with previous psychiatric disturbances at the personal or family level.

So in the medical centre we had a team that took care of psychiatric cases. This work increased exponentially, to the point that I decided to discuss the situation with Neelam. I asked her if I could have more precise guidelines from the Master, but a few days later Neelam called and told me Osho had not given any response.

After a few months, in which the situation continued to get worse, I went back to Neelam, this time with some therapists in order to give more force to my requests. Neelam asked Osho again, but he just started laughing and again gave no directive. Finally, when the work of contacting the embassies and families of these people, to ask for their help, became really intense, I let Neelam and Hasya know we weren't going to do this work anymore, since this activity was monopolizing our time.

Either they needed to give us a department with more personnel that could take care of the mental cases, or we would throw in the towel. So Hasya explained to Osho that the situation had become really serious and we needed guidance.

This was his response:

My work is not that of helping people who are sick, or re-establishing a precarious equilibrium that the normal world calls 'wellbeing.' My work is that of helping people who are already well to become Realized Beings. Therefore, we are not here to take people from the unconscious to the ordinary level of consciousness, but rather to take people who are already at the normal level to a state of super-consciousness. For this reason, send these people back to their own countries and, for those who are nonviolent and believe themselves to be enlightened, give them a space where they can meet together so that they can confront their own madness.

When Hasya gave me this message outside Lao Tzu gate, where I was waiting for an answer, I felt liberated from a great burden that was hanging on my shoulders. It was, in fact, exactly what I wanted to hear and exactly what my own intelligence was telling me.

28 The Blows Keep Coming

Krishna House became the place where I spent my year of trauma due to forced separation from Nandi. I'd been so affected by these events with the Master that my world shrank into two rooms, where I worked and where I slept. I rarely went out of the ashram, except occasionally to go to a restaurant in the city with some close friends.

I worked all day long, and sometimes into the night, when I was often called to deal not only with cuckoos but with someone in the ashram who had fallen sick, or when some accident had happened. As the local doctor, I had to stitch up many sannyasin friends during this time, healing small wounds to the forehead, or the hands, that resulted from riding in rickshaws, the small three-wheel taxis that were unleashed at full speed in the course of the night – when the streets were empty of traffic – racing on their insane paths through Pune.

When the cases were more serious, I was forced to take the unlucky ones to local hospitals. In this way, I started to have more contact with Indian doctors in different hospitals. Often, I personally accompanied residents of the ashram into the operating room in order to help them. In fact, my days were more than full and this helped dull the pain of the wounds caused by the blows of the Master. Emotionally I hadn't fully recovered, so my heart wasn't open to a new relationship.

At about this time, Osho started to complain about pain in his arms and shoulders, and his body began to show the first signs of breaking down. Gradually, Osho and those around him came to suspect that he had been poisoned while in jail in the United States, perhaps with substances that could no longer be traced in his body and which nobody knew how to treat. I told Neelam and Amrito there was a system called Mora, with which they could detect the presence of poisons in the body and perhaps create a specific detoxifying therapy. Neelam showed a lot of interest in this, but Amrito had no trust in me, nor in any alternative medicine, so he said nothing about it to Osho.

After a couple weeks, I was told that Vivek wanted to see me, so I went to meet her in the house where I used to live. Vivek was a strange and unusual woman who was difficult to read and could be very surly, bordering on the misanthropic. She saw almost no one except Osho, whom she cared for day and night.

The whole time I lived in Lao Tzu I'd met her very few times. She was a woman with long, dark, chestnut-coloured hair, straight and fine, which went down her back. Small, with a very English face that was long and white, she gave an initial impression of veiled sadness or of a wild animal nature, with penetrating blue eyes that many were afraid of meeting. She looked like a cat, a wild lynx, and she was rarely seen in public in the various communes we built.

Everybody knew her as the companion of Osho, but very few talked to her in all those years and it couldn't be said she was very talkative. She asked me how I'd come to know about this machine and if its use could really help Osho. So I laid out to her in very simple and concrete terms the basic concepts and explained to her how this device could help identify the presence of poisons and indicate suitable therapeutic approaches. I had hardly finished speaking when she disappeared from my sight. She limited herself to saying "Okay!" and disappeared down the corridor.

It was obvious that she wanted Osho to experiment with the Mora system. For my part, I never forced the issue, knowing there were several different opinions in that house about how to treat Osho. Having had the experience of living in this hothouse, I didn't want to interfere. I limited myself to communicating the opportunity Mora presented in Osho's medical case. If they needed me, they would call me.

About two months passed and then one day Jayesh called me into his private room in Krishna House. Jayesh had made his appearance in the world of Osho during the last year of the Ranch, brought by Hasya, who presented him to the Master as a competent businessman. When Osho was arrested in North Carolina, Jayesh was on the plane with him along with members of his personal staff and was arrested along with everyone else.

In the space of a few months, he was in direct contact with the Master, accompanying him on the world tour and back to Pune, where he was busy soothing the political waters swirling around Pune, Mumbai and Delhi, helping to secure Osho's continuing presence in the ashram. Shortly before his death, Osho created an 'Inner Circle' with Jayesh at its head, making him primarily responsible for continuing his work at many levels.

For the record, Osho didn't leave anyone in his place as a spiritual leader, simply because it was impossible to replace him. Neither did he want his sannyasins confined within any form of institutionalized religious structure after his death. For this reason, there aren't any bosses, managers or leaders charged with the continuing growth of the neo-sannyas movement around the world in the years since Osho's departure.

The Master was aware that, once he was gone, it would be necessary to collect and disseminate the big collection of books and videos he'd created over the years. It was the basis of a unique teaching that would be of tremendous value to humanity for centuries to come.

Osho also knew that, in material terms, this legacy had great financial value, which is why he created the Inner Circle, appointing Jayesh as its head, supervising the publication and distribution of his books and tapes, and maintaining the working structure of the commune in Koregaon Park. This is how the spiritual heritage could continue to be accessed: through the Master's words and face, along with the fragrance of divine grace that will stay in the air in the Pune ashram and other Osho centres for hundreds of years, although it can be perceived only by those sensitive enough to receive it.

Already, at the beginning of Pune Two, Jayesh was becoming a point of reference for many aspects of the commune, including both its financial organization and its protection from Indian politicians. He had charisma and a natural talent for persuading people to see things his way, as well as an acute business sense, plus the support of his own considerable personal wealth, which he used on many occasions over the years to help the commune or people living in it.

I went to his room in Krishna House, which was located two doors down the corridor from mine. The whole team was there: Vivek, Amrito and Jayesh. One of Jayesh's qualities was to make you feel instantly at ease, respecting your presence and your opinions without creating difficulties. He asked me to explain the Mora approach to healing and help them understand exactly what it could do.

So, for the third time, I explained these machines, only this time employing more technical language, mainly because Amrito was there with his sceptical scientific nature. Nevertheless, Jayesh understood the potential of these machines and told Amrito, in a tone that was more an order than a suggestion, to take all the information I had given them to Osho. I detected in Vivek's expression a faint smile of satisfaction beneath her subtle veil of impenetrability.

That same evening, Amrito brought the brochures to the Master, explaining to him the basic mechanisms. The next morning Jayesh called me to his office, telling me that Osho had great appreciation for the machines and wanted all of them within five days!

At that time, in 1987, there were three devices on the market: the Mora Machine itself, which was the main device; the Mora Colour, which sent out bands of electromagnetic fields of different frequencies according to colour spectrum; and the Indumed, which sent out frequencies according to the 'Schumann Fields' – the natural magnetic fields of Planet Earth.

Osho wanted everything immediately, as was his custom. At the time, these devices had only been on the market for a few years in

Germany. Ordering them in Europe would take some months. How to get them in India in five days?

Jayesh gave me the keys to his office, telling me I could use it all day, making as many calls as I needed, spending whatever money I required without limits. But the machines had to be there in five days. I sat down at his desk and started calling sannyasins in Europe who might be able to help me. Those in the Cologne commune were the most available. I asked them to contact the German firm immediately in order to buy the machines but, as I suspected, the company replied they would need a few weeks to assemble the machines. After that, they had to be sent to India...more days lost.

I searched other avenues without success. Then, after two days, I remembered that my Swiss colleague, who'd been working with me at the beginning of Pune Two, knew these machines well and might even have bought them. I looked for him everywhere, but eventually discovered he had gone to Goa to do a yoga retreat in isolation. No one knew where he was, or how long he would stay there.

I looked for his wife, who'd stayed in the commune. I explained to her the urgency of the situation and she understood perfectly. She confirmed the machines had been purchased, knew their whereabouts, came with me to the office, called her mother-in-law in Geneva and told her some friends would come and take the machines because they were needed in the commune immediately.

Wow! It was done. I called the Cologne commune and told the organizers to send a sannyasin to Geneva to get the machines and bring them to Pune. On the fourth day, a sannyasin flew from Frankfurt to Geneva, collected the machines and left for India. On the fifth day the machines were here. I informed Amrito that the machines had arrived, but I also told him I wanted their inventor, Dr Franz Morell, to be the one who would treat the Master.

Even though I knew very well how to use the machines, I wanted the best for Osho. So I returned to Jayesh's office and called Cologne to get the number of Dr Morell. His wife answered the phone and told me that her husband was seriously ill in hospital and didn't have much time to live. I asked her if she had the names of those doctors who were closest to him. She gave me five names: an English doctor, three Germans and a Swiss. I called them, one by one. They all said it was too much to leave with such short notice, except the last one, the Swiss doctor. When he heard the name Osho he was happy to come and visit the Master. He was reading his books and was struck by what he called his 'spiritual philosophy.' So he decided to come and that very same day I made a ticket available for him at Geneva airport, paying all his expenses plus his fee.

Amrito and I went to the Pune airport to pick him up, took him to the ashram, to a room that had been arranged for him in Krishna House, and the next day I accompanied him to Lao Tzu for the visit. There, Amrito told me I couldn't enter. He would take the man to Osho. I could wait outside the gate and talk to him after the medical visit.

So, about two hours later I sat down in the Zorba bar with the Swiss doctor, where he informed me about everything he'd done. The same scenario repeated itself for five consecutive days in which Dr Gerard explained to me all the tests, the treatments and the follow-up that needed to be done once a week for a few months.

Osho liked bio-resonance therapy, as this system is now called, which uses electromagnetic waves, and made it known that he would willingly continue the sessions. When Dr Gerard left, everyone expected that, in the natural order of things, I would be giving the sessions to the Master, since I had organized the whole thing and was the only one who understood these new systems. But the Master hit my ego even harder than before, pulling out the rug from under my feet once again, with a message I knew was illogical and would take years for me to understand.

I arrived at the Lao Tzu gate a little early, anxious about treating the Master. After a little while Amrito arrived with a big bright smile on his face — a mix of satisfaction, madness and amusement. To conduct the sessions, Osho had chosen Anubuddha, one of the two massage therapists who had been leading the training in Tuscany at the time when I met Nandi. Anubuddha was a skilled body worker but had absolutely no understanding of alternative medicine.

But I knew better than to argue with Osho's decision, so I had to enter Lao Tzu with Anubuddha, explain everything to him, then wait outside the door of the treatment room in case he didn't understand, or forgot to do something.

I had not yet recovered from the blow of forced separation from Nandi and being thrown out of his house, yet, almost immediately, Osho was giving me another gift that would be very difficult to digest, but would certainly save my soul from any egotistical fantasy of being the Master's doctor – not only the Master's doctor, but also the doctor who perhaps succeeded in curing him with alternative medical systems.

For weeks, we continued with this farce...me accompanying Anubuddha to the door of what was known as the 'dental room.' Inside Lao Tzu House, a small operating room had been constructed, where Osho underwent various medical checks and procedures by specialists: the care of his dentist, his eye doctor, and others.

I have to acknowledge that Anubuddha was very kind to me, assuring me of his support, respect and esteem. There was no doubt that he was embarrassed by this role of 'temporary specialist' he'd been asked to play. Fortunately, he was a very intelligent person and quickly understood how the machines worked. After a couple months, he was capable of doing the work himself, rarely asking me for further explanations.

For many months, Osho received the bio-resonance treatments in order to strengthen his immune system, and also the Indumed treatments for pains in his back and shoulders. However, he never recovered from the thallium and radiation to which, we suspected, his body had been subjected while in jail.

Dr Gerard and I shared the same hypothesis: that Osho had been irradiated by radioactive seeds with long frequencies that penetrated his body without leaving any trace of their biochemical component. In keeping with this diagnosis, Osho's organism started to progressively degenerate on the left side of his body, starting from the shoulder, arms and neck, then extending to the face, especially the jaw and inner ear.

In the course of the last year, he was operated on by two great Indian surgeons: Dr Jyog for his ear problem and Dr Modi for his jaw.

They were called in because his bones had been infected, producing a breeding ground for disease that expanded rapidly and damaged nerve fibers, provoking strong pains. Maybe there was also an old diabetic component, a disease that is widespread among Indians, especially the well-off, which facilitated the spread of the infections. In any case, after his time in America, Osho's body started to degenerate in the bones on one side of the body.

My ego had again been put under pressure. Nevertheless, there wasn't time to understand the significance of what the Master was doing to me. I felt a deep trust that the Master was taking care of me and my spiritual growth, personally and directly. I also felt he was using me in some way to send a message to other sannyasins whose essence was hidden, like mine, under the same masks. I needed more than a year to absorb the blow of the separation and more than three years to understand the enormous gift he'd given me by crushing my doctor ego.

In Krishna House, I woke up every morning at six o'clock with the gong of Dynamic Meditation in nearby Buddha Hall and went downstairs for breakfast after yawning and stretching on my bed to the music of the meditation. During this time, I was meeting a huge number of people, and I became an integral part of the commune, whereas in Lao Tzu I saw only the few people who lived in the house of the Master.

After many months of listening to Dynamic while stretching on my bed, I finally decided it would be nice to do the meditation, along with everyone else, participating directly in the catharsis that happened every morning. I did it continuously for three months, triggering a process that helped me transform the shock from all of Osho's hits into vital and creative energy.

Jayesh personally paid for the new machines, and for other therapeutic equipment that Osho requested, as well as for another Mora machine for me to use in the medical centre as a form of collateral therapy.

Soon sannyasins were asking for Mora sessions and in the course of a few months I found myself loaded with requests. As a result, I was doing less and less acupuncture, leaving it in the hands of Abhiyana, an American expert in Chinese medicine with whom I'd always been in agreement.

My Argentine colleague was a beautiful woman with a grown child who also lived in the ashram, and with whom I worked shoulder-to-shoulder. Nirupo had a lot of experience in practical medicine and I relied on her for my allopathic decisions. She was attractive, tall, with dark hair, an athletic body and strong features characteristic of the South Americans. She had a lot of energy, was tireless in the work and managed to defuse even critical situations, making everyone relax, including doctors, nurses and above all the patients who were now flocking to the centre.

Mostly we had cases that were relatively simple to resolve, but once in a while we had really serious situations. The most extreme case was probably Rakesh, a body worker – in fact, the most expert and experienced among all of our body workers – who since Pune One had been teaching the practice of Rolfing, an intense deep-tissue technique.

Rakesh was a big, slow-spoken, humorous fellow and one of the great characters of the commune, very much part of the colourful scenery of our stylish ashram. Canadian by birth, he became a disciple of Osho in the early '70s and had never gone away, except for very brief periods. Rakesh was loved by everyone in the community.

One afternoon, he came to the medical centre and told me that since the night before he'd been having abdominal pains. I gave him some pain relief pills followed by injections, but after an hour the pain was still getting stronger. I was alone that afternoon and after few hours, when I saw that no medical treatment was working, I ran like a madman into the offices in order to get a car to take him immediately to the hospital.

At the hospital, I had a series of tests done right away, the results of which didn't justify the symptoms he was experiencing, which continued to develop dramatically. That night Rakesh was no longer mentally present, his pains increasing so much they rendered him semiconscious. The next morning, the situation had not improved and the sonogram showed faint signs of internal bleeding. The surgeon, the pathologist and I met in the office of the hospital. One wanted to operate immediately, the other preferred to wait for the results of other tests, so that in the end they passed me the ball, saying that I was his doctor and I had to decide.

Listening to what was going on inside me, I was aware of a big fear of losing Rakesh, so I asked for immediate surgical intervention. I went into the operating room with them, having called the ashram, asking them to contact his family in Canada. The surgeon took out metres and metres of intestine that was perforated with tiny ulcers capable of bringing death to Rakesh very quickly. He decided to cut out about two-and-a-half feet of intestine, the part that was most perforated, although the rest wasn't in good condition either.

When I exited from the operating room, Rakesh's girlfriend was waiting outside. I hugged her and told that everything had gone well, but his general condition was not reassuring. After a slight improvement in the late morning, the pains started to come back in the afternoon and Rakesh went into a pre-coma. I spent the afternoon in the office, refusing to accept that we couldn't understand what was happening.

I began to study all the medical books we had with us and after a few hours my eyes, my heart and my mind were all fixed on two small lines that were reporting a case of poisoning by *Clostridium perfrigens*, a bacteria that invades the intestine, producing a toxin that creates small ulcers that soon result in death. I felt a strong energy explode inside my body – I was sure this was the situation with Rakesh.

I went to the office and called Germany, searching for a colleague in Cologne whose opinion I respected. I asked him if he was familiar with the European Institute of Toxicology, which prepares antidotes to bacterial toxins, explaining to him our urgent need to have the antidote within 24 hours. The German commune went into action immediately and by next morning at seven o'clock an Indian sannyasin knocked on my door. He had just come from the airport with two vials of the antitoxin coming from Berne.

Meanwhile, the night before, I decided to let Osho know that Rakesh could die at any moment. I went to Anando in Lao Tzu and informed her of the situation. She went and told the Master and returned with one of Osho's towels, white and medium size, and a brown teddy bear that was exactly like the energy of Rakesh. They were gifts for him.

She and I left by car, to bring these things to 'Rocky,' as we affectionately called him. Rocky was unconscious. Two or three sannyasins were keeping him company. Anando approached the bed and put the two gifts near Rakesh's body. The teddy bear was a perfect match – it felt like his little brother.

The next morning I was happy to wake up early to receive the life saving package. If my diagnosis was right, I could still save him, otherwise there wasn't any hope. I ran through the hospital to talk to the head doctor, explaining to him my diagnosis. He told me he had only seen one case of *Clostridium perfrigens* but that certainly this could fit Rakesh's situation.

We decided to administer the anti-toxin as a drip, very slowly, drop by drop. In the afternoon Rakesh started to get better and in the evening he opened his eyes. The next morning, after having spent a quiet night, he had his first morning of celebration, coming back to life. His parents were there, his girlfriend, and a few sannyasins who came from the ashram. Finally, I could relax, after several intense days spent looking for ways to keep Rakesh with us. The diagnosis proved to be correct, the head doctor congratulated me and, more importantly, Rakesh started to make jokes about his impromptu trip into another dimension.

"What the hell did you eat?" I asked him a few days later, when he had recovered. "It's a mystery to me, because that particular bacteria grows only on rusty metal!"

Rakesh remembered that the night before he got sick, he had opened the refrigerator and eaten from a can of sardines that had been open for days. That was the culprit – a can of sardines that had taken him to the edge of the grave. I don't think Rakesh has eaten sardines again since that night.

29 The Osho Robes

In the period during which he opened the gates to the separation of couples in Lao Tzu, I asked Osho four questions, all of which he answered. Among these questions was one that was very different from those on male-female relations. It was: "Can it be said that the real moment of anarchy begins only with our choice of a spiritual path?"

After the discourse, Maneesha came to tell me that the Master was really pleased with my question and found it very profound, and that he wanted to let me know. Here was one of the few caresses that came from him in that year, along with, of course, the big gift of having accepted me in his house for six months.

When the discourse was over, Nandi and I made our way slowly toward our room. I always arrived in the room before Nandi because she paused along the way to talk or to hug with friends. Hardly had I opened the door when I was completely disoriented, with the doorknob and my heart in my hand, seeing two magnificent Osho robes spread out elegantly on our bed, one next to the other. On Nandi's side of the bed there was a black robe and on my side was a sea-blue robe.

Osho's clothes changed a lot over the years. In the first years of Pune One he wore a very simple white robe, but with time he began to wear more and more stylish and sophisticated clothing, finally ending up with 'the Star Wars look' he enjoyed wearing on the Ranch. Already, at the end of Pune One he'd started to wear caps, which from then on he never relinquished, even on his death bed. His robes were tunics that were long and colourful, more often with shoulder pads, the material becoming more and more refined with time.

But it was on the Ranch that he reached apex of his *haute couture*, wearing robes decorated with gold and rhinestones, made of velvet and synthetic materials, using a succession of colours that changed with every discourse he gave.

The robe he sent me as a gift was dark blue with large shoulder pads that extended well past the shoulders. It reminded me of the Jedi Masters in *Star Wars*. From the elevated shoulders, the material came down in broad strips, in different tones of blue. The neck was raised with a piece of pleated elastic material that came up to the chin. It was a winter robe, obviously, because it also had an inner lining of black velvet. It was one of the robes he wore most often at the Ranch in winter, as Vivek told me later, giving me a sweet smile of complicity.

The Master had really given me an intimate gift and I think it was for that reason Vivek felt closer to me. I never expected to receive anything of the kind, not only because it was highly unusual – Osho centres around the world received such things, but individual disciples rarely did – but also because it confirmed to me that Osho was working with me on the astral plane.

During my very early days as a sannyasin, after I was initiated in '78, whenever I closed my eyes in meditation, I started to see the Master, usually with his hands in the *namaste* gesture, wearing a blue robe. He also appeared in my dreams, on different occasions, depending how my unconscious was playing, and always with the blue robe. But at that time, in the first commune, Osho dressed exclusively in a plain white tunic. It seemed to be so much part of him that none of us could have guessed that one day he would dress in a whole variety of colours.

Nine years later, coming into the room where he'd invited me to stay, I found the blue robe on my bed that I'd always seen in my dreams, or my visions. I was shocked by this and didn't understand what these clothes were doing in our room. In the meantime, behind me, two or three people who knew about the gift were laughing gently at my great surprise.

I turned to them and said, "I think Krishna Priya (one of the Lao Tzu cleaners) got confused about the rooms. Osho's robes are on our bed!" Everyone started to laugh and Devageet hugged me, saying these were gifts from the Master for Nandi and me. I was astonished by the gift, but above all by the colour of the robe he'd sent. We all hugged while I broke out in tears.

From that day on, and for years to come, I never understood why Osho gave Nandi a black robe. Certainly, it was very beautiful, but to me it seemed very sorrowful and too serious for a woman like her. Besides, black didn't suit her and she never wore it. I imagined a robe with all the colours of spring, or the elegance of a peacock, for her, but surely not black.

Nandi was a woman full of life and loved by all. She was a joyous person and her daughter Disha was even more energetic and joyful than her. Brought up in the commune of the Master since she was a child, Disha was less than twenty and breathtakingly beautiful. She had a freshness, spontaneity and *joie de vivre* that bubbled around her, spreading wherever she went. The two women together were a winning couple on all levels, having been able to receive so much from life because they were so open and pure. Energy flowed in them like water rising from a spring; everyone wanted to dive in, in order to refresh themselves.

At that time, Nandi was separated from her first husband, with whom she had her daughter, Disha. He had never become a sannyasin, but nevertheless maintained good relations with his ex-wife and above all with his daughter.

A few years after the death of Osho, two tragically sorrowful events marked Nandi's life: the suicide of her first husband, and then the death of her daughter from an ectopic pregnancy. The loss of such a wonderful daughter, still young and full of life, must have been terribly difficult for her, as it was for all of us who knew Disha and found it hard to accept that this most beautiful flower in the field of the Master had departed so early.

Those two robes, given in 1987, contained in themselves the past and the future, dimensions the Master was able to perceive all the time, as if they were both part of an eternal present. Many times, in fact millions of times, Osho said the only existential reality is the present; the past and future exist only in the mind. My direct personal experience of these events verified for me that he was living on a completely different level from our own.

❏❏❏

30   My New Identity

Months after Dr Gerard's visit, Amrito called me and said he had talked with Osho, who decided I should dedicate myself exclusively to Mora Therapy sessions and leave the leadership of the medical centre to Indivar, an American doctor who'd run the medical centre at the Ranch.

I had to leave everything behind that I'd built, and the medical team with whom a beautiful atmosphere had been created in our little centre. All this, in order to take on another role that would be, although I didn't yet know it, my final role in this commune and, in time, the role through which I would present myself to the world after twelve years of communal life.

I was very unhappy about giving up my role as head doctor, but by now I'd started to understand that beyond the momentary blows of the Master there was always something afterwards that was much bigger and more valuable than the reactions of my little ego.

The loss of my position put me into uncertainty; I had no idea what would happen to me. I saw myself alone, in a small dark room, giving sessions to one person at a time. This vision didn't make me particularly happy. At the same time, I now knew that with the Master the path was one of dissolving the ego, not beautifying it.

So I continued to give sessions in the medical centre without being able to take care of the medical aspect of the work. It seemed strange not to be able to decide anything and not to share the joy of collaborating with Nirupo and my other colleagues anymore. I felt isolated and diminished, and both confused and trustful at the same time – trusting that all that happened to me through the Master had to be for my own growth, even if I didn't understand in the moment.

I continued like that for a few weeks until one day Jayesh called me into his office. He asked me how it was going with the Mora machine. I told him that I had recently increased the number of sessions and that people were really happy with this system of therapy, using non-invasive electromagnetic waves for healing and for testing for allergies and food intolerances.

He told me that Osho wanted me to expand the work. Not only that, he wanted me to create a healing centre separate from the allopathic medical centre, a new place where all unconventional medical techniques would be used. As a first step, the commune had purchased a villa on the other side of the street, that could be converted into a health centre, with saunas and two floors of rooms used for therapy.

I would be the leader of this endeavour and could go right now to see the space in order to decide the best way to use it. So far as the machines were concerned, if I needed more of them I could order whatever was necessary. Jayesh would buy whatever we needed. Wow! What a hit! Osho always played for high stakes and big projects. I never saw him opt for projects that were medium sized. He wanted everything to be the best, for him and for us, and always as soon as possible.

Yet again, my acceptance of events had permitted the most beautiful flowers to spring up in my life. I hadn't avoided the shredding and the blows of the Master, I hadn't closed my heart. I hadn't blamed anyone. Now, suddenly, I found myself in charge of a healing space twenty times bigger than the medical centre.

In that property, besides the healing centre, the ashram quickly created a space for theatre, sculpture and painting, a post office, a Japanese restaurant and a big tent that served as a beer garden in the evening after the meditations.

I went immediately to the villa, which was really beautiful and big. On the second floor, I chose the biggest room in the corner of the structure, with a window that overlooked the gardens. I had *carte blanche* for everything, so I had a big desk built where I could put the machines and a series of movable cabinets that could hold all the vials of homeopathic products.

The room was insulated against humidity during the monsoon and it had air conditioning. It was like a dream, but Osho made sure we were living so much better than in a dream. He had us living reality at the highest level of our potential energy. In all this time, for almost two years now, Osho had worked on me continuously, breaking down old masks and helping me to live in closer contact with my essence.

A few months would pass before 'Omar Khayyam,' the name Osho gave to the new villa, was ready to house the healing centre and its staff. The opening of this new space had added a certain feverishness to the work in the commune, which was already on full throttle. Following Osho's guidance, Jayesh was expanding the ashram, rapidly transforming it into an ultramodern centre for spiritual growth, with many new rooms for meditation, therapy groups and sessions, as well as new residential spaces, a large park, a swimming pool, health centres, centres for creative and martial arts, and more. Everything was changing, growing bigger, as new properties were being added to the original setup.

In addition, Osho was preparing, without anyone being aware of it, a temple for the period after his departure. He asked for a 'new bedroom' inside Lao Tzu, to be located in Chuang Tzu Auditorium, the place where he gave discourses in the early days of the commune, and the place where I had received my initiation in 1978.

The auditorium contained a space that was really big for one bedroom and many of us thought the Master was hiding something, but certainly none of us – not I, nor most of the residents – could think this would be his *samadhi*, the place where his ashes would be kept. And for his part, he did everything to keep us from realizing that he was constructing the space where the ashes of his body would be placed. But as the work went on, for almost two years, more and more people understood that in this huge space, with white Italian marble floor and high walls, absolutely empty and with high, tinted windows reaching from the ground more than 20 feet high, he would never make his bedroom.

The work inside Lao Tzu accelerated, and was done in continuous shifts. Osho was pushing to finish it quickly, so there was a steady increase in the number of bricklayers and carpenters to complete the project. Everything was in turmoil and it seemed like we had returned to the times of the Ranch, when frantic construction was the basis of our being together.

Jayesh did a great job making property deals and gaining the cooperation of Indian authorities and so, within two years, the ashram quadrupled in size. The energy was very high and Osho was pushing us deeper in his daily discourses, too, which lasted longer and longer. Everything was going at full speed in this very positive and creative period.

But at the very moment when the energy was flying higher than ever, I had a completely different experience. I was still living in Krishna House in my tiny room, almost a monk's cell, a refuge into which I was happy to withdraw and rest in the evenings. Suddenly, one day at dawn, my body and my mind woke up with an experience of great energy that forced me to sit up in bed. In the first moment, I thought it was time for Dynamic and that my body, which was used to getting up early, had been activated by itself. But soon I understood that it wasn't really about waking up. Along the wall in front of me, my eyes began to see a series of images that gradually became clearer, displaying my own vision as if someone was projecting a film behind my back.

****

I saw a big house, like a castle in the English style or a large English manor house, with big woods behind the residence. All around the main building, there were extensive English lawns that were almost phosphorescent.

Suddenly, from this scene devoid of human beings, the figure of Osho appeared, coming out of the house. My observation point was far away, very far away from the house, probably about two hundred yards away, and the space was empty except for green grass. The image of Osho was small from my perspective, but coming

MY LIFE WITH OSHO

toward my point of observation, and his body started to get bigger as it came nearer.

Behind him, in small groups, his disciples were coming out and following him at a respectful distance. He was walking slowly, as he did in real life, and the image took some time to arrive at my observation point. When he was really near, a few steps from me, an armchair appeared, on which he sat like he did in discourse. The disciples that had followed him, little by little as they came closer, grew in number as they arrived around the chair, sitting down in a semicircle of silence around him. There were about 1,000 people seated on the English lawn. The scene was very bucolic, but the sensation received was that of being in front of something solemn, very solemn, as if the Master had come out to make an important declaration.

When everyone was seated, the Master started to speak. He said that in a little while he would be dead and that it would not be a natural death but that he would be killed by one of his disciples. This person, along with others, would organize his death right in the middle of the commune, before the eyes of everyone.

He knew already that this would happen but he wouldn't interfere in these events. He went on to speak about betrayal and that we all needed to be very aware because the enemy was hiding among us. He spoke again very intensely about the situation that would be created and then, at a certain point, he pointed toward me, saying: "From now on Azima you will always be seated at my right side!" After that he rose slowly and moved toward the big English house. The image was absorbed in the dissolving light that made it smaller and smaller on the horizon.

The next images were inside the ashram in Pune, where thousands of people were walking as usual along the main road. Everyone was busy with their own affairs, only the looks they exchanged were not the usual looks full of loving confidence, open to hugs and sharing. The atmosphere was very tense and people where looking each other with reticence. Disciples where suspicious of each other, even with friends. Groups of people where talking with animosity and accusing each other of something. Panic and *fear was everywhere and was increasing like an avalanche, becoming bigger and bigger. Everybody suspected everybody else and living inside the ashram was impossible. I saw myself running here and there, looking for some place to hide, but in vain.*

In the next scene I found myself in a sauna with Kaveesha and Yogi, two American sannyasins who were involved with the Mystery School and other ashram projects. There, I could finally relax. I felt secure and shared with them the events that had happened. Kaveesha, with her usual calm, told me that everything would go the right way and that we could remain protected there until the epidemic of mistrust had passed. For the rest, there was nothing we could do.

****

The images suddenly disappeared and I found myself sitting on the bed as before the experiences had started. My body returned to normal and the intense burst of energy I had felt vibrating inside me had vanished. Once again I was seeing the room how it actually was, being conscious of real time, while knowing nothing of how much time had elapsed during the vision. It could have been a few minutes or a lot longer. The images were so clear, I had no doubt that my body/mind had seen a vision of what would happen in the future. I couldn't do anything but go to Kaveesha and share my vision with her.

Kaveesha was an American woman with a very robust body and energetic presence that left no doubt about her meditative state and her charisma. She was always calm and most of time I met her she was seated in an armchair. She worked closely with Yogi, who was a friend of hers from her pre-sannyas life as a therapist in America.

When they arrived in Pune Two, they soon created a stream of therapy so effective that Osho put Kaveesha in charge of 'The Academy of the Mystery School,' which became the most successful therapy department in the ashram.

The Mystery School groups used esoteric methods focusing directly on the growth of human consciousness, and were completely different from the therapy groups like Primal and Encounter. These new groups helped people develop sensitivity to subtle things like *prana* and the chakras, and trained people to read the energy of others in order to help them become more conscious of whatever is keeping them separate from the light. These groups were very successful and brought a lot of money to the ashram's coffers.

Kaveesha wasn't seen much around the ashram. She stayed in her room all day. Everything and everyone circled around her and she behaved like a real master inside the commune of the Master, but in a space of total devotion toward Osho. For many, Kaveesha became an embodiment of the truth and more and more people began to follow her. She also lived in Krishna House, along with others of her entourage. I didn't have much contact with them, but every time I did have contact, my trust was fully repaid.

Now, having had this vision, it was clear to me that these were the only persons with whom I could share it. I had to let them know what had happened. So after Dynamic, I went to Yogi's room, which was adjacent to mine.

Yogi was also a medical doctor but had left his clinical career in order to become an expert in hospital organization and in this way had made a lot of money. From the time he became a sannyasin he was dedicated solely to meditation and was working with Kaveesha to create new therapeutic programs.

He was a man of medium height, with brown hair and dark brown eyes that reflected a sharp intelligence, set in a face that inspired calm and trust. Always dressed in sober and elegant clothes, he was a man of few words who knew how to listen, which made it easy to open up to him when sharing ideas or confiding problems.

After hearing my story, Yogi didn't hesitate. He brought me to Kaveesha's room, where she listened to my vision in silence, stretched out on her favourite sofa. At the end of my brief account she said the vision should be referred to Osho right away, because two days ago a friend of hers in Hollywood, a medium but not a sannyasin, had called to warn them to be on guard, because she'd had a vision of someone making an attempt on the Master's life.

My vision coincided with another, completely separate vision, which occurred on another continent but only a few hours apart — the same message coming from two sources that didn't know each other.

Kaveesha assured me she would call Anando, who saw Osho every morning, asking her to report to him as soon as possible the two visions. She would call to inform me as soon as she had an answer from the Master. We hugged and in this hug I felt all the strength of this woman who had a very pronounced male energy coupled with an enormous maternal compassion. In that hug, her energy expanded and my body was filled with an intense heat that made me feel immediately at home.

I left and slowly made my way toward the medical centre, where I was immediately swept away by events that, as usual, came tumbling towards me, one right after the other.

Two days passed and then I got a call from Kaveesha asking me to come to her room. Anando had reported to Osho exactly what had happened to me and to the medium in America. The Master's answer was an intense and prolonged silence. Anando had attempted to press for an answer, but his answer was a continued and absolute silence. Certainly, if our visions were simply inventions of our minds, he would have made a joke, as he usually did, in order to downplay the circumstances. But he remained silent and, to me, that silence implicitly confirmed the authenticity of our visions.

The experience of this vision affected me deeply, but I preferred not to talk about it with anyone in order not to give rise to paranoid gossip within the commune. Kaveesha and I saw each other rarely and on the few occasions when we did meet we avoided talking about this subject. But a year and a half after my vision, it was discovered that negative vibrations were somehow being turned against the Master.

One evening in December 1989, Osho made it known, through an announcement by Amrito, that someone was intoning mantras that were hitting him in the energy centre of the *hara*, weakening him so much that they were bringing him toward certain death. In these days, when he stepped onto the podium, he was tottering like

I'd never seen before and his body was clearly suffering. In the space of two years he had visibly aged: he looked more like an old man of a hundred than a man in his fifties. He was no longer able to give discourses, but continued to join us most evenings, to share his silence with us for twenty minutes. After the meditation he left like a cloud disappearing in the sky without leaving a trace.

The first evening that Amrito relayed the message of the Master, I think many sannyasins didn't take it seriously, but for me it was a heavy blow received from a still sky. These words brought back the vision that I'd had a year and a half before. In the following evenings, Osho made it known through Amrito that, according to his information, this energy attack on him through the mantras was intensifying and that soon it would be impossible to escape from it. In record time, slabs of lead were installed around his chair, in the hope that the vibrations couldn't reach him then, but during the following nights his messages didn't change.

Osho let us know that he also knew mantras that could cause death and that if necessary he could use them. However, the next night his message was clear: "In my philosophy of life there is no place for violence. Even though I know mantras that are stronger than theirs, I would absolutely not use them, preferring death rather than going against the ideal of non-violence I have professed and lived by."

Every evening we waited anxiously for the message from Amrito, nevertheless the essence of what was being communicated didn't improve. The Master let us know that only Indians and Tibetans knew mantras that were this powerful and we needed to look among ourselves. A distrustful paranoia that I had seen clearly in my vision, took over the ashram. At the entrance of Buddha Hall and sprinkled around the crowd, the sensitive ones among us were asked to 'feel' the presence of possible suspect persons.

Energetic 'corridors' were created to defend the Master from mantras and even outside the commune, near the park, Indians who looked like they might be able to send messages from farther away were followed. During the day, many channellings were done to try to find out where the sounds were coming from, but it was futile:

MY LIFE WITH OSHO | 341

we didn't discover anything that could stop these sounds from weakening the Master.

As the days passed, people became more and more worried, and while the commune continued to function normally, we felt helpless against this invisible energy that was taking our Master away. The trust and friendship we once enjoyed was replaced by suspicion. As Kaveesha had said in the vision, we could only wait.

In all of this period, from the vision I had in Krishna House in 1988 to the death of the Master in 1990, every evening we sat in Buddha Hall to meditate with him, I had my place at the right side of his chair, up until the night they brought his corpse to the podium, before the cremation.

This was unusual. In the hall where we meditated with him, about 3,000 people entered. Seats in the first few rows were reserved and assigned by the office. The first two rows were generally reserved for the people in Lao Tzu and for old sannyasins residing in the ashram. Behind them were residents of Krishna House and therapists; behind them sat the rest of the workers. The remaining part of the hall was free seating and whoever entered first could sit nearer to the podium. The seats for us residents were changed regularly. It was almost impossible to be assigned a seat in the same area for so long, but for over a year I had a place at the right side of the podium, as it had been in the vision.

None of us, especially those who worked in the commune, suspected that the Master was really leaving his body. Even Neelam, who continued to see him regularly, thought he would stay with us for another year. Nevertheless, the vision materialized in all its little details. One more shock was in store. In the same period, a little before the mysterious 'mantra' events, Vivek, the woman who had taken care of the Master meticulously for so many years, died.

She died from an overdose of sleeping pills and it seems likely she intended to take her own life, or send a signal of distress that was not heard by anyone until her body was discovered in the morning and it was too late. She arrived at the hospital in a coma and died soon afterwards.

My first-hand experience with her gave me the feeling that the whole saga of Osho's travels outside India, including the attempts by Sheela to isolate her, and the poisoning of Osho by the US Government, then being expelled and hounded from country to country, all served to make her withdraw into a mistrustful sadness that only succeeded in isolating her more from the rest of us.

Besides, I am sure she felt that Osho was leaving the body very soon. I think the idea of seeing Osho die was unbearable to her.

Osho's response to her death was to ask us to place a photo of her, inset into the wall of one of the ashram's pyramid-shaped buildings, with an inscription in her memory that added, "who died an untimely death."

Vivek's death was, for me, a powerful reminder that it doesn't matter how physically close you are to a Buddha. All that matters, in the end, is the depth of your own meditation and the totality of your determination to reach your inner being.

31   Meeting with Poonjaji

In 1989 when the new healing centre started to function well, they called me to the office to tell me my new residential room would be outside the original ashram, in the building Jayesh had bought for the healing centre and arts department. The room was even smaller than in Krishna House. This time there wasn't even a bathroom inside – I had to go to the end of the corridor to use the bathroom and shower, which was also used by the other residents.

There was only enough space for a bed, a wardrobe and a tiny chest of drawers. A small window looked out the back of the villa, toward the garden surrounding the house. It was from this window, less than a year later, that Pragito and I understood the Master had left his body.

In this year, Osho personally reduced the number of resident workers because he didn't want people putting down roots in Pune, and for this reason the office started to hire local workers for construction and masonry.

I remained head of Mora Therapy, which started to make more and more profit for the commune, so much so that in a few months, after the first courses I gave on bio-resonance, there was a team of four people with me, who carried out the follow-up procedures I established. Two new rooms were added for sessions. My main assistant was the German doctor who'd been the last person to leave the Oregon Ranch, staying on for two years to take care of everything.

It was a pleasure to work with Puri; he had a fantastic totality in everything he did. When he arrived from the Ranch in '88, he was immediately taken in by the ashram. He was tired of machines, transport vehicles, broken pumps and trying to maintain all the equipment that remained on the Ranch. Not surprisingly, he wanted to do something totally different.

So he asked me if he could learn bio-resonance. I was happy to have another doctor with me because my other assistants weren't trained medically. They were sannyasins who were fascinated by the system and the techniques they'd learned in my courses.

Puri became my right hand man and together we tried out a lot of new ideas. My small but profitable department became a kind of flower in the button hole of the ashram. It was a futuristic scene, our room full of machines: Mora Colour, Indumed, Mora, Bicom {?sp?}, Crystal Therapy, Coloured Light Sources and so on.

Several Indian journalists who came to write articles on Osho and the ashram were sent to me to experience the quality of alternative therapy that was available in the ashram. They were so impressed they wrote articles about me and the medical devices I was using, and in a short time 'Dr Azima' was a well-known personality in the State of Maharashtra.

Neelam sent famous people from Indian public life to me for medical visits, especially people from the arts. I had a visit from Hari Prasad Chaurasia, the well-known master of the Indian bamboo flute, known as *bansuri*, whom Osho, on several occasions, described as the greatest flute player who ever existed. There was also Shivkumar Sharma, the country's best player of a stringed instrument called a *santoor*, played with wooden sticks, as well as many other artists who came to the commune to give concerts and pay their respects to Osho.

From then on, Osho gave me a lot of attention and even started to include me in some of his jokes, which he told every evening at the end of his discourses to make us laugh and relax before participating in the 'gibberish' and 'let go' meditations. 'Dr Azima' became a personality in several jokes and this was one of the most beautiful gifts he gave me, because it put me in the small entourage of disciples of whom he liked to make fun, knowing well their devotion to him.

In the meantime, I started to test workers for food intolerance and proposed the ashram create a line for non-dairy food at our daily meals. So they created two service lines in the restaurant, one dairy and one non-dairy. For this decision, at least in the beginning, many people were unhappy with me, thinking it to be completely unnecessary. But with the passage of time, this initiative became widespread in our communes throughout the world. Nowadays, a diet without dairy or without wheat is increasingly popular in the ordinary world.

When we introduced the diet for food intolerance in 1988, no one in India had heard about a diet without milk products or sugar and it wasn't easy for someone to follow such a diet in this country. The typical Indian diet relies a lot on dairy products and sugar – so much sugar that a lot of Indians suffer from diabetes. Osho himself had a mild form of this disease.

This reminds me of Poonjaji, the Advaita Master whom I visited after Osho's death and who was also affected by this disease in a serious way. I meditated with him for a few weeks in Lucknow in '92 and he also wanted a medical visit with me. Poonjaji, also known as Papaji, was already old when I met him, about 80, and his body was affected by diabetes, which was now in an advanced state, with circulation problems that caused difficulties walking. He was a man with an imposing stature and even though he was old and limping he had a physical presence that was felt in the whole room.

The first time I saw him, seated Indian style on his raised platform, a golden halo extended from his face and filled the space around his body with a yellow-gold light that made him seem like an old Tibetan monk, as seen in the ancient paintings of Tibet. I had seen the same aura of yellow gold in '78 when I met Krishnamurti in Mumbai and immediately that experience came to my mind.

His big round face was always engraved with a smile full of compassion that made you feel immediately welcome, received and embraced by a halo of joy. He joked frequently during his teachings, even just by moving his big clear eyes, and serious people couldn't get much traction with him.

Whatever question came to him from disciples, he initiated the mental torture by asking the person: "Who is asking the question?" And the longer you tried to stay standing on this meagre tightrope he put you on, the more he pushed you toward the abyss of the ultimate question, "Who am I?"

I never asked Poonjaji a question, seeing as I already recognized my not knowing who I was. It seemed useless for me to ask him questions and I stayed in the room where he was giving *satsang*, meditating and enjoying the light energy that his presence created during those weeks.

Two days before leaving Lucknow, one of Papaji's closest disciples came to my apartment, which wasn't far from his house, to tell me that Papaji had asked for a medical consultation with me before I left. I didn't expect this gift from him, primarily because we had never spoken to each other and I had never asked a question during the teachings. I hadn't tried to put myself in a place where I could be seen during this period, but as usual the masters respond spontaneously to events without interference from their minds. So the next morning, after he had had his breakfast in his room, I entered for this so called 'medical visit.'

It was a modest apartment in a completely Indian style, with a big living room at the entrance, where Papaji gave his teachings. At the end of the corridor to the right, there was his room, a bathroom and another room. In his room, all the events of the day unfolded in these few square metres, except for *satsang* that was held in the big room. There was a small kitchen in the back with a Western woman who took care of preparing his food, who was at that moment washing dishes.

To the right, there was a simple bed with springs and a mattress where he slept and where he welcomed people who came to talk to him. Around him there were three or four people who were cleaning the floor, talking on the telephone and taking care of relations with the outside world. They were coming and going continuously. Everything happened with an unusual harmony that made the atmosphere similar to an orchestra where everyone played their own instrument in perfect harmony with the others.

Papaji was clearly the director of this orchestra and he continued to joke and give instructions when asked practical questions. He greeted me with a big smile and had me sit down next to him on the bed. He talked to me about absurd things without any real sense, continuing to joke and laugh at whatever happened in the moment.

I was already familiar with the Indian mind, particular that of the guru, who didn't do anything but talk of little things, totally in the present moment, as if nothing existed outside this room and this moment. So I willingly dived into this flow of energy that had no logical sense but which was nevertheless endowed with the vital presence that was so strong around him and immediately made me joyous and playful with him.

After half an hour or so, I told him that I had come as a doctor to visit him and that I would ask him some questions. He laughed again, saying it was a fixation of his disciples to have him see doctors and that in recent years the strangest doctors had come to see him in order to pull his legs, examine his eyes, clean his energy, insert their hands in his abdomen and do a lot of other manoeuvres that had no other effect but to amuse him a lot.

He started to imitate aura cleaning with the goofy gestures that an American doctor had used to treat him a few years ago. Everyone present started to pretend to clean the aura of someone else and immediately we were all laughing together in chorus. It was impossible to be serious in his presence.

We stayed together a couple hours and at the end I suggested that he eliminate white sugar from his diet, substituting cane sugar, and I gave him some herbal medicine, which I knew could be easily obtained in India, to help the circulation in his legs. Before I left he looked into my eyes and said: "Everyone tries to cure my diabetes, but if it weren't for my illness I wouldn't have met a wonderful man like you."

I hugged him from my heart and thanked him tearfully for all he'd given me in these few hours we spent together. Once again I had experienced that a real Master goes beyond appearances and goes directly to the heart of people, to the essence that pervades everything, without wasting time with mental frills and moralistic games.

Poonjaji simply wanted to see me and spend time with me, and he used his ailing body and his illness to live something deeper and more essential than a simple symptom or a simple medical treatment. I stayed a few more days, and on my last day, at the end of the *satsang*, while he was going to his room and everyone made a small opening for him to pass, he stopped in front of me and said with a lot of love in his voice:

"Is it really true you have to leave tomorrow?"

"Yes, but I will stay in contact with you and continue to give you treatment for your legs."

"Oh! My legs are already better, so I quit taking the medicine!"

We burst out laughing and with a *namaste* I thanked him while in tears for all the love he had shared with me. Poonjaji continued to give teachings until the last days of his life, in this dimension of joy and awareness. He died in *samadhi* in Lucknow in 1997. I didn't see him again, because after that I went back to Italy and disappeared into the life of the West, throwing myself totally into my medical practice.

❐❐❐

32 The White Robe Brotherhood

In the middle of 1989, Osho decided that inside the ashram we would again wear specific colours. Outside we were free to wear any type of clothes we liked, but during the day, inside the ashram, we were asked to wear maroon robes, which were a mixture of wine red and blue, with a bit more shade of red, rather like the robes of Tibetan monks. During the evening meditations with him, we were asked to wear robes that were completely white. The therapists, when working in groups and individual sessions, now had to wear black robes with a white belt at the waist.

In this way, the ashram filled up with colour and seemed like one of those old Tibetan monasteries full of monks arriving from all over the place to attend one of their annual celebrations. With respect to the orange robes we wore in Pune One, the energy was now clearly different. In those days, the explosion of energy was much more concentrated on the physical and sexual level, whereas now we all breathed a more meditative air, sweeter and more focused inward.

The change brought about by the robes was really tangible, just like all the big experiences Osho had us live through in these last years. But it wasn't only a question of that. Lately, more meditation groups had been added to the program and many sannyasins went around the ashram wearing badges that said 'In Silence.' So, once

350 | MY LIFE WITH OSHO

again, Osho gave the signal to move toward a new dimension, as he had many times in the past.

The energy in the ashram was growing, opening up to new paths that started to flow in new streams that fed the river. The streets of the ashram filled with new disciples and with old friends who reappeared in the *Buddhafield* after many years of absence. Osho was pushing us to the maximum and joy, creativity and meditation were at their height in these last two years of his presence in the physical body.

From Pune One, in which the work had been centered on releasing sexual energy and repressed anger, and from the Ranch, where he had us living fully the power of the third chakra, we had travelled to Pune Two, where Osho started to focus on a more refined energy, working with the fourth and fifth chakras: love and creativity.

The explosion that followed was unforgettable. There were no limits and participation in the ashram was total and unconditional. The first time Osho sat with us, with all of us dressed in white, it provoked an emotion so deep and intense that many of us burst out crying. Osho called this evening meditation the *Meeting of the White Robe Brotherhood*, asking us to dress in white wherever we did this meditation around the world, reaffirming the idea that after his death, whenever five or more of us were meditating together, he would be there with us.

Osho was plugging us into an underground energetic current that had never died, dating from the time of Christ. Often Osho had spoken to us about the life of Jesus, telling us it wasn't exactly like it has been recorded in the New Testament. Osho's version of these events has been confirmed by archaeological finds and by various books, both modern and ancient, which confirm that Jesus didn't die on the cross and after his 'resurrection' he left for the Orient.

In Osho's version, Pontius Pilate had a lot of admiration for Jesus, partly because his wife was a follower, and she had begged Pilate not to condemn her Master to death. So Pilate spoke to Jesus, offering him a way out, an escape route that could get him out of Jerusalem safe and sound, but Jesus answered: "My father wills it," indicating his intention to end his days on the cross.

In order to save him from certain death, Pilate organized the crucifixion for the afternoon before the Sabbath, the day when the Jews observed their religious ceremonies. He knew Jesus would have to be taken down from the cross before the Sabbath began. So he stayed on the cross for only a few hours. Recent scientific studies by researchers at American universities have demonstrated that it would take at least 24-36 hours to die on the cross.

Once his disciples had taken him down, they took him to a secret place in order to wait for his astral body to re-enter his physical body. When he was ready, he left Galilee and headed for the Orient, along with his mother and Mary Magdalene, his companion.

From that time on, Jesus and his disciples dressed in white, creating the *White Robe Brotherhood*, and making many converts on the way to India. Many ancient Arabic texts talk about a certain Jesus and the *White Robe Brotherhood* that stopped along the way to India and preached a new doctrine. Often, they stopped for a few months and then continued toward the East. Among other things, these texts report the precise names of some of his disciples.

The tomb of his mother Mary is located in Pakistan, with her name carved on it. The main group went on to Kashmir, to the village of Pahalgam, which means 'the village of the shepherd.' Here Jesus stopped and established his community, which became very well known and full of followers who dressed in white robes. He lived to the venerable age of more than 80 years old. His tomb can be found to this day in this village, with his name inscribed and a carved impression of his feet.

Two thousand years later, Osho reconstructed an energy field that had become an underground movement with the passing of the centuries, mainly due to persecution, and that a few followers had secretly kept alive. Osho was now opening up this energetic field to hundreds of thousands of people. It was as if he was bringing together different esoteric spiritual traditions in one vessel that didn't have a name or specific rules, but that was ready to sail the seas of the unknown dimensions, the seas of 'religiousness' and no longer those of exclusive sectarian doctrines.

Seen from the perspective of the Buddhist tradition, Osho was the Master who has again turned the 'Wheel of the Dharma,' nearly

2,500 years after Gautama Buddha, opening a new dimension, a global dimension that includes both the spiritual and material life, without any separation. He did this by putting all the religious traditions into a single global vision.

If we look at his life more closely, we can see that his message and his teachings include not only ultra modern psychological insights and the ancient paths of Buddha and of Zen, but also those of Jesus and esoteric Christianity, as well as Taoist, Zoroastrian and Socratic traditions. Osho had the capacity to unite all the religions of the past under one umbrella, under which he himself was just an empty space, a vacuum that permitted the different subtle energies that govern the visible world to come together.

In the coming years of the twenty-first century, the cathartic energy of religious fanaticism will get stronger. Sectarian religions will use their power in the name of their faith, bringing whole populations into conflict and destruction, with millions of deaths. Now is the time that Osho's message needs to be absorbed by more and more people. And hopefully, one day, what remains of this world will give birth to a new dimension, no longer based on power, but on love and compassion.

It is our human destiny to live in love, but in order to realize this, existence has structured itself in an illogical, absolutely mysterious way. A Master like Osho comes to this planet to help millions of people cross the threshold of this quantum leap, in this case, from the third chakra to the fourth. This can advance the human race, which, as it is behaving now, has lowered itself to a subhuman level.

In his last years, the Master did everything he could to organize things before leaving the physical body. He did everything so that there would be no spiritual power structure around his teachings after he had left. In fact, up until today, twenty years after his death, there is no trace of a spiritual power structure constructed in his name.

So far as I was personally concerned, in the last years of the Master's life, my medical creativity exploded and opened me up to all kinds of experimentation, to paths that were both possible and impossible. For example, a few sannyasins who were involved in the work started by Wilhelm Reich, the pioneering psychotherapist, started asking for my collaboration in their research. So we regularly shared our experiences in exploring new energetic structures that served to protect the physical body from pollution and strengthen the immune system.

We constructed an 'orgone box,' inspired by Reich's work, in which you could sit to receive cosmic energy accumulated through its special layers and in this way become more vital and healthy. We explored systems for protecting against ultraviolet rays from the sun, mixed with substances for detoxifying the body and other systems for regenerating the body.

Therapists who worked with crystals and channelling in the Mystery School also came to explore my system of diagnosis and therapy. With them, I experimented with a wide range of medicines created on my machines in alignment with the frequencies of different crystals. I created a mix of crystals to detoxify the intestines, to strengthen the immune system, to stimulate the thyroid and to help the vision of the third eye – remedies that hundreds of people experienced voluntarily in the therapy groups happening in the commune, reporting their results to me.

As a diagnostic tool, in addition to the bio-resonance machine, I also used a Kirlian photography machine built by a sannyasin. Osho had spoken often of this technique, which could photograph the electrical field around the physical body, and could be used to diagnose an illness many months before it became manifest. He was very happy with the results of our first photo taken with the Kirlian machine and encouraged us to go ahead with this work.

Through using these new systems, we succeeded in cutting in half the amount of antibiotics that up to now had been used prolifically to treat every minor infection. I no longer set foot in the medical centre, now permanently in the hands of Amrito, who, through Indivar, was freely distributing antibiotics for even the smallest infections.

I had total freedom of expression for my scientific creativity and the same thing was happening in other departments, especially in the art department, which was expanding exponentially, offering groups on painting, sculpture, singing, theatre and music, all of which had been the arts most favoured in the commune of the Master since the beginning.

Even in the sphere of therapy, new groups were created with a direct push from Osho. And, in addition to the two processes he created for men and women's liberation that I have already mentioned, he personally created three new techniques, which he called 'meditative therapies'. These were *No Mind*, *Born Again*, and *Mystic Rose*. He also created a process that used hypnosis to heal the body; this he called *Reminding Yourself of the Forgotten Language of the Body*.

One morning, all of the therapists were called together and informed that Osho wanted to experiment with new techniques. We would do these techniques together and report back, giving feedback about our reactions on a daily basis. So, each morning, about 50 of us gathered in a room, where we were invited to laugh continuously for three hours. We were all friends, many of us with a lot of therapy experience, so we really had a good time together. This happened every day for seven days. Then, for the next seven days, we were asked to cry uninterruptedly for three hours every day.

After this deep cleansing process, when many people reported that they felt a deep desire to simply sit in silence, Osho added a third stage to this process, which he had named the *Mystic Rose*. This third stage he called 'the watcher on the hill,' sitting silently for three hours a day for one week. This completed the three-week meditative therapy, which became one of the ashram's most powerful tools for cleansing and transformation.

The next meditative therapy to be created was *No Mind*, in which we were invited to spend one hour talking loudly in complete gibberish, followed immediately by one hour of silent meditation.

Gibberish as a spiritual method comes from the Sufi tradition, from a strange Sufi mystic called Jabbar, who lived several centuries ago. Jabbar became famous for the fact that he never spoke a word that people could understand. He just spoke nonsense. It was his way of bypassing the mind and connecting with people at a deeper level.

So the room was like a madhouse. We were busy articulating sounds that made no sense, sometimes like babies make when they are playing, before they have learned to speak properly, saying words without significance, and sometimes shouting at the tops of our voices, uttering sounds without any inhibition whatsoever. For us, it was a verbal catharsis, a vomiting of guttural sounds and consonants that effectively emptied the mind before entering into a meditative state.

And, as I mentioned earlier, the Mystery School led by Kaveesha also exploded in a whirlwind of new esoteric groups that made her department the most popular and consequently the most lucrative therapy section in the ashram. Everything was expanding like a chain reaction and every creative idea was welcomed.

Along with many others, I didn't fully appreciate at the time that we were living in such a special, magical moment, where the temporal space between an idea and its practical realization was minimal, thanks to the support of all our friends in the ashram. In fact, it often happened that when we shared an idea it was multiplied a hundred times by the suggestions and creative support of others.

So I found myself totally involved in fantastic experiments, discussions, and futuristic projects that made me forget the 'female' component of my life, even though I had many beautiful open-minded lovers during this period. Until one day, when...

I had gone to our Mariam Canteen for lunch. Lunch was the most popular meal and the tables were really crowded. Usually, in order to avoid the long lines, I extended my sessions so that I arrived at the canteen late, at a time when I could eat in peace.

I was seated alone at a table that day, and had almost finished my meal when, looking up from my plate, I saw a woman who seemed unsure of where to go, standing between the serving area and the table opposite me. She stopped, as if lost, looking around without really searching for anything specific. She was tall, with olive skin and black hair falling in waves over her shoulders, and dark brown eyes that were very intense. Her body was feminine, full and round, in perfect proportions that were difficult to take your eyes off. Her ample breasts were very natural and gave her a maternal look.

I saw her as confused, evidently not knowing what to do or where to go, or maybe she'd just had an argument with her man. I knew nothing about her and had never seen her before. She must have been a new arrival. Suddenly, I saw my body impulsively stand-up and without any preconceived idea move toward her and hug her, as if she was an old friend who'd returned after a long time and I was welcoming her. It was a long hug, very warm, both energetic and sexual, and after a while we let go of each other. I looked her in the eyes and said to her: "Don't worry. I will take care of you."

I returned to my table without adding anything more and without expecting a response. I think I was more shocked than she was. I couldn't explain this sudden reaction, these words that came out of the emptiness of my mind. I tried to finish my meal, but the warmth of her body still filled my soul, far more than this bland meal filled my body. I returned to work and her energy stayed with me all day, a loving warmth and sweetness that accompanied me like a perfume that had seeped into the tissues of my body.

That night, coming out of the evening meditation, we met casually in a crowd of people heading out the gate for different restaurants in the city. We hugged again and it was so beautiful to squeeze each other that we ended up in bed in her house behind the ashram without being able to say a word. We walked there without having exchanged the slightest information about each other and stayed together overnight.

Pragito was an American woman who had lived in Central America for the first fifteen years of her life. Her father was a geological engineer and when she was small he was transferred to Costa Rica for his work. Their house was near the forest, where he worked, and she lived in a way that was absolutely wild and natural.

In a short time, she was accepted as part of a local tribe that still lived 'wild' in nature. So, she spent her first years naked and wild among the tribal people, learning respect for plants, animals and nature in general, feeling like an integral part of nature itself. As she told me later, she often spent the entire day immersed in observing the nature around her, spontaneously getting used to the silence and the state of non-doing. The space of mental emptiness was for her a natural experience that she lived for years as a child, so when she encountered meditation through Osho, a deep part of her felt she was returning home.

After fifteen years of living in the wild forest with its rhythms, its innate music and its spontaneity, her father was transferred to California and Pragito found herself catapulted into the dreamland of the '70s, among young hippies, musicians, artists and alternative people who were trying to live in a different way than in the sclerotic structure of the marketplace. Because of these experiences, Pragito was an impressive mixture of a natural woman, with an ego that was simple and spontaneous without tricks, and a mind that was open, intelligent and modern. She was the first and only partner of mine who shared the same astrological sign as me: Aquarius.

Few words were exchanged between us. It was more like we were communicating through physical energy that bypassed the verbal mind. Making love with her was like diving into a river, a big calm river that carried you gently along unknown shores, allowing you to see colours and images that you had never seen before and that you would never be able to dream up. She had a siren's body and when she undressed that first night, I felt my flesh slowly melt inside of her like warm wax. I let myself go in that warmth and that sweetness that tasted like a wild and uncontaminated land, a land of which the scental one was enough to nourish me.

The morning after, I woke up to find she had already gone. I was stunned. I hadn't opened up like that to a woman since I had been with Nandi. Again, I felt the sweetness flowing delicately inside my body, like walking on fresh snow, and with that same lightness I walked toward the ashram to have breakfast. When things are meant to happen, they do so easily, and so we met spontaneously. It was only then we started to use words in order to know each other in a more superficial, intellectual way.

Pragito was one of those Americans who'd arrived in big numbers at the Ranch and who remained there the whole time with her partner in order to work on the creation of 'Rancho Rajneesh.' At that time, she'd been with a German man who was one of the real characters in the communes of Osho. His name was Haridas –

meaning 'the servant of God' – who'd been one of the very first disciples of the Master.

Osho loved Haridas and always kept him nearby in the communes, speaking often about him in his public discourses to make fun of the German ego – especially the Teutonic inability to understand jokes. Haridas was a big man, powerful, with red hair and a red beard. He resembled a brave Viking warrior, but his sweet blue eyes were in marked contrast to this initial impression. Haridas, who had been staying in America with Pragito and her daughter, came back to Pune about a year after Osho's return. He was immediately reintegrated in the new energy the Master had created. For months, he tried to convince Pragito to return to the commune, but without results.

Pragito was one of the many American disciples who remained disappointed after the Ranch, because she felt abandoned by the Master, and had no intention of entering into a new project. She also had a young child, then about thirteen or fourteen years old, whom she didn't want to involve in another uncertain adventure. She wanted to give her daughter security, to have her study and be with other American adolescents in order to be integrated in the world.

Pragito told me how Haridas did everything to convince her to return to the commune, explaining that it was no longer the old story of the Ranch, and that now the energy was concentrated on meditation and on creativity, and that old disciples and friends were coming back to live with the Master. Finally, after many months, she gave in to the insistence of her partner and left for Pune with her daughter, thinking to stay for a brief period.

When we met, she'd arrived just a few days before and that air of confusion I saw in the restaurant was the state of her soul in that moment, because she didn't expect to find this drastic change in the energy of the commune. She was very touched by the human warmth that had been created between us all. Like a lot of Americans, Pragito hadn't met Osho before the Ranch.

On the Ranch, life was all about the work, construction and being busy without pause, day and night, whereas now she found herself in an energyfield with a lot of space and silence, with meditation and creativity. She was disoriented, looking for common ground between her image of the Master at that time and this one in Pune.

The afternoon of our first meeting I understood intuitively her state of confusion and with my hug and my words she felt welcome in the ashram and in the new space the Master had created. So we became ardent lovers, while her relationship with Haridas, her former companion, was being transformed into a friendship between ex-partners.

One day I met her with Haridas and her daughter, and the meeting was so simple and loving that it touched me deeply. Haridas had no resentment toward Pragito or me and accepted her choice with naturalness and spontaneity. In fact, from that day on, he and I started to meet more often, becoming rather good friends, until one day he asked me if I could teach him the bio-resonance technique because he was tired of being an electrician, a role he'd played since the time of the first commune.

So he participated in my trainings and later I accepted him as part of my staff. He learned a lot within a short time and his interest was total, as only a German's can be, so much so that after Osho died Haridas took classes at a German naturopathy school and in the space of four years became a very good naturopath, a healing skill that he still exercises today.

The relationship between Pragito and me had a simplicity that I'd never experienced before with a woman and it continued like that, without obstacles, without conflict, in the most totally relaxed way. Pragito wasn't a woman who expressed her emotions, nor did she involve others in her worries, so we found ourselves together without any problems: friends, lovers and partners, sharing the last year of the life of the Master.

Her presence relaxed me deeply, lifting me out of the stress of the medical practice. Pragito was for me a great 'Mother Earth' in the form of a woman; with her I melted and was regenerated.

She didn't go back to America after a few weeks, as was her intention, but stayed to the end of Osho's days on Planet Earth. I was with her when we, together with the whole commune, burned the body of our beloved one.

Meanwhile, the meditations with the Master were reaching peaks never before seen by his sannyasins. While his body was deteriorating more and more, his energy was expanding immensely. The ashram was vibrating with his love and in the lanes around Koregaon Park we went around drunk with his energy.

In India, a new culture was arising that had succeeded in vanquishing some of the old, fixed, traditional attitudes and as a result people were becoming increasingly interested in Osho's modern teachings. The more modern-minded Indians continued to arrive the ashram and listen to his teachings, unlike the times of the first commune where the major part of the Indian middle class shunned his message as being too audacious.

In these years, Osho experienced a radical re-evaluation in his own country, becoming the most influential Master on the Indian subcontinent. His books appeared in all the major libraries, including the official library of the Indian Parliament, where he was given his own section – a distinction hitherto given only to Mahatma Gandhi.

His vision, which to most Indians was almost science fiction in the '70s, came to be immortalized in his first book to be published in India, *From Sex to Superconsciousness*. This, and books like it, were now being carried around by the new, emerging middle class that had opened up to material wealth, to the equality of women and to a more open sexuality that was no longer repressed. In addition, Indian women finally began to show interest in the path opened up by women in the West decades ago.

Artists, writers, politicians, actors and other famous people came to the ashram, which was enriched even more thanks to the support of wealthy Indians. India was changing and Pune, which had been a sleepy, military city in the first years of the '70s, full of mansions in the English style, with big parks and lanes used by bicycles and rickshaws, was now rapidly transforming into an industrial metropolis, with factories that spread out across the formerly verdant land of the surrounding Deccan Plateau. Money and business were now as equally important as Hindu gods, and industrial 'progress' hit the city with a bang, distorting it within a few short years into something unrecognizable by us, the Western spiritual seekers who'd arrived in the 1970s.

In short, many of these new middle class Indians were interested in the teachings of Osho and today, twenty years after his death, Osho's vision has become a magnet for all those who'd maintained inside their souls the memory of the Master-disciple relationship as part of their own spiritual tradition.

It wasn't only the general public that was changing its tune, but also the authorities themselves, who from the '60s to '80s had tried in every way to oppose him. Particularly in the years immediately following the end of his physical life, Osho was recognized as a great philosopher and genius of the 20th century, even being considered as one of ten greatest men in the history of modern India, along with Mahatma Gandhi and other national figures.

33 The Last Teaching

During the last year of his public teaching, Osho introduced a new meditation technique at the end of his discourses. First came his jokes, loosening us up, then we plunged into gibberish, speaking nonsense, then came a drumbeat heralding sudden and total silence in Buddha Hall. At this point, Osho would speak a few words, guiding us deeper inside ourselves, and then, accompanied by another drumbeat, he would invite us to 'let go' and relax totally, falling back on the floor, as if almost dead. At this stage, Osho would continue speaking, urging us to penetrate even more deeply within ourselves. This was a technique that took us like an arrow straight to our centre:

"Remember that you are all Buddhas. In this precise moment you are the Buddha. Let yourselves go, relax, letting go of all of the tension, letting your body fall to the ground."

While we were completely relaxed and stretched out on the floor, reclining on each other, his magnetic voice carried us into a state of silence we had never experienced before, reminding us constantly, night after night, meditation after meditation, that our essence is that of the Buddha.

Without frills, stories, explanations or spiritual lessons, Osho took us straight to our centre, reminding us that Buddhahood is not something to get but simply to remember: remembering a state that we already know and have forgotten because of an unnatural society that directs all its resources toward nourishing a monstrous ego, in which greed never ends, destroying the planet and the minds of thousands of human beings, in order to possess more power and more money.

In order to *appear* perfect and magnificent, young and strong, the ego is ready to accept whatever compromises and distortions are required in order to show others its power. Narcissism today is predominant. Narcissus is the new god, the god that is worshipped and loved by the overwhelming majority of human beings.

The direction Osho indicated to us was diametrically opposite: at the end of a long path begun in the '60s, after 30 years of hypnotic discourses, he had brought us directly inside ourselves, in that natural space where life flows without obstacles, with an inherent music and a celestial rhythm that keeps everything in harmony.

The 'hidden harmony' of which the Master spoke, as did Pythagoras millennia ago, is a harmony that pervades existence. We sentient beings rush away from this natural state every day in order to move toward the abyss of a mind that always wants more and in the end brings us nothing but a great collective madness in which man destroys himself.

Osho knew he was going to leave his physical body and so, in the preceding year, he pushed us energetically to the maximum, focusing solely on Zen, which contains the essence of all meditative practices. Zen teaches the pure presence of the moment, the awareness of our every act, every instant of our day, including, at the end, our nocturnal rest. With Zen, Osho pushed us to experience directly this 'full emptiness,' which is a space without time, where the speaking mind disappears and makes it possible to experience the peace and quiet associated with the depths of the sea, without any superficial wave being able to touch its tranquillity.

Thousands of people of all races, from every continent of this fantastic planet, came together every night to explore the depths of the heart and consciousness of the Master, who until the last breath of his body stayed with us in order to help us experience the essence of life. He persevered, coming to be with us even though his body was sick, wounded, disintegrating from having been poisoned. Every evening he sat with us to share his space of meditation, with all his majestic presence, even when it was coming close to the very last days of his existence on this earth.

In April 1989, Osho concluded his last public discourses with a series called *The Zen Manifesto – Freedom from Oneself*, which started on the 20th of February and ended on the 10th of April. His last public comments, which presaged a long period of silence that lasted for the nine months before his ultimate departure, were given on April 10, 1989. The discourse began with a Zen *sutra* that went like this:

"Tozan had a question about whether inanimate objects could spread the Dharma. So Tozan visited Master Isan, who suggested he visit Master Ungan. With Ungan, Tozan became aware of reality for the first time, and he composed this *gatha* in order to remember his experience: How marvellous! How marvellous! The inanimate spreads the Dharma, that ineffable, indescribable reality! If you try to hear it with your ears you will never understand it. Only when you hear it through your eyes can you really know it."

Osho started by saying:

"Friends...The tradition of Zen is hard. It takes twenty to thirty years of constant meditation, withdrawing from every type of social life and using all our energy to meditate. That tradition comes directly from Gautama Buddha. He himself found enlightenment after twelve long years of hard work.

I am completely changing the traditional spiritual path of Zen, because I don't see how modern man can devote twenty or thirty years of his life only to meditation. If Zen remains so hard it will disappear from the world completely. It has already disappeared from China, as it is disappearing from Japan, and it disappeared from India long ago.

In fact, it only remained in India for five hundred years after Gautama Buddha. In the sixth century it reached China and stayed for only a few centuries before moving toward Japan. Now it is almost extinct in both China and Japan. You will be surprised to know that my books are read and studied in the Zen monasteries. Zen has to be transformed in a way that modern man can be interested in it. It needs to be easy and relaxed, not hard. That old kind of tradition is no longer possible and no longer necessary.

Once it is explored, once someone gets enlightened, the path will be easier. You don't need to discover electricity every time you need to use it. The awakening of Buddha is a very easy and relaxed phenomenon. So now that many people are awakened the path has become clear, it is no longer arduous and difficult. You can playfully enter into and lucidly experience the awakening of consciousness and of awareness."

His last talk continued for about an hour and a half, taking us into the space of silence that we were experiencing every evening. None of us were conscious of the fact that this would be his last discourse and the mind took his presence for granted, as always.

"Come back peacefully, silently, like a Buddha. And when you open your eyes remember the path you have travelled, the source you have found and the divine nature you have experienced.

In this moment you are the most blessed people on this Earth. Remember yourself as a Buddha and this precious experience, because it is your own eternity, your immortality. It is your real experience.

You are one with the stars, the trees, the sky and the ocean. You are no longer separate. Remember that you are Buddhas.... Sammasati."

The last word of Gautama Buddha was also *sammasati*. The last word that Osho pronounced in public...the same as Buddha's.

My life flowed on intensely, like that of all the disciples around Osho, every hour of the day. Our ashram was really full during the last year of Osho's life, and walking along the lanes of the various properties meant having a series of meetings and hugs with dozens of friends with whom you were sharing this amazing experience that is 'the death of a Buddha.'

Notwithstanding that we didn't know his death was near, many of us felt a particularly intense energy in the commune, an atmosphere that was especially bubbly, like the air you breath at high altitude when you go beyond six or seven thousand feet. We felt drunken, light and yet revitalized by an impalpable loving force. At the same time, many of us felt a fundamental concern and we often shared our intuition and our premonitions about him. I knew Osho was sick, knew about his recurring infections, and everyone knew that his body couldn't last for long, but no one suspected it would happen so fast. I was thinking, perhaps more hopefully than others, that he would live another couple of years. I didn't really think the time would be so short.

We took care of him in all the ways we could. In addition to the bio-resonance therapy that was undertaken for a year or so, Osho agreed to receive different kinds of massage to ease the pain in his joints, which was increasing partly because he was no longer moving his body, staying all day seated in his armchair or lying on his bed. As far as I know, he also took a lot of allopathic drugs to relieve pain, infections and the difficulty he had in allowing the physical body to sleep.

As he said many times in his discourses, once you have reached the peaks of consciousness where he and other Buddhas resided, the mind no longer became unconscious, not even in the night, and thus the necessary recuperation of the physical body was missing.

He no longer had any connection to the so-called real world. Time was escaping from his dimension and Anando had to inform him of the time of his appointments, seeing how in his space there was only an intense present.

Various small operations on his teeth were done and also two bigger operations, one of which I was involved in indirectly because I was a good friend of the doctor who operated.

Dr Modi was a specialist who operated on the bones of the jaw. He had studied in London and was specialized in surgery on the face, working for many years in England. In Pune he had a private clinic and was considered one of the great Indian surgeons. His wife Zareen had become a disciple of Osho many years before and between us a very deep friendship was born, which continues up to the present, decades later. So I got to know him through her. His mentality was very Western, and his English sounded more like Oxford than Pune. He had never accepted Osho as a Master, unlike Zareen, who left the family and came to live in the commune.

Dr Modi loved horses, and had a sizeable mansion in the city in the colonial style of the English, with a beautiful garden. Being with him nourished me a lot due to his great culture and intelligence. We often talked for hours, passing on information about anything from pharmaceutical drugs to Indian philosophy and gardening.

He had the face of a North Indian, with a wide forehead and small lips that were clearly articulated and often bathed in a glass of whiskey, then busy with a cigarette, and very big black eyes that shone with the light of an intelligence that separated him from the rest of the world. Modi was out of place in India and in his depths he felt like a Westerner who was forced to live there. He didn't like all the poverty or the religious aspects that characterized the continent. In his soul, he was much closer to European existentialism than to the Hinduism of the Indian masses.

Since Osho's time in American prisons, the infections that had begun in his ear and jawbone were spreading dangerously toward the cerebral cavity. So Amrito decided to call Dr Modi. After a medical visit, he decided to operate as soon as possible. That morning, before entering Lao Tzu, Modi came to see me and shared the tension he felt in having to operate on a man like Osho. After a brief exchange he asked me where he could find me after the surgery was over, because he wanted spend a little time with me before leaving the ashram.

He came to see in my office after about three hours. He was very shaky and vulnerable, as I had never seen him before. After all, he was a surgeon with a firm hand and an iron will. He hugged me, breaking out in tears in my arms. He wasn't able to understand how it was possible, what he had experienced in that small operating theatre. He told me that when everything was ready, he told Osho that he would give him an anaesthetic injection and that after a few moments he wouldn't feel anything, and then he would start operating. But Osho refused to receive the injection.

Modi responded with all the authority of a famous surgeon and said to him: "Here I am the surgeon and I say we have to give you the anaesthetic and it is not a matter of discussion." But Osho looked at him and answered: "You are the surgeon but I am the Master and I am telling you to operate without an anaesthetic, starting when I give you the signal with my finger."

Modi felt cornered. From one side he knew that surgery on the face was extremely painful and that it wasn't practical to do it without anaesthetic, but from the other side he couldn't refuse because, after all, Osho was the master of his own body and also a spiritual Master who knew what was happening beyond the physical body and the mind. Modi was petrified by the idea of operating without an anaesthetic on open bones, but he followed Osho's orders and performed the whole operation without a drop of anaesthetic.

Osho, shortly after closing his eyes, made a movement with his finger, giving the okay to start the operation, leaving his physical body in the hands of Dr Modi. After the operation, Osho re-entered his body and calmly opened his eyes. Modi was shaken, knowing that what had just happened wasn't understandable within the realm of normal science and that Osho's behaviour had put in question all his medical convictions about operating without an anaesthetic.

He continued to repeat to me, like a recording, "It's not possible." He was absolutely shocked at having operated without an anaesthetic and he continued to be agitated for a long time.

As soon as he managed to relax, we went together for a drink at one of the ashram bars. It was an interesting moment, watching Dr Modi recover from this experience that could have changed his life forever. But instead, his ego reclaimed control with explanations generated by his strong rational mind.

The truth is, Osho was always a Master, not only when he came to speak with us and share his state of meditation. Osho was permanently in a state of total disconnection from the false reality of the ego and he took advantage of every situation in order to be able to teach something to people who came near him, even to the detriment of his body.

Osho respected Dr Modi very much and privately told Zareen a few times he would be happy if her husband took sannyas. But in spite of all these doors being opened in front of him, Modi never became a disciple. Because of his intellectual ego, he never could make the jump from the mind to the heart, the jump from the outsider to the disciple, the jump of a lover who lets go into existence, without any resistance.

We remained good friends, but our meetings became less

frequent and slowly I stopped seeing him as he reduced his visits to the ashram to almost zero. The small operating room prepared for Osho continued to be busy, with the coming and going of various doctors and surgeons who visited him, doing their best to help with the various problems that came up from time to time.

Osho's body was sick and weak and his consciousness had a lot of difficulty staying in his body. This, as he told us on more than one occasion, is a difficulty that faces many Masters. The process of enlightenment breaks identification with the body, as well as the mind, and few have the capacity to remain in the body after such an experience. The physical body is heavy, gross and difficult to manage once you have entered into divine consciousness. There, the experience of bliss is so great there is no other choice but to stay in that state, not having any interest in physical activity.

Nevertheless, for 36 years, Osho had stayed in the body and its my feeling – in the last few years especially – that if it hadn't been for our enormous love for him he would have left us years before. Our love was his anchor. It kept him alive and connected him energetically with his consciousness in order to build a bridge to us; an interwoven bridge of light, thanks to thousands of individual sannyasins who were weaving their devotion to support him and prevent him from disappearing into the void of death.

From May '89 till the end of that year there were many interruptions in his public appearances that lasted a few days, in which Osho couldn't leave his room to come to us in Buddha Hall. But for the rest of the evenings, he came every night to meditate together with us in silence, without his incredible discourses, without his wonderful sense of humour, without his jokes and that mischievous smile.

We sat with him in silence. After long silences, interspersed with brief musical pieces, he had us do the gibberish meditation, then silence again, sharing with us the state of pure presence of the Buddha.

He went on like that until the end.

34   The Last Celebration

    These months that passed without discourses from the Master were more intense than usual. Osho saw only Anando, Amrito and Jayesh in his room, and appeared before us all in silence most evenings in Buddha Hall. Every night after the meditation, Jayesh rose from his seat in order to join the Master in his room, receiving the latest guidance for the temple that was growing bigger and bigger.

    Osho gave instructions for creating a new Buddha Hall – in the form of a pyramid, whose shape would support our meditation – and explained to Jayesh with meticulous details what to do with the enormous organization that had grown up around him. I don't think even Jayesh suspected the Master would leave his body soon; perhaps the only person who knew was his private doctor, Amrito, who was busy the whole day taking care of him.

    In one of our few friendly meetings, he told me that in these last months he'd recorded five to seven heart attacks in a single day and that he himself didn't understand what was going on. And yet, notwithstanding these regular heart attacks, Osho continued to come out in the evenings to share his space with us.

    Medically, his body was a series of scientific impossibilities and any normal person who had only ten per cent of his suffering would have been in bed in hospital, with a team of doctors performing emergency treatments. But he did everything for us until the end, as if his body didn't belong to him any longer. On a few evenings, we saw him leaning to one side when he entered Buddha Hall, and every time my heart – and the hearts of all the others – jumped with fear at seeing him so fragile. His body steadily became more like an empty package, and from the outside it looked almost like a marionette whose puppeteer was dozing off. Sometimes an arm or leg went in the wrong direction. One night while Osho was greeting us, his right foot wobbled in empty space beyond the edge of the podium, making him stagger...and also us.

We had arrived at the end of his path, but Osho continued to live as if death didn't interest him. Hundreds of times over the years, he had spoken to us about death and the intensity of this final moment in which the explosion, or implosion, is total and atomic, saying that only if this abyss is accepted during life can we consciously face this moment of eternity that is the total dissolution of the body.

Now he was showing us in practice how a realized being faces this moment and he was facing it in a way that was so detached and natural that none of us realized how short was the time remaining. We had gone beyond the shock of Vivek's death and also the trauma of the mantras disturbing his body.

During the early days of January 1990, we often didn't see him because his health was so poor he didn't manage to come out in the evenings to meditate with us. Pragito, with the sensitivity of someone used to living in the forest, said that something big was happening that would upset the ashram in a short time. We were no longer able to make love. The energy was so strong that we often stayed in bed hugging in silence, waiting for the body to relax enough so we could go to sleep.

It was the evening of January 19. The previous evening Osho hadn't managed to come out for the meditation. The last time we'd seen him, Osho looked extremely wobbly on the podium, far more than before. So on the night of the 19th, we decided not to go to the meditation because we were sure he wouldn't come. We chose to go to bed and, as we usually did, we showered and stayed in bed holding each other and breathing together.

Some hours earlier, walking in the main street, I had met my dear American friend Zeno. We were hugging in silence, as if one of our parents had died this day, and after the embrace we talked about our feelings. They were exactly the same, both of us feeling that the atmosphere of death had spread in the commune and we were very worried about the Master, but no one had said anything so we were asking ourselves if someone among the sannyasins had died in the commune.

Now it was about seven in the evening and Pragito and I were hugging in silence when we heard screams in the garden. We jumped up and went to the window that looked out on the garden. We didn't understand what they were saying, but sannyasins were running toward Buddha Hall and they were all screaming something different. In a few seconds, I felt a crashing inside my chest, and strong physical pain produced by an invisible force.

Pragito didn't hesitate a moment, putting on a white robe and running outside saying, "He left!" I stayed alone at the window and watched all the sannyasins running toward Buddha Hall and inside me a voice said, "Whatever happens stay aware." I moved very slowly, putting on a white robe and going down the stairs, trying not to lose my focus on my gestures and my breathing. I walked toward Buddha Hall, entering from the main gate and went toward the podium.

Now it was clear the Master had left. Many were crying: "He's dead! He's dead!" I entered the hall, full of people who were crying, dancing, jumping, hugging each other, meditating with eyes closed…. Thousands of disciples were expressing from their centre the emotions of this news that exploded like an atomic bomb in the commune.

It was an unforgettable scene. The music was playing at high volume, as was usual in the hall, this time celebrating what all of us didn't ever want to happen. I managed to be centered until I got inside the hall. Then seeing an Italian friend who was guarding the podium, my detachment melted away like snow in the sun. Grabbing the guard by the robe, I asked him, screaming, if it was true that the Master was dead. He was taken by surprise and in a very gentle and calm way he looked at me and said, "All of us must die."

I burst out crying and it was a cry of liberation, as when I met Osho for the first time in Buddha Hall in 1978. Twelve intense years had gone by. I had lived the impossible, thanks to him – adventures that I would never have dreamed of living when I was still a good little boy in Palermo. I was born and born again at different times with Osho and now he had left us, tired of a body that hadn't really belonged to him for years. He had squeezed the juice of his life to the maximum and just as water evaporates when fully heated, so he decided to let go of the body and evaporate in the air of consciousness.

I didn't stop crying. The crowd of disciples who were there pushed me toward the right side of the podium, where I managed sit down and continue my crying. All around they were celebrating, singing and exploding with energy, just as he had always asked us to do: "Celebrate death, celebrate life, celebrate every event. Be total."

Certainly, we had learned to celebrate with him, but in this unique circumstance, I wasn't ready to sing and be joyful, although I knew the exhortations of the Master were different. When they brought out his body on a stretcher of bamboo, hastily made by a few devotees, Amrito gave the official notice of his death and reminded us that the Master, before going, had asked us to celebrate, singing and dancing. But my heart burst out in continuous crying, even more when his body was put on the podium.

He was dressed in blue, the same colour as the robe he'd given to me three years before. The stretcher was already laden with flowers and you could only see his face, peaceful, serene, as we had always seen it. His feet were sticking out slightly from the end of the stretcher. His shoes were the same black velvet thongs he had always worn. His clothes changed a lot over the years, but his model of shoes never changed. His hands were placed one on top of the other on his chest, all covered with rose petals that were swirling around, happy to have also been blessed by the death of a Buddha.

They kept him on the podium for a brief period, maybe fifteen minutes in all, and then lifted him up. Then started the long procession outside the ashram and along the streets that led to the burning ghat and funeral pyre, which was located by the river about a mile and a half from the commune. I continued to cry all the way, in the midst of 5000 people who were following the body of their beloved Master. I continued to hug friends and cry, and the more I cried the more I felt that my being was emptying out something that took years to understand. In all that confusion along the road I met Pragito. We hugged and together followed the long line of disciples who were singing while following their Master to the funeral pyre. With the fresh air and all the friends nearby, I also started to sing.

We arrived at banks of the river where the funeral pyre had already been organized. Indians are wonderful in celebrations, especially in funerals. It's a ritual that has been handed down for centuries and has reached perfection. The members of Osho's biological family were there, and his spiritual family – all of us – were strung out along the river in order to let everyone enter into the space where the fire would be lit.

It was dark, with thousands of people from all over the world dressed in white robes singing and celebrating death, the death of their beloved. Their songs drowned out the sounds of nature. The river and the birds that usually sing so intensely in these places weren't heard any more. The guitars and the tambourines prevailed over everything, but the centre of this circle of energy that we created around the fire was still Osho, as always majestic, serene, blissful, totally realized.

He was an emperor who had reigned in the best way over the biggest of all realms – his own life. He didn't want anything special for his death. When Amrito asked him what we should do on the occasion of the death of a great Master like him, he simply answered: "Nothing special. Take my body to my people in Buddha Hall, celebrate and remind everyone that it's good to celebrate everything in life, then take the body to the river and burn it."

The *burning ghat* is a simple place, out in the open, used by all kinds of people, but he didn't make any distinction between his body and that of any ordinary man. We started to cover the corpse with wood and the last thing you could see was his face – very serene. Then his brother set light to the wood, and the flames took over everything. We continued singing, singing and singing, crying and laughing and hugging, all together around his pyre, the pyre of the Buddha, which was burning more and more intensely.

After about two hours, Pragito wanted to leave. It was late and she was tired, but I had no intention of leaving his body while it was burning. I returned to the room with Pragito, who went to bed. I put on Western clothes, including pants and a brown leather jacket to protect me from the cold of the night, having no intention to go to bed. I told Pragito I couldn't sleep knowing that the body of the Master was burning. So I said goodbye to her and returned to the bank of the river.

It must have been about one o'clock in the morning and the number of people had diminished significantly. The musicians had gone away and with them went most of the disciples. It was very intimate now in the dark of night. You could hear the birds, the river, the wind and all of nature expressing its constant joy. The flames were no longer high, but the pyre was burning steadily and there were still big pieces of wood at the base of the fire. There were about a hundred of us and a few more were far away near the river, enjoying the magnificent experience of the silence of nature.

I crossed my legs and sat in meditation. Before me the fire glowed. In the ashes there remained, incredibly, the perfect imprint of his feet, outlined by the ashes. It was magical, a circle of disciples sitting in the darkness around the glowing remains of their Master, on the banks of a river under the starry Indian sky.

I observed the form of the feet of the Master, which remained intact, the fire continuing to go around it without destroying this castle of coals that magically remained. And so, observing, my mind became calm, the thoughts dwindled and everything inside started to become still and empty, but full of energy. Quiet, immobile, nothing inside moved, not the body nor the mind, nor my breathing, which slowed down more and more, finally almost stopping, the eyes looking inward, the body still, aware of birds cawing once in a while, total silence inside and a peace that I had never felt so deeply in all my life.

A peace that didn't know about emotions, going beyond both the mind and feelings, a peace that doesn't have warmth, nor passion, nor time. A peace that is beyond space and all possible verbal descriptions, and **in this peace I lost myself completely, absolutely.**

When I opened my eyes again, the morning had come and the

life of the city had already begun. Around me, the number of people had diminished to about fifty, many of whom, including me, were still around the fire, and a few along the river. The heat of the day brought me back, because I hadn't heard the noises and thought it was still night. But the strong Indian sun made itself felt on my leather jacket and the sweat made me return from a space in which my ego had completely disappeared – melted in the space of the Master, which had dissolved in the universe.

I remained there, stunned and dazzled by what had happened to my soul during this marvellous Indian night, this historical night that had taken away a Buddha who had turned the wheel of the dharma. In that peace and tranquillity of silent disciples I remained there until the body shook and came to life, returning to its old self, as I had always known it.

Before getting up, I spontaneously took some ashes of the Master. As if by magic, I found myself looking at a small plastic container. There I deposited a handful of ashes. I put it in my pocket, stood up, bowed down again before the Master, or what remained of him – the 'flowers' as the tiny fragments are called – which would be put in an urn and brought to the ashram next day.

I started to move, observing around me the scene that remained of the celebration the night before. Then slowly I walked toward the road and then toward the ashram. On the way, my body was strangely light and my mind so calm that the sounds of the traffic passed through me silently.

While walking, a strange sensation took form inside me, like an opening, or a mist that was disappearing. I started to see my future, not as an image but as sensations, and the most prominent was of a full and complete circle, the circle of my life, past and future, and in the future I no longer recognized my old self.

In the middle of the circle, roots had started to grow inside me, roots that would protect me for the years ahead, allowing me to face the world that, since childhood, I'd always felt to be foreign to me, with which I'd never felt identified, this society that doesn't have space for much except for profit and gratuitous violence. A society that has never nourished the spiritual component and the wonder of life, but thinks only about violent survival.

I saw myself in the future, alone, walking in the world. I saw myself with other women, in other spaces. I saw myself as a successful doctor in a world of sick souls. These were more sensations than images, and in all these sensations the roots were growing and held me steadily on the ground. Indirectly, Osho had made these roots grow, the Master with his presence and his joy, showing the path of light in a world moving in the darkness of the mind.

These twelve years had given me an emotional stability and a life that wouldn't have been possible without the Master. I had lived the joy of real freedom that resides inside our hearts and not in external objects. The light coming through him made many people run away, remaining blind to the strength of the energy of a living Buddha. Their minds found all kinds of reasons to justify their objections. But the 'reasons' that the mind can create to close itself off are simply petty in the presence of a being of that stature. For sure, Osho offered us the opportunity to live through many experiences that could be questioned and criticized. Those of us who stayed, stayed because our hearts were totally with him.

We can live with a Master only if the heart has been given to him totally, without regret or doubts, without any judgments whatsoever. Then the Master does nothing but guide us toward the door, opening it and making us see that which is real, this world that all the Masters have spoken about for millennia. It exists inside us. So the Master is nothing other than a vehicle, an empty space through which we can begin to see the vast universe of pure consciousness.

As I walked slowly that morning, along the streets that brought me to the ashram, the roots became steadily stronger. Inside, it felt like I had finished the apprenticeship and now I had to put it into practice, alone in the world. I felt that my time in the commune would end soon and I would leave India forever. India had given much more than I expected. But the journey I started in 1978, on my way to the Orient in rusty vehicles that brought me to India, was now over.

The journey had started as a young, left-wing intellectual who went to India in order to look for a little peace and clarity in his confused mind. It was a trip that had brought me farther than India itself. Of all the routes possible on this wonderful planet, this trip had taken me to the threshold of the luminous door of my inner silence, a door that isn't found in any physical place on this planet, that doesn't have corporeal dimensions or mechanisms, but that resides in the depth of the heart in every human being.

It's a door that many have gone through and then come back, to share their experience with other humans who continue to wander around in confusion and despair. It's a door that you have to go through alone and with your own strength, your own intelligence and your own awareness. And, paradoxically, in order to develop this art of being alone on this inner journey that is both very long and very short, a Master is indispensable.

The mazes of the mind are infinite, like a labyrinth of tunnels that is impossible to get out of without a guide who has already walked the path and knows how to come out into the pure light of day. The mind itself doesn't have any existential reality and it clings to its own images in order to be able to survive the light of love. So without a guide, mind always reflects a new image of yourself that justifies your choices. Yet that door is always open and lives inside us like a small flame that is only waiting to be fed by the wind of awareness.

As I walked slowly that morning, along the lanes that brought me to the ashram, all these inner experiences were going on in a simple way. The roots were growing more solid during that brief walk without time, roots that can make it possible for us to face life and all its mystery, so that the tree of truth can flower. Many people today make the mistake of trying to make the flower of consciousness grow without having developed the deep roots of the tree of life. Life must be lived totally in all its facets, until the day we have to leave the false images, without any repentance or regret. "Live your life intensely and totally," Osho told us a million times. Now I understood why.

He was dead, his body burned a few hours before, ashes at my back. But in that morning there wasn't the slightest regret about my life with the Master. I had given myself totally, at the risk of my own life, at the risk of losing my family, my social image as a doctor, all my friends, risking to live without money and without a future. I hadn't held back anything. I had burned my past behind me and I had thrown myself into the hands and into the eyes of the Master I hadn't seen for many centuries.

Now the emptiness I felt was no longer an empty emptiness but rather an empty fullness in which I began to see the tree of my own life, with all of its powerful roots. The door had opened and I felt a reality that was beyond space and time.

As I walked slowly that morning, along the lane to the ashram while the light of day shone brightly, I entered the commune like a new man, relaxed, more mature than before, so mature that I didn't feel anything except my own individuality. I was without any identification, without thirst, without family, religions, political parties, clubs or whatever other infernal things man has created in order to *not* see his individuality in its majestic unity. I was reborn in another life, again, thanks to the big gift the Master had given us: the gift of our freedom – including freedom from Osho himself.

He was gone forever and I felt free as never before and at the same time full, full of the infinite love that I had received for many years, a love that stayed with me like a door of light that was now open, open for eternity. If you recognize the Master along the path of infinite lives, it means that you met at other times. All the experiences that are lived with a true Master last forever, so you can recognize the Buddha or the Christ that is in you, or in front of you.

As I walked slowly that morning, I became aware, entering the ashram, of a reality that stayed with all of us for many months to come. The nectar of Osho was dispersed in our hearts and was visible on the faces of all the disciples in the ashram. The love that I felt in everyone was majestically palpable and the embraces, which had always been popular in all the communes of Osho, became really long, so long that for days all appointments were missed and rules were suspended. Everything went on, but with a slow pace and a relaxation never seen before.

Everyone, without exception, fell into the heart. Everyone, from that night, was completely opened up, and stayed open for a long time, until each of us went back into the tunnels of our personal lives, keeping in our hearts the experience of that openness, the openness of the Eighth Door:

The door of love that allows us to see beyond time, beyond space, beyond the mind.

The following days were unforgettable in their beauty. The celebration continued next day when the 'flowers' were brought from the burning ghat in a big brass urn, carried by Osho's brother Vijay, followed by a festive procession of thousands of disciples. I was in the commune when two lines of disciples formed spontaneously to let Vijay pass.

The crowd of people swelled like an ocean inside the ashram, thousands were coming in, singing and celebrating behind the urn that contained the ashes. It became impossible to walk or to move and there was nothing left to do but dance and sing your own joy while millions of rose petals were thrown toward Vijay who was patiently trying to reach Lao Tzu gate in order to deliver Osho's 'flowers' to the *samadhi*.

We sang for hours during the simple ceremony of depositing his ashes and from that day on we continued to live, all of us, by our own strength, from the roots that each of us had developed in order to face alone the marvellous path of life on this planet. To continue to walk toward the wide open door that the Master had reopened after centuries of lies and power games.

The Eighth Door
Love

The door from which we are able to see the essence of our existence, the essence that lives in the here and now – in the eternity of this unsolvable mystery that is life.

☐☐☐

ABOUT THE AUTHOR

Azima V. Rosciano studied medicine at Palermo University in Sicily, graduating *summacum laude* in Medicine & Surgery in 1977. After a short period of working in conventional hospitals he left Europe.

He studied homeopathy and ayurvedic medicine in India, where he was an honorary professor at an ayurvedic college in Pune. From 1987 when Osho returned to Pune, Azima was the founder and director of a pioneering multi-disciplinary healing centre, where different types of medicine and healing methods were combined in a holistic approach to health and well-being.

Returning to Italy in 1992, he specialized in Bio-Resonance Medicine, becoming a well-known expert in the field. Three years later he published his book, *Biorisonanza: La Medicina Del Futuro* (Bio-resonance: The Medicine of the Future) *(Edizioni Cerchio della Luna Pavia 1995)*.

Later he began to focus more on classical homeopathy in both his clinical and teaching work. In 2007 he published the book, *Unicismo Omeopatico (Edizioni Tecniche Nuove Milano)* (The Uniqueness of Homeopathy).

In 1996 he published his first work of music therapy, a best-selling CD called *L'Armonia Dei Chakra* (The Harmony of the Chakras), Edizioni Red, Milano 1996.

His second CD, *Musica Dal Profondo* (Music from the Depths), was published in 2008 byEdizioni Red, Milano.

Azima's spiritual memoir, *La Mia Vita Con Osho,* was published in 2011 by Edizioni Xenia, Milano. It sold out in the first year and is now being republished concurrent with this English edition.

Azima has now retired from the practice of medicine, and dedicates his time to writing books and teaching meditation.

OSHO LITERATURE

- The Osho Upanishad
- Sermons in Stones 
- Tantric Transformation 
- The Psychology of The Esoteric 
- I Say Unto You (Vol -I) 
- I Say Unto You (Vol -II) 
- The Divine Melody 
- And The Flowers Showered 
- Be Silent And Know 
- The Mystery Beyond Mind 
- Love And Meditation 
- The Ultimate Adventure 
- Turning In 
- Tantra Vision : An Invitation to Silence 

DIAMOND BOOKS
X-30, Okhla Industrial Area, Phase-II New Delhi-110020
Tel : 91+11-40712100, 40716600 Fax : 011-41611866
email : sales@dpb.in   www.dpb.in

OSHO BOOKS

- The Alchemy of Enlightenment
- Secret of Disciplehood
- The Centre of the Cyclone
- Fly Without Wings
- Be Oceanic
- Rising in Love 
- Inner Harmony
- Towards The Unknown
- A Taste of The Divine
- The Mystery Beyond Mind
- The Greatest Gamble
- Ecstasy: The Language of Existence

OSHO BOOKS

- BLESSED DAYS WITH OSHO
- THE INWARD JOURNEY
- TWO HUNDRED TALES for TEN THOUSAND BUDDHAS
- Our Beloved Osho
- New Vision For The New Millenium — Dr. Vasant Joshi
- The Calm Way
- Allah to Zen
- My Dance with a Madman — Anand Subhuti
- The Art of Living — Osho Quotes to Eternal Life
- OSHO Nirvana the last nightmare
- Osho's Vision on Education
- Be Silent and Know — OSHO

OSHO LITERATURE

- The Alchemy of Yoga
- Moving To The Center 
- The Ever present Flower 
- The Birth of Being 
- Singing Silence 
- The Royal Way 
- A Lotus of Emptiness 
- Glory of Freedom 
- The Great Challenge 
- I am the Gate 
- A Cup of Tea 
- Meditation : The Art of Ecstasy 
- Zen : Take It Easy 
- Zen : The Art of Living 
- Zen : The Art Of Meditation 
- Zen : The Art of Enlightenment 

DIAMOND BOOKS X-30, Okhla Industrial Area, Phase-II New Delhi-110020
Tel : 91+11-40712100, 40716600 Fax : 011-41611866
email : sales@dpb.in www.dpb.in